Obenaus/Weidacher

•

Dictionary and User's Guide to the NEW Handbook of Business English

Dictionary and User's Guide

to the

NEW Handbook of Business English

Keywords in Context

Wolfgang Obenaus
Josef Weidacher

Linde
international

Bibliografische Information Der Deutschen Bibliothek

Die Deutsche Bibliothek verzeichnet diese Publikation in der Deutschen Nationalbibliografie; detaillierte bibliografische Daten sind im Internet über http://dnb.ddb.de abrufbar.

ISBN 10: 3-7143-0078-3
ISBN 13: 978-3-7143-0078-9

1210 Wien, Scheydgasse 24, Tel.: 0043/1/24 630
www.lindeverlag.at

Druck: Hans Jentzsch & Co. Ges. m. b. H., 1210 Wien, Scheydgasse 31

PREFACE

The main purpose of the *Dictionary and User's Guide* is as an aid in the use of the *New Handbook of Business English*. This is to be achieved in two ways. First, the guide provides the German equivalents of all technical terms and phrases as well as of a fairly large number of less common (mainly Latin-based) non-technical expressions occurring in the *Handbook*. The reader will therefore not have to consult specialised and general dictionaries when working with the book. Second, the guide offers users a list of keywords classified according to subject matter, which is intended to enable them to obtain a coherent view of the various topics covered in the *Handbook* in spite of the alphabetical arrangement of the entries.

To avoid misunderstandings, it may be necessary to point out that the first part of this supplement is not a general dictionary of business English, and that, although it might prove helpful in dealing with other economics and business texts, its entries are geared strictly to the terms as they are used in the *Handbook*.

July 2006

Wolfgang Obenaus
Sepp Weidacher

LIST OF ABBREVIATIONS

adj.	– adjective / Adjektiv / Eigenschaftswort
adv.	– adverb / Adverb / Umstandswort
am.	– amerikanisch
brit.	– britisch
fig.	– figurative / bildlich / metaphorisch
pl.	– plural / Plural / Mehrzahl
prep.	– preposition / Präposition / Vorwort
s.	– substantive / Substantiv / Hauptwort
sby.	– somebody / jemand
sthg.	– something / etwas
v.	– verb / Verb / Zeitwort
UK	– United Kingdom
US	– United States

A

AAA rating – s. AAA-Einstufung (höchste Bonitätsstufe)
ABA – Austrian Business Agency (siehe)
abandon – v. aufgeben, preisgeben
abandonment – s. Aufgeben / Aufgabe / Eliminierung (eines Produktes)
aberration – s. Abweichung, Fehlleitung
abolish – v. abschaffen, aufheben
abolition – s. Abschaffung, Aufhebung
abortion – s. Fehlgeburt, Abtreibung, totaler Fehlschlag
abscence – s. Abwesenheit
absenteeism – s. (unentschuldigtes) Fernbleiben von der Arbeit, Absentismus, Blaumachen
absolute advantange – s. absoluter (Kosten-)Vorteil
absolute disadvantage – s. absoluter (Kosten-)Nachteil
absolute market share – s. absoluter Marktanteil
absolute standard – s. allgemein gültiger / absoluter / firmenunabhängiger / Richtwert
absorb – v. absorbieren, auffangen, dämpfen
absorb a tariff increase – eine Zollerhöhung auffangen / nicht auf die Kunden/Kundinnen abwälzen
abstention – s. (Stimm-)Enthaltung
abundant – adj. reichlich vorhanden, häufig vorkommend
ACA – Associated Chartered Accountant (siehe)
accede – v. beitreten
accede to a convention – einer Konvention beitreten
accelerate – v. beschleunigen, forcieren
accelerated cost recovery – s. vorzeitige Abschreibung
accelerated depreciation
s. vorzeitige Abschreibung
s. degressive Abschreibung
accelerated depreciation allowance – s. Betrag der vorzeitigen Abschreibung
accelerator principle – Akzeleratorprinzip
accept – v. annehmen, akzeptieren
accept goods – Waren annehmen
acceptance
s. Annahme / Akzept (eines Wechsels)
s. akzeptierter Wechsel, Akzept
s. Annahme (eines Antrages)
s. Annahme (von Waren)
acceptance credit – s. Akzeptkredit
acceptance house – s. Akzept-, Außenhandelsbank
acceptor – s. Akzeptant/in, Annehmer/in
access – s. Zutritt, Zugriff, Zugang
access – v. zugreifen, Zugriff nehmen
to access data – auf Daten zugreifen
accessible – adj. zugänglich
accessory contract – s. Nebenvertrag, akzessorischer Vertrag
access time – s. Zugriffszeit
accident – s. Unfall, plötzlich eintretendes Ereignis mit Schadenswirkung auf Menschen und/oder Sachen
accidental damage – s. Unfallschaden
accidental death – s. Unfalltod
accidental loss – s. Verlust aufgrund eines Unfalls, Unfallschaden
accommodation – s. Unterkunft, Unterbringung, Wohnung
accord – s. Übereinkunft, Abkommen, Abmachung
accord – v. gewähren, verleihen, zuerkennen
account
s. Konto
s. (pl.) Buchhaltung (im Sinne der Geschäftsbücher)
s. (Rechnungs-)Abschluss, Jahresabschluss
s. Bilanz (im Sinne der volkswirtschaftlichen Gesamtrechnung)
s. Rechnung
s. Kunde/Kundin, Klient/in
s. Werbeetat, Kundenetat
s. Geschäfts-, Kundenbeziehung, Kundschaft
debit an account – ein Konto belasten
credit an account – ein Konto erkennen, einem Konto gutschreiben
keep an account – ein Konto haben / unterhalten
handle an account – ein Konto führen
handling an account – Kontoführung
pay an amount into an account – einen Betrag auf ein Konto einzahlen
settle an account – eine Rechnung begleichen
for sby's account – auf jemandes Rechnung
for his own account – auf (seine) eigene Rechnung
revive an inactive account – eine eingeschlafene Geschäftsbeziehung reaktivieren
we have lost the Shell account – wir haben Shell als Klienten (unserer Werbagentur) verloren
current account – Leistungsbilanz
accountable – adj. verantwortlich, rechenschaftspflichtig
be accountable to one's stakeholders – den Anspruchsberechtigten gegenüber verantwortlich / rechenschaftspflichtig sein
accountant
s. (Bilanz-)Buchhalter/in, Fachmann/Fachfrau des Rechnungswesens
s. Buchsachverständige/r, Wirtschaftstreuhänder/in, Wirtschaftsprüfer/in, Buchprüfer/in, Steuerberater/in
account balance – s. Kontostand, Guthaben
account balance inquiry – s. Kontostandanfrage, Anfrage nach dem Kontostand, Abrufen des Kontostandes
account charge – s. Kontoführungsgebühr, Buchungsgebühr
account executive – s. Kundenbetreuer/in, (Werbe-)Kontakter/in, Etatdirektor/in
account for
v. verbuchen, bilanzieren
v. entfallen auf
accounting for bad debts – Verbuchung / Bilanzierung uneinbringlicher / dubioser Forderungen
accounting for stock options – bilanzielle Behandlung von Aktienoptionen
Futures account for 95% of total volume. – Auf börsenmäßige Terminkontrakte entfallen 95 % des Gesamtvolumens.
account form – s. Kontoform
account holder – s. Kontoinhaber
accounting – s. Rechnungswesen, Bilanzierung
accounting body – s. Berufsverband für Wirtschaftsprüfer u. ä. Berufe, Wirtschaftsprüferkammer (z. B. Institute of Chartered Accountants)
accounting concept – s. Begriff / Element der Buchhaltung / des Rechnungswesens
accounting conventions– s. Gewohnheiten / Gepflogenheiten / Usancen im Rechnungswesen / in der (Finanz-)Buchhaltung
accounting cycle – s. Buchungszyklus (vom Beleg bis zum Jahresabschluss)
accounting date – s. Bilanzstichtag
accounting (exchange) gain – s. nicht realisierter (Währungs-)Umrechnungsgewinn

accounting (exchange) loss – s. nicht realisierter (Währungs-) Umrechnungsverlust
accounting exchange risk – s. (Währungs-)Umrechnungs-, buchhalterisches Wechselkursrisiko
accounting information – s. Buchhaltungsdaten
accounting period – s. Rechnungsperiode
accounting practice – s. Verfahrensweisen / Praktik(en) / Gepflogenheiten im Rechnungswesen / in der (Finanz-)Buchhaltung
accounting principles – s. Grundsätze ordnungsgemäßer Buchführung und Bilanzierung
accounting process – s. Rechnungswesen-, Bilanzierungs-, Buchhaltungsverfahren, Abläufe im Rechnungswesen, in der Bilanzierung / Buchhaltung
accounting records – s. Bücher, buchhalterische Aufzeichnungen
accounting rules – s. Buchhaltungs- und Bilanzierungsvorschriften
accounting statement – s. Periodenrechnung, Periodenabschluss, Jahresabschluss, Finanzausweis
accounting system – s. Rechnungswesen-, Buchhaltungssystem
accounting value – s. Buchwert
account management – s. Kunden-, Etatbetreuung
account management department – s. Kontaktabteilung / Abteilung für Kundenbetreuung (einer Werbeagentur)
account manager – s. Kundenbetreuer/in, (Werbe-)Kontakter/in, Etatdirektor/in
Accounts – s. Buchhaltungsabteilung
account sales – s. Verkaufsabrechnung eines Kommissionärs / Konsignatars
accounts payable – s. (Buch-)Verbindlichkeiten (aufgrund von Warenlieferungen und Leistungen)
accounts payable to trade creditors
s. Verbindlichkeiten aufgrund von Warenlieferungen und Leistungen
accounts receivable – s. (Buch-)Forderungen (aufgrund von Warenlieferungen und Leistungen)
accounts receivable accounting – s. Debitorenbuchhaltung
account supervisor – s. Kontaktgruppenleiter/in, Etatdirektor/in, Gruppenleiter/in Kundebetreuung
accrual basis – s. Prinzip der Periodenreinheit / Periodenabgrenzung
accruals and deferrals – s. Rechnungsabgrenzungsposten
accrue – v. zufließen, erwachsen, auflaufen, anfallen, entstehen
gains accrue to a company – Gewinne entstehen für eine Gesellschaft
benefits accruing to ldcs – der den ärmsten Entwicklungsländern erwachsende Nutzen
accrued expense – s. antizipatives Passivum (Rechnungsabgrenzungsposten), sonstige Verbindlichkeit
accrued income – s. antizipatives Aktivum (Rechnungsabgrenzungsposten), sonstige Forderung
accrued interest – s. der Berichtsperiode zuzurechnende / noch nicht vereinnahmte / anteilige Zinsen, Zinsforderung(en)
accrued item – s. antizipativer Rechnungsabgrenzungsposten, sonstige Forderung / Verbindlichkeit
accrued liability – s. antizipatives Passivum (Rechnungsabgrenzungsposten), sonstige Verbindlichkeit
accrued revenue – s. antizipativer Ertrag(-sposten)
accumulated depreciation – s. kumulierte Abschreibung, gesammelte Abschreibungsbeträge, Summe der auf dem Konto Wertberichtigung zum Anlagevermögen gesammelten Abschreibungsbeträge
Accumulated Depreciation – s. (das Konto) Wertberichtigung zum Anlagevermögen, Erneuerungskonto
achieve – v. erreichen, erzielen
achieve a goal – ein Ziel erreichen
achieve results – Resultate / Ergebnisse erzielen
acid – s. Säure
acid – adj. sauer
acid rain – s. saurer Regen
acid precipitation – s. saurer Niederschlag
acid-test ratio – s. Liquidität 2. Grades
acknowledge
v. bestätigen
v. anerkennen, eingestehen, zugeben
acknowledge defeat – Niederlage eingestehen
acknowledge receipt – Erhalt bestätigen
acknowledgement
s. Bestätigung
s. Anerkennung, Anerkenntnis, Zugeständnis
ACP – African Caribbean Pacific (countries) (siehe)
acquire
v. erwerben, kaufen, übernehmen
v. sich (etwas) aneignen
v. akquirieren
acquire a company – eine Firma erwerben / übernehmen
acquire knowledge – sich Wissen aneignen, Wissen erwerben
acquire customers – Kunden akquirieren
acquisition
s. Erwerb, Ankauf, Aneignung
s. Übernahme, Erwerb, Akquisition
acquisition of customers – Kundenakquisition
acquisition of a company – Übernahme / Erwerb / Akquisition einer Gesellschaft
acquisition cost – s. Anschaffungswert, -kosten
across the board – adj. / adv. generell, allgemein, „durch die Bank"
act
s. Tat, Handlung
s. Gesetz
act of parliament – Parlamentsgesetz, vom Parlament verabschiedetes Gesetz
acting president – s. stellvertretende/r Generaldirekto/r / Vorstandsvorsitzende/r
action
s. Handlung, Vorgehen, Maßnahme
s. Klage, Prozess
bring an action against sby. – jemanden klagen / verklagen, gegen jemanden Klage erheben
action for damages pending – anhängige Schadenersatzklage, schwebendes Schadenersatzverfahren
a piece of the action – ein Stück vom Kuchen
active partner – s. geschäftsführende/r Gesellschafter/in einer Personengesellschaft
activity – s. Tätigkeit, Beschäftigung
activist approach – s. Aktivismusstrategie
act of God – s. Naturereignis, höhere Gewalt
actual cost(s) – s. Istkosten
actual delivery – s. effektive Lieferung, körperliche Übergabe
actual insolvency – s. Überschuldung, Insolvenz (auf Grund von Überschuldung), Zahlungsunfähigkeit
actual result – s. Istgröße, tatsächliches Resultat
actuals – s. Warentermingeschäfte mit effektiver Lieferung
actual total loss – s. tatsächlicher Totalverlust
actuary – s. Versicherungsmathematiker
ad – advertisement (siehe)

adapt – v. (sich) anpassen
adaptation – s. Anpassung
address
v. adressieren, anschreiben, ansprechen, sich wenden an
v. sich befassen mit, angehen
address target groups – Zielgruppen ansprechen
address a problem – sich mit einem Problem befassen, sich einem Problem zuwenden
addressing machine – s. Adressiergerät
adduce – v. anführen, beibringen, erbringen
adduce proof – Beweis(e) erbringen
adhere – v. befolgen, einhalten, sich halten
adhere to a delivery date – einen Liefertermin einhalten
adhesive tape – s. Klebeband
ad hoc – adj./ adv. ad hoc, kurzfristig, ohne Weitblick, vom Augenblicksbedarf bestimmt, ungeplant
convened ad hoc – kurzfristig einberufen
adhoc purchasing – Einkaufspolitik ohne Weitblick
ad hoc discount – s. kurzfristiger / kurzzeitiger Preisnachlass
adjacent – adj. benachbart, nebeneinander liegend
adjourn – v. vertagen, (zeitlich oder örtlich) verlegen
adjudge – s. entscheiden, erkennen, erklären
adjudge sby. bankrupt – jemanden als zahlungsunfähig erklären, über jemanden das Konkursverfahren eröffnen
adjust
v. anpassen, bereinigen, korrigieren, berichtigen
v. umbuchen, nachbuchen
adjust for price changes – preislich bereinigen
adjustable peg – s. stufenflexibler Wechselkurs, stufenflexibles Wechselkurssystem
adjustable peg (with bands) – s. stufenflexibler Wechselkurs (mit Bandbreiten)
adjusted – adj. (statistisch) bereinigt, berichtigt
adjusted time series – s. bereinigte Zeitreihe
adjusted trial balance – s. (um Um- und Nachbuchungen) berichtigte Rohbilanz (Summen und/oder Saldenbilanz)
adjusting entries – s. Um- und Nachbuchungen
administered price – s. (staatlich oder durch Unternehmen) regulierte Preise, administrierte Preise
administration
s. Verwaltung, Administration
s. -wirtschaft(-slehre)
s. Regierung
s. (brit.) Ausgleichsverfahren
personnel administration – Personalwirtschaft
US administration – US-Regierung
administrative barriers (to trade) – s. administrative Handelshemmnisse
administrative cost(s) – s. Verwaltungskosten
administrative expense(s) – s. Verwaltungsaufwand, -kosten
administrative overhead(s) – s. Verwaltungsgemeinkosten
admissible – adj. zulässig, erlaubt, einfuhrberechtigt
be admissible duty free – zollfrei einführbar sein, zollfrei importiert werden können
admission – s. Zulassung, Einfuhr, Import
admit
v. zugeben, eingestehen
v. einlassen, zulassen, (Import) erlauben
adopt – v. annehmen, einführen
adopt a new system – ein neues System einführen
ADR – alternative dispute resolution (siehe)
ad valorem – adv. auf Wertbasis
ad valorem duty – s. Wertzoll
advance
s. Vorauszahlung, Anzahlung, Vorschuss, Bevorschussung
s. (kurzfristiger) Kredit
advance on documents – Bevorschussung von Dokumenten
make an advance – einen kurzfristigen Kredit gewähren
make an advance on receivables bought – erworbene Forderungen bevorschussen
advance
v. erhöhen, hinaufsetzen, anziehen, steigen
v. Fortschritte machen, fortschreiten
v. vorschießen, Vorschuss leisten, bevorschussen
advance prices – Preise erhöhen
advance a percentage of the value of accounts – Forderungen zu einem Prozentsatz bevorschussen
advance payment – s. Vorauszahlung
advance payments from customers – s. vom Kunden geleistete Anzahlungen, erhaltene Anzahlungen
adverse – adj. ungünstig, passiv
adverse balance of trade – s. passive Handelsbilanz
advertisement – s. Werbemittel, Inserat, Annonce
advertisement for bids – s. Ausschreibung (im engeren Sinn), Einladung zur Anbotslegung
advertiser – s. Werbungstreibende/r, Inserent/in, Anzeigenkunde/-kundin
advertising
s. Werbung
s. Werbemittel, Werbematerial
advertising agency – s. Werbeagentur
advertising campaign – s. Werbefeldzug, -kampagne
advertising copy – s. Werbetext
advertising department – s. Werbeabteilung
advertising effect – s. Werbewirkung
Advertising Expense – s. Werbeaufwand(-skonto)
advertising manager – s. Werbeleiter/in, -manager/in, -chef/in, Leiter/in der Werbeabteilung
advertising medium – s. Werbeträger
advertising research – s. Werbeforschung
advertising schedule – s. Werbeterminplan, Einschaltplan
advice
s. Ratschlag, Ratschläge, Beratung
s. Nachricht, Benachrichtigung, Aviso, Avisierung, Anzeige, Mitteilung
advice note – s. Versandanzeige
advice of dispatch – s. Versandanzeige
advice of shipment – s. Versandanzeige
advise
v. (be-)raten, empfehlen
v. benachrichtigen, verständigen, informieren, ankündigen, avisieren, mitteilen
advising bank – s. Avisobank
advisory services – s. Beratungsdienste, -tätigkeit, Konsulententätigkeit
advocate – v. befürworten, eintreten für
aerospace industry – s. Luft- und Raumfahrtsindustrie
affect – v. einwirken auf, (negativ) beeinflussen, betreffen, angehen, beeinträchtigen
affiliated company – s. Konzernunternehmen, verbundenes Unternehmen
affirm – v. bestätigen, bekräftigen, versichern
affluent – adj. wohlhabend, begütert, im Überfluss schwimmend
affluent lifestyle – s. Leben im Überfluss
affluent society – s. Überfluss-, Wohlstandsgesellschaft
afford
v. sich (etwas) leisten,
v. bieten, gewähren
We cannot afford this. – Wir können uns das nicht leisten.
afford protection – Schutz bieten

affordable – adj. bezahlbar, erschwinglich
AFL-CIO – American Federation of Labor and Congress of Industrial Organisations (siehe)
African Caribbean Pacific countries – s. afrikanische, karibische und pazifische Länder
AFTA – ASEAN Free Trade Area (siehe)
after-tax – adj. / adv. nachsteuerlich, versteuert, nach Steuern
after-tax rate of return – s. Rentabilität bezogen auf das Ergebnis nach Steuern
age allowance – s. Altersfreibetrag
agency – s. Agentur, Vertretung
agency broker – s. reine/r Börsenmakler/in (ohne Transaktionen auf eigene Rechnung)
agenda – s. Tagesordnung
agent
s. Handelnde/r, Akteur/in, Schaffende/r
s. Handlungsbevollmächtigte/r, Vertreter/in
s. (selbständige/r) Handelsvertreter/in
s. Gesellschaftsorgan
s. Sammelbesteller/in
free agent – Freischaffende/r
agent carrying stock – s. Vertreter/in mit Auslieferungslager
age structure – s. Altersstruktur, Altersaufbau
aggravate – v. erschweren, verschlimmern, verschärfen
aggregate – s. volkswirtschaftliche / makroöknomische Größe, Aggregat, Gesamtgröße, -summe
aggregate – v. aggregieren, zusammenlegen, zusammenzählen
aggregate
adj. gesamt, Gesamt-
adj. aggregiert, gesamtwirtschaftlich, makroökonomisch
aggregate demand – s. gesamtwirtschaftliche Nachfrage
AGM – annual general meeting (siehe)
agreed takeover – s. freundliche (mit der Geschäftsleitung der Zielgesellschaft abgestimmte) Übernahme
agreed takeover bid – s. freundliches (mit der Geschäftsleitung der Zielgesellschaft abgestimmtes) Übernahmeangebot
agreement – s. Übereinkunft, Abmachung, Vertrag
honour an agreement – sich an eine Übereinkunft halten
Agreement on Trade-Related Aspects of Intellectual Property Rights – s. Abkommen über handelsbezogene Aspekte geistiger Eigentumsrechte
agribusiness – s. Agrobusiness, Argibusiness, industriell betriebene Landwirtschaft
agricultural commune – s. landwirtschaftliche Kommune
agricultural co-operative – s. landwirtschaftliche Genossenschaft
agricultural marketing co-operative – s. landwirtschaftliche Absatzgenossenschaft
agricultural subsidy – s. Landwirtschaftssubvention
AICPA – American Institute of Certified Public Accountants (siehe)
aid – s. Hilfe, Hilfeleistung, Hilfsmittel
aid through trade – s. Hilfe durch Handel, Handel anstatt Hilfe, Handelshilfe
airborne trade – s. Luftfrachtverkehr
air cargo – s. Luftfracht(-gut)
air cargo insurance – s. Luftfrachtversicherung
air cargo policy – s. Luftfrachtversicherung(-spolizze)
air carrier – s. Luftfrachtführer, Fluggesellschaft
air-conditioning system – s. Klimaanlage
air consignment note – s. Luftfrachtbrief
air container – s. Luftfracht-Container
aircraft – s. Flugzeug/e
aircraft hull insurance – s. Luftkaskoversicherung
air freight
s. Luftfracht(-gut)
s. Luftfracht(-gebühr)
air freighter – s. Frachtflugzeug
air line booking system – s. Fluglinien-, Flugticketreservierungssystem
airline operator – s. Linienfluguntemehmen, -firma
airline schedule – s. Flugplan
air mail – s. Luftpost
air pollution – s. Luftverschmutzung
airport of departure – s. Abflughafen
airport of destination – s. Bestimmungsflughafen
air shipment – s. Luftfracht(-sendung)
air transport – s. Luftfrachtverkehr, Luftverkehr
air waybill – s. Luftfrachtbrief
ALGOL – Algorithmic Language (Programmiersprache)
alienation – s. Entfremdung
allocate – v. zuteilen, zuweisen, widmen, (den Einsatz) steuern, zurechnen, zumessen, zuschlagen, verteilen, umlegen, dotieren
allocate costs – Kosten zurechnen / verteilen / umlegen
allocate resources – den Einsatz von Produktionsfaktoren / Mitteln steuern, Produktionsfaktoren einsetzen
allocated quota – s. Länderkontingent
allocation
s. Allokation, Steuerung des Faktoreinsatzes, Faktoreinsatz
s. Zurechnung, Zuteilung, Zuschlag, Umlegung, Verteilung (bes. von Kosten), Dotation
put customers on allocation – Kundenaufträge rationieren
allocations from profits – s. Dotation (der Rücklagen) aus den Gewinnen
allocation of machines – s. Maschinenbelegung
allocation of resources – s. Ressourcen-, Mittelallokation, Allokation (volkswirtschaftlicher) Ressourcen
allocation to retained earnings accounts – s. Dotierung der Rücklagen
allotment of shares – s. Zuteilung / Repartierung von Aktien
allowance
s. ausgesetzter Betrag, Monatsgeld, Taschengeld
s. Zuschuss, Zuwendung, Beihilfe
s. (Preis-)Nachlass
s. (Steuer-)Freibetrag
s. Abschreibung(-squote), Wertberichtigung
Allowance for Bad Debts – s. (das Konto) Wertberichtigung zu Forderungen, Delkredererückstellung(-skonto)
Allowance for Depreciation – s. (das Konto) Wertberichtigung zum Anlagevermögen
Allowance for Doubtful Accounts – s. (das Konto) Wertberichtigung zu Forderungen Delkredererückstellung(-skonto)
Allowance for Uncollectible Accounts – s. (das Konto) Wertberichtigung zu Forderungen, Delkredererückstellungskonto
allowance method – s. Pauschal-, Sammelwertberichtigung
allow for – v. berücksichtigen, ins Kalkül ziehen
all-risk clause – s. Allgefahrenklausel
all-risks cover – s. Allgefahrendeckung
all-risks policy – s. Allgefahrenpolizze
alternative dispute resolution – s. alternative / außergerichtliche Streitbeilegung, alternative Verfahren zur Streitbeilegung
alternative marketing organisation – s. alternative Handels- / Vertriebsorganisation, Importorganisation des Fairen Handels/ Fair-Trade-Handelshaus
alternative trading organisation – s. alternative Marketing- / Vertriebsorganisation, Importorganisation des Fairen Handels, Fair-Trade-Handelshaus

amalgamation
s. (brit.) Fusion durch Neugründung
s. (am.) echte Fusion
amenable – adj. zugänglich
amendment – s. (Ab-)Änderung, Ergänzung, Nachtrag, Berichtigung, Novelle
amenity – s. Annehmlichkeit, Ausstattungsdetail, -merkmal
American Federation of Labor and Congress of Industrial Organisations – Dachverband der US-Gewerkschaften
American Institute of Certifled Public Accountants – s. Berufsorganisation der amerikanischen Wirtschaftsprüfer
American option – s. amerikanische (Devisen-)Option
American Stock Exchange – s. American Stock Exchange (Wertpapierbörse im Besitz der NASDAQ)
American-style option – s. amerikanische Option, Option amerikanischen Stils
AMEX – s. American Stock Exchange (siehe)
amicable – adj. gütlich, einvernehmlich, freundlich
ammunition – s. Munition
amortisation
s. Abschreibung auf immaterielle Vermögenswerte
s. Tilgung, periodische Rückzahlung, Bedienung einer Schuld
AMOs – alternative marketing organisations
amount due – s. geschuldeter Betrag, Schuldbetrag
amount owed – s. geschuldeter Betrag, Schuldbetrag
analogue – adj. analog
analogue computer – s. Analogrechner
ancillary products – s. Zubehör, Verbrauchsmaterial
animal manure – s. Tierdünger, Mist
announcement – s. Bekanntmachung, Anzeige
annual accounts – s. Jahresabschluss
annual general meeting – s. Jahreshauptversammlung (AG), jährliche Gesellschafterversammlung (GmbH)
annual meeting of shareholders – s. Jahreshauptversammlung(AG), jährliche Gesellschafterversammlung (GmbH)
annual meeting of stockholders – s. Jahreshauptversammlung (AG), jährliche Gesellschafterversammlung (GmbH)
annual rental value – s. Bemessungsgrundlage für die ehemalige UK-Gemeindesteuer
annual transit policy – s. (Binnentransport-) Pauschalversicherung / Pauschalpolizze
annual writing-down allowance – s. jährlicher steuerlicher Abschreibungsbetrag
antecedents – s. Vorgeschichte, Vorläufer
anti-business – adj. wirtschaftsfeindlich
anticipated expense – s. antizipatives Passivum (Rechnungsabgrenzungsposten), sonstige Verbindlichkeit
anticipated profit – s. imaginärer Gewinn
anti-dumping duty – s. Antidumpingzoll
anti-dumping measures – s. Antidumpingmaßnahmen
anti-dumping tariff – s. Antidumpingzoll
antifreeze – s. Frostschutzmittel
antifreeze – adj. frostgeschützt, -resistent
anti-subsidy duty – s. Antisubventionszoll
antitrust law – s. Antitrustrecht, US-Kartell- und Monopolgesetzgebung
APEC – Asia-Pacific Economic Cooperation (siehe)
APL – A Programming Language (Programmiersprache)
apparent – adj. augenscheinlich, offensichtlich, Anscheins-
apparent good order and condition – augenscheinlich (äußerlich) gute Beschaffenheit (Konnossementsklausel)
appeal
s. Anreiz, Attraktivität, Anziehungskraft, Anklang
s. Anrufung
appeal to the WTO – Anrufung der Welthandelsorganisation
appeal
v. wirken, Eindruck machen, beeindrucken, ansprechen
v. anrufen
appeal to customers – Kunden ansprechen / beeindrucken
appealing – adj. anziehend, attraktiv, ansprechend
appearance
s. Erscheinen, Auftauchen, Entstehen
s. Aussehen, äußeres Erscheinungsbild
append – v. anfügen, hinzufügen
append to a contract – einem Vertrag hinzufügen, als Vertragsanhang anfügen
applicable – adj. anwendbar, geltend, zutreffend
where applicable – falls zutreffend
applicable law – s. anzuwendendes Recht
applicant
s. (Stellen-)Bewerber/in
s. Antragsteller/in
s. Akkreditivsteller/in, Akkreditiv-Auftraggeber/in, Anweisende/r
s. Garantieauftraggeber
applicant for a credit – s. Kreditwerber/in, -antragsteller/in
applicant for a guarantee – s. Garantieauftraggeber/in
application
s. Antrag, Anmeldung, Bewerbung, Gesuch
s. Anwendung, Verwendung, Geltung
application for foreign currency – s. Antrag für den Erwerb oder die Ausfuhr von Fremdwährungen
application for listing – s. Antrag auf Börsenzulassung / Börsennotierung
application of funds – s. Mittelverwendung
application package – s. Anwendungssoftwarepaket
application program – s. Anwendungsprogramm
application software – s. Anwendungssoftware
application to open a (documentary) credit – s. Akkreditivantrag
applied science – s. angewandte Wissenschaft
apply
v. anwenden, gebrauchen, einsetzen
v. gelten, passen, zutreffen
v. sich wenden (an)
v. beantragen, bewerben
quotas apply to certain goods – Kontingente gelten für bestimmte Waren
a section applies to sthg. – ein Paragraph gilt für etwas
apply for a job – sich um einen Posten bewerben
apply to sby. – sich an jemanden wenden
appoint – v. ernennen, einsetzen
appoint an arbitrator – einen Schiedrichter ernennen
appointment
s. Ernennung, Bestellung, Berufung
s. Termin, Verabredung
appreciate
v. wertschätzen, zu danken wissen
v. im Wert steigen, im Kurs steigen, aufwerten (bes. bei einer Währung mit flexiblem Wechselkurs)
We appreciate your business. – Wir danken Ihnen für Ihren Besuch.
The US dollar has appreciated. – Der US-Dollar hat aufgewertet.
appreciation
s. Wertschätzung
s. Wertsteigerung
s. (Wechsel-)Kursanstieg, Aufwertung (bes. einer Währung mit flexiblem Wechselkurs)
apprentice – s. Lehrling

apprenticeship – s. Lehre, Lehrverhältnis
approach
s. Annäherung, Zugang
s. (Theorie-/Denk-)Ansatz, Methode, Weg, Verfahren, Rechnungsart
appropriate – adj. geeignet, entsprechend, passend, angepasst
appropriate – v. zuordnen
appropriate goods to a contract – Kaufvertrag konkretisieren
appropriate technology – s. angepasste Technologie
appropriation
s. Aneignung,
s. Verwendung, Zuteilung, Zweckbestimmung
appropriation account – s. Gewinnverwendungskonto, buchmäßige Gewinnaufteilung
appropriation of profits – s. Gewinnverwendung, buchmäßige Gewinnaufteilung, Zweckbindung von Gewinnen
approval – s. Billigung, Genehmigung, Zustimmung
on approval – auf Probe
sale on approval – Kauf auf Probe
approval period – s. Billigungsfrist
approximate – adj. annähernd, ungefähr, etwa
aptitude test – s. Eignungstest
arb – arbitrager (siehe)
arbitrage
s. Arbitrage
s. Börsenspekulation (im Zusammenhang mit Firmenübernahmen)
arbitrager
s. Arbitrageur/in
s. Börsenspekulant/in (im Zusammenhang mit Firmenübernahmen)
arbitrageur (siehe *arbitrager*)
arbitration
s. Schiedsgerichts-, Schiedsverfahren
s. (arbeitsrechtliches) Schlichtungsverfahren
arbitration award – s. Schiedsspruch
arbitration clause – s. Schiedsklausel
arbitration proceedings – s. Schiedsgerichts-, Schiedsverfahren
arbitrator – s. Schiedsrichter
arch board file – s. Hebelordner
arch (lever) file – s. Hebelordner, Büroordner mit Hebelmechanik
arch unit – s. Hebelmechanik (bei einem Büroordner)
ardent – adj. begeistert, glühend
area code – s. Ortsvorwahlnummer
arise – v. entstehen, sich ergeben
disputes arising from the contract – die sich aus dem Vertrag ergebenden Streitigkeiten
arithmetic-logic unit – s. Rechenwerk, arithmetisch-logische Einheit, ALU
arithmetic mean – s. arithmetisches Mittel
arm
s. Arm
s. Sparte, Geschäftszweig
keep sbdy. at arm's length – jemanden auf Distanz halten
arm's length transaction – s. marktkonformes Geschäft, marktkonformer Geschäftsabschluss
armament industry – s. Rüstungsindustrie
armchair shopping – s. Homeshopping, Heimkauf
arrangement for payment – s. Zahlungsmethode
arrear – s. (meist pl.) Rückstand, Schulden
in arrear(s) – im Rückstand, in Verzug
arson – s. Brandstiftung
articles of association – s. der das Innenverhältnis regelnde Teil des Gesellschaftsvertrages / der Satzung / der Statuten einer UK- *registered company*
articles of incorporatlon – s. Gründungsurkunde einer US-*corporation*, der das Außenverhältnis regelnde Teil des Gesellschaftsvertrages / der Satzung / der Statuten
articles of partnership – s. Gesellschaftsvertrag (einer Personengesellschaft)
articulated lorry – s. Sattelzug, Sattelkraftfahrzeug
artificial fertiliser – s. Kunstdünger
artificial person – s. juristische Person
ascertain – v. erfassen, feststellen, ermitteln
ASEAN – Association of Southeast Asian Nations (siehe)
ASEAN Free Trade Area – s. Freihandelszone des Verbandes Südostasiatischer Staaten
Asia-Pacific Economic Cooperation – s. Asiatisch-Pazifische Wirtschaftsgemeinschaft, Asiatisch-Pazifische Wirtschaftszusammenarbeit
ask – s. Brief-, Verkaufs-, Devisenbrief-, Devisenverkaufskurs, Angebot
ask price – s. Brief-, Verkaufs-, Devisenbrief-, Devisenverkaufskurs
ask rate – s. Brief-, Verkaufs-, Devisenbrief-, Devisenverkaufskurs
asked price – s. Brief-, Verkaufs-, Devisenbrief-, Devisenverkaufskurs
asked rate – s. Brief-, Verkaufs-, Devisenbrief-, Devisenverkaufskurs
assembler – s. Assembler, Assemblierer, Assemblierprogramm
assembling
s. Zusammenstellung (von Aufträgen oder Sortimenten)
s. Assembling, Montage, Zusammenbau
assembly – s. Montage, Zusammenbau
assembly language – s. Assembler-, Assembliererssprache, maschinenorientierter Symbolcode
assembly line – Fertigungsstraße, Fließband, Montageband
assess
v. beurteilen, bewerten, einschätzen
v. festsetzen, bemessen, vorschreiben, veranlagen
assess customs duties – Zölle / Zollgebühren bemessen
assess a premium – eine Versicherungsprämie festsetzen
assessable – adj. steuerbar
assessable income – s. steuerbares Einkommen
assessed value – s. Einheits-, Steuerwert
assessment
s. Beurteilung, Bewertung, Einschätzung, Prüfung
s. (steuerliche) Veranlagung; Bemessung; Festsetzung; Vorschreibung von Abgaben, Zöllen, Steuern etc.; Steuervorschreibung
environmental impact assessment – Umweltverträglichkeitsprüfung
assessment centre – s. Assessment Center, Assessment-Center-Verfahren
assessment district – s. Steuerbezirk
assessment of import duty – s. Bemessung des Einfuhrzolls
assessor – s. (Grund-)Steuerveranlagungsbeamter
asset
s. Vermögenswert, Aktivposten
s. (pl.) Aktiva, Aktiven, Vermögenswerte
asset account – s. aktives Bestandskonto
asset-backed securities – s. Asset-Backed Securities, (sekundär) verbriefte Finanzaktiva
asset-based finance – s. Asset-Based Finance (ABF), durch Unternehmensaktiva besicherte Finanzierung(-sstrukturen)
asset value – s. Substanz- / Buchwert (einer Aktie)
assign
v. zuweisen, zuteilen, umlegen

v. zedieren, abtreten
assignment
s. Zuteilung, Aufgabe
s. Zession, Abtretung
assistance programme – s. Förder-, Hilfsprogramm
Associated Chartered Accountant – s. assoziiertes Mitglied des Institute of Chartered Accountants
associated company – s. assoziiertes Unternehmen
associated country – s. assoziiertes Land
association – s. Vereinigung, Zusammenschluss, Verband, Verein
Association of Southeast Asian Nations – s. Verband Südostasiatischer Staaten
assume
v. annehmen, unterstellen
v. übernehmen
assume a risk – ein Risiko übernehmen
assurance – s. Lebensversicherung
astray – adv. abseits des rechten Weges, auf dem Irrweg, im Irrtum
go astray – vom rechten Weg abkommen, fehlgeleitet werden, an die falsche Adresse geschickt werden
AT – advanced technology (personal computer)
ATA carnet – s. Carnet ATA, internationales Zollpassierscheinheft (für die vorübergehende Einfuhr und Ausfuhr von bestimmten Waren)
ATM – s. automated teller machine (siehe)
ATO – alternative trading organisation (siehe)
atomic fission – s. Kernspaltung
atomic fusion – s. Kernfusion
attach
v. anheften, beifügen, beilegen
v. anhaften, gelten
attached documents – beigefügte Dokumente
attached to this letter – als Anlage zu diesem Brief
insurance attaches as soon as .... – die Versicherung gilt, sobald ....
attend – v. teilnehmen an, besuchen
attend a meeting – an einer Sitzung teilnehmen
attend a course – einen Kurs besuchen
attendee – s. (Sitzungs-)Teilnehmer/in
attract – v. anziehen, auf sich ziehen, unterliegen
attract tax – steuerpflichtig sein
attract income tax – einkommensteuerpflichtig sein
Gains attract a tax rate of 5%. – Gewinne unterliegen einem Steuersatz von 5 % / werden mit 5 % besteuert.
attrition rate – s. Versager-, Flopquote
auction – s. Auktion, Versteigerung, Auktionsmethode (für Wertpapieremissionen)
auctioneer – s. Auktionator/in, Versteigerer, Versteigerin
auction (off) – v. versteigern
audience – s. Publikum, Leserschaft, Zuhörerschaft, Zuschauerschaft
audio typist – s. Phonotypist/in
audit– s. Rechnungs-, Buch-, Abschlussprüfung, Revision
audit – v. prüfen, Rechnungsprüfungen durchführen
audited balance sheet – s. testierte / geprüfte Bilanz
auditee – s. geprüfte / zu prüfende Firma / Organisation
auditing – s. Rechnungs-, Buch-, Abschluss-, Revision
auditor – s. Rechnungs-, Abschlussprüfer/in, Revisor/in, Revisionsfachmann, -fachfrau
auditor's report – s. Prüfungsbericht / Bestätigungsvermerk
audit team – s. Prüfergruppe
auspices – s. Schirmherrschaft
under the auspices of the WTO – unter der Schirmherrschaft der WTO
austere – adj. spartanisch (eingerichtet), sparsam
austerity – s. (drastisches) Sparprogramm, Austerity
Austrian Business Agency – (offizielle) österreichische Betriebsansiedlungsorganisation
autarky – s. Autarkie, wirtschaftliche Unabhängigkeit
authenticate – s. authentisieren, identifizieren, (behauptete Identität) nachweisen / bestätigen, beglaubigen
authorise – v. autorisieren, genehmigen, bewilligen, freigeben
authorised capital – s. Grund-/Stammkapital plus genehmigtes Kapital
authoritarian management style – s. autoritärer Führungsstil
authority
s. Befugnis, Vollmacht, Ermächtigung
s. Behörde
automated teller machine – s. automatischer Bankschalter, erweiteter Geldausgabeautomat
automatic dialler – s. automatischer Rufnummernbeantworter, Wählautomat
automatic selling – s. Automatenverkauf
automatic vending – s. Automatenverkauf
automatic vending machine operator
s. (Verkaufs-)Automatenbetreiber/in, -aufsteller/in
automation – s. Automation
automobile insurance – s. Kraftfahrzeugversicherung
automotive industry – s. Fahrzeugindustrie
autonomous expenditure – s. autonome / exogene / exogen bestimmte Ausgaben
auxiliary – adj. Hilfs-, Neben-, unterstützend
auxiliary functions – s. Hilfsdienste, unterstützende Dienste / Bereiche / Tätigkeiten
avail (oneself of sthg.) – v. (von etwas) Gebrauch machen
available – adj. verfügbar, zu haben, erhältlich, benutzbar
L/C available by a draft – ein durch einen Wechsel benutzbares Akkreditiv
availability – s. Verfügbarkeit
aval – s. Aval, Avalbürgschaft
average
s. Durchschnitt (arithmetisches Mittel)
s. (ungewichteter) Index
s. Havarie, durch Unfall verursachte Beschädigung an Schiff und Ladung
with average – mit Deckung der Partikularhavarie
average – adj. durchschnittlich, Durchschnitts-
average – v. im Durchschnitt ausmachen / betragen
average adjustment – s. Dispache, Adjustierung, urkundliche Feststellung der Havarie-grosse-Schäden
average tax rate – s. Durchschnittssteuersatz
aviation insurance – s. Lufttransport-, Luftfahrtversicherung
award – v. zuerkennen, zuschlagen
award a contract – einen Auftrag zuschlagen / erteilen
awarding of the contract – s. Zuschlag, Auftragserteilung
awareness – s. Bewusstsein, Bewusstheit, Bekanntheit
awareness of environmental problems – Umweltbewusstsein
awareness of product differences – Bewusstsein für Produktunterschiede
AWB – s. air waybill (siehe)

B

B2B – business-to-business (siehe)
B2B sell-side storefront – s. anbieterseitiges internetbasiertes Geschäftsportal für Business-to-Business-Transaktionen
B2B buy-side procurement – nachfrageseitiges internetbasiertes Beschaffungssystem für Business-to-Business-Transaktionen
B2B market place – s. (Business-to-Business) Handelsportal, (Business-to Business)
Handelsplattform, Business-to-Business-Marktplatz, B2B-Marktplatz, Internet-Marktplatz, Internet-Handelsplattform
B2C – Business-to-Customer (siehe)
B2E – Business-to-Employees (siehe)
B2G – Business-to-Government (siehe)
backfire – v. sich als Rohrkrepierer erweisen, in die Hose gehen
backlog of unfilled orders – s. Auftragsbestand, Bestand an unerledigten Aufträgen
back to basics – *zurück zu den Wurzeln*, Rückbesinnung auf die Kernkompetenz(en)
bad debt expense – s. Kreditverlust(e)
bad debts – s. dubiose und/oder uneinbringliche Forderungen (aus Warenlieferungen und Leistungen)
bads – s. negative Güter / externe Effekte
bad timekeeping – s. Unpünktlichkeit
balance
s. Gleichgewicht, Equilibrium
s. Saldo, Kontostand, Restbetrag, Restschuld, Rest
in balance – im Gleichgewicht, ausgeglichen
on balance – per Saldo, unter dem Strich
balance – v. saldieren, Saldo feststellen
balance inquiry – s. Kontostandanfrage, Anfrage nach dem Kontostand, Abrufen des Kontostandes
balance of payments – s. Zahlungsbilanz
balance of payments deficit – s. Zahlungsbilanzdefizit, -passivum
balance of payments format – s. Zahlungsbilanzsystem, -gliederung
balance of payments on capital account
s. Kapitalverkehrsbilanz
balance of payments on current account – s. Leistungsbilanz
balance of payments surplus – s. Zahlungsbilanzüberschuss, -aktivum
balance of trade – s. Handels-, Warenverkehrsbilanz
balance out – v. ausgleichen
balance sheet – s. (Unternehmens-)Bilanz
draw up a balance sheet – eine Bilanz erstellen
prepare a balance sheet – eine Bilanz erstellen
balance sheet date – s. Bilanzstichtag
balance sheet equation – s. Bilanzgleichung
balance sheet item – s. Bilanzposten
balance sheet ratio – s. Bilanzkennzahl
balance sheet risk – s. (Währungs-)Umrechnungsrisiko, buchhalterisches Wechselkursrisiko
bale – v. in Ballen verpacken
baled goods – in Ballen verpackte Waren
ban – s. Verbot
bank acceptance – s. Bankakzept, (pl.) Privatdiskonten
bank charge – s. Bank-, Kontoführungs-, Manipulationsgebühr
bank commission – s. Bankprovision
bank counter – s. Bankschalter
pay in over the bank counter – beim Bankschalter einzahlen
bank deposits – s. (Bank-)Einlagen, Depositen
bank draft – s. Banken-, Institutsscheck
banker's reference – s. Bankreferenz
bank giro – s. Zahlungs- und Überweisungsverkehr der UK-Banken
bank guarantee – s. Bankgarantie
banker's draft – s. Banken-, Institutsscheck
banking – s. Bankgeschäft, -wesen, -fach
banking habit – s. habituelle Nutzung von Bankdienstleistungen durch Kleinkunden
banking hours – s. Banköffnungszeiten
banking office – s. Bank
banking services – s. Bankdienstleistungen
bank lending – s. Kredit- / Aktivgeschäft der Banken
bank loan – s. Bankkredit
bank rate – s. Bankrate, Leitzinsen
bank reference – s. Bankreferenz
bankrupt – s. Konkurs-, Insolvenzschuldner/in
bankruptcy – s. Insolvenz-/ Konkurs- / Ausgleichs(-verfahren)
bankruptcy petition – s. Antrag auf Eröffnung eines Insolvenz- / Konkurs- / Ausgleichsverfahrens
bankrupt's estate – s. Konkurs-, Insolvenzmasse
bankrupt's property – s. Konkurs-, Insolvenzmasse
bank statement – s. Konto-, Bankauszug
bank transfer – s. Banküberweisung (ins Ausland)
banner – s. (Werbe-)Banner / Spruchband / Transparent
bar – s. Balken, Säule, Strich
bar chart – s. Säulen-, Stabdiagramm
bar code – s. Strichcode
bargain
s. Geschäft, Transaktion, Abschluss, Übereinkunft
s. Gelegenheitskauf, günstiges Geschäft, billige Ware, Schäppchen
bargaining position – s. Verhandlungsposition
barge – s. Last-, Frachtkahn
barrage – s. Trommelfeuer, Bombardement
barrel – s. Fass, (als Maßeinheit) 159 Liter
barter
s. Tausch(-handel), Tauschgeschäfte
s. Gegengeschäfte, Eigenkompensation
barter transaction – s. Tauschgeschäft
based
adj. basiert, begründet, bezogen, beruhend
adj. mit (Firmen-)Sitz
US-based firms – Firmen mit Sitz in den USA
base (lending) rate
s. Basiszinssatz der UK-Geschäftsbanken, (etwa) Zinssatz für erste Adressen
s. Zinssatz der Bank von England für Kredite an die Diskontbanken, UK-Leitzinsatz
base value – s. (Index-)Basiswert
base period – s. Basisperiode, -zeitraum, Bezugsperiode
BASIC – Beginner's All-purpose Symbolic Instruction Code (Programmiersprache)
basic accounting principles – s. (allgemeine) Grundsätze ordnungsgemäßer Buchführung und Bilanzierung
basic period – s. Grundmietzeit
basis
s. Basis, Grundlage
s. Basis, Basis-Differenz, Differenz zwischen Termin- und Kassakurs
basis point – s. Basispunkt, bp, 0.01 Prozent
30 basis points over LIBOR – 30 Basispunkte über LIBOR

basis swap – s. Basisswap
batch – s. Stoß, Stapel, Partie, Los, Charge
batch processing – s. Stapelverarbeitung
batch production – s. (Klein-)Serienfertigung, Chargenfertigung
battle-cry – s. Schlachtruf, Motto
bp – basis point (siehe)
B/E – bill of exchange (siehe)
bear – s. Bär, Baisse-Spekulant, Baissier
bearer – s. Inhaber, Überbringer
bearer bill – s. Inhaberwechsel
bearer cheque – s. Inhaberscheck
bearer instrument – s. Inhaberpapier
bearer share – s. Inhaberaktie
bearish – adj. Baisse-, pessimistisch
bearish sentiment – Baissestimmung
bear market – s. B Bärenmarkt, Baisse
bear out – v. bestätigen, bekräftigen
bear strategy – s. Bärenstrategie, Baisse-Strategie
beef up – v. stärken, kräftigen
beeper – s. Piepserl, Radio Pager
beginning inventory – s. Anfangsbestand
below-average – adj. unterdurchschnittlich
belt-tightening – s. „den Gürtel enger schnallen"
benchmark – s. Benchmark, Richt-, Referenz-, Pegel-, Vergleichswert
benchmark interest rate – s. Leitzinssatz, Leitzinsen
benefactor – s. Wohltäter, Erblasser, Schenker
beneficial – adj. dienlich, förderlich, nutzbringend, vorteilhaft
beneficiary
s. Begünstiger, Anweisungsempfänger (eines Akkreditivs)
s. (Anspruchs-)Berechtiger
beneficiary of a guarantee – Garantiebegünstigter, -nehmer
beneficiary of a trust – Treuhandbegünstigter, Treunehmer
benefit
s. Nutzen, Vorteil, Gewinn, Wohltat
s. (Sozialversicherungs-)Leistung
s. (betriebliche) Nebenleistung / Vergünstigung
benefit period – s. Erfolgs-, Anfallsperiode (Rechnungsperiode, der die erfolgsmäßigen Konsequenzen von Einnahmen oder Ausgaben zuzurechnen sind)
benign – adj. günstig, mild, zuträglich, freundlich
environmentally benign – umweltfreundlich, -verträglich
bereavement allowance – s. Todesfall-Freibetrag
berth – s. Liegeplatz (eines Schiffes)
best-efforts – s. *best efforts*, angemessene / vertretbare / zumutbare Anstrengungen zur Erreichung eines Vertragszieles (US-Verpflichtungsklausel ohne Entsprechung im deutschen / österreichischen Recht)
betting – s. Wetten, Abschließen von Wettverträgen
beverage – s. Getränk
bid
s. Gebot, Angebot, Submissionsangebot (bei Ausschreibungen)
s. Geld-, Devisengeld-, Devisenankaufskurs, Geld, Nachfrage
bid – v. bieten, lizitieren (bes. bei einer Auktion)
bid-ask spread – s. Spanne (zwischen Geld- und Briefkurs), Marge (zwischen Geld und Brief)
bid bond – s. Bietungs-, Ausschreibungsgarantie
bidder – s. Bieter/in (bei einer Auktion, bei einem Firmenübernahmeangebot), Anbieter/in, Bewerber/in, Submittent/in (bei einer Ausschreibung)
bidding
s. Ausschreibung (im weiteren Sinn)
s. Angebotsabgabe, Unterbreitung von Submissionsangeboten, Teilnahme an einer Ausschreibung, Lizitieren
bidding consortium – s. Bieter-, Bietungskonsortium, Bietergemeinschaft
bid guarantee – s. Bietungs-, Ausschreibungsgarantie
bid-offer spread – s. Spanne (zwischen Geld- und Briefkurs), Marge (zwischen Geld und Brief)
bid price – s. Geld-, Ankaufs-, Devisengeld-, Devisenankaufskurs
bid rate – s. Geld-, Ankaufs-, Devisengeld-, Devisenankaufskurs
bid up – v. hinauflizitieren
Big Bang
s. Urknall
s. Big Bang (Reform des britischen Finanzmarktes 1986)
bilateralism – s. Bilateralismus, Prinzip der Zweiseitigkeit
bilateral trade accord – s. (bilaterale) Präferenzzone, bilaterales Handelsabkommen
bill
s. Rechnung, Faktura
s. Wechsel
s. Konnossement, Seefrachtbrief
s. Gesetzesvorlage
s. Handzettel
s. (Gesamt-)Kosten
The total bill came to €20 million. – Die Gesamtkosten beliefen sich auf 20 Millionen Euro.
bill – v. in Rechnung stellen, fakturieren
bill book – s. Wechsel-, Wechselkopierbuch
bill broker – s. Wechselmakler(-firma)
billing – s. Rechnungslegung, Fakturierung
billings – s. Umsatz(-erlöse)
billion – s. Milliarde, 10^9
bill of exchange – s. Wechsel
accept a bill of exchange – einen Wechsel akzeptieren
bill of exchange for €2,000 – s. Wechsel über / lautend auf 2.000 €
discount a bill of exchange – einen Wechsel diskontieren
dishonour a bill of exchange – einen Wechsel nicht honorieren / nicht akzeptieren / nicht einlösen
draw a bill of exchange on sby. – einen Wechsel auf jemanden ziehen
present a bill of exchange – einen Wechsel vorlegen
present a bill of exchange for payment – einen Wechsel zur Zahlung vorlegen
protest a bill of exchange – einen Wechsel protestieren / protestieren lassen
bill of lading – s. Konnossement, begebbarer Seefrachtbrief, Seeladeschein
issue a bill of lading – ein Konnossement ausstellen
bill payable – s. Schuldwechsel, Wechselverbindlichkeit
bill receivable – s. Besitzwechsel, Rimesse
bills books – s. Wechselbuch
bin – s. Lagerbehälter
binary digit – s. Binärzeichen, Bit
binary notation – s. Binärschreibweise, -darstellung
binary number – s. Binär-, Dualzahl
binary system – s. Dual-, Binärsystem
biodegradable – adj. biologisch abbaubar
biogas converter – s. Biogasreaktor, -fermenter
biogas digester – s. Biogasanlage, -fermenter, Biomassekonverter
biomass – s. Biomasse
biosphere – s. Bio-, Ökosphäre
biotechnology – s. Biotechnologie

birth control – s. Geburtenregelung, -kontrolle
birth defect – s. Geburtsfehler
birth rate – s. Geburtenziffer, -häufigkeit
bit – s. Bit
B/L – bill of lading (siehe)
black – s. Gewinnzone
be in the black – in der Gewinnzone / aktiv sein, schwarze Zahlen schreiben
black economy – s. Schatten-, Schwarz-, Untergrundwirtschaft
blacklist – v. auf die schwarze Liste setzen, einem Lieferboykott unterwerfen
blacklist – s. schwarze Liste, Negativ-, Ausschlussliste
black market – s. schwarzer Markt
blank cheque
s. leeres Scheckformular
s. Blankoscheck
blank endorsed – adj. mit einem Blankoindossament versehen, blanko indossiert
blanket brand – s. Produktgruppen-, Dach-, Familienmarke
blanket guarantee – s. Pauschalgarantie
blank indorsement – s. Blankoindossament
blanket requisition – s. pauschale Materialanforderung
blast furnace – s. Hochofen
bleep – s. Piepston, Piepser
bleeper – s. Piepserl, Radio Pager
blend – v. mischen, verschneiden (bei Getränken)
blind person's allowance – s. Blindenfreibetrag
block – s. (Daten-)Block, physischer Satz
block ot flats – s. Wohnblock
blog – Blog, (Kurzform von) Weblog
blood-clotting agent – s. Blutgerinnungsmittel
blow up – v. hochrechnen, auf die Grundgesamtheit umlegen
blue chips – s. erstklassige Aktien, Standard-, Spitzenwerte
blue chip stock – s. erstklassige Aktie, Standard-, Spitzenwert
blue-collar employee – s. Arbeiter
blurred – adj. verschwommen, unscharf
board
s. (Führungs-)Gremium, (Leitungs-)Stab, Direktorium
s. Führungsgremium einer UK-/US-Kapitalgesellschaft, Verwaltungsrat
board appointments – s. Bestellung von Mitgliedern des Verwaltungsrates
board meeting – s. Sitzung des *board of directors* / Verwaltungsrates
Board of Customs and Excise – s. (ehemalige) UK-Steuerbehörde / Ministerialabteilung für Zölle und indirekte Steuern
board of directors – s. Führungsgremium einer UK-/US-Kapitalgesellschaft, Verwaltungsrat
Board of Inland Revenue – s. (ehemalige) UK-Finanzverwaltung / Steuerbehörde / Ministerialabteilung für direkte Steuern
board of management – s. Vorstand (einer österr. / deutschen Aktiengesellschaft)
board of trade
s. Handelskammer
s. Warenbörse (z. B. Chicago Board of Trade)
board of trustees – s. Treuhänderausschuss, Kuratorium
boardroom participation – s. Mitbestimmung auf der Unternehmensebene / im Aufsichtsrat
bodily injury – s. Körperverletzung
body – s. Körperschaft, Gremium
body corporate – s. juristische Person, Körperschaft
body of law – s. Gesetzessammlung, Kodex
bona fide
adj. gutgläubig
adj. ernstmeinend, ernstgemeint, seriös
bona fide holder – gutgläubige/r Inhaber/in
bona fide tenderer – ernstmeinende/r Bieter/in
bond
s. Anleihe, Schuldverschreibung, Obligation, Rente, (börsengängiges) schuldrechtliches Wertpapier
s. (Bank-)Garantie
call a bond – eine Bankgarantie in Anspruch nehmen
bonded goods – s. Zolllagergut
bonded warehouse – s. Zolllager
bond fund – s. Anleihe-, Rentenfonds
bondholder – s. Anleiheinhaber/in, Inhaber/in einer Schuldverschreibung
bond issuer
s. Anleihe-Emittent/in, Emittent/in einer Anleihe, Anleihebegeber
s. Garantiegeber/in, -aussteller/in, Aussteller/in einer Bankgrantie, Garant/in
bond market – s. Anleihe(n)markt, Rentenmarkt
bond price – s. Anleihe(n)kurs, Rentenkurs
Bonds Payable – s. (das Konto) Anleihenschuld
bonus – s. (Leistungs-)Prämie, Zugabe, Bonus
bonus element – s. Prämienkomponente
bonus share – s. Gratisaktie
bonus system – s. Prämien-, Prämienlohnsystem
book-building – s. Bookbuilding, Bookbuilding-Verfahren
bookkeeper – s. (nicht bilanzfähiger) Buchhalter, Kontenführer
bookkeeping – s. Buchhaltung (ausschließlich Rechnungsabschluss und vorbereitende Arbeiten)
bookkeeping records – s. buchhalterische Aufzeichnungen
book of original entry – s. Grundbuch, Journal
book value – s. Buchwert
boom – s. Hochkonjunktur, Boom, Hausse
BOOT – build-own-operate-transfer (siehe)
booth
s. (Messe-, Ausstellungs-)Stand
s. Telefonzelle
borrow – v. borgen, ausborgen, ausleihen
borrow money from sbdy. – von jemandem Geld borgen / ausleihen
borrowed capital – s. (mittel- bis langfristiges) Fremdkapital
borrower – s. Kreditnehmer
borrower's call option – s Zins-Call
borrowing – s. Kreditaufnahme
botched – adj. verpfuscht, vermasselt
bottle bank – s. Glas-, Flaschencontainer
bottom line
s. (Rein-)Gewinn, Jahresüberschuss, Bilanzergebnis
s. Endergebnis, Resultat, was bei einer Sache herausschaut
bottom out – v. Tiefpunkt erreichen und überschreiten, Talsohle überwinden
bought deal – s. feste Übernahme (einer Emission durch ein – auf eigene Rechnung handelndes – Übernahmekonsortium)
bounce – v. platzen
cheque bounces – Scheck platzt / wird nicht eingelöst
bound
adj. gebunden, broschürt
adj. gebunden, verpflichtet
adj. vorherbestimmt
bound by contract – vertraglich gebunden
This was bound to happen. – Das musste (zwangsläufig) so kommen.
bought-in goods – s. zugekaufte Ware(n)
box
s. Schachtel, Kiste

s. (Diagramm-)Feld / Kasten
bracket – s. Klammer, Stufe, Intervall
bracket creep – s. kalte Progression, progressive Abschöpfung, inflationsbedingtes Hineinwachsen in höhere Steuerstufen
branch – s. Filiale, Zweigniederlassung, Zweiganstalt
branch factory – s. Zweigwerk
branchless banking – s. filialloses (Direkt-)Banking, filialloser Vertrieb von Bankdienstleistungen
branch of economic activity – s. Wirtschaftszweig
branch office – s. Filiale, Zweigniederlassung, -anstalt
branch out – v. ausdehnen, erweitern, ausweiten
branch out into currency trading – Geschäftstätigkeit auf Devisenhandel ausweiten / ausdehnen
brand – s. (Produkt-)Marke
brand awareness – s. Bekanntheitsgrad einer Marke, Markenbekanntheitsgrad
branded article – s. Markenartikel
brand equity – s. Markenwert
brand extension – s. Markenerweiterung, Markentransfer (auf ein Produkt in einer neuen Produktkategorie)
brand image – s. Markenimage
branding – s. Markenpolitik
brand loyalty – s. Markentreue
brand manager– s. Marken-, Produktmanager, Brand-Manager
brass-plate company – s. Briefkastenfirma
breach of contract – s. Vertragsbruch, -verletzung
breadth of range – s. Breite des Produktionsprogramms / Sortiments, Sortimentsbreite
breakdown
s. Panne, Defekt
s. Aufgliederung, Aufschlüsselung
breakdown by product line – s. Aufgliederung nach Artikelgruppen
breakdown according to country of destination – Aufgliederung nach Bestimmungsländern
break down
v. kaputt gehen, eine Panne haben
v. aufspalten, abbauen,
v. zerlegen, zergliedern, aufgliedern, aufschlüsseln
break down plastic materials – Plastikstoffe (chemisch) aufspalten / abbauen
break down aggregates – Gesamtzahlen aufschlüsseln
break even – v. ausgeglichen bilanzieren, eine schwarze Null schreiben
break-even analysis – s. Gewinnschwellenanalyse, Break-Even-Analyse
break-even point – s. Gewinn-, Nutzschwelle, Kostendeckungspunkt, Break-Even-Punkt
break-even sales – s. Gewinn-, Nutzschwelle, Kostendeckungspunkt, Break-Even-Punkt; Umsatzwert oder -marge, bei der weder Gewinn noch Verlust entsteht
break out – v. ausgliedern, separat ausweisen, herausnehmen
break up – v. zerteilen, aufteilen, auseinander nehmen
Bretton Woods Agreement – s. Bretton-Woods-Abkommen
bribery – s. Bestechung
bricks and mortar – adj. (wörtlich) aus Ziegeln und Mörtel (bestehend), traditionell, nicht internetgestützt
bricks-and-mortar firm – konventionelles Unternehmen ohne internetgestützte Vertriebskanäle, Bricks-and-Mortar-Firma
brief – v. briefen, instruieren
brief – adj. kurz, bündig
briefcase – s. Aktenkofferformat, Computer im Aktenkofferformat, Portable (im engeren Sinn)
Brititsh Retail Price Index – s. UK-Verbraucherpreisindex
broadband – s. Breitband
broad-based index – s. breiter / umfassender Index
broad-based tax – s. umfassende / generelle Steuer, Steuer mit breiter Bemessungsgrundlage
broadcasting – s. Rundfunkübertragung, -wesen, -sendung(en)
broadcast signal – s. Rundfunksignal
brochure – s. Broschüre, gebundener / gehefteter Prospekt
broker – s. (Handels-)Makler
brokerage
s. Maklergebühr, -provision, Courtage
s. Maklerfirma
brokerage firm – s. Maklerfirma
brokerage house – s. Maklerfirma
brokerage transaction – s. Maklergeschäft, durch Maklerfirma abgewickeltes Geschäft
broker-dealer – s. Broker-Dealer, Wertpapierfirma mit Händler- und Maklerfunktion
browse – v. durchblättern, durchstöbern, durchsuchen, browsen
browser – s. Browser, Surf-Software
buck – s. Dollar
make a fast buck – einen schnelllen Dollar machen, schnelles Geld machen
budget – s. Budget, Haushaltsplan
budget – v. budgetieren, planen, vorgeben
budgetary – adj. budgetär, budgetmäßig
budgetary control – s. Budget-, Planungskontrolle
budgetary policy – s. Budgetpolitik
budget balance – s. Budgetsaldo
budget cut – s. Ausgabenkürzung, Senkung der Staatsausgaben, Reduktion des staatlichen Ausgabenvolumens
budgeted figure – s. Soll-, Planzahl, vorgegebene Größe
budgeting – s. Budgetierung, (kurz- bis mittelfristige) Planung(-srechnung)
budgeting process – s. Budgetierung, Planerstellung
budgetminded – adj. sparsam, haushälterisch
buffer stock – s. Puffer-, Marktausgleichslager
building block – s. Baustein, -element
building design – s. Bauweise, architektonische Gestaltung
Buildings – s. Gebäude(-konto)
building society – s. UK-Bausparkasse
building society savings account – s. UK-Bausparkonto
building trade – s. Baugewerbe, -wirtschaft
build-own-operate-transfer – s. (das Finanzierungsmodell) Bau-Besitz-Betrieb-Übertragung, BOOT-Finanzierungsmodell
built-in obsolescence – s. geplante Produktveralterung
bulk
s. Volumen, Größe, Menge, Masse, Umfang
s. Hauptteil, Großteil
supply goods in bulk – Waren lose / unverpackt / alla rinfusa liefern
bulk buying – s. Großabnahme, -einkäufe, Mengenkäufe
bulk cargo – s. Massen-, Schüttgüter
bulk commodities – s. Massen-, Schüttgüter
bulk discount – s. Mengenrabatt
bulk goods – s. Massen-, Schüttgüter
bulk liquid container – s. Tankcontainer
bulk powder container – s. Staubgutcontainer
bulk purchase – s. Großeinkauf
bull – s. Bulle, Hausse-Spekulant, Haussier
bullet repayment – s. endfällige Rückzahlung
bullish – adj. Hausse-, optimistisch
bullish mood – Haussestimmung
bull market – s. Bullenmarkt, Hausse, Börsenboom
bunds – s. (internationaler Ausdruck für) deutsche Bundesschuldverschreibungen

burden – s. Gemeinkosten, indirekte Kosten
burden on the environment – s. Umweltbelastung
burglary – s. Einbruchsdiebstahl
bushel – s. Scheffel (etwa 36 Liter)
business
s. Geschäfte, Transaktionen, Geschäftstätigkeit, Betrieb
s. Geschäft, Betrieb, Unternehmen, Firma
s. Sparte, Branche, Gewerbe
s. Geschäftsbereich, Division,
adj. W/wirtschafts-, U/unternehmer- , U/unternehmens-, B/betriebs-, betrieblich
The firm makes a business of buying and selling goods. – Die Firma kauft und verkauft Waren gewerbsmäßig.
transact business – Geschäfte tätigen / abwickeln
anti-business – wirtschaftsfeindlich
business communication – Wirtschaftskommunikation
business accounting – s. betriebliches Rechnungswesen
business administration – s. Betriebswirtschaftslehre
business analysis – s. Wirtschaftlichkeitsanalyse, ökonomische Analyse
business angel – s. Business Angel, (unternehmerisch erfahrene/r, unabhängige/r) Privatinvestor/in, Firmenpate / -patin
business assets – s. Geschäfts-, Gesellschaftsvermögen
business communication – s. Wirtschaftskommunikation, betriebliche Kommunikation
business consultant – s. Betriebs-, Unternehmensberater, Betriebsberatungs-, Unternehmensberatungsfirma
business consulting – s. Unternehmens-, Betriebsberatung
business cycle – s. Konjunktur-, Wirtschaftszyklus
business document – s. Beleg
business enterprise – s. Unternehmen
business establishment – s. Betrieb, Betriebsstätte
business finance – s. betriebliche Finanzierung / Finanzwirtschaft, Unternehmensfinanzierung
business format – s. Business-, Betriebs-, Geschäftskonzept
business indicator – s. Konjunkturindikator
business information company – s. Auskunftei, Wirtschaftsdatengesellschaft
business interruption – s. Betriebsunterbrechung
business interruption insurance – s. Betriebsunterbrechungsversicherung
business logistics – s. Unternehmenslogistik, -logistik, betriebliche Logistik
business organisation – s. Unternehmen, Firma
business park – s. Business-, Industrie-, Gewerbepark
business portfolio – s. Geschäftsfeldportfolio
business rate – s. UK-Gemeindesteuern auf Büro-, Geschäfts- und Industrieobjekte
Business School – s. Business School, betriebswirtschaftliche Universität / Fakultät, Management-Hochschule
business statistics – s. Betriebsstatistik, betriebswirtschaftliche Statistik
business studies – s. Betriebswirtschaftslehre
business-to-business – s. Geschäfts- / Kommunikationsbeziehungen zwischen Unternehmen, Business-to-Business, B2B
business-to-customer – s. Geschäfts- /oder Kommunikationsbeziehungen zwischen Unternehmen und Kunden, B2C
business-to-employees – s. Geschäfts- / Kommunikationsbeziehungen zwischen Unternehmen und Mitarbeitern
business-to-government – s. Geschäfts- / Kommunikationsbeziehungen zwischen Unternehmen und staatlichen Stellen
business transaction – s. Geschäftsfall, Transaktion
business unit – s. Unternehmen, Geschäftsfeld
business variable – s. betriebswirtschaftlich Größe / Variable
button – s. Knopf, Programmschaltfläche
buyer
s. Käufer/in, Kunde/Kundin, Nachfrager
s. Einkäufer/in, Einkaufschef/in (z. B. in einem Warenhaus)
buyer credit – s. Käufer-, Bestellerkredit, gebundener Finanzkredit
buyer of the option – s. Optionsnehmer
buyer records – s. Einkaufs-, Beschaffungsunterlagen
buyers' market – s. Käufermarkt
buy-in – s. Buyin, Buy-in, Firmenübernahme durch externe Manager
buying rate – s. Geld-, Devisengeld-, Ankaufs-, Devisenankaufskurs
buyout – s. Buyout, Unternehmensaufkauf, Übernahme eines Unternehmens, Firmenübernahme
buy out – v. ankaufen
buy out a firm – eine Firma aufkaufen
buy-side – adj. nachfrageseitig
buzzword – s. Schlag-, Modewort
bylaws – s. der das Innenverhältnis regelnde Teil des Gesellschaftsvertrages / der Satzung / der Statuten einer US-*corporation*
byproduct – s. Nebenprodukt
byte – s. Byte

C

cable – s. Kabel, Überseetelegramm
by cable – telegraphisch
cable transfer – s. telegraphische Auszahlung
CAD – cash against documents (siehe)
CAD – s. computer-aided design (siehe)
C. & F. – COST AND FREIGHT (siehe)
CAFTA – Central American Free Trade Area (siehe)
calibrate – v. dimensionieren, die (richtige) Größe wählen
call
s. (Zahlungs-)Aufforderung
s. Nachfrage, Inanspruchnahme
s. Kaufoption
s. (Vertreter-)Besuch
s. Telefonanruf, -gespräch
call
v. nennen, bezeichnen
v. einberufen
v. abrufen, in Anspruch nehmen
call a bond – eine (Bank-)Garantie in Anspruch nehmen / abrufen
call a meeting – eine Sitzung einberufen
call for – v. erfordern, fordern
This calls for careful planning.– Das erfordert eine sorgfältige Planung.
call money – s. tägliches / täglich fälliges Geld, Geldmarktsichteinlagen
call policy – s. Besuchspolitik (für Vertreter)
call premium – s. Kaufoptionprämie, Call-Preis
call seller – s. Verkäufer/in einer Kaufoption, Stillhalter/in (in Devisen), Call-Verkäufer/in
call writer – s. Verkäufer/in einer Kaufoption, Stillhalter/in (in Devisen), Call-Verkäufer/in
CAM – s. computer-aided manufacturing (siehe)
cancel – v. stornieren, widerrufen, aufheben, ungültig erklären, löschen, streichen, kürzen
cancel an order – einen Auftrag stornieren
cancel an undertaking – eine Zusage widerrufen / rückgängig machen
cancellation – s. Stornierung, Storno, Widerruf, Aufhebung, Löschung, Streichung
cancellation of an order – s. Auftragsstornierung, -storno
cancer rate – s. Krebsrate. -häufigkeit
C.& F. – COST AND FREIGHT (siehe)
cap
s. Obergrenze
s. Zins-Cap, börsenfähige Vereinbarung einer Zinsobergrenze
cap – v. nach oben hin limitieren
cap rates – Steuersätze / Zinssätze nach oben hin limitieren
capacity
s. Fähigkeit
s. Geschäftsfähigkeit
s. (Produktions-)Kapazität
s. Eigenschaft, Funktion
work at full capacity – voll ausgelastet sein / arbeiten
work to capacity – voll ausgelastet sein / arbeiten
work at 30% of capacity – zu 30% ausgelastet sein
capacity constraint – s. Kapazitätsbeschränkung, -engpass
capacity to contract – s. Geschäftsfähigkeit
capacity utilisation – s. Kapazitätsauslastung, -nutzungsgrad, Beschäftigungsgrad
cap buyer – s. Cap-Käufer/in
cap holder – s. Cap-Käufer/in
capital
s. (Geld-)Kapital
s. (Real-)Kapital
Capital is one of the factors of production. – Das Kapital ist einer der Produktionsfaktoren.
capital account
s. Kapitalverkehrs-, Kapitalbilanz (altes Zahlungsbilanzsystem)
s. Bilanz der Vermögensübertragungen (neues Zahlungsbilanzsystem)
s. Kapitalkonto (Rechnungswesen)
capital accumulation account – s. Vermögensänderungskonto
capital aid – s. Kapitalhilfe
capital allowance – s. steuerliche / steuerrechtliche Abschreibung, steuerlicher / steuerrechtlicher Abschreibungsbetrag
capital asset
s. Vermögenswert
s. (pl.) materielles Anlagevermögen
capital base – s. (Eigen-)Kapitalbasis
capital equipment – s. Anlagegüter
item of capital equipment – Anlagegut
capital expenditure – s. Investition(-saufwand), Ausgaben für Investitionen
capital expenditure budget – s. Investitionsplan, -budget
capital finance account – s. Kreditänderungskonto, volkswirtschaftliche Finanzierungsrechnung
capital flow – s. Kapitalbewegung, -strom
capital formation – s. Kapitalbildung, Investition
capital gain – s. Veräußerungs-, Spekulationsgewinn, (realisierter) Wertzuwachs / Kursgewinn
capital gains tax – s. Steuer auf Veräußerungsgewinne, Wertzuwachs-, Kursgewinn-, Spekulationsgewinn-, Spekulationssteuer
capital gearing
s. Finanzierungsstrukturkennzahl, Kapitalstrukturkoeffizient
s. Verschuldungskoeffizient, -grad
capital goods – s. Investitions-, Kapitalgüter
capital inflow – s. Kapitalzustrom, -zufluss
capital-intensive – adj. kapitalintensiv
capital investment analysis – s. Investitionsrechnung
capitalisation
s. (Gesamt-)Kapital / Kapitalausstattung (eines Unternehmens)
s. Kapitalstruktur (eines Unternehmens)
s. (Gesamt-)Kurswert (eines Unternehmens an der Börse), Marktkapitalisierung
s. Kapitalisierung, Aktivierung
s. Umwandlung in Aktienkapital
s. Großschreibung
capitalisation of reserves – s. Umwandlung von Rücklagen in Aktienkapital
capitalise
v. aktivieren
v. in (formelles) Aktienkapital umwandeln
v. groß / mit großem Anfangsbuchstaben schreiben
capitalise reserves – Rücklagen in Aktienkapital umwandeln
capital item – s. Vermögensgegenstand, Anlagegut
capital-labour ratio – s. Kapitalintensität
capital letter – s. Großbuchstabe
capital loss – s. Spekulationsverlust, (realisierter) Wertverlust / Kursverlust

capital market – s. Kapitalmarkt
capital movement – s. Kapitalverkehr, -fluss, -bewegung
capital note – s. kurz- bis mittelfristige Schuldverschreibung
capital outflow – s. Kapitalabfluss
capital outlay – s. Investition(-saufwand)
capital output ratio – s. Kapitalkoeffizient (K/Y)
capital project – s. Investitionsvorhaben, -projekt
capital (project) evaluation – s. Investitionsrechnung
capital project planning – s. Investitionsbudgetierung
capital ratio – s. Kapitalstrukturkoeffizient, Verschuldungsgrad
capital reserve – s. gebundene Rücklage, Kapitalrücklage
capital stock
s. Grund-, Stamm-, Aktienkapital
s. Kapitalstock, Produktionsfaktor Kapital, volkwirtschaftliches Anlagevermögen
Capital Stock – s. Kapital(-konto)
capital structure – s. Kapitalstruktur
capital transaction
s. Kapitaltransaktion
s. (pl.) Kapitalverkehr
capital transfer
s. Vermögensübertragung / Übertragung von Vermögenswerten (durch Erbfall und/oder Schenkung)
s. Kapitaltransfer, -fluss, -export, -import
capital transfer tax – s. UK-kombinierte Schenkungs- und Nachlasssteuer
cap seller – s. Cap-Verkäufer
caption – s. (Bilanz-)Position, Titel, Überschrift, Bezeichnung
captive – adj. firmenintern, -eigen
captive consulting unit – s. (firmen-)interne Betriebsberatungsabteilung, -sparte, -division
captive leasing company – s. konzerninterne Leasinggesellschaft
captive product – s. Verbundprodukt, Zubehör, Verbrauchsmaterial
captive-product pricing – s. Preisgestaltung für Verbundartikel, Verbundkalkulation
capture (of data) – s. (Daten-)Erfassung
capture – v. erfassen, erobern
cap writer – s. Cap-Verkäufer/in
carbon – s. Kohlenstoff
carbon dioxide – s. Kohlendioxid
carbon fuel – s. Kohlenwasserstoff-Kraftstoff / -Brennstoff
carbon paper – s. Kohlepapier
card
s. Karte, Karteikarte
s. Pappe
cardholder – s. Karteninhaber
card index system – s. Kartei(-system)
care – s. Sorgfalt
exercise care – Sorgfalt üben
cargo – s. Fracht(-gut)
cargo-aircraft – s. Frachtflugzeug
cargo container – s. Container, Frachtcontainer
cargo handling – s. Umschlag von Frachtgut, Güterumschlag, Cargo Handling
cargo insurance – s. Güter-, Warentransportversicherung
cargo policy – s. Gütertransport-, Seefrachtversicherungspolizze
cargo reception – s. Frachtgutannahme
cargo space – s. Frachtraum
cargo terminal – s. Frachtterminal, Frachtabfertigungshalle, -gelände, -anlage
carload – s. Wagenladung
carnage – s. Blutbad
carpenter – s. Zimmermann, Bautischler
car rental business – s. Mietautobranche
carriage
s. Transport, Beförderung
s. Fracht, Frachtgebühr, Transportgebühr
carriage by sea – s. Seetransport
carriage of goods by air – s. Luftfrachtverkehr
carriage of goods by rail – s. Eisenbahnfrachtverkehr
carriage of goods by road – s. Straßenfracht-, Straßengüter-, Güterkraftverkehr
carriage of goods by sea – s. Seefrachtverkehr
carriage of goods on inland waterways – s. Binnenschifffahrtsfrachtverkehr
carriage return – s. Wagenrücklauf
carrier – s. Frachtführer/in, Verfrachter/in, Transportunternehmer/in
carry forward – v. vortragen, übertragen
carry forward a balance – einen Saldo vortragen
carrying – s. Lagerhaltung, Lagerung
cost of carrying – Lagerhaltungs-, Lagerkosten
carrying device – s. (innerbetriebliches) Transportmittel, Fördereinrichtung
cartel – s. Kartell
car telephone – s. Autotelefon
cartel syndicate – s. Syndikat
carve up – v. zerteilen, aufteilen
cascade tax – s. Bruttoallphasenumsatzsteuer, kumulative Allphasenumsatzsteuer
case
s. Kiste
s. Fall
s. Argumente
case in point – (passendes) Beispiel
case against sthg. – Argumente gegen etwas, was gegen etwas spricht
case for sthg. – Argumente für etwas, was für etwas spricht
cash
s. Bargeld, Barmittel
s. (Bilanzposten) Kassenbestand (unter Einschluss von Schecks, Besitzwechseln und frei verfügbaren Sichtguthaben bei Kreditinstituten)
s. (prompte / sofortige) Bezahlung
cash – v. einlösen
cash a cheque – einen Scheck einlösen
cashable – adj. einlösbar
be cashable – eingelöst werden können
cash account – s. Kassakonto
cash-and-carry price – s. Abholpreis
cash-and-carry wholesaler – s. Abholgroßmarkt, -großhandlung, Cash-and-Carry-Markt
cash against documents – s. Kassa gegen Dokumente, Zahlung gegen Dokumente
cash at bank – s. (Bilanzposten) Sichtguthaben bei Kreditinstituten
cash basis – s. (Prinzip der) Einnahmen-/ Ausgabenrechnung
cash bid – s. Bar-Übernahmeangebot (für ein Unternehmen)
cash book – s. Kassabuch
cash budget – s. Einnahmen-Ausgabenplan, Liquiditätsplan
cash call – s. Griff in die Taschen der Aktionäre (bei einer Kapitalerhöhung)
cash card – s. Bankomat-, Bezugskarte
cash collection – s. Inkasso
cash cow – s. Cash Cow, Melkkuh
cash crops – s. Cash-Crops, Marktfrüchte, (landwirtschafliche) Marktprodukte
cash discount – s. Skonto

take / avail oneself of a cash discount – Skonto in Anspruch nehmen
cash dispenser – s. Geldausgabeautomat, Bankomat
cash dispensing machine – s. Geldausgabeautomat, Bankomat
cash dividend – s. Bardividende
cash grant – s. (private oder staatliche) Finanzhilfe, finanzielle Unterstützung
cash flow
s. Cash Flow
s. Zahlungsstrom
cash-flow-based finance – s. Cash-Flow-basierte Finanzierung(-sstrukturen), Projektfinanzierung
cash flow exchange gain – s. zahlungsstromwirksamer / liquiditätswirksamer Kursgewinn
cash flow exchange loss – s. zahlungsstromwirksamer / liquiditätswirksamer Kursverlust
cash flow statement
s. Cash-Flow-Rechnung, Kapitalflussrechnung
s. (Abkürzung für) statement of changes in financial position on a cash basis), Bewegungsbilanz
cashier – s. Kassier
cashless – adj. bargeldlos
cashless society – bargeldlose Gesellschaft
cash market – s. Kassa-, Devisenkassamarkt
cashier's check – s. Institutsscheck
cash inflow – s. Barzufluss, Einzahlung
cash in hand – s. Kassenbestand inklusive Schecks und Besitzwechsel
Cash in Hand and at Bank – s. (Bilanzposten) Kassenbestand (unter Einschluss von Schecks, Besitzwechseln und frei verfügbaren Sichtguthaben bei Kreditinstituten)
cash management – s. Cash Management, Kassenmanagement, Kassenhaltung
cashless society – s. bargeldlose Gesellschaft
cash on delivery – s. (gegen) Nachnahme
cash on hand – s. Kassenbestand inklusive Schecks und Besitzwechsel (Bilanz)
cash outflow – s. Barabfluss, Auszahlung
cash rebate – s. Barvergütung (bei der Einlösung von Rabattmarken)
cash register – s. Registrierkasse
cash sale – s. Barverkauf
cash withdrawal – s. Barabhebung
cash with order – s. Zahlung bei Auftragserteilung
cast
v. werfen, abgeben
v. eine Rolle zuweisen, präsentieren, positionieren, „verkaufen"
cast a vote – eine Stimme abgeben
cast doubts on sthg. – etwas in Zweifel ziehen / anzweifeln
cast a product as "expensive but reliable" – ein Produkt als „teuer aber verlässlich" positionieren
casting vote – s. Dirimierungsrecht; Recht des Vorsitzenden, bei Stimmengleichheit zu entscheiden
CAT – customer-activated terminal (siehe)
catalogue – s. Katalog
catalogue firm – s. Katalogfirma,
catalogue operator – s. Katalogfirma
catalogue retailing – s. Katalogeinzel-, Kataloghandel, Kataloggeschäft
catalogue selling – s. Kataloghandel, -geschäft
catalogue shopping – s. Katalogkauf
catch-all – adj. alles umfassend, ganz allgemein
catchment area – s. Einzugsgebiet
cater – v. versorgen, (Bedürfnisse) decken, befriedigen
cater to the final consumer – die Bedürfnisse des Letztverbrauchers decken
cater for a need – ein Bedürfnis decken / befriedigen
catering – s. Bewirtung, Verkauf von Speisen und Getränken, Gastronomie
cathode-ray tube – s. Kathodenstrahlröhre, Bildröhre
cattle-grazing – s. (Nutzung als) Viehweide
cause
s. Ursache, Grund, Anlassfall
s. Sache, Anliegen
support the cause of fair trade – die Sache des Fairen Handels unterstützen
caution mark – s. Vorsichtsmarkierung
CBOT - Chicago Board of Trade (siehe)
CD – certificate of deposit (siehe)
CD – compact disc (siehe)
CD-burner – s. CD-Brenner
CD-ROM – Compact Disc Read-Only Memory (siehe)
CD-ROM drive – s. CD-ROM Laufwerk
ceiling – s. Obergrenze, oberer Interventionspunkt
cell nuclei – s. Zellkerne
cell nucleus – s. Zellkern
cellphone – s. Mobiltelefon, Handy
cell production – s. (flexibles) Zellenfertigungssystem
cellular phone – s. Mobiltelefon, Handy
census – s. Vollerhebung, Volkszählung
Central American Free Trade Area – s. Zentralamerikanische Freihandelszone
central bank – s. Zentralbank, Notenbank
central government – s Zentralregierung, Bund
central institution – s. Zentral-, Führungsstelle. Leitinstitution
centralised filing – s. zentrale Schriftgutablage
centrally planned economy – s. Zentralverwaltungs-, Planwirtschaft
central processing unit – s. Zentraleinheit
central processor – s. Zentral-, Befehlsprozessor
CEO duality – s. (eine nur im angelsächsichen Recht mögliche) Doppelfunktion als Vorstandsvorsitzender und Ausichtsratspräsident
certificate of deposit – s. Kassenschein, -obligation
certificate of incorporation – s. Gründungsbescheinigung, Nachweis der Eintragung ins Handelsregister / Firmenbuch als Kapitalgesellschaft
certificate of insurance – s. Versicherungszertifikat
certificate of origin – s. Ursprungszeugnis
certified check – s. bestätigter Scheck
Certified Public Accountant – s. Wirtschaftstreuhänder, Wirtschaftsprüfer, Steuerberater, (konzessionierter) Buchprüfer
certify – v. bestätigen, zertifizieren
CET – common external tariff (siehe)
ceteris paribus – adj./adv. ceteris paribus, unter sonst gleichen Umständen
ceteris paribus condition – s. Ceteris-paribus-Bedingung
CFR – interntionaler Code für C.&.F. (siehe)
CFCs – chlorfluorcarbons (siehe)
chain – s. (Laden-, Einzelhandels-)Kette
chain of command – s. Befehlsweg, -kette
chain of distribution – s. Distributions-, Verteilungskette; Distributionskanal, Absatzweg
chain store – s. Kettenladen, Filialgeschäft
chair – s. Vorsitz, Vorsitzende/r
take the chair – s. den Vorsitz übernehmen
chair – v. den Vorsitz führen

chair a meeting – bei einer Sitzung den Vorsitz führen
chairman
s. Vorsitzende/r
s. Präsident/in des Verwaltungsrates einer UK-/US-Kapitalgesellschaft
chairperson
s. Vorsitzende/r
s. Präsident/in des Verwaltungsrates einer UK-/US-Kapitalgesellschaft
chamber of commerce – s. Handelskammer
champion – s. Verfechter, Unterstützer, Vorkämpfer
champion – v. favorisieren, verfechten, sich einsetzen für, sich auf die Fahnen heften
champion free trade – sich den Freihandel auf die Fahnen heften
Chancellor of the Exchequer – s. UK-Finanzminister
channel – s. Kanal, Eingabekanal, Ausgabekanal
channel of distribution – s. Distributionskanal, Absatzweg, Distributions-, Verteilungskette
character – s. Zeichen
characteristic – s. Merkmal
charge
s. Gebühr, in Rechnung gestellter Betrag
s. Kosten, Aufwendung, Aufwand, Lastschrift, Belastung
s. (Vermögens-)Belastung, (Grund-)Pfandrecht, Last
s. Obhut, Sorge, Leitung, Verantwortung
s. Anklage(-schrift), Anklagepunkt
be in charge of sthg. – etwas leiten, die Verantwortung für etwas haben, etwas über haben
incur a charge – eine Gebühr zahlen müssen
free of charge – kostenlos, unentgeltlich
charge
v. berechnen, (als Preis) fordern / verlangen, verrechnen
v. anlasten, belasten, aufrechnen, anschreiben
v. beauftragen, betrauen
v. anklagen, beschuldigen
v. elektrisch aufladen
charge for the cost of handling the account – die Kosten der Kontoführung berechnen
charge an account – ein Konto belasten
charge a bill to a credit card – einen Rechnungsbetrag mit der Kreditkarte bezahlen
Charge it! – (Schreiben Sie es an!) Ich zahle mit Kreditkarte!
charge an item against current income – einen Posten gegen die Periodenerträge aufrechnen / zu Lasten der Periodenerträge verrechnen / als Periodenaufwand verbuchen
charge with a task – mit einer Aufgabe betrauen
be charged with sthg. – mit etwas betraut sein / werden
chargeable
adj. steuerbar, steuerpflichtig
adj. zurechenbar, zuzurechnen
This tax is chargeable on all supplies. – Diese Steuer gilt für / erfasst alle Leistungen.
chargeable supplies – steuerbare / steuerpflichtige Leistungen
costs chargeable to a unit – einem Kostenträger zuzurechnende Kosten
charging period – s. Abrechnungsperiode (für Bankgebühren)
charitable – adj. wohltätig, mildtätig, karitativ, gemeinnützig
for charitable purposes – für wohltätige Zwecke
charitable donation – s. mildtätige / karitative Spende
charity – s. Wohtätigkeitsorganisation, gemeinnützige Organisation
charity event – s. Wohltätigkeitsveranstaltung
chart – s. Diagramm, Graphik, tabellarische Darstellung
charter – s. Gründungsurkunde einer US-*corporation* (siehe), der das Außenverhältnis regelnde Teil des Gesellschaftsvertrages / der Satzung / der Statuten
charter party – s. Charter Party, Charter-Vertrag
Chartered Accountant – s. Wirtschaftsprüfer, (konzessionierter) Buchprüfer
chartered company – s. durch den Freibrief der Krone errichtete Gesellschaft
chartist – s. Chartist, technischer Analyst, technisch orientierter Analyst
chart of accounts – s. Kontenrahmen, -plan
chattel mortgage – s. Mobiliarhypothek, Pfandrecht an beweglichen Sachen
chattels – s. bewegliche Sachen und Rechte
check
s. (am.) Scheck
s. (kleine) Rechnung, Kassenbon, Verkaufsbeleg, Kassenzettel
s. Überprüfung, Kontrolle
s. Hemmnis, Hindernis, Riegel, Barriere, Bremse
check
v. überprüfen, kontrollieren, nachrechnen, als richtig ankreuzen
v. hemmen, hindern, aufhalten, Einhalt gebieten, eindämmen, zügeln, drosseln, bremsen
check A against B – A mit B vergleichen (und auf ihre Übereinstimmung prüfen)
checking account – s. Kontokorrent-, Giro-, Scheckkonto
checking operation – s. Prüfung, Prüfvorgang
checking procedure – s. Prüfvorgang, Prüfverfahren
checkout counter – s. (Supermarkt-)Kasse, Kassenplatz
checkout operation – s. Kundenabfertigung an der Kassa
checkout person – s. (Supermarkt-)Kassierer/in
cheque – s. Scheck
honour a cheque – einen Scheck bezahlen / einlösen / honorieren
make out a cheque – einen Scheck ausstellen
draw a cheque – einen Scheck ziehen / ausstellen
write out a cheque – einen Scheck ausstellen
cheque account – s. Kontokorrent-, Scheckkonto
cheque card – s. Scheckkarte
cheque drawing facility – s. Scheckverkehr(-smöglichkeit); Möglichkeit, Schecks auszustellen
cheque form – s. Scheckformular
cheque guarantee card – s. Scheckkarte
cheque rate – s. Scheckkurs, Wechselkurs für Schecks
Chicago Board of Trade (CBOT) – s. Chicago Board of Trade (weltgrößte Rohstoff-, Futures- und Optionsbörse).
chief executive officer – s. Generaldirektor, Vorstandsvorsitzender
chief financial officer – s. Finanzdirektor, Finanzvorstand, Vorstandsmitglied für Finanzen.
chief information officer – s. leitender Informtionsmanager, Informationsvorstand
chief operating officer – s. (etwa) Generaldirektorstellvertreter, stellvertrender Vorstandsvorsitzender
child allowance – s. Kinderfreibetrag
child mortality – s. Kindersterblichkeit
chip
s. (Spiel-)Jeton
s. Chip, Halbleiterblättchen, integrierter Schaltkreis
chip card – Wertkarte, Chipkarte
chloracne – s. Chlorakne
chlorfluorocarbon – s. Fluorchlorkohlenwasserstoff
chore – s. (mühsame) Arbeit, Plackerei

CHS – Conference on Human Settlements (siehe)
C.I.F. – COST, INSURANCE, FREIGHT (siehe)
on a c.i.f. basis – auf C.I.F.-Basis
CIF – internationaler Code für C.I.F. (siehe)
c.i.f. contract – s. C.I.F.-Kontrakt, C.I.F.-Vertrag
C.I.F. landed – s. CIF gelandet
c.i.f. value – s. cif-Wert
CIM – s. Convention for the International Carriage of Goods by Rail (siehe)
CIP – FREIGHT/CARRIAGE AND INSURANCE PAID TO (siehe)
circuit – s. Schaltung, Leitung
circular – s. (Werbe-)Rundschreiben
circular flow of the economy – s. Wirtschaftskreislauf
circular letter – s. (Werbe-)Rundschreiben
circulate – v. (durch Rundschreiben) verteilen / zukommen lassen
circumvent – s. umgehen
city code – s. Ortsvorwahlnummer
civil commotion – s. Volksaufruhr, -aufstand
civil-law partnership – s. Gesellschaft bürgerlichen Rechts
civil war – s. Bürgerkrieg
CL – carload (siehe)
claim
s. Forderung, Anspruch, Klagebegehren, Reklamation
s. Schadenersatzanspruch, Versicherungsanspruch, Schadensfall
s. Behauptung, Aussage
make a claim – eine Forderung erheben, einen Anspruch anmelden, eine Reklamation machen / vorbringen
substantiate a claim – eine Behauptung / Aussage begründen / beweisen
claim
v. fordern, beanspruchen, Anspruch erheben auf, verlangen
v. behaupten
claim delivery of the goods from sby. – von jmdm. die Ausfolgung der Ware verlangen
claims experience – s. Schadensverlauf
clamour – v. (lautstark) rufen
clash – s. Zusammenstoß
class 'A' share – s. (Stamm-)Aktie ohne Stimmrecht, A-Aktie
class 'B' share – s. (Stamm-)Aktie mit Stimmrecht, B-Aktie
classical system – s. klassisches (Körperschaftsteuer-)System
classification format – s. Klassifikationsformat, Präsentation / Anordnung von Daten nach einem inhaltlich-logischen Klassifikationsschema
classified ad – s. Kleinanzeige
claused bill of lading – s. unreines Konnossement
clean bill of lading – s. reines Konnossement
clean collection – s. einfaches / nichtdokumentäres Inkasso
clean draft – s. einfache / nichtdokumentäre Tratte
clean floating – s. sauberes / reines Floaten, System völlig freier Wechselkurse
clean floating rate – s. völlig flexibler / völlig freier Wechselkurse
cleaning – s. Reinigung(-sdienste)
clean payment – s. Zahlung gegen (einfache) Rechnung
clear
v. (zollamtlich) abfertigen, freimachen
v. räumen, abverkaufen
v. genehmigen
v. gegenseitig aufrechnen
clear through customs – zollamtlich abfertigen
clear for import – für den Import abfertigen / freimachen
clear-cut – adj. abgeholzt, kahlgeschlagen
clear-cutting – s. Kahlschlag, Abholzung
clearing – s. Clearing, Abrechnung(-sverkehr), Aufrechnung von gegenseitigen Forderungen
clearing bank – s. UK-Geschäftsbank, Clearing-Bank
clearing house – s. Abrechnungsstelle, Girozentrale
clearing system – s. Clearing-System, (wechselseitiges) Verrechnungssystem
clerk – s. (Büro-)Angestellte/r, Beamter/Beamtin / Sekretär/in, Referent/in
senior clerk – Referatsleiter/in
click-and-mortar firm – s. Firma mit konventionellen und internetgestützen Vertriebswegen, Click-und-Mortar-Unternehmen
click economy – s. Internetwirtschaft, Online-Wirtschaft, Click-Wirtschaft
click firm – s. (reine) Internetfirma, (reines) Online Unternehmen
client – v. Klient/in, Kunde/Kundin, Abnehmer/in
clinch
v. sicher befestigen, festmachen
v. (endgültig) abschließen
clinch a deal – Geschäft (endgültig) abschließen
clock rate – s. Taktfrequenz (eines Prozessors)
close – v. schließen, stilllegen, abschließen
close an account to / into the income statement – ein Konto gegen die V+G abschließen
close corporation – s. (etwa) Gesellschaft mit beschränkter Haftung
close corporation statute – s. (US-einzelstaatliches) GmbH-Gesetz
closed economy – s. geschlossene Volkswirtschaft
closed-end fund – s. (am.) geschlossener Investmentfonds, Investmentfonds nach dem Gesellschaftsprinzip
close out – v. glattstellen
close out a futures contract – einen börsengehandelten Terminkontrakt glattstellen
close-out rate – s. Glattstellungskurs
close-out transaction – s. Glattstellungstransaktion, -geschäft
closing date
s. Ladeschluss, Frachannahmeschluss
s. Einsendeschluss, Endtermin
closing exchange rate – s. (Bilanz-)Stichtagskurs, Kurs am Bilanzstichtag
closing out of a futures contract – s. Glattstellung eines börsengehandelten Terminkontraktes
closing rate (of exchange) – s. (Bilanz-)Stichtagskurs, Kurs am Bilanzstichtag
closing rate method – s. Stichtagskursmethode
closing sale transaction – s. kompensierender Verkauf, Glattstellungsverkauf
closing stock – s. Schlussbestand
closing transaction – s. Glattstellungstransaktion
clutch – s. Kupplung
clutter – s. Durcheinander, Wirrwarr
CMR – s. *Convention relative au contrat de transport international de Marchandises par Route*, Convention for the International Carriage of Goods by Road (siehe)
Co. – company (siehe)
coarse – adj. grob, grobfasrig
coal-fired power plant – Kohlekraftwerk
coal gasification – s. Kohlevergasung
coal liquefaction – s. Kohleverflüssigung
coat – v. überziehen, beschichten
COBOL – Common Business Oriented Language (Programmiersprache)
C.O.D. – cash on delivery (siehe)

code
s. Gesetzbuch, Gesetzsammlung
s. Code, Telegrammschlüssel, Codewort, Codenummer
s. (ethischer) Kodex, Sammlung von Verhaltensnormen
co-generation – s. Kraft-Wärmekopplung, Kraft-Wärme-Kupplung
coincide – v. (zeitlich) zusammenfallen
The expiry date of the option coincides with the rollover date. – Der Verfallstag der Option fällt mit dem Zinsanpassungsdatum zusammen.
coincident indicator – s. synchroner Konjunkturindikator, Präsens-Indikator
coin-operated vending machine – s. (mit Münzen betriebener) Warenautomat, Münzautomat
cold call – s. unangemeldeter Besuch (eines Vertreters/einer Vertreterin)
collaboration – s. Zusammenarbeit
collage – s. Collage, Mischbild, bunte Zusammenstellung
collate – v. zusammentragen, sortieren und stapeln
collateral
s. (Kredit-)Besicherung
s. Faustpfand
collateral – adj. zusätzlich, Neben-
collateral security
s. (Kredit-)Besicherung
s. Pfand an beweglichen Sachen und Rechten, Besicherung durch bewegliche Sachen und Rechte
collect
v. abholen, einsammeln
v. einziehen, kassieren, Inkasso durchführen
collect call – s. R-Gespräch, Rückgespräch
collectible
adj. fällig, zahlbar
adj. einbringlich
collecting bank – s. Inkassobank
collective will – gemeinsamer Wille, Willensübereinstimmung
collection
s. Inkasso, Zahlungseinzug
s. Abholung, Sammlung
handle a collection – ein Inkasso / einen Zahlungseinzug durchführen
collections made on accounts written off – Inkasso von bereits abgeschriebenen Forderungen
collection agency – s. Inkassobüro
collection and delivery service – s. Hausabfuhr und -zufuhr
collection arrangement – s. Inkassoverfahren
collection cost(s) – s. Inkassospesen, -gebühr, Einzugsspesen, Erhebungskosten
collection letter – s. Mahnschreiben, Mahnung
collection period – s. Außenstandsdauer der Forderungen, Forderungsdauer, Zahlungsdauer
collection ratio – s. Debitorenumschlag(-shäufigkeit), Forderungsumschlag(-häufigkeit)
collection service – s. Abholdienst, Hausabfuhr
collective bargaining – s. Kollektivvertrags-, Tarifverhandlungen
collect method – s. dekursive Verzinsung
collect on delivery – s. gegen Nachnahme
collector – s. Kollektor
collision – s. Kollision, Zusammenstoß
collusion – s. Kollusion, geheime Absprache (zum Nachteil Dritter), geheime (betrügerische) Verabredung, Verdunkelung
coloured ribbon – s. Farbband
combat – s. Kampf, Bekämpfung, Kampfhandlungen
combat – v. bekämpfen
combined certificate of value and origin – s. kombiniertes Wert- und Ursprungszeugnis (Zollfaktura)
combined transport – s. kombinierter Verkehr, gebrochener Güterverkehr
combined transport document – s. kombiniertes Transportdokument, CT-Dokument
combined transport operator – s. Frachtführer im kombinierten Verkehr, CTO
combustible – s. brennbar
combustion – s. Verbrennung
combustion process – s. Verbrennungsprozess
COMESA – Common Market for Eastern and Southern Africa (siehe)
come – v. erhältlich / verfügbar sein, geben, existieren
It comes in different sizes. – Es ist in verschiedenen Größen erhältlich.
come in – v. hineinpassen, relevant sein, zutreffen, anwendbar sein, seinen Platz haben
This is where the accelerator principle comes in. – Hier hat das Akzeleratorprinzip seinen Platz.
command
v. befehlen, anordnen
v. erzielen
command higher prices – höhere Preise erzielen
land commands a price – für Grundstücke wird ein Preis verlangt, Grundstücke erzielen einen Preis / sind Wirtschaftsgüter
commerce – s. Handel (im weiteren Sinn, mit Einschluss der notwendigen Hilfsfunktionen)
commercial – s. Werbesendung
commercial agent – s. (selbständige/r) Handelsvertreter/in
commercial artist – s. Werbegraphiker/in, Gebrauchsgraphiker/in
commercial bank – s. Geschäfts-, Kommerz-, Universalbank
commercial credit risk – s. kommerzielles Risiko
commercial establishment – s. (gewinnorientiertes) Unternehmen, (gewinnorientierter) Betrieb
commercial insurance – s. private Versicherung
commercial insurer – s. privater Versicherer
commercial invoice – s. Handelsrechnung, -faktura
commercialisation
s. Produkteinführungsphase (im weiteren Sinn), Kommerzialisierungsphase
s. Kommerzialisierung, Überhandnehmen wirtschaftlicher Gesichtspunkte
commercial logic – s. wirtschaftliche Sinnhaftigkeit / Logik
commercial paper
s. Handelspapiere (Scheck, Wechsel etc.)
s. Commercial Paper, Finanzierungswechsel, Geldmarktpapiere privater Emittenten, kurzfristige Schuldverschreibungen
Commercial paper is issued by large corporations. – Diese Geldmarktpapiere werden von Großfirmen begeben.
commercial property – s. Büro- und Geschäftsgebäude
commercial rates – s. Gemeindesteuern auf Büro- und Geschäftsgebäude
commercial risk – s. kommerzielles Risiko
commercial traveller – s. Handelsreisende/r, Reisende/r
commercial treaty – s. Handelsabkommen
commission – s. Provision
commit
v. zusagen, verpflichten
v. (sich) verpflichten, sich (voll) einsetzen, sich festlegen, sich verschreiben, hinter (einer Sache) stehen
funds committed – zugesagte / verplante Mittel
be committed to improvement – voll hinter einem Verbesserungsprogramm stehen

v. begehen
commit a crime – ein Verbrechen begehen
commit oneself – sich verpflichten, sich einsetzen
commitment – s. Zusage, (eingegangene) Verpflichtung, Festlegung, Bindung, Bereitstellung
commitment fee – s. Bereitstellungsprovision
commitment underwriting – s. Emissionsgarantie, Underwriting (im engeren Sinn)
committee – s. Komitee, Ausschuss
commodity
s. Ware, (Wirtschafts-)Gut
s. (international gehandelter) Rohstoff, Welthandelsgut
s. Massenartikel, -ware, massengefertigter Standardartikel
commodity agreement – s. Rohstoffabkommen
commodity chemicals – s. Grundchemikalien
commodity chip – s. massengefertigter Chip, Standardchip
commodity exchange – s. Waren-, Rohstoffbörse
commodity forwards – s. Warenterminkontrakte, -geschäfte
commodity futures – s. börsenmäßige / standardisierte Warenterminkontrakte
commodity market – s. Waren-, Rohstoffbörse
commodity pact – s. (internationales) Rohstoffabkommen
common external tariff – s. gemeinsamer Außenzoll
common external trade policy – s. gemeinsame Handels- / Außenhandelspolitk (der EU)
common fund – s. Gemeinschaftsfonds, gemeinsame Kassa
common market – s. Gemeinsamer Markt (der EU)
Common Market for Eastern and Southern Africa
s. Gemeinsamer Markt für Ost- und Südafrika
common stock – s. Stammaktien(-kapital)
communal property – s. Gemeinschaftseigentum, Eigentum aller
commune – s. Kommune
communicate – v. mitteilen
communication
s. Kommunikation
s. Nachricht, Mitteilung
s. (pl.) Nachrichtenwesen
communication link – s. (Daten-)Übertragungsleitung, (Daten- /Nachrichten-)Verbindung
communications mix – s. Kommunikationsmix
communication protocol – s. Kommunikationsprotokoll
communication satellite – s. Nachrichtensatellit
communication skills – s. Kommunikationsfähigkeit, kommunikative Fertigkeiten
community – s. Gemeinwesen, Gemeinschaft, Gemeinde, Welt, Kreise
commercial community – Geschäftswelt
the English-speaking community – die englische Sprachgemeinschaft
the international community – die internationale (Staaten-)Gemeinschaft
investing community – Anlegerkreise
community charge – s. UK-Lokalsteuer / Gemeindeabgabe / Kopfsteuer
compact disc – s. CD, Compact Disc (optisches digitales Speichermedium)
Companies Act – s. UK-(Kapital-)Gesellschaftsgesetz
Companies Acts – s. US-(Kapital-)Gesellschaftsrecht
company
s. (Kapital-)Gesellschaft
s. Unternehmen, Firma
set up / establish / form a company – eine Gesellschaft gründen / errichten
company car – s. Firmen-, Dienstwagen
company law – s. UK-(Kapital-)Gesellschaftsrecht
company legislation – s. UK-(Kapital-)Gesellschaftsrecht
company limited by guarantee – s. Gesellschaft mit beschränkter Nachschusspflicht
company limited by shares – s. UK-Kapitalgesellschaft
company promoter – s. Firmengründer/in, Gründer/in einer Gesellschaft
company secretary – s. „Gesellschaftssekretär" (Position, die Wesenszüge eines Prokuristen, Syndikus und eines geschäftsführenden Aufsichtsratsmitgliedes vereint)
company train – s. Firmenzug, für Firmenkunden reservierter Güterzug
comparative advantage – s. komparativer Vorteil
comparative advertising – s. Vergleichs-, Komparativwerbung
compatible – adj. kompatibel, widerspruchsfrei, vereinbar
compel – v. zwingen
compensate
v. kompensieren, ausgleichen
v. entschädigen
v. entlohnen, vergüten
compensation
s. Kompensation, Ausgleich
s. Ersatz, Schadenersatz, Entschädigung
s. Entgelt, Vergütung
employee compensation – Arbeitsentgelte
executive compensation – Vergütung für Führungskräfte, Vorstand-, Managervergütung
compensatory – adj. ausgleichend, Ausgleichs-, entschädigend, Entschädigungs-,
compensatory balance – s. Liquiditätsbeitrag (Teil eines Bankkredites, der nicht in Anspruch genommen werden darf und damit den Effektivzinssatz erhöht)
compensatory cash payment – s. Ausgleichszahlung
compensatory damages – s. im Vorhinein festgesetzter Schadenersatz, Vertragsstrafe / Konventionalstrafe in der Höhe des zu erwartenden Schadens
compete
v. konkurrieren, im Wettbewerb stehen,
v. an einer Konkurrenz / an einem Preisausschreiben / Wettbewerb teilnehmen
compete on price – über den Preis konkurrieren / verkaufen / kaufen
compentent – adj. kompetent, qualifiziert, zuständig
competent court of jurisdiction – s. zuständiger Gerichtshof
competition
s. Konkurrenz, Wettbewerb, Wettkampf
s. Preisausschreiben, Gewinnspiel
meet competition – der Konkurrenz entgegentreten
participate in a competition – an einem Gewinnspiel teilnehmen
competition law – s. Wettbewerbsrecht
competitive
adj. konkurrierend, Konkurrenz-
adj. konkurrenzfähig, wettbewerbsfähig
competitive advantage – s. Konkurrenzvorteil
competitive devaluation – s. Abwertungskonkurrenz, konkurrenzmotivierte Abwertung, Abwertung aus Konkurrenzgründen
competitiveness – s. Konkurrenz-, Wettbewerbsfähigkeit
competitive product – s. Konkurrenzprodukt, konkurrenzfähiges Produkt
compile – v. zusammenstellen, aufstellen, erstellen
compiler – s. Compiler, Übersetzer(-programm)
complaint – s. Beschwerde, Mängelrüge, Reklamation
settle a complaint – Beschwerde regeln / in Ordnung bringen
complete
adj. vollständig

adj. gültig
a complete contract – ein gültiger Vertrag
complete
v. fertigstellen, beenden, abschließen, vollenden
v. abschließen, tätigen
v. ausfüllen
complete a sale – einen Kauf abschließen / tätigen
complete a form – ein Formular ausfüllen
compliance – s. Einhaltung, Befolgung, Erfüllung
in compliance with – gemäß, entsprechend, in Übereinstimmung mit, unter Einhaltung von
comply – v. entsprechen, nachkommen, einhalten, erfüllen, sich halten an
comply with a request – einer Bitte nachkommen
comply with conditions / terms – Bedingungen erfüllen
component – s. Bestand-, Bauteil
composite currency – s. Mischwährung
compound – s. (chemische) Verbindung
compound arbitrage – s. indirekte Arbitrage, Mehrwährungsarbitrage
compound duty – s. Mischzoll
compound interest – s. Zinseszinsen
comprehensive – adj. umfassend
comprehensive guarantee – s. Pauschalgarantie
comprehensive tax – s. umfassende / generelle Steuer
compressor – s. Niederhalter (eines Büroordners)
comprise – v. umfassen, beinhalten
compromise – v. gefährden, aufs Spiel setzen, kompromittieren
comptroller – s. Controller
compulsory – adj. zwingend, verbindlich, verpflichtend, Zwangs-, Pflicht-
compulsory arbitration – s. Schlichtungszwang, staatlich vorgeschriebenes Schlichtungsverfahren bei arbeitsrechtlichen Konflikten / Tarifverhandlungen
compulsory levy – s. Zwangsabgabe
compulsory liquidation – s. Zwangsliquidation
compulsory surrender – s. Ablieferungspflicht
computation – s. Berechnung
compute – v. berechnen
computer – s. Computer, Rechenanlage, Elektronenrechner
computer-aided – adj. computer-, rechnergestützt
computer-aided design – computer- / rechnergestütztes Entwerfen und Konstruieren, CAD
computer-aided manufacturing – s. rechner- / computergestützte Produktion(-ssteuerung), CAM
computer application – s. Computeranwendung
computer-coded – adj. computergerecht kodiert / verschlüsselt
computer-assisted – adj. computer-, rechnergestützt
computer graphics – Computergraphik
computer language – s. Programmiersprache
computer memory – s. (elektronischer Daten-)Speicher
computer program – s. Computerprogramm
computer tape – s. Magnetband
computer-type information – s. computergerechte / -fähige Daten
computer-type memory – s. elektronischer Datenspeicher
conceive – v. ersinnen, (sich) ausdenken, erfinden, entwerfen
conceive an idea – auf eine Idee kommen, sich etwas ausdenken
concept of conservatism – s. Grundsatz der Bilanzvorsicht
concept of prudence – s. Grundsatz der Bilanzvorsicht
concern
s. Angelegenheit, Sache
s. Sorge, Bedenken
s. Unternehmen, Geschäft, Betrieb
his main concern – seine größe Sorge, sein wichtigstes Anliegen
famly-run concern – Familienbetrieb
concerned
adj. betroffen, betreffend
adj. besorgt
adj. beschäftigt, befasst, engagiert
the committee concerned – der betroffene / zuständige Ausschuss
the activities concerned – die Aktivitäten, um die es sich handelt
be concerned about sthg. – über etwas besorgt sein, sich über etwas Sorgen machen
be concerned with sthg. – mit etwas beschäftigt / befasst ein
concerned citizens – engagierte Bürger
concession – s. Zugeständnis, Vergünstigung, Vorteil, Nachlass
concessional – adj. günstig, Vorzugs-, günstiger als marktwirtschaftlich, mit einem Schenkungselement
concessionary – adj. günstig, Vorzugs-, günstiger als marktwirtschaftlich, mit einem Schenkungselement
on concessionary terms – zu Vorzugskonditionen / günstigeren als marktwirtschaftlichen Bedingungen
conciliation – s. Schlichtung(-sverfahren), Versöhnung
conciliator – s. Schlichter/in, Vermittler/in
conclusion – s. Schluss(-folgerung)
conclusion of a contract – s. Abschluss eines Vertrages
concurrent – adj. gleichzeitig, nebeneinander bestehend
on concurrent terms – Zug um Zug
condition
s. Bedingung, Voraussetzung, Auflage, Einschränkung
s. (Vertrags-)Bedingung, (wesentliche Vertrags-) Bestimmung
comply with a condition – eine Bedingung einhalten / erfüllen
relax a condition – eine Bedingung / Einschränkung lockern
conditional acceptance – s. eingeschränkte Annahme
conditional bond – s. bedingte Bankgarantie
conditional – adj. abhängig
conditional sale – s. (Raten-)Kauf mit Eigentumsvorbehalt
condition of payment – s. Zahlungsbedingung
conditions of cover – s. Versicherungsbedingungen
condone – v. verzeihen, dulden, durchgehen lassen
conduct – s. Verhalten, Betragen, Handlung oder Unterlassung
conduct – v. durchführen, abwickeln
conduct a survey – eine Studie / Erhebung durchführen
Conference on Human Settlements – s. (UN-) Konferenz für menschliche Ansiedlungen
conference shipping line – s. Konferenzlinie
confidential – adj. vertraulich
confirm – v. bestätigen
confirmation – s. Bestätigung, Schlussnote, -brief
confirmed irrevocable (documentary) letter of credit
s. bestätigtes, unwiderrufliches Dokumentenakkreditiv
confirming bank – s. bestätigende Bank
conflicting goals – s Konfliktziele, Zielkonflikt(e)
conflict of interest – s. Interessenskonflikt
conflict of law
s. internationales Privatrecht
s. Rechtskollision
conformity – s. Übereinstimmung
in conformity with – in Übereinstimmung mit, übereinstimmend, gemäß
in conformity with the contract – vertragsgemäß
conformity with the contract – s. Vertragsgemäßheit

conglomerate – s. Misch-, Konglomeratskonzern
conglomerate group – s. Misch-, Konglomeratskonzern
conglomerate merger – s. laterale Fusion
coherent – adj. zusammenhängend, verständlich, stimmig, kohärent
consanguinity – s. Grad der (Bluts-)Verwandtschaft
conscious parallelism – s. abgestimmtes Verhalten (im Sinne des Kartellrechts)
consent – s. Zustimmung, Einwilligung
consequent – adj. folgend, sich daraus ergebend
a consequent reduction – eine sich daraus ergebende Reduzierung
consequential costs – s. Folgekosten
consequential loss insurance – s. Betriebsunterbrechungsversicherung
consequential loss policy – s. Betriebsunterbrechungsversicherungspolizze
conservation
s. Schonung, schonende Behandlung, schonender Umgang, Bewahrung, Schutz
s. Sparen, Spargedanke, Anti-Verschwendungsphilosophie
conservation measure – s. (Energie-)Sparmaßnahme
conservation of nature – s. schonender Umgang mit der Natur, Naturschutz
consideration
s. Berücksichtigung, Erwägung, Erörterung
s. Gegenleistung
consignee
s. (Waren-)Empfänger
s. (Verkaufs-)Kommissionär/in, Konsignatar/in
consignment
s. Warensendung, Posten
s. Kommission(-sgeschäft)
on a consignment basis – auf Kommissionsbasis
on consignment – in Konsignation
consignment contract – s. Konsignationsvertrag
consignment note – s. Frachtbrief
consignment stock – s. Konsignationslager
consignment transaction – s. Konsignations-, Kommissionsgeschäft
consignor
s. (Waren-)Absender
s. Kommittent/in, Konsignant/in, Auftraggeber/in
consistency – s. Kontinuität, Konsequenz, Folgerichtigkeit
consistency principle – s. Prinzip der Bilanzkontinuität, Stetigkeitsprinzip
consistent – adj. konsequent, folgerichtig, ohne (inneren) Widerspruch, stetig
consolidate
v. konsolidieren
v. zu einer Sammelladung / zu Sammelladungen zusammenstellen
consolidated accounts – s. konsolidierter (Konzern-)Abschluss
consolidated balance sheet – s. konsolidierte (Konzern-)Bilanz
consolidated financial statements – s. konsolidierter Perioden- / Jahres- / Konzernabschluss
consolidated group accounts – s. konsolidierter Perioden- / Konzernabschluss
consolidated income statement – s. konsolidierte Gewinn- und Verlustrechnung / Erfolgsrechnung
consolidated shipment – s. Sammelladung
consolidated transport – s. Sammeltransport
consolidation
s. (am.) Fusion durch Neugründung
s. Erstellung eines konsolidierten Rechnungsabschlusses / Konzernabschlusses
s. Zusammenstellung einer Sammelladung / von Sammelladungen
constituency – s. Wählerschaft, Kundenkreis
constraint
s. Einschränkung, Engpass
s. (Rand-)Bedingung
construction
s. Bau, Errichtung, Bau, Bautätigkeit
s. Bauwirtschaft
s. Montageindustrie
construction lag – s. verzögerte Kapitalstockanpassung
constructive total loss – s. angenommener / fingierter Totalverlust
consular fee – s. Konsulatsgebühr
consular invoice – s. Konsulatsfaktura
consular mission – s. konsularische Vertretung
consultant – s. Konsulent/in, Berater/in
consulting services – s. Beratungsdienste, Beratung
consumables – s. Hilfs-, Verschleiß-, Verbrauchsmaterial
consumer – s. Konsument, Verbraucher
consumer confidence – Konsumentenvertrauen
consumer co-operative – s. Konsumgenossenschaft
consumer credit – s. Konsum-, Konsumentenkredit
consumer demand – s. Konsumnachfrage, Nachfrage nach Konsumgütern
consumer durables – s. Gebrauchsgüter, langlebige Konsumgüter
consumer goods – s. Konsumgüter
consumer goods lease – s. Konsumgüterleasing(-vertrag)
consumer lending – s. Vergabe von Konsumkrediten, Konsumkreditgeschäft
consumerism
s. Konsumerismus, Konsumentenschutzbewegung
s. Konsumideologie, konsumorientierte Lebensphilosophie
consumer-led – adj. konsuminduziert, durch den Konsum hervorgerufen
consumer-led recovery – konsuminduzierter Konjunkturaufschwung
consumer price index – s. Index der Verbraucherpreise, Lebenshaltungs-Preisindex
Consumer Price Index – s. US-Verbraucherpreisindex
consumer promotion – s. konsumentenorientierte Verkaufsförderung
consummate – v. vollziehen, abschließen
consumption – s. Verbrauch, Konsum, Verzehr
consumption effect – s. Konsumeffekt
consumption pattern – s. Verbrauchs-, Konsumstruktur
container
s. Behälter, Verpackung
s. Container
container bill – s. Containerkonnossement
containerisation – s. Containerisierung, Umstellung auf Container, Einführung von Containern
container service(s) – s. Containerverkehr
container vessel – s. Containerschiff
contend – v. behaupten, (Meinung) verfechten / vertreten
content provider – s. Content-Provider, Inhaltslieferant, -anbieter
contest
s. Wettbewerb
s. Preisausschreiben
contest – v. beeinspruchen, anfechten, Einwendung(-en) erheben

contested takeover bid – s. feindliches (d. h. nicht mit der Führung der Zielfirma abgestimmtes) Übernahmeangebot
contingency – s. Eventualfall, von Zufall oder Bedingung abhängiges Ereignis, Eventualität, unvorhergesehener Fall
contingency fee – s. Erfolgshonorar
contingent – adj. abhängig, bedingt, Eventual-
contingent liability – s. Eventualverbindlichkeit, Rückstellung für eine dem Bestand nach unsichere Verbindlichkeit
continuous caster – s. Stranggussanlage
contract – s. (privatrechtlicher) Vertrag
make a contract – einen Vertrag abschließen / errichten
conclude a contract – einen Vertrag abschließen / errichten
procure a contract – einen Vertrag vermitteln
enter into a contract – einen Vertrag abschließen
perform a contract – einen Vertrag erfüllen
rescind a contract – einen Vertrag rückgängig machen / aufheben
manufacturing under contract – s. Lohnfertigung
contract
v. Vertrag abschließen, kontrahieren, sich vertraglich verpflichten
v. einengen, beschränken, reduzieren, schrumpfen
contract for the carriage of goods – einen Frachtvertrag abschließen
contract the money supply – die Geldmenge reduzieren / schrumpfen lassen
contract currency – s. Vertragswährung
contract date
s. Vertragsdatum, Zeitpunkt des Vertragsabschlusses, Abschlusstag (eines Export- bzw. Importvertrages)
s. Abschlusstag (eines Devisenkontraktes)
contract delivery date – s. Liefertag / Liefertermin / Erfüllungstag / Erfüllungstermin (eines börsengehandelten Terminkontraktes)
contract for forward delivery – s. Terminkontrakt (mit effektiver Lieferung)
contract for services – s. Dienstleistungvertrag, Werkvertrag
contracting party – s. Vertragspartei
contraction – s. Kontraktions- / Abschwungphase
contract negotiations – s. Vertragsverhandlungen
contract of agency – s. Agentur-, Vertretungsvertrag
contract of apprenticeship – s. Lehrlingsvertrag, Lehrvertrag
contract of carriage – s. Frachtvertrag
contract of carriage by air – s. Luftfrachtvertrag
contract of employment – s. Arbeitnehmervertrag, Dienstvertrag
contract of insurance – s. Versicherungsvertrag
contract of sale – s. Kaufvertrag
contract of service – s. Arbeitnehmervertrag, Dienstvertrag,
contractor
s. Vertragschließende/r, Kontrahent/in
s. Lieferant/in, Auftragnehmer/in, Unternehmer/in
contract penalty – s. Vertrags-, Konventionalstrafe
contract size – s. Kontraktgröße
contractual – adj. vertraglich, Vertrags-
contractual arrangement – s. vertragliche Abmachung
contractual joint venture – s. Contractual Joint Venture, Gemeinschaftsunternehmen in Vertragsform
contractual obligation – s. vertragliche Verpflichtung, Vertragspflicht
contract value – s. Vertragswert, -summe
contribution margin – s. Deckungsbeitrag
contribution margin method – s. Deckungsbeitragsrechnung
contributor – s. Beitragszahler
control
s. Kontrolle
s. Lenkungs-, Beschränkungsmaßnahme, Restriktion, Bewirtschaftung
s. Verfügungsgewalt, Kontrolle
s. Steuervorrichtung, Bedienungseinrichtung, Schalter
government controls – staatliche Lenkungsmaßnahmen
impose controls – Restriktionen usw. einführen
tighten controls – Restriktionen usw. verschärfen
relax / loosen controls – Restriktionen usw. lockern
abolish / lift controls – Restriktionen usw. abschaffen / aufheben
exercise control – Verfügungsgewalt ausüben
under control – unter Kontrolle
control
v. steuern, lenken, leiten
v. beschränken, einschränken, restringieren, bewirtschaften
v. kontrollieren, beherrschen
control bit – s. Kontroll-, Prüfbit
control circuitry – s. Kontrollbus, -schaltkreise
controller – s. Controller
controllership – s. Aufgabenbereich eines Controllers
controlling – adj. beherrschend, maßgeblich, mehrheitlich, steuernd, lenkend, Lenkungs-
controlling interest – s. beherrschende Beteiligung
controlling company – s. herrschendes Unternehmen, Obergesellschaft
controlling interest – s. beherrschende Beteiligung
controls – s. Lenkungs-, Beschränkungsmaßnahmen, Restriktionen, Bewirtschaftung
control unit
s. Leitwerk, Steuerwerk,
s. Lenkungstelle
convene – v. einberufen
convene a meeting – eine Sitzung einberufen
convenience – s. Annehmlichkeit, Bequemlichkeit, Komfort
convenience goods – s. kurzlebige Konsumgüter, Güter des täglichen Bedarfs
convenience store – s. Nachbarschaftsladen, Greißler, Tante-Emma-Laden
Convention for the International Carriage of Goods by Rail
s. Vertrag über die internationale Eisenbahnbeförderung von Gütern
Convention for the International Carriage of Goods by Road
s. Vertrag über den internationalen Gütertransport auf Straßen
convergence – s. Konvergenz, Zusammenwachsen
convergence criteria – s. Konvergenzkriterien
conversion – s. Konvertierung, (Währungs-)Umtausch
conversion efficiency – s. (Energie-)Umwandlungseffizienz
conversion gain – s. (Währungs-)Transaktionsgewinn, (Währungs-)Umwechslungsgewinn
conversion loss – s. (Währungs-)Transaktionsverlust, (Währungs-)Umwechslungsverlust
conversion risk – s. Währungsumrechnungs-, Transaktions-, Konvertierungsrisiko
convertibility – s. Konvertibilität, Konvertierbarkeit
convertible bond – s. Wandelschuldverschreibung
convertible currency – s. (voll) konvertierbare / konvertible Währung
convertible debenture – s. Wandelschuldverschreibung
convey
v. befördern, versenden
v. übermitteln
v. besagen, bedeuten
conveyance
s. Transport, Beförderung
s. Transportmittel, Fahrzeug

COO – chief operating officer (siehe)
co-operative – s. Genossenschaft, Kooperative, Cooperative
co-operative society – Genossenschaft
cooling off – s. (zeitlich begrenztes) Recht des Vertragsrücktrittes bei Haustürgeschäften
co-op – s. consumer co-operative (siehe)
co-operative – s. Genossenschaft
co-operative management style – s. kooperativer / partizipativer Führungsstil
co-operative movement – s. Genossenschaftsbewegung
co-operative society – s. Genossenschaft
copier – s. Kopierer, Kopiergerät
copy
s. Kopie, Duplikat, Durchschrift
s. Exemplar, Ausfertigung
s. Werbetext
run off copies – Kopien (auf einem Vervielfältigungsapparat) machen
copying
s. Kopier-(tätigkeit)
s. (unautorisierte und/oder gesetzwidrige) Vervielfältigung
copyright – s. Urheberrecht
copywriter – s. Werbetexter/in
cord – s. (Telefon-)Schnur, (Telefon-)Kabel
cordless telephone – s. schnurloses Telefon
core – s. Kern, Haupt-, Zentral-
core business – s. Kerngeschäft(-sfeld)
core competency – s. Kernkompetenz
core period – s. Kernzeit
core value – s. Kernwert, zentraler Wert
corn
s. Getreide
s. (am.) Mais
corner shop – s. Laden an der Ecke, Greißler, Nahversorgungsgeschäft
Corp. – s. Abkürzung *für corporation* (siehe) in Firmennamen
corporate – adj. zu einem Unternehmen mit eigener Rechtspersönlichkeit / zu einer Kapitalgesellschaft / zu einem (Groß-)Unternehmen gehörend, Unternehmens-
corporate bond – s. Unternehmens-, Privatanleihe, private Anleihe, Industrieanleihe, -obligation
corporate cash management – s. Cash-Management für (Groß-)Unternehmen
corporate chain store – s. Filialunternehmen, Filialist, Ladenkette
corporate culture – s. Unternehmenskultur
corporate director – s. körperschaftliches Mitglied des erweiterten Aufsichtsrates / Verwaltungsrates einer UK-/US-Kapitalgesellschaft
corporate entity – s. juristische Person, Unternehmen als eigener Rechtsträger
corporate finance – s. betriebliche Finanzierung / Finanzwirtschaft, Unternehmensfinanzierung,
corporate finance advice – s. Finanzberatung für Großunternehmen
corporate governance – s. Corporate Governance, (Gestaltung und Umsetzung der) Unternehmensverfassung
corporate hierarchy – s. Unternehmenshierarchie
corporate image – s. Firmen-, Unternehmensimage
corporate income tax – s. Körperschaftsteuer, Gewinnsteuer für Kapitalgesellschaften
corporate note – s. Finanzierungswechsel, Geldmarktpapier eines privaten Emittenten, kurzfristige Schuldverschreibung
corporate officer – s. Organ / Mitglied der Geschäftsleitung einer Kapitalgesellschaft
corporate personality – s. juristische Person
corporate philosophy – s. Unternehmensphilosophie
corporate planning – s. Unternehmensplanung, Langfristplanung im Unternehmen, strategische Planung
corporate profit – s. Unternehmensgewinn, Gewinn einer Kapitalgesellschaft
corporate restructuring – s. Unternehmensumstrukturierung
corporate savings – s. Unternehmensersparnisse
corporate seal – s. (vom UK- und US-Gesellschaftsrecht vorgeschriebenes) offizielles Siegel einer Kapitalgesellschaft, offizielles Erkennungs- und Beglaubigungszeichen einer Kapitalgesellschaft
corporate secretary – s. „Gesellschaftssekretär" (Position, die Wesenszüge eines Prokuristen, Syndikus und eines geschäftsführenden Verwaltungsratsmitgliedes vereint)
corporate sector – s. Unternehmenssektor, Sektor der Kapitalgesellschaften
corporate social accounting – s. gesellschaftsbezogenes Rechnungswesen, Sozialbilanzen
corporate social responsibility – s. Corporate Social Responsibility, CSR, soziale Verantwortung von Unternehmen
corporate stock option – s. Mitarbeitaktienoption, Aktienoption als Vergütungselement
corporate world – s. Unternehmerkreise, Geschäftswelt, Wirtschaft
corporation
s. Körperschaft, juristische Person
s. Kapitalgesellschaft, Aktiengesellschaft
s. wirtschaftliche Unternehmung der öffentlichen Hand
s. Konzern
corporation aggregate – s. aus mehreren natürlichen und/oder juristischen Personen bestehende juristische Person, Körperschaft
corporation income tax – s. Körperschaftsteuer, Gewinnsteuer für Kapitalgesellschaften
corporation statute – s. (US-einzelstaatliches) (Kapital-)Gesellschaftsgesetz
corporation statutes – s. US-(Kapital-)Gesellschaftsrecht
corporation stock – s. Kommunalschuldverschreibung
corporation tax – s. Körperschaftsteuer
correct – v. korrigieren, bereinigen
correct for price changes – preislich bereinigen
correction feature – s. Korrektureinrichtung
correction fluid – s. Korrekturflüssigkeit, „Tip-ex"
correspondent – s. Korrespondent/in, Geschäftsfreund/in (im Ausland), befreundete Bank / Firma / Organisation (im Ausland)
correspondent bank – s. Korrespondenzbank
cost
s. Kosten
s. Aufwand, Aufwendungen
s. Wert
s. Herstellungskosten
s. Anschaffungs und/oder Herstellungskosten
s. Anschaffungs- und/oder Herstellungswert
s. Selbstkosten, Selbstkostenpreis
at the lower of cost or market – zum Niedrigstwert
at cost – zum Selbstkostenpreis, zum Einstandspreis, zum Anschaffungs- und/oder Herstellungswert
incur costs – Kosten verursachen
costs are incurred – Kosten entstehen / fallen an
cost – v. (durch-)kalkulieren
cost a project – ein Projekt kalkulieren
cost a product – ein Produkt / den Preis eines Produktes kalkulieren
cost accounting – s. Kostenrechnung
cost accounts – s. Kostenrechnung(-ssystem)

cost allocation – s. Kosten-, Aufwandsverteilung, Umlegung / Zurechnung von Kosten
cost centre – s. Kostenstelle
cost control – s. Kostenkontrolle und -lenkung
cost escalation clause – s. Preissteigerungs-, Kostenschwankungsklausel
COST, INSURANCE, FREIGHT – KOSTEN, VERSICHERUNG, FRACHT
cost leadership strategy – s. Kostenführerschaftsstrategie
cost of acquisition – s. Anschaffungswert, -skosten
cost of capital – s. Kapitalkosten
cost of collection – s. (Steuer-)Erhebungskosten, (Steuer-)Inkassokosten
cost of goods sold – s. Wareneinsatz, Herstellungskosten der Absatzleistung, Umsatzkosten
cost of sales – s. Wareneinsatz, Herstellungskosten der Absatzleistung, Umsatzkosten
cost of storage – s. Lagerhaltungs-, Lagerkosten
cost of the goods – s. Kosten der Ware (im Sinne der INCOTERMS, d. h. Transport- und sonstige Nebenkosten)
cost price – s. Selbstkosten-, Einstandspreis
cost principle – s. Anschaffungswertprinzip
cost-push inflation – s. kosteninduzierte Inflation
cost recovery – s. Kapitalrückgewinnung, Wiedereinbringung der Anschaffungs- / Produktionskosten von Anlagegütern, (Verdienen der) Abschreibung
cost(s) of production – s. Herstellungskosten
costs pertaining to the procurement and receipt of goods
s. Bezugskosten der Ware
cost unit – s. Kostenträger
cotton – s. Baumwolle
cotton subsidy – s. Baumwollsubvention, -förderung
count
s. Zählung, Auszählung, Erhebung
s. (Anklage-)Punkt, Hinsicht
full count – Vollerhebung, (Volks-)Zählung
be criticised on several counts – in mehrfacher Hinsicht krtisiert werden
counter
s. Zähler, Zählwerk
s. Ladentisch, (Bank-)Schalter
counteract – v. bekämpfen, entgegentreten
counter-claim – s. Gegenforderung
counter-culture – s. Gegenkultur, alternative Lebensformen
counter-cyclical policy – s. antizyklische Konjunkturpolitik
counterfeiting – s. (Ident-)Fälschung; gewerbsmäßige Fälschung; unerlaubter Gebrauch von geschützten Designs, Marken, Herkunftsangaben und Patenten
counter-indemnity – s. Rückgarantie
counter-inflationary policy – s. Antinflationspolitik, (Maßnahmen zur) Inflationsbekämpfung
countermeasure – s. Gegenmaßnahme
counter-offer – s. Gegenangebot
counterpart – s. Gegenstück, Entsprechung, (Amts-)Kollege
counterparty – s. Gegenpartei, -seite, die andere Transaktionspartei
counter-productive – adj. kontraproduktiv, die gegenteilige Wirkung erzielend
counterpurchase – s. Parallel-, Kopplungsgeschäft
counter-retaliation – s. Gegenvergeltung, Vergeltung für Vergeltung
countersign – v. gegenzeichnen
counter-signature – s. Gegenzeichnung, korrespondierende Unterschrift
countertrade – s. Gegengeschäfte, Abwicklung von Gegengeschäften
countervailing duty – s. Ausgleichszoll, -abgabe
countervailing tariff – s. Ausgleichszoll, -abgabe
country code – s. Landesvorwahlnummer
country of origin – s. Ursprungsland
county – s. Grafschaft (England)
couple – v. (an-)kuppeln
coupon – s. (Werbe-)Kupon, Gutschein, Bon
coupon swap – s. Kuponswap, Zinsswap
course of business – s. Abwicklung eines Geschäftes / einer Transaktion, geschäftliche Vorgangsweise, Geschäftsverlauf
Courier – s. Kurier, (Eil-)Bote
courier service – s. Kurierdienst
court of arbitration – s. Schiedsgericht
court of law – s. (ordentlicher) Gerichtshof, (ordentliches) Gericht
cover
s. (Versicherungs-)Deckung, Versicherungsschutz
s. Briefumschlag
s. Umschlag, Schutzhülle
under separate cover – unter besonderem Umschlag, mit gleicher Post (aber in separatem Kuvert)
cover – v. decken, abdecken
cover costs / risks – Kosten / Risken (ab)decken
coverage
s. Anwendungsbereich, Umfang
s. (Versicherungs-)Deckung / Schutz
s. Reichweite (von Medien)
covered container – s. gedeckter Container
covered wagon – s. gedeckter Güterwagen
covering
s. Kurssicherung (im engeren Sinn), Abdeckung des Währungsumwechslungsrisikos
s. Kurssicherung (im weiteren Sinn), Abdeckung des Wechselkursrisikos
covering in the spot market – s. Abdeckung des Währungsumwechslungsrisikos über den Geldmarkt, Kurssicherung über den Geldmarkt / durch Fremdwährungskreditaufnahme und/oder Fremdwährungsveranlagung
covering letter – s. Begleitbrief, -schreiben
covering technique – s. s. Kurssicherungstechnik, -maßnahme, Maßnahme zur Preissicherung
cover note – s. vorläufige Deckungszusage
CPI – Consumer Price Index (siehe)
CPT – FREIGHT/CARRIAGE PAID TO (siehe)
CPU – central processing unit (siehe)
cradle – s. Wiege
cradle-to-grave – „von der Wiege bis zur Bahre", auf den gesamten (ökologischen Produkt-)Lebenszyklus bezogen
craft
s. Fahrzeug(e)
s. Handwerk, Gewerbe, Beruf
craft union – s. Berufsgewerkschaft
crate – s. Lattenkiste, Steige, Verschlag
crate – v. in Lattenkisten / Steigen / Verschlägen verpacken
crawl – v. kriechen
crawling peg – s. Gleitkurs, Gleitparität, Wechselkurssystem mit gleitender Paritätsanpassung
creation of utilities – s. Nutzenstiftung
creative department – s. Kreativ-, Gestaltungsabteilung
creative director – s. Kreativdirektor/in, Leiter/in der Kreativabteilung einer Werbeagentur
creator – s. Schöpfer/in, Urheber/in
creator of intellectual property – Urheber geistigen Eigentums
creche – s. Kinderkrippe, Krabbelstube

credit
s. Kredit, Darlehen
s. Zahlungsziel
s. Haben(-buchung), Gutschrift
s. Akkreditiv
grant / extend credit - Kredit gewähren
six months credit - Zahlungsziel von sechs Monaten
a credit to Accounts Receivable - eine Habenbuchung auf dem Forderungskonto
on credit - auf Ziel
credit - v. erkennen, gutschreiben
credit an account - v. ein Konto erkennen
credit an account with an amount - v. einen Betrag einem Konto gutschreiben / ein Konto mit einem Betrag erkennen
credit an amount to an account - v. ein Konto mit einem Betrag erkennen, einen Betrag einem Konto gutschreiben
credit agreement - s. Kreditvertrag
credit and collection policies - s. (etwa) Kredit- und Mahnwesen, Vorgangsweise im Kredit- und Mahnwesen
credit application - s. Kreditantrag
credit balance - s. Habensaldo, (Bank-)Guthaben
credit bureau - s. (genossenschaftliche) Auskunftei, Kreditschutzverband
credit card - s. Kreditkarte
credit card scheme - s. Kreditkartenorganisation
credit clearing system - s. Abrechnungs- / Clearingsystem für den bargeldlosen Überweisungsverkehr
credit co-operative - s. Kreditgenossenschaft
credit crunch - s. scharfe Kreditrestriktion, starke Kreditverknappung
credit entry - s. Habenbuchung
credit facility - s. Kreditfazilität
credit information - s. Kredit-, Bonitätsauskunft, Kreditinformation
credit inquiry - s. Erkundigung(-sschreiben), Auskunftsgesuch, Anfrage um Bonitätsauskunft
credit inquiry agency - s. Auskunftei
credit limit - s. Kreditlimit
credit line - s. Kreditlinie, Kreditrahmen
credit loss - s. Kreditverlust
credit memorandum - s. Gutschriftsanzeige
credit multiplier - s. Kreditmultiplikator
credit note - s. Gutschriftsanzeige
creditor
s. Gläubiger/in, Fremdkapitalgeber/in
s. (pl.) Verbindlichkeiten auf Grund von Warenlieferungen und Leistungen
creditors' funds - s. Fremdmittel, Fremdkapital
creditorship - s. Gläubigerverhältnis
creditorship rights - s. Gläubigerrechte
credit period - s. Zahlungsziel, Kreditlaufzeit
credit rating - s. Bonitätsbeurteilung, Bonitätseinstufung, Bonitätsbewertung, Rating, Kreditwürdigkeit
credit reporting agency - s. Auskunftei
credit requirement - s. Akkreditivverfordernis, -bedingung
credit risk - s. Delkredere-, Kredit-, Zahlungsrisiko
credit sale
s. (zwischen Kaufleuten) Zielverkauf, Verkauf auf Ziel
s. (in Verträgen mit Endverbrauchern) Ratenkauf (ohne Eigentumsvorbehalt), Kauf / Verkauf mit Stundung des Kaufpreises
credit side - s. Habenseite
credit squeeze - s. Kreditrestriktion(en), Kreditbremse
credit standing - s. Kreditwürdigkeit, Bonität
credit terms - s. (Zahlungs-)Ziel, Kredit
sell on credit terms - auf Ziel / Kredit verkaufen
credit hours - Zeitgutschrift, gutgeschriebene Arbeitsstunden
credit multiplier - s. Kreditmultiplikator
credit transfer - s. Überweisung
credit transfer form - s. Überweisungsformular
creditworthiness - s. Kreditwürdigkeit, Bonität
creditworthy - adj. kreditwürdig
creed - s. Glaubensbekenntnis, Credo
creeping inflation - s. schleichende Inflation
criminal offence - s. strafbare Handlung, Straftat
criteria - s. Maßstäbe, Kriterien
criterion - s. Maßstab, Kriterium
CRM - customer relationship management (siehe)
crop - s. Ernte, Feldfrucht
crop residues - s. Ernterückstände
crop rotation - s. Fruchtfolge
crop failure - s. Missernte, Ernteausfall
cross-border - adj. grenzüberschreitend
cross-border leasing - s. grenzüberschreitendes Leasing
cross-breeding - Kreuzzüchtung, Kreuzung, Hybridisierung
cross-currency basis swap - s. Basis-Währungsswap
cross-currency coupon swap - s. Zins-Währungsswap
cross-currency fixed/fixed swap - s. Zins-Währungsswap fest/fest
cross-currency fixed/floating swap - s. Zins-Währungsswap fest/variabel
cross-currency floating/floating swap - s. Zins-Währungsswap variabel/variabel
cross-currency swap - s. Zins-Währungsswap
crossed cheque - s. gekreuzter Scheck, (etwa) Verrechnungsscheck
cross-sell - v. im Verbund verkaufen
cross-selling - s. Verbundverkauf, Cross-Selling
crossing - s. Kreuzvermerk, Kreuzung
crowd out - v. verdrängen, hinausdrängen
CRT - cathode-ray tube (siehe)
crude - s. Rohöl
crude - adj. roh, (statistisch) unbereinigt, ungewichtet
crunch - v. zermalmen, verarbeiten
CT - cable transfer (siehe)
CTO - combined transport operator (siehe)
CT rate - s. Wechselkurs für telegraphische und Telex-Auszahlungen, Devisenkurs
cubic capacity (of an engine) - s. Hubraum
cue - s. Hinweis, Fingerzeig
Production should take its cue from marketing. - Die Produktion sollte sich am Marketing ausrichten / orientieren.
cue stick - s. (Billard-)Queue, Billardstock
culprit - s. Schuldige/r
cultural event - s. kulturelle Veranstaltung
cumulative preference share - s. kumulative Vorzugsaktie, Vorzugsaktie mit Dividendennachbezugsrecht
cumulative quantity discount - s. Umsatzrabatt, -bonus, -bonifikation
curb - v. beschränken, drosseln, bremsen
currency
s. Währung
s. Bargeldumlauf, Münzen und Banknoten, Papiergeld
currency basket - s. Währungskorb
currency adjustment clause - s. Kurssicherungs-, Währungsklausel
currency basket - s. Währungskorb
currency clause - s. Kurssicherungs-, Währungsklausel
currency cocktail - s. Mischwährung
currency control - s. Devisenbewirtschaftung

currency dealer – s. Devisen-, Währungshändler/in
currency escalator clause – s. Kurssicherungs-, Währungsklausel
currency forwards – s. Währungstermingeschäfte, -kontrakte, Devisentermingeschäfte, -kontrakte
currency fluctuation – s. Wechselkursschwankungen
currency futures – s. börsengehandelte Währungsterminkontrakte, Währungsfutures
currency futures contract – s. Währungsterminkontrakt, Währungsfuture
currency hedging – s. Devisenkurssicherung, Wechselkurssicherung, Absicherung gegen das Wechselkursrisiko
currency market – s. Devisen-, Währungsmarkt
currency of the credit – s. Akkreditivwährung
currency option – s. Devisen-, Währungsoption
currency parity – s. Währungsparität,
currency protection clause – s. Kurssicherungs-, Währungsklausel
currency rate – s. Mengennotierung
currency risk – s. Wechselkurs-, Devisenkurs-, Kurs-, Währungsrisiko
currency swap – s. Währungs-, Devisenswap
currency union – s. Währungsunion
current account
s. Leistungsbilanz
s. Kontokorrentkonto, Girokonto, Scheckkonto
current account balance – s. Sicht-, Kontokorrentguthaben, Guthaben auf Girokonto
current account deficit – s. Leistungsbilanzdefizit, -abgang
current account deposit – s. Sicht-, Kontokorrenteinlage
current account surplus – s. Leistungsbilanzüberschuss, -aktivum
current-account terms of trade – s. Terms of Trade auf der Basis der Leistungsbilanz
current assets – s. Umlaufvermögen
current debt – s. kurzfristige Verbindlichkeit(-en), kurzfristiges Fremdkapital
current bond yield – s. Sekundärmarktrendite von Anleihen
current creditor – s. Fremdkapitalgeber mit kurzfristiger Forderung, Lieferkreditgeber
current investment income – s. Kapitalerträge
current liabilities – s. kurzfristige Verbindlichkeiten
current liabilities to capital (or owners' equity) ratio – s. Anteil der kurzfristigen Verbindlichkeiten am Eigenkapital, kurzfristige Verbindlichkeiten zu Eigenkapital
current price – zur Zeit geltender / aktueller Preis
current ratio – s. Liquidität 3. Grades, Deckungsgrad 3
current replacement cost – s. Wiederbeschaffungs-, Tageswert (am Beschaffungsmarkt)
current replacement value – s. Wiederbeschaffungs-, Tageswert (am Bechaffungsmarkt)
closing rate method – s. Stichtagskursmethode
current rate (of exchange)– s. (Bilanz-)Stichtagskurs, Kurs am Bilanzstichtag
current rate method – s. Stichttagskursmethode
current transfers –s. laufende Transfers, laufende Transaktionen ohne Gegenleistung
current transfers account – s. Bilanz der laufenden Transfers
current yield – s. Sekundärmarktrendite
custodianship for customers' securities – s. Wertpapierdepot(-verwaltung)
custody – s. Gewahrsam, Verwahrung, Aufbewahrung, Obhut, Depot
custom – s. Brauch, Sitte
customary – adj. gewohnheitsmäßig, üblich, usuell
customer relationship management – s. Management von Kundenbeziehungen, Kundenbeziehungsmanagement, Customer Relationship Management, CRM-Management
customer-segment pricing – s. segment-orientierte Preisgestaltung, Preisdifferenzierung nach Kundensegmenten, persönliche Preisdifferenzierung
customised globalisation – s. transnationale (Marketing-)Strategie, transnationales Marketing
customised option – s. Freiverkehrsoption, nicht-börsenotierte Option, bankmäßige (Devisen-)Option
customer – s. Kunde/Kundin, Klient/in, Abnehmer/in
customer-activated terminal – s. (Bank-)Kundenterminal
customer perception – s. Kundenwahrnehmung, -perzeption
customer relationship management – s. Kundenbeziehungsmanagement, Customer Relationship Management, CRM
customs authorities – s. Zollbehörden
customs border – s. Zollgrenze
customs clearance – s. Zollabfertigung
customs custody – s. Zollgewahrsam
customs duty – s. Zoll, Zollgebühr, -abgabe
customs entry – s. Zollanmeldung, -erklärung, -antrag
file a customs entry – eine Zollanmeldung einbringen, (etwas) zur Verzollung anmelden, einen Zollantrag stellen
customs examination – s. Zollbeschau
customs invoice – s. Zollfaktura
customs office – s. Zollamt, -stelle
customs procedure – s. Zollbehandlung, -verfahren, -abfertigung
customs tariff – s. Zolltarif
customs territory – s. Zollgebiet
customs union – s. Zollunion
customs valuation – s. Zollwertfeststellung, -festsetzung, Festlegung / Ermittlung des Zollwertes
customs value – s. Zollwert
cut-price store – s. Diskontladen, Diskonter
cut-throat competition – s. ruinöse Konkurrenz, Verdrängungswettbewerb
cutting – s. (Zeitungs-)Ausschnitt, Stoffstück, -muster
C.W.O. – cash with order (siehe)
cyberspace – s. virtueller Erlebnisraum, Cyberspace
cyclical – adj. konjunkturell, konjunkturbedingt, kurzfristig
cyclical unemployment – s. konjunkturelle / konjunkturbedingte Arbeitslosigkeit

D

D/A – documents against acceptance (siehe)
DAF – DELIVERED AT FRONTIER (siehe)
dairy product – s. Molkereiprodukt
daisy-wheel – s. Typenrad, Schreibrad
damage
s. Schaden, Schäden, Beschädigung
s. (pl.) – s. Schadenersatz
loss of, or damage to, the goods – Verlust oder Beschädigung der Ware
sue for damages – auf Schadenersatz klagen
damages clause – s. Schadensersatz-, Vertragsstrafenklausel
damage to property – s. Sachschaden
data bit – s. Datenbit
data processing – s. Datenverarbeitung
data transmission – s. Datenübertragung
data transmission line – s. Datenübertragungsleitung
data transmission link – s. Datenübertragungsleitung, Datenverbindung
date of issue – s. Ausstellungsdatum
date of maturity – s. Fälligkeitsdatum
date of payment – s. Zahlungstermin, -datum, Datum der Zahlungsleistung
date of settlement
s. Zahlungstermin, -datum, Datum der Zahlungsleistung / des Zahlungseinganges
s. Fälligkeits- Erfüllungs-, Valutatag (eines Devisengeschäftes)
s. Liefertag, -termin, Erfüllungstag (eines börsengehandelten Devisenterminkontraktes)
DATEX -Data Exchange (altes deutsches Datennetzwerk)
daunting – adj. abschreckend, beängstigend
day care centre – s. (Kinder-)Tagesstätte
day-to-day management – s. Abwicklung der laufenden Geschäftsangelegenheiten, laufende Geschäftsführung, laufende Geschäftsabwicklung, Tagesgeschäft
DCF method – discounted cash flow method (siehe)
DCF technique – discounted cash flow technique (siehe)
DCP – FREIGHT / CARRIAGE PAID TO (siehe)
DDP – DELIVERED DUTY PAID (siehe)
DDU – DELIVERED DUTY UNPAID (siehe)
deadlock – s. toter Punkt, Stillstand, Blockierung
break the deadlock – den toten Punkt überwinden
dead-weight tonnage– s. Tragfähigkeitstonnage, Gesamtzuladungsgewicht eines Schiffes in Tonnen
deal
s. Geschäft, (Geschäfts-)Abschluss, Abmachung
s. Behandlung, Vorgangsweise
It's a deal! – Abgemacht!
unfair deal – unfaire Behandlung / Vorgangsweise
dealer – s. (Einzel-)Händler/in
dealer brand – s. Eigen-, Haus-, Händler-, Handelsmarke
dealer sales contest – s. Händlerverkaufswettbewerb, Verkaufswettbewerb für Händler/innen
dealer's brand – s. Eigen-, Haus-, Händler-, Handelsmarke
dealing centre – s. Devisenhandelszentrum, internationaler Finanzplatz
dealing room – s. Dealing Room, Handelsraum
dealing system – s. (Wertpapier-)Handelssystem
death tax – s. Erbschaftssteuer
debenture – s. (brit.) Unternehmensanleihe, Industrieobligation, (am.) nicht besicherte Unternehmensanleihe
debenture holder – s. Inhaber / Besitzer einer (besicherten oder nicht besicherten) Unternehmensanleihe
debit – s. Soll, Sollbuchung
a debit to cash – eine Sollbuchung auf dem Kassakonto
debit – v. belasten, auf Soll buchen
debit an account – v. ein Konto belasten
debit an account with an amount – v. ein Konto mit einem Betrag belasten
debit an amount to an account – v. ein Konto mit einem Betrag belasten, einen Betrag auf einem Konto auf Soll buchen
debit balance – s. Sollsaldo, Minus (auf dem Bankkonto)
debit card – s. Debit-, Lastschriftkarte
debit entry – s. Sollbuchung
debit memo – s. Lastschriftanzeige
debit memorandum – s. Lastschriftanzeige
debit note – s. Lastschriftanzeige
debit side – s. Sollseite
debt
s. Schuld, Schulden, geschuldeter Betrag
s. Fremdkapital, -mittel
s. Forderung(en)
meet debts – Schulden begleichen / bezahlen
export debts – Exportforderungen
debt-equity ratio – s. Verschuldungsgrad, -koeffizient
debt finance – s. Kredit-, Fremdmittelfinanzierung
debt forgiveness – s. Schuldenerlass, -nachlass
debt fund – s. Debt-Fonds, Rentenfonds, Fonds für verzinsliche Anlagen (Anleihen, Schatzwechsel etc.)
debt market – s. Fremdkapital-, Anleihen-, Rentenmarkt
debt ratio – s. Fremdkapitalanteil, -quote, Anspannungskoeffizient
debtor
s. Schuldner
s. (pl.) Schuldner, Forderungen
debt securities – s. (börsengängige) schuldrechtliche Wertpapiere
decapitalise – s. klein schreiben, mit kleinem Anfangsbuchstaben schreiben
The word should be decapitalised. – Das Wort sollte klein geschrieben werden.
decay – s. Verfall, Verwitterung, Verrottung
December call – s. Dezember-Call
deceptive – adj. irreführend, täuschend
deceptive advertising – s. irreführende Werbung
decision-maker – s. Entscheidungsträger/in, Verantwortliche/r, Entscheidungsinstanz
decision-making – s. Entscheidungsprozess/e
decision trees – s. (Methode der) Entscheidungsbäume
declaration
s. Dividendenbeschluss, -erklärung
s. Meldung, Anmeldung (z.B. einer Sendung im Rahmen einer Pauschaldeckung)
declaration policy – s. Abschreibpolizze
decline
s. Rückgang, Abnahme
s. Degenerations-, Abschwungphase
decline stage – s. Niedergangsphase
declining-balance method – s. (geometrisch) degressive Abschreibung, Buchwertabschreibung
decoupling – s. Entkoppeln
decreasing-charge method – s. degressive Abschreibung

dedicated – adj. spezifisch, ohne alternative Verwendungsmöglichkeit, Spezial-
dedicated equipment – s. Spezialgeräte
deductible – s. Selbstbehalt, Abzugsfranchise
deduction
s. Abzugsbetrag, Abzugsposten
s. Freibetrag, Sonderausgabe
deed – s. gesiegelter, förmlicher Vertrag
deed of protest – s. Protesturkunde
deem – v. halten für, betrachten als, erachten als
be deemed to be insured – als versichert gelten
deep discount bond – s. (unter pari ausgegebene) Null-Kupon-Anleihe
deep-sea container services – s. Hochseecontainer-Dienste
deep-sea trade – s. Hochseeschifffahrt
default – s. Nichterfüllung (einer gesetzlichen oder vertraglichen Verpflichtung, bes. der Zahlungsverpflichtung), Unterlassung, Versäumnis, Verzug, Zahlungsverzug, Nichtzahlung, Säumigkeit
in default – säumig, in Verzug
in default of sthg. – in Ermangelung einer Sache
default – v. vertraglichen Verpflichtungen nicht nachkommen, Termin versäumen, in (Zahlungs-)Verzug geraten, nicht bezahlen
default on a debt – Schuld nicht bezahlen (können)
default on the payment of interest – mit der Zinsenzahlung in Verzug geraten
default bond – s. bedingte (Bank-)Garantie mit Effektivklausel
defect – s. Fehler, Mangel
defective – adj. mangelhaft, fehlerhaft, beschädigt
defective goods – s. mangelhafte Waren
defence industry – s. Rüstungsindustrie
defer – v. aufschieben, verschieben
deferred credit – s. transitorisches Passivum (Rechnungsabgrenzungsposten)
deferred expense – s. transitorisches Aktivum (Rechnungsabgrenzungsposten)
deferred expense and accrued income – s. aktiver Rechnungsabgrenzungsposten
deferred income – s. transitorisches Passivum, transitorische Passiva (Rechnungsabgrenzungsposten)
deferred income and accrued expense – s. passive/r Rechungsabgrenzungsposten
deferred item – s. transitorischer Posten der Rechnungsabgrenzung
deferred profit-sharing plan – s. Gewinnbeteiligung mit Sperrfrist/ Sperrklausel, Investivlohn
deferred revenues – s. transitorische Passiva (Rechnungsabgrenzungsposten)
deferred share – s. Nachzugsaktie
deferred terms – s. (Zahlungs-)Ziel, Kredit
buy on deferred terms – v. auf Ziel / Kredit kaufen
deficit – s. Defizit, Abgang
settle a deficit – ein Defizit ausgleichen
meet a deficit – ein Defizit ausgleichen
show a deficit – ein Defizit aufweisen, passiv sein
be in deficit – ein Defizit aufweisen, passiv sein
deficit on invisibles – s. Dienstleistungsdefizit, Defizit in der Dienstleistungsbilanz
deficit spending – s. Defizitspending
deflate
v. eindämmen, restringieren, restriktive Wirtschaftspolitik betreiben
v. die Inflation herausrechnen, (bei Vorliegen einer Preissteigerung) auf reale Zahlen umrechnen, preislich bereinigen
deflation
s. restriktive Wirtschaftspolitik, Deflation
s. Deflation, Nachfragelücke
s. Inflationsbereinigung
deflationary
adj. deflationär, restriktiv, kontraktiv, (die gesamtwirtschaftliche Nachfrage) einschränkend
adj. deflatorisch, durch eine Nachfragelücke gekennzeichnet
deflator – s. Deflator(-index), Paasche Preisindex
deforestation – s. Entwaldung, Abholzung
defraud – v. betrügen, hinterziehen
defray – v. tragen, übernehmen, bestreiten
defray costs – Kosten tragen / übernehmen
degree of vertical integration – s. Fertigungstiefe, Ausmaß der vertikalen Integration
de-industrialisation – s. Entindustrialisierung, Deindustrialisierung
delay – s. Verzögerung, Verzug
without delay – unverzüglich
delay in delivery – s. Lieferverzug
delay in payment – s. Zahlungsverzug
del credere – s. Delkredere, Inkassogarantie, Haftung / Garantie für die Zahlungsfähigkeit des Schuldners
del credere agent – s. Delkredereagent/in, Handelsvertreter/in mit Delkrederefunktion
del credere commission – s. Delkredereprovision
del credere risk – s. Delkredere-, Inkassorisiko, Risiko des Forderungsausfalls
deliberate – adj. absichtlich, bewusst
deliver
v. liefern, ausliefern, zustellen, abliefern
v. übergeben, aushändigen
v. Erwartungen erfüllen
DELIVERED AT FRONTIER – GELIEFERT GRENZE
DELIVERED DUTY PAID – GELIEFERT VERZOLLT
DELIVERED DUTY UNPAID – GELIEFERT UNVERZOLLT
DELIVERED EX QUAY – GELIEFERT AB KAI
DELIVERED EX SHIP – GELIEFERT AB SCHIFF
delivery
s. Lieferung, Auslieferung, Zustellung, Ablieferung
s. Übergabe, Aushändigung
take delivery of goods – Waren übernehmen / abnehmen
make or take delivery of a currency amount – einen Währungsbetrag liefern or abnehmen
by indorsement and delivery – durch Indossament und Übergabe
delivery charge – s. Zustellungs-, Lieferkosten
delivery date
s. Liefertermin, -frist
s. Fälligkeits-, Erfüllungs-, Valutatag (eines Devisengeschäftes)
s. Liefer-, Erfüllungstag Liefermin (eines börsengehandelten Devisenterminkontraktes)
delivery date option – s. Termingeschäft mit Laufzeitoption
delivery fleet – s. Lieferwagenfuhrpark
delivery period – s. Lieferfrist, Lieferzeit
delivery van – s. Lieferwagen
demand
s. Forderung, Anforderung, Verlangen, Sicht, Vorlage
s. Nachfrage
meet a demand – einer Forderung nachkommen / entsprechen
make a demand – eine Forderung erheben
payable on demand – zahlbar bei Vorlage, zahlbar bei Sicht
generate demand – Nachfrage erzeugen / schaffen / kreieren

demand
v. verlangen, fordern
v. nachfragen
quantity demanded – nachgefragte Menge
demand curve – s. Nachfragekurve, -funktion, Preisabsatzkurve, -funktion
demand deposit – s. Sichteinlage
demander – s. Nachfrager/in
demand function – s. Nachfragefunktion
demand-pull inflation – s. nachfrageinduzierte Inflation
demand-shift inflation – s. strukturelle Inflation
demarcation line – s. Trennungslinie, Abgrenzung
demeaning – adj. erniedrigend, herabwürdigend
demijohn – s. Korbflasche, Glasballon
demodulation – s. Demodulation, Empfangsgleichrichtung
demodulator – s. Demodulator, Empfangsgleichrichter
demographic factor – s. demographischer Faktor
demurrage – s. Überliegegeld, Liegegeld, (Waggon-)Standgeld
denationalise – s. entstaatlichen, privatisieren
denominated in – adj. lautend auf
denominated in a foreign currency – auf eine Fremdwährung lautend, Fremdwährungs-
denominated in a given currency – auf eine bestimmte Währung lautend
denomination – s. Stückelung, Nennwert
denominator – s. Nenner (einer Bruchzahl)
denote – s. bezeichnen
density – s. Dichte, Häufigkeit
density of solar facilities – s. Solaranlagendichte
deny
v. verneinen, dementieren, bestreiten
v. verweigern
deny payment – die Zahlung verweigern
deoxyribonucleic acid – s. DNA, Desoxyribonukleinsäure
departmental filing – s. dezentrale Schriftgutablage
Department of Employment – s. UK-Arbeitsministerium
Department of Trade and Industry – s. UK-Handels- und Industrieministerium
department store – s. Kauf-, Warenhaus
dependent employment – s. unselbständige Erwerbstätigkeit / Arbeit
dependent variable – s. abhängige / endogene / erklärte Variable
depletable – adj. erschöpfbar, nicht erneuerbar, der Substanzveringerung unterworfen
depletable asset – s. der Substanzverringerung unterliegender / natürlicher / nicht reproduzierbarer / nicht erneuerbarer Vermögensgegenstand
deplete – v. erschöpfen, (vollständig) ausschöpfen / aufbrauchen / leeren
our stocks are depleted – unser Lager ist erschöpft / geleert
depletion
s. Substanzverringerung, Schwund, Erschöpfung, vollständige Ausbeutung
s. Substanzwertabschreibung, Absetzung für Substanzverringerung
depletion charge – s. Aufwand für Substanzwertabschreibung, Substanzwertabschreibungsquote
depletion rate – s. Betrag der Substanzwertabschreibung pro abgebaute Mengeneinheit (z.B. abgebaute Tonne, abgebauten Kubikmeter usw.)
deploy – v. verwenden, anwenden, einsetzen
deposit
s. Einzahlung, Einlage (bei einer Bank)
s. (Bank-)Einlage
s. Hinterlegung
s. Anzahlung
s. Kaution
s. Pfand (für eine Mehrwegpackung)
s. Lagerstätte, Vorkommen
ore deposit – Erz-, Erzvorkommen
deposit
v. – einzahlen, einlegen, anlegen
v. – deponieren, hinterlegen
money deposited in a bank – das bei einer Bank eingelegte Geld
deposit account – s. Depositen-, Sparkonto
deposit money – s. Buch-, Giralgeld
depositor
s. Einleger/in, Einlagenkunde/-kundin (bei einer Bank)
s. Einlagerer
depository institution – s. Kreditinstitut
deposit rate – s. Habenzinssatz, Zinssatz für (Spar-)Einlagen
deposit taking – s. Entgegennahme von Einlagen, Passivgeschäft
depreciable assets – s. abnutzbare / abschreibungsfähige Wirtschaftsgüter
depreciation
s. Wertminderung, Kurs-, Preisrückgang, (Geld-)Entwertung
s. Abschreibung, ordentliche Abschreibung auf das Anlagevermögen
depreciation account – s. Abschreibungskonto
depreciation allowance – s. Abschreib-, Abschreibungsquote, Absetzung für Abnutzung, AfA
depreciation charge – s. Abschreibungsaufwand
depreciation computation – s. Berechnung des Abschreibungsaufwandes
Depreciation Expense – s. Abschreibungsaufwand(-skonto), (das Konto) ordentliche und außerordentliche Abschreibung vom Anlagevermögen
depreciation for tax purposes – s. Abschreibung im steuerlichen Sinn, steuerrechtliche Abschreibung
depreciation method – s. Abschreibungsmethode
depreciation of the internal value of a currency – s. (innere) Geldentwertung
depression – s. Depresson; scharfe, langanhaltende Rezession, Wirtschaftskrise
depth of the range – s. Tiefe des Produktionsprogrammes / Sortimentes, Sortimentstiefe
deputise – v. (jemanden) vetreten
deputy – s. Stellvertreter/in
DEQ – DELIVERED EX QUAY
derailment – s. Entgleisung
deregulation – s. Deregulierung, Abbau staatlicher Lenkungsmaßnahmen
deregulatory – adj. Deregulierungs-
derivative instrument – s. Derivat, derivatives Finanzinstrument
derivatives market – s. Derivativmarkt, -börse, Markt für derivative Finanzprodukte
derived demand – s. abgeleitete Nachfrage
derogatory – adj. abfällig, abschätzig
DES – DELIVERED EX SHIP (siehe)
desalination – s. Entsalzung
design
s. Entwurf, Zeichnung, Plan, Modell
s. Muster, Design
s. Konstruktion(-sweise)
design
v. entwerfen, konzipieren, entwickeln
v. konstruieren
designation – s. Bezeichnung

designed – adj. bestimmt, gedacht, geplant, zugeschnitten
desk research – s. Schreibtischforschung, Sekundärerhebung
desktop computer – s. Tischcomputer
desktop publishing – s. Desktop Publishing
destabilise – v. destabilisieren
destination – s. Bestimmungsort
destination principle – s. Bestimmungslandprinzip
detachable – adj. abtrennbar
deteriorate – v. sich verschlechtern, sich verschlimmern, schlecht werden, verderben
deterioration
s. Verschlechterung, Verschlimmerung
s. Verschleiß, Verderb, Wertminderung
determinable – adj. feststellbar, bestimmbar
determinant – s. Determinante, bestimmender Faktor, Bestimmungsgröße
deterrent – s. Abschreckung(-smittel), Abschreckungswaffe
devaluation – s. Abwertung (einer Währung – besonders: bei einer Währung mit festem Wechselkurs)
devalue – v. abwerten (besonders: eine Währung mit festem Wechselkurs)
develop
v. entwickeln,
v. ausarbeiten, erstellen
v. verwerten
v. erschließen
v. bebauen
develop estimates – Schätzungen / Prognosen ausarbeiten
develop a site – ein Grundstück erschließen / bebauen
developing country – s. Entwicklungsland
development
s. Entwicklung,
s. Ausbau
s. Erschließung, Baureifmachung
s. Bebauung,
s. Bauprojekt, Bauobjekt
development agency
s. Betriebsansiedlungsorganisation, -gesellschaft
s. Entwicklungs-, Entwicklungshilfeorganisation
development aid – s. Entwicklungshilfe
development co-operation – s. Entwicklungszusammenarbeit
development corporation – s. Entwicklungs-, Betriebsansiedlungsgesellschaft
development economics – s. Entwicklungsökonomie, Wirtschaftstheorie der Entwicklungsländer
development fund – s. Entwicklungsfonds
device – s. Vorrichtung, Gerät, Methode
diagram – s. Diagramm
dial – s. Wählscheibe
dictator – s. Diktatgeber/in, Diktierende/r
differential tariff – s. Differenzialzoll, unterschiedlicher Zoll
differentiation strategy – s. Differenzierungstrategie
diffuse – adj. diffus, verschwommen, verwaschen
digit – s. Stelle (in einem Zahlensystem), Ziffer
double-digit inflation – zweistellige Inflation
digital – adj. digital
digital circuit – s. digitale Schaltung, Breitbandleitung
digital computer – s. Digitalrechner
digitalisation – s. Digitalisierung
digital versatile disc – s. DVD, digitale, vielseitig einsetzbare Diskette, optisches Speichermedium
digital video disc – s. DVD, digitale, vielseitig einsetzbare Diskette, optisches Speichermedium
dilute – v. verwässern
dilution – s. (Gewinn- / Beteiligungs-)Verwässerung
diminishing-balance method – s. (geometrisch) degressive Abschreibung, Buchwertabschreibung
diminishing returns – s. abnehmender Ertragszuwachs
dinkies – double-income, no-kids households (siehe)
dioxin – s. Dioxin, Sevesogift
diplomatic mission – s. diplomatische Vertretung
direct access memory – s. Direktzugriffspeicher, direkt adressierbarer Speicher
direct access storage device – s. Direktzugriffspeicher, direkt adressierbarer Speicher
direct arbitrage – s. direkte Arbitrage, Zweiwährungsarbitrage
direct banking – s. Direkt-, Online-, Internet-Banking
direct costing – s. (echtes) Direct Costing
direct cost(s) – s. Einzelkosten
direct debit form – s. Einzugsformular
direct debiting – s. Lastschrift-, Abbuchungsverfahren, Lastschrift-Einzugsverkehr
direct debits – s. Lastschrift-, Abbuchungsverfahren, Lastschrift-Einzugsverkehr
direct dialling – s. Selbstwähl-, Selbstwählfernverkehr
direct exporting – s. direkter Export
direct insurance – s. Direktversicherung
direct intervention – s. direkte Intervention
direct investments – s. direkte Investitionen, Direktinvestititonen
direct invitation to the pubilc – s. Selbstemission (von Wertpapieren)
direct labour – s. Einzellöhne, Fertigungslöhne
direct leasing – s. direktes Leasing
direct mail
s. Direct Mail, Briefwerbung, Postversandwerbung
s. direkter Postversand
direct materials – s. Einzelmaterial(-kosten)
direct marketing – s. Direktmarketing, direktes Marketing
director – s. Mitglied des Führungsgremiums einer UK-/US-Kapitalgesellschaft, Aufsichtsratsmitglied (mit oder ohne Vorstandsagenden), Verwaltungsratsmitglied
directors' report – s. Bericht der Geschäftsleitung / des Verwaltungsrates
directory – s. Adressbuch, Telefonbuch
direct quotation – s. Preisnotierung
direct subsidy – s. direkte Subvention / Finanzhilfe
direct tax – s. direkte Steuer
direct write-off method – s. Einzelwertberichtigung (bei Forderungen)
dirty bill of lading – s. unreines Konnossement
dirty floating – s. kontrolliertes / schmutziges / manipuliertes Floaten
disabled – adj. behindert, arbeitsunfähig
disabled person – Behinderter, Invalide
diasblement benefit – s. Behinderten-, Arbeitsunfähigkeitsgeld, Invaliden-, Behinderten-, Arbeitsunfähigkeitsrente
disaggregate – v. disaggregieren, entflechten
disburse – v. flüssigmachen, zuzählen, auszahlen
disburse loans – Kredite flüssigmachen / zuzählen / auszahlen
disbursement – s. Zuzählung / Flüssigmachung / Auszahlung (von Krediten)
discharge – s. Entladung, Abladen
discharge
v. entladen, löschen
v. entlasten, entbinden, entlassen
v. tilgen, bezahlen, begleichen
discharge from liability – aus der Haftung entlassen / entbinden, entlasten

disclaimer of opinion – s. Versagen des Bestätigungsvermerks
disclosure – s. Offenlegung, Publizität(-spflicht)
discount
s. Preisnachlass (Skonto, Rabatt)
s. Deport, (Termin-)Abschlag
s. Disagio, Abschlag
s. Wechseldiskont
grant a discount – einen Preisnachlass gewähren
sell at a discount – mit einem Preisnachlass verkaufen
The currency is at a discount. – Die Währung weist einen Deport auf.
This share stands at a discount to its asset value. – Die Aktie notiert unter ihrem Substanzwert.
discount
v. diskontieren
v. abzinsen
discount a bill of exchange – einen Wechsel diskontieren
discount cash flows – Zahlungsströme abzinsen
discounted cash flow method – s. dynamische Investitionsrechnungsmethode
discounted cash flow technique – s. dynamische Investitionsrechnungsmethode
discount house
s. Diskontladen, Diskonter
s. Diskontbank, Spezialbank für das Wechselgeschäft
discounting (of a bill of exchange) – s. (Wechsel-) Diskontierung
discount loan – s. Diskontkredit
discount method – s. antizipative Verzinsung
discount period – s. Skontofrist, Kassarespiro
discount rate
s. (Re-)Diskontsatz, Bankrate
s. Kalkulationszinsfuß
discounts
s. diskontierte Wechsel, Diskontkredite
s. Skonti und Rabatte
discount store – s. Diskontladen, Diskonter
discrepancy – s. Diskrepanz, Unterschied
discrepancies between legal systems – s. Rechtsunterschiede, unterschiedliche Rechtssysteme
discrete – adj. diskret, durch endliche Intervalle getrennt
discretion
s. Diskretion, Takt
s. Ermessen, Belieben, Gutdünken
at the buyer's discretion – im Ermessen des Käufers
discretionary power – s. Ermessenspielraum, -freiheit
discretionary provision – s. Kannbestimmung
discrimination
s. unterschiedliche / differenzielle Behandlung
s. Diskirminierung, diskriminierende / benachteiligende Behandlung
discriminatory
adj. unterschiedlich, differenziell
adj. diskriminierend, benachteiligend, wettbewerbsverzerrend
discriminatory government procurement – s. Benachteiligung von Firmen im öffentlichen Beschaffungswesen, diskriminierende Praktiken im öffentlichen Beschaffungswesen
discriminatory pricing – s. Preisdifferenzierung, -diskriminierung
discriminatory treatment
s. unterschiedliche / differenzielle Behandlung
s. diskriminierende / benachteiligende Behandlung
diseconomies of scale – s. Kostenprogression, überproportionale Kostenerhöhung
disequilibrium – s. Ungleichgewicht, fehlendes Gleichgewicht
dishonest – adj. unehrlich
dishonour – s. Nichthonorierung, Nichtannahme, Annahmeverweigerung
dishonour by non-acceptance – s. Nichtannahme, Annahmeverweigerung (bei einem Wechsel)
dishonour by non-payment – s. Nichtzahlung (eines Wechsels)
dishonour – v. nicht honorieren, Not leiden lassen
dishonour a bill of exchange – Wechsel nicht akzeptieren / nicht einlösen
dishonoured bill of exchange – s. notleidender Wechsel
disincentive – s. leistungshemmender Faktor, Abschreckung
disincentive – adj. leistungshemmend, abschreckend, lähmend
disinflation – s. Disinflation, Entflationierung, Zurückführung der Inflation auf ein „Normalmaß"
disintermediation – s. Ausschaltung von Mittlern / der Banken als Mittler zwischen Letztkreditgeber(n) und Letztkreditnehmer/n)
disk drive – s. Platten-, Diskettenlaufwerk
disk storage – s. Platten, Diskettenspeicher
dismiss – v. entlassen
dismissal – s. Entlassung
disparagement – s. Herabsetzung, Verunglimpfung
dispatch – v. absenden, versenden, verschicken
dispatching station – s. Versandbahnhof
dispel – v. zerstreuen
dispense
v. verteilen, ausgeben, bereitstellen, abgeben
v. dispense (with sthg.) – (ohne etwas) auskommen, (etwas) überflüssig machen, auf (etwas) verzichten, (etwas) entbehren, (von etwas) Abstand nehmen
display
s. Ausstellung, Zurschaustellung, optische Anzeige
s. (Waren-)Auslage
s. Entfaltung, Vorführung, Darstellung
display – v. darstellen, zeigen, anzeigen, zur Schau stellen, aufweisen, herzeigen, sichtbar machen
display rack – s. Auslagen-, Vollsicht-, Warenauslageregal
display screen – s. Bildschirm
disposable bottle – s. Einwegflasche
disposable (personal) income – s. verfügbares (persönliches) Einkommen
disposal
s. Veräußerung, Verkauf, Abstoßen
s. Beseitigung, Wegschaffen, Entsorgung
s. Verfügung(-sgewalt)
place / put sthg. at sby's disposal – etwas jemandem zur Verfügung stellen
dispose of – v. veräußern, verkaufen
dispose of assets – Vermögenswerte verkaufen
dispute settlement – s. Streitbelegung
disqualification – s. Entfallen der persönlichen Voraussetzungen (für einen *director*)
disregard – s. Missachtung, Vernachlässigung
dissemination – s. Streuung, Verbreitung
dissociation – s. Absonderung, Distanzierung, Isolierung
policy of dissociation – (wirtschaftliche) Isolationspolitik, Importsubstitutions-Strategie
dissolution – s. Auflösung, Liquidation
dissuade – v. abraten, abbringen
distort – v. verzerren
distorting effect – s. (wettbewerbs-)verzerrende Wirkung
distribute
v. verteilen, austeilen, zusenden, aussenden, versenden
v. ausschütten, auszahlen
v. absetzen, verkaufen, in Umlauf bringen
distribute circulars – Rundschreiben aussenden

distributed data processing – s. dezentralisierte Datenverarbeitung
distributing agent – s. Vertreter/in mit Auslieferungslager
distribution
s. Distribution, Vertrieb, Absatz, Auslieferung
s. (Einkommens- / Vermögens-)Verteilung
s. statistische Verteilung
s. Ausschüttung, Dividendenzahlung
distribution channel – s. Distributions-, Marketingkanal, Absatzweg
distribution channels studies – s. Distributionskanalforschung, distributionspolitische Analysen
distribution cost studies – s. Absatzkosten-, Vertriebskostenanalyse
distribution depot – s. Auslieferungslager
distribution network – s. Vertriebssystem, -apparat
distribution of income – s. Einkommensverteilung
distribution subsidiary – s. Marketing-, Vertriebstochter
distributive trade – s. Handel, (Gesamtheit aller) Handelsunternehmen, Absatzwirtschaft
distributor
s. (am.) Großhändler
s. (brit.) Vertragshändler (Groß- oder Einzelhändler)
distributor's brand – s. Eigen-, Haus-, Händler-, Handelsmarke
distributor service – s. Zustelldienst, -verkehr
district heating – s. Fernwärme(-system)
disutility – s. negativer Nutzen, Leid
diverse – adj. verschiedenartig, unterschiedlich
diversification – s. Diversifizierung, Diversifikation
divestiture – s. Abstoßen / Veräußerung von Firmenteilen oder Beteiligungen
divestment – s. Desinvestition, Freisetzung von Kapital
divi – s. Rückvergütung
dividend
s. Dividende
s. Rückvergütung
declare a dividend – eine Dividende festsetzen / beschließen
pass a dividend – keine Dividende festsetzen / beschließen, Dividende ausfallen lassen
dividend arrears – s. Dividendenrückstände
dividend cover – s. Dividendendeckung
dividend per share – s. Dividende pro Aktie
dividends distributed – s. ausgeschütteter Dividendenbetrag, ausgeschüttete Dividende
dividends earned – s. Dividendenerträge
dividend yield – s. Aktienrendite (auf Basis der letztgezahlten Dividende), Dividendenrendite
dividing – s. Teilung, Aufteilung (von Großsendungen zur Weiterveräußerung an die nächste Handelsstufe)
division – s. Geschäftsbereich, Sparte, Division
divisional organisation – s. divisionale Organisation, Sparten-, Geschäftsbereichsorganisation
division of labour – s. Arbeitsteilung, Arbeitsteiligkeit
divorce – s. Trennung, Scheidung
DIY sector – do-it-yourself sector (siehe)
DNA – deoxyribonucleic acid (siehe)
dockage – s. Hafengeld, -gebühren
dock dues – s. Hafengeld, -gebühren
docker – s. Hafenarbeiter/in
docks – s. Hafen(-anlagen)
doctrine – s. (fundamentaler) Grundsatz, Lehrmeinung, Doktrin
documentary collection – s. Dokumenteninkasso
documentary credit – s. Dokumentenakkreditiv
documentary credit operation – s. Geschäft auf der Basis eines Dokumentenakkreditivs
documentary draft – s. Dokumententratte
documentary letter of credit – s. Dokumentenakkreditiv
document of title – s. Traditions-, Dispositionspapier
documents against acceptance – s. Dokumente gegen Akzept
documents against payment – s. Dokumente gegen Zahlung
dog – s. Hund, Problemprodukt, Auslaufprodukt
do-it-yourself sector – s. Heimwerkerkerbranche
dollar assets – s. auf Dollar lautende Forderungen / Finanzaktiva
dollar bananas – s. Dollarbananen (die von US-Großfirmen auf Plantagen in Lateinamerika produzierten Bananen)
domestic consumption – s. freier (Inlands-)Verkehr (im zolltechnischen Sinn)
domestic heating system – s. Hausheizungs-, Wohnungsheizungssystem
domestic marketing – s. Inlandsmarketing
domestic market price – s. (vergleichbarer) Inlandspreis
domestic servants – s. Haushaltspersonal
domestic trade – s. Binnenhandel
domestic value – s. (vergleichbarer) Inlandspreis
domiciled bill – s. domizilierter Wechsel, Domizilwechsel
donation – s. Schenkung, Zuwendung
donee – s. Beschenkte/r, Schenkungsempfänger/in
donee country – s. Empfängerland
donor – s. Schenkungsgeber/in, Schenker/in, Spender/in
donor country – s. Geberland
door panel – s. Türfüllung
door-to-door selling – s. Haustürverkauf
door-to-door service – s. Haus-Haus-Verkehr
dormant partner – s. von der Geschäftsführung und Vertretung ausgeschlossener, voll haftender Gesellschafter einer UK-Personengesellschaft
dot-com bubble – s. (spekulative) Dotcom-Blase
double
v. verdoppeln
v. doubeln, Doppelrolle spielen
Cheque cards can double as debit cards. – Scheckkarten können auch die Rolle als Lastschriftkarten übernehmen.
double bottom – s. Doppeltief(-formation)
double coincidence of wants – s. doppelte (Bedürfnis-)Koinzidenz
double-edged – adj. zweischneidig
double-entry bookkeeping system – s. System der doppelten Buchhaltung, doppelte Buchhaltung
double glazing – s. Doppelverglasung
double-income, no-kids households – s. Dinkies, Zwei-Personenhaushalte mit zwei Einkommen
double residence – s. Doppelwohnsitz
double-spread ad – s. doppelseitige Anzeige
double taxation – s. Doppelbesteuerung
double taxation agreement – s. Doppelbesteuerungsabkommen
Dow Jones Industrial Average – s. Dow-Jones Industrieaktienindex
Dow Jones Industrial Index – s. Dow-Jones Industrieaktienindex
downmarket – adj. weniger hochwertig, für weniger kaufkräftige Kunden, Massen-
move downmarket – sich auf ein weniger hochwertiges Sortiment / Massenmarktssortiment umstellen
downmarket goods – s. (billige) Massenware
down payment – s. Anzahlung
downsizing – s. Downsizing, Gesundschrumpfen, Verschlankung

downstream – adj. nachgelagert
downstream from the point of production – der Produktion (in der Wertschöpfungskette) nachgelagert
downward-sloping – adj. (ab-)fallend, nach unten geneigt
D/P – documents against payment (siehe)
DPS – dividend per share (siehe)
draft
s. Entwurf, Konzept
s. Wechsel, Tratte
draw a draft – einen Wechsel ziehen
present a draft – einen Wechsel vorlegen
drag – s. Hemmschuh, Bremseffekt, Bremswirkung
drainage – s. Entwässerung
draw
v. – (auf sich) ziehen
v. – ziehen, ausstellen
draw fire – (scharfe) Kritik auf sich ziehen
draw a cheque – einen Scheck ausstellen
draw a cheque against an account – einen Scheck auf ein Konto ausstellen
drawee – s. Bezogener (Scheck, Wechsel)
drawee bank – s. bezogene Bank, Zahlstelle
drawee of a bill of exchange – s. Wechselbezogene/r
drawee of a cheque – s. (Scheck-)Bezogener, bezogenes Kreditinstitut
drawer
s. Schublade
s. (Wechsel-)Aussteller/in, (Scheck-)Aussteller/in
drawer of a bill of exchange – s. Wechselaussteller/in
drawer of a cheque – s. (Scheck-)Aussteller/in
drawing
s. Zeichnung, Skizze
s. Gewinn-, Privatentnahme
draw up – v. erstellen
draw up the agenda – die Tagesordnung erstellen
draw up a balance sheet – eine Bilanz erstellen
drill bit – s. Bohrkrone, Bohrerspitze
drive – s. Laufwerk
drive – v. antreiben, vorantreiben
driver
s. Lenker
s. Antriebsmoment, Antriebsfaktor, Beweggrund
drive train – s. Drivetrain, Antriebsstrang (Getriebe bis einschließlich Hinterachse eines Fahrzeugs)
driving force – s. Antrieb(-skraft), Motivation
drug dealing – s. Drogenhandel
drum – s. zylindrischer Behälter
dual capacity – s. Prinzip der Doppelfunktion, Vereinigung der Funktionen eines Effektenmaklers und Effektenhändlers in einer Person / Firma, Selbsteintrittsrecht eines Effektenmaklers / Börsenmaklers
dub – v. bezeichnen, benennen, titulieren
due
adj. ordnungspemäß, gebührend
adj. zurückzuführen, verursacht
adj. geschuldet, zu leisten
adj. fällig, zahlbar
duly endorsed – ordnungsgemäß indossiert
in due course – zu gegebener Zeit, rechtzeitig
due to A – zurückzuführen auf A, wegen A
amount due – geschuldeter Betrag
an exporter due to receive payment – ein Exporteur, dem ein Betrag geschuldet wird
due from banks – Forderungen an Kreditinstitute
payments due under the contract – auf Grund des Vertrages zu leistende Zahlungen
fall due – fällig werden
due date – s. Fälligkeitstermin, Verfallstag
due diligence
s. Due Diligence, Feinprüfung (z.B. eines Übernahmeangebotes)
s. gebührende / verkehrsübliche Sorgfalt
dummy – s. Strohmann
dump
v. Dumping betreiben, zu Schleuderpreisen verkaufen / ausführen, unterbieten
v. abladen, verklappen, (wild) deponieren
dumped goods – s. Dumpingware, gedumpte / vom Dumping betroffene Ware
dumping – s. Dumping
dumping margin – s. Dumpingmarge, -spanne
duplicate – s. Kopie, Durchschrift, Duplikat, Ausfertigung
in duplicate – in doppelter Ausfertigung
duplicate – v. vervielfältigen, kopieren
duplicating – s. (mechanische) Vervielfältigung
duplicating system – s. Durchschreibebuchführung
duplication
s. (mechanische) Vervielfältigung
s. Doppelzählung
s. Zweigleisigkeit
duplicator – s. Vervielfältigungsapparat
durability
s. Verwendungshäufigkeit (eines Gutes)
s. Dauerhaftigkeit, lange Nutzungsdauer
durable consumer goods – s. Gebrauchsgüter, langlebige Konsumgüter
durable item – s. Gebrauchsgut, -gegenstand
durable producer goods – s. Investitions-, Kapitalgüter
duration – s. Dauer, Laufzeit
duration of a licence – Laufzeit einer Lizenz
duration of a loan – Laufzeit eines Kredites
duty
s. Pflicht, Verpflichtung, Obliegenheit, Aufgabe
s. Abgabe, Steuer, Zoll(-gebühr)
dutiable – adj. zollpflichtig
duty free – adj. / adv. zollfrei
duty-levying nation – s. Zolland, das den Zoll einhebende Land
DVD – digital versatile disc (siehe)
dwarf – v. in den Schatten stellen, klein erscheinen lassen
dwelling – s. Wohnhaus, Wohnung
d.w.t. – dead-weight tonnage (siehe)

E

E.&O.E. – errors and omissions excepted (siehe)
earmark – v. kennzeichnen, zweckbinden, vormerken, bereitstellen
earn – v. verdienen, erwirtschaften, realisieren
earn revenues – Erträge erwirtschaften / realisieren
revenue is earned – Erträge entstehen / fallen an / werden realisiert / gehören zu / beziehen sich auf
interest income earned – erwirtschaftete Zinserträge
earned income allowance – s. Arbeitnehmerfreibetrag
earned income tax credit – s. Arbeitnehmerabsetzbetrag
earned surplus – s. (offene) Rücklagen
earnings
s. Ertrag, Erträge
s. (Rein-)Gewinn
s. Einkommen, Einkünfte, (Gesamt-)Verdienst
earnings before interest and tax – s. Ergebnis vor Zinsen und Steuern, (etwa) Betriebsergebnis, EBIT-Gewinn
earnings of management – s. Unternehmerlohn
earnings per share – s. Gewinn pro Aktie
earnings yield – s. Aktienrendite auf der Basis des Gewinnes pro Aktie, Gewinnrendite
earpiece – s. Hörmuschel
easy money – s. Politik des leichten Geldes, expansive Geld- und Kreditpolitik, Niedrigzinspolitik
EBA – Everything but Arms (siehe)
EBIT – earnings before interest and tax (siehe)
EBIT elasticity of earnings per share – s. EBIT-Elastizität des Gewinns pro Aktie, Maßzahl für die Reaktion des Gewinns pro Aktie auf Änderungen im EBIT-Ergebnis
e-business – s. E-Business, E-Geschäft, elektronische Geschäftsabwicklung
EC – European Community (siehe)
ECB – European Central Bank (siehe)
ECGD – Export Credits Guarantee Department (siehe)
eco-dumping – s. Öko-, Umweltdumping
eco-fanatic – s. Umweltfanatiker/in, Ökospinner
eco label – s. Ökosiegel, -zeichen, -gütezeichen
ecological balance – s. ökologisches Gleichgewicht
eclogical thinking – s. ökologische Denkweise / Einstellung
ecology – s. Ökologie
e-commerce – s. E-Commerce, elektronischer Handel, Internethandel, Online-Handel
econometric model – s. ökonometrisches Modell
economic – adj. wirtschaftlich, zur Wirtschaft gehörig
economic agent – s. Wirtschaftssubjekt, -einheit
economical – adj. wirtschaftlich, sparsam, haushälterisch
economic and monetary union – s. Wirtschafts- und Währungsunion
economic entity – s. Wirtschaftseinheit, -subjekt
economic exposure – s. ökonomische Währungsposition
economic goods – s. Wirtschaftsgüter, wirtschaftliche Güter
economic growth – s. Wirtschaftswachstum
economic indicator – s. Konjunkturindikator
economic integration – s. Wirtschaftsintegration,
economic life – s. betriebswirtschaftliche Nutzungsdauer / Nutzungszeit
economic order quantity – s. optimale Bestellmenge
economic partnership agreement – s. wirtschaftliches Partnerschaftsabkommen
economic policy – s. Wirtschafts-, Konjunkturpolitik
economic policy-making – s. Gestaltung und Durchführung der Wirtschaftspolitik, wirtschaftspolitische Aktivitäten
economic risk – s. ökonomisches (Wechselkurs-)Risiko
economics
s. Volkswirtschaftslehre, Wirtschaftswissenschaften
s. (volks-)wirtschaftliche Aspekte, Rentabilitätsfaktoren, Rentabilität, Wirtschaftlichkeit, wirschaftliche Sinnhaftigkeit
economic system – s. Wirtschaftssystem
economic thought – s. volkswirtschaftliche Lehrmeinung
economic union – s. Wirtschaftsgemeinschaft, -vereinigung, wirtschaftlicher Zusammenschluss
economic unit – s. Wirtschaftssubjekt, -einheit
economic welfare – s. wirtschaftliche Wohlfahrt, wirtschaftliches Wohlergehen
economies of integration – s. Integrationssynergien
economies of scale – s. Economies of Scale, Kostendegression, Betriebsgrößenersparnis, Größenersparnis
economies of scope – s. Economies of Scope, Verbundersparnisse, Verbundvorteile, Synergieeffekte
economise – v. sparsam umgehen, sparsam sein, sparsam verwenden
economise on raw materials – mit Rohmaterial sparsam umgehen
economy
s. (Volks-)Wirtschaft
s. Einsparung, Sparmaßnahme, Wirtschaftlichkeit
practice economy – Einsparungen machen, sparsam sein
make economies – Einsparungen machen, sparsam sein
economy in transition – s. Übergangs-, Reformwirtschaft, Reformland
ecosphere – s. Öko-, Biosphäre
e-cruiting – s. Online-Personalbeschaffung
ECU – European Currency Unit (siehe)
edit – v. editieren, herausgeben, redigieren, druckfertig machen
educational services – s. Bildungseinrichtungen, -aktivitäten
EEC – European Economic Community (siehe)
EEMU – European Ecomic and Monetary Union (siehe)
e-economy – s. netzgestützte / internetgestützte Wirtschaft, netzgestütztes Wirtschaftssystem
effective – adj. wirksam, geltend, in Kraft
be effective – gelten, in Kraft sein
effective demand – s. effektive / durch Kaufkraft gestützte Nachfrage
efficiency
s. Effizienz, Wirksamkeit, Leistungsfähigkeit
s. Produktivität
s. Wirtschaftlichkeit, Wirkungsgrad
s. Rentabilität
EFT – electronic funds transfer (siehe)
EFTA
European Fair Trade Association (siehe)
European Free Trade Association (siehe)
EFTPOS – electronic funds transfer at point of sale (system) (siehe)
EFTPOS terminal – s. Datenerfassungskassa mit elektronischer Überweisungsmöglichkeit
egalitarian – adj. egalitär, partnerschaftlich, auf dem Prinzip der Gleichberechtigung fußend, dem Grundsatz der Gleichberechtigung verpflichtet
egg – s. Ei
put all one's eggs in one basket – alles auf eine Karte setzen
ego-sensitive goods – s. Lifestyleprodukte, Snob-Artikel

eke out an existence – v. sich durchschlagen,
elaborate – v. im Detail ausarbeiten
elaborate – adj. detailliert, im Detail ausgearbeitet
elasticity – s. Elastizität
elasticity of substitution – s. Substitutionselastizität
electricity generating – s. Elektrizitätserzeugung
electricity utility – s. Elektrizitätsversorgungsunternehmen, Elektrizitätsgesellschaft
electric (resistance) heating – s. Elektroheizung
electric signs – s. Leuchtreklame
electronic banking – s. elektronische Zahlungsverkehr- und Informationsleistungen
electronic commerce – s. E-Commerce, elektronischer Handel, Internethandel
electronic funds transfer – s. elektronischer Zahlungsverkehr
electronic funds transfer at point of sale (system) – EFTPOS System, Kassensystem mit elektronischer Überweisungsmöglichkeit
electronic letter of credit – s. elektronisches Akkreditiv, Online-Akkreditiv
electronic mail – s. elektronische Post
electronic mail box – s. elektronisches Postfach
electronic money – s. elektronisches Geld, Computergeld
electronic retailing – s. Electronic Retailing, elektronischer (Einzel-)Handel
eligible – adj. geeignet, in Frage kommend, (anspruchs-)berechtigt, fähig
eligible for a guarantee – garantiefähig
eligible for cover – deckungsfähig
eligibility – s. Fähigkeit, Eignung, Anspruch
eligibility for discounting – s Diskontfähigkeit
elusive – adj. schwer fassbar
e-mail – s. E-Mail, elektronische Post, elektronisches Poststück
e-mail terminal – s. E-Mail-Terminal
emanate – v. hervorgehen, entstehen
e-marketing – s. E-Marketing, elektronisches Marketing, Online-Marketing, Internet-Marketing
embodiment – s. Verkörperung, Verbriefung
embody – v. verkörpern, repräsentieren, verbriefen
rights embodied in an instrument – in einer Urkunde verkörperte / verbriefte Rechte
emboss – v. prägen, aufprägen
emerge – v. entstehen, auftauchen, sich ergeben
emergence – **s.** Entstehen, Auftauchen
emergency aid – s. Katastrophen-, Soforthilfe
emission – s. Emission (im technischen – nicht im finanziellen – Sinn)
gas emissions – Gasemissionen
employed – s. Beschäftigte
employee – s. Arbeitnehmer, Mitarbeiter
employee benefit – s. (betriebliche) Nebenleistung / Sozialleistung
employee buyout – s. Mitarbeiter-Buyout
employee compensation – s. Arbeitsentgelte
employee participation – s. Arbeitermitbestimmung
employer
s. Arbeitgeber
s. Auftraggeber
employers' association – s. Arbeitgeberverband
employment – s. Beschäftigung, Arbeit, Beschäftigungsverhältnis, Arbeitsverhältnis
employment agency – s. Arbeitsvermittlungsstelle, (private) Stellenvermittlung
employment grant – s. Beschäftigungs-, Arbeitsplatzsubvention
employment office – s. Arbeitsamt
employment services – s. Arbeitsmarktverwaltung
employment subsidy – s. Beschäftigungs-, Arbeitsplatzsubvention
EMS – European Monetary System (siehe)
EMS – environmental management system (siehe)
EMU – Economic and Monetary Union (siehe)
enact – v. verabschieden
enact a law – ein Gesetz verabschieden
enclose – v beilegen, beifügen, als Anlage / Beilage senden
enclose an invoice in the parcel with the goods – den Waren im Kollo / Paket eine Rechnung beilegen
enclosed please find – in der Anlage übermitteln wir Ihnen
We are enclosing a cheque. – Als Beilage übermitteln wir Ihnen einen Scheck.
encode – v. kodieren
encroachment – s. Übergreifen, Übergriff
encumbrance – s. Belastung (eines Vermögenswertes), Rechte eines Dritten / Dritter (an einem Vermögenswert) (z. B. die hypothekarische Belastung eines Grundstückes)
enabling clause – s. (GATT) Ermächtigungsklausel
end
s. Ende
s. Zweck
s. Marktsegment
s. Stelle, Ort
receiving end – Angerufene/r, Empfänger/in
to this end – zu diesem Zweck
The end justifies the means. – Der Zweck heiligt die Mittel.
ending inventory – s. Schlussbestand
end-of-season sale – s. Saisonschlussverkauf
endorse
v. indossieren
v. bestätigen, (werblich) unterstützen
endorsee – s. Indossatar
endorsement – s. Indossament
endorser – s. Indossant
end-user – s. Endverbraucher, Endanwender
energy conservation – s. Energiesparen
energy consumption – s. Energieverbrauch
energy crisis – s. Energiekrise
energy efficiency – s. Energieeffizienz, Wirkungsgrad des Energieeinsatzes
energy input – s. Energieeinsatz
energy needs – s. Energiebedarf
energy source(s) – s. Energieträger, -quelle
energy waste – s. Energievergeudung, -verschwendung
enforceable – adj. (im Rechtsweg) durchsetzbar, vollstreckbar, einklagbar
enforceability – s. Durchsetzbarkeit, Vollstreckbarkeit, Klagbarkeit
enforcement – s. Durchsetzung, Vollziehung, Vollstreckung
engage
v. sich verpflichten, sich einlassen
v. abschließen, tätigen
v. einstellen, anstellen, engagieren
engage in a transaction – ein Geschäft tätigen / abschließen
engagement – s. Versprechen, Zusage, (eingegangene) Verpflichtung
engineer – v. (aus-)gestalten, umarbeiten, arrangieren
enjoin – v. auferlegen, vorschreiben
enlarge – v. sich verbreitern
enlarge on sthg. – sich über etwas verbreitern / auslassen
enlargement – s. Vergrößern, Vergrößerung
en route – adv. unterwegs, während des Transports
enshrine – v. niederlegen
enshrined in Article 85 – im Artikel 85 niedergelegt

entail – v. mit sich bringen, involvieren, sich handeln um, um (etwas) gehen
Portfolio investment entails the acquisiton of financial assets. – Bei indirekten Auslandsinvestitionen handelt es sich um den Erwerb von Finanzanlagen.
enter
v. eintragen, buchen
v. eingeben, eintippen
enter an item on the debit side – einen Posten auf Soll buchen
enter data – Daten eingeben / eintippen
enter into – v abschließen, eintreten in
enter into a contract – einen Vertrag abschließen
enter into a transaction – ein Geschäft abschließen
enter into business relations – in Geschäftsverbindung treten
enterprise – s. Unternehmen, Firma
entitle
v. betiteln, bezeichnen, benennen
v. berechtigen
be entitled to sthg. – zu etwas berechtigt sein, auf etwas Anspruch haben
entity – s. (juristische) Person, (organisatorische) Einheit, Organisation
entrepreneur – s. Unternehmer, Geschäftsmann
entropy – s. Entropie
entrust – v. anvertrauen, beauftragen
entry
s. Eintritt, Zutritt
s. Buchung, Eintragung
s. Zollantrag, -anmeldung
entry for warehousing – Zollantrag auf Abfertigung zur Zollagerung
enumerate – v. (einzeln) aufzählen, zählen, erfassen
envelope – s. Kuvert, Briefumschlag
envelope-sealing machine – s. Briefschließmaschine
environment
s. (natürliche) Umwelt
s. Systemumwelt, Umfeld, Rahmenbedingungen
economic environment – wirtschaftliche Rahmenbedingung
environmental – adj. die Umwelt betreffend, Umwelt-
envirnomental auditing – s. Umweltprüfung, Öko-Prüfung, Umwelt-Auditing, Öko-Auditing, Erstellung von Umwelt-Audits
environmental dumping – s. Öko-, Umweltdumping
environmental expenditure – s. Umweltschutzaufwand, Ausgaben für den Umweltschutz
environmental impact – s. Umweltbelastung, -verträglichkeit
environmental impact assessment – s. Umweltverträglichkeitsprüfung
environmental management system – s. Umweltmanagementsystem
environmentally benign – adj. umweltfreundlich, -verträglich
environmentally-minded – adj. umweltbewusst
environmental organisation – s. Umweltorganisation
environmental protection – s. Umweltschutz
environmental record – s. Umweltbilanz, Umweltleistung
environmental tariff – s. Umweltzoll, Öko-Zoll
epitomise – v. kurz darstellen, zusammenfassen
equal – v. entsprechen, gleich (groß, hoch) sein, gleichkommen
equate – v. gleichsetzen
equation – s. Gleichung
equation method – s. Gewinnpunktrechnung nach der Gleichungsmethode
equilibrium – s. Equilibrium, Gleichgewicht
equipment – s. Maschinen und maschinelle Anlagen
equipment lease – s. Maschinenleasing(-vertrag), Leasingvertrag für Ausrüstungsgegenstände
enquiry – s. Anfrage
EPS – earnings per share (siehe)
EPZ – export processing zone (siehe)
equitable – adj. gerecht, fair
equity
s. Eigenkapital
s. Aktienkapital
s. Stammaktienkapital
s. (pl.) /Stamm-)Aktien
s. Gerechtigkeit, Fairness
equity capital
s. Eigenkapital
s. Aktienkapital, das durch Stammaktien und Vorzugsaktien repräsentiertes Kapital
s. Stammaktienkapital, das durch Stammaktien repräsentiertes Kapital
equity fund – s. Aktienfonds
equity joint venture – s. Equity Joint Venture, Gemeinschaftsunternehmen in Gesellschaftsform
equity market – s. Aktienmarkt
equity position – s. Beteiligung, Anteil
equity ratio – s. Eigenkapitalanteil. -quote
equity securities – s. Beteiligungspapiere, Aktien
equity share – s. Stammaktie
equivalent – s. Äquivalent, (Gegen-)Wert
equivalent – adj. gleichwertig, entsprechend, äquivalent
be equivalent to sthg. – einer Sache gleichkommen / entsprechen
era – s. Ära, Zeitalter
ergonomics – s. Ergonomie, Arbeitswissenschaft
erroneous – adj. irreführend, falsch
errors and omissions excepted – Irrtümer und Auslassungen vorbehalten, vorbehaltlich Irrtümer und Auslassungen
escalation clause – s. (Preis-)Gleit-, Wertsicherungsklausel
escalator clause – s. (Preis-)Gleit-, Wertsicherungsklausel
escape clause
s. Schutz-, Ausstiegs-, Befreiungsklausel
s. Escape-Klausel, Schutzklausel gegen Warenimporte nach Art. XIX des GATT
ESCB – European System of Central Banks (siehe)
e-shopping – s. E-Shopping, Internet-Shopping, Internetkauf
establishment – s. Unternehmen, Geschäft, Betrieb
estate – s. Vermögen(-smasse), Erbmasse, Nachlass, Konkursmasse
eatate duty – s. (1975 abgeschaffte) UK-Erbschaftssteuer in der Form einer Nachlasssteuer
estate tax – s. Erbschafts-, Nachlasssteuer
esteem need – s. Anerkennungsbedürfnis
estimate
s. Schätzung
s. Kostenvoranschlag
estimate – v. schätzen, veranschlagen, beurteilen, bewerten
estimated liability – s. Rückstellung für eine der Höhe nach ungewisse Verbindlichkeit
estuary – s. Trichtermündung
e-tailer – s. Internet-Einzelhändler, Internet-Kaufhaus
e-tailing – s. E-Tailing, e-Tailing, elektronischer (Einzel-)Handel
ethical fund – s. ethischer (Investment-)Fonds, SRI-Fonds
EU Environmental Audit Directive – s. EU-Öko-Audit-Richtlinie
euphemism – s. Euphemismus, beschönigender Ausdruck
euphemistic – adj. euphemistisch, beschönigend

eurobond – s. Euroanleihe, auf Euros lautende Anleihe
Euro-bond – s. Euro-Anleihe, auf eine der Euro-Währungen / Auslandswährungen lautende Anleihe
eurocheque – s. Euroscheck
Euro-currency – s. Euro-Währung (Währungspositionen in einem Fremdland)
Euro-currency credit – s. Euro-Währungskredit
Euro-currency markets – s. Euro-Währungsmärkte, Euro-Devisenmärkte
Euro-dollar – s. Euro-Dollar (Dollarpositionen in einem Fremdland)
Euro-dollar loan – s. Euro-Dollar-Kredit
Euro-euro bond – s. Euro-Euro-Anleihe
Euro-markets – s. Euro-Märkte
European Central Bank – s. Europäische Zentralbank, EZB
European Community – s. Europäische Gemeinschaft
European Currency Unit – s. Europäische Währungseinheit
European Economic Community – s. Europäische Wirtschaftsgemeinschaft, EWG
European Economic and Monetary Union – Europäische Wirtschafts- und Währungsunion, EWWU
European Fair Trade Association – s. European Fair Trade Association (Dachverband der Fair-Trade Handelshäuser in Europa)
European Free Trade Association – s. Europäische Freihandels-Assoziation
European Monetary Syatem – s. Europäisches Währungssystem
European option –s. europäische (Devisen-)Option
European-style option – s. europäische (Devisen-)Option, Option europäischen Stils
European System of Central Banks – Europäisches System der Zentralbanken, ESZB
Euro-speak – s. Eurosprache, Euro-Speak
eurozone – s. Eurozone, Euro-Währungsgebiet, Euroraum, Eurogebiet
exchange risk guarantee – Wechselkursrisikogarantie
exclusive importer – s. Alleinimporteur
expenditure approach –s Verwendungsrechnung (BSP / BIP)
evade – v. ausweichen, hinterziehen
  evade taxes – Steuern hinterziehen
evaluate – v. bewerten, beurteilen
even – adj. eben, gleichmäßig, ausgeglichen, gerade
  even income distribution – gleichmäßige Einkommensverteilung
  even number – gerade Zahl
event
  s. Ereignis, Fall
  s. Veranstaltung
event insured against – s. Versicherungsfall
Everything But Arms – s. „Alles außer Waffen“ (Präferenzprogramm der EU für die ärmsten Entwicklungsländer)
evidence
  s. Beweise, Beweismaterial, Zeugenaussage
  s. (urkundlicher) Nachweis
evidence – v. nachweisen, beurkunden
evolve – v. sich entwicklen
excess
  s. Übermaß, Überschuss, Überschreitung
  s. Selbstbehalt, Abzugsfranchise
  amounts in excess of current needs – über den laufenden Bedarf hinausgehende Beträge
exchange
  s. (Leistungs-)Austausch, (Leistungs-)Verkehr, Handel (im weitesten Wortsinn)
  s. (bes. in Zusammensetzungen) Devisen, Fremdwährung
  s. (Effekten- / Waren-)Börse
exchange clause – s. Kurssicherungs-, Währungsklausel
exchange control(s) – s. Devisenbewirtschaftung, devisenrechtliche Bestimmungen
exchange control form – s. (Antrags-)Formular der Zentralbank für devisenrechtliche Bewilligungen
exchange gain – s. (Wechsel-)Kurs-, Währungsgewinn
exchange-listed option – s. börsengehandelte / standardisierte Option, Börsenoption
exchange loss – s. (Wechsel-)Kurs-, Währungsverlust
exchange operator – s. Telefonvermittlung, Fernamt
exchange rate – s. Wechsel-, Devisen-, Fremdwährungskurs
exchange rate differential – s. (Wechsel-)Kursdifferenz, Wechselkursgefälle
exchange rate quotation – s. Devisen-, Kursnotierung
exchange rate system – s. Wechselkurssystem
exchange risk – s. Wechselkurs-, Kurs-, Währungsrisiko
exchange risk guarantee – s. Kursrisikogarantie
exchange risk protection – s. Devisenkurs-, Wechselkurssicherung, Absicherung gegen das Wechselkursrisiko
exchange-traded interest rate option – s. börsengehandelte / standardisierte Zinsoption
exchange-traded option – s. börsengehandelte / standardisierte Option, Börsenoption
excise duty – s. (spezielle) Verbrauchsteuer
excise tax – s. (spezielle) Verbrauchsteuer
exclusion of liability – s. Haftungsausschluss
exclusive agency – s. Alleinvertretung
exclusive agent – s. Alleinvertreter/in, Gebiets- oder Bezirksvertreter/in
exclusive dealer – s. Vertragshändler/in
exclusive dealership – s. exklusiver Händlervertrag, Exklusivvertrag für Vertragshändler
exclusive distributor – s. Exklusiv-Vertragshändler/in, Alleinvertriebsberechtigte/r, Exklusivhändler/in, Generalvertreter/in
exclusive distributorship – s. Alleinvertrieb(-srecht), Generalvertretung
exclusive importer – s. Generalimporteur
exclusive licence – s. ausschließliche Lizenz
exclusive territorial rights – s. Alleinverkaufs / -Alleinvertretungsrechte für ein Gebiet
ex-directory number – s. Geheimnummer
executive – s. Führungskraft, Spitzenmanager/in, leitende/r Angestellte/r
executive committee
  s. geschäftsführender Ausschuss des Verwaltungsrates einer UK/US-Kapitalgesellschaft
  s. Geschäftsführungsgremium, Vorstand
executive compensation package – s. Vergütungspaket für Führungskräfte
executive director – s. geschäftsführendes Mitglied des Führungsgremiums einer UK- / US-Kapitalgesellschaft, Geschäftsführer, Vorstandsmitglied mit Aufsichtsratsfunktion, Aufsichtsratsmitglied mit Vorstandsagenden
executive jet – s. Firmenflugzeug, Vorstandsjet
executive search – s. Personalberatung für Führungskräfte, Headhunting
executive search organisation – s. Personalberater/in / Personalberatungsfirma für Führungskräfte, Headhunter
executive suite – s. Räume der Gesellschaftsleitung, Chef-, Vorstandsetage
executive washroom – s. Cheftoilette, Vorstandsklo
exempt – adj. befreit, frei

exempt – v. befreien, entbinden
exempt sby. from an obligation – jemanden von einer Verpflichtung entbinden
exempt from duty – adj. zollfrei
exempt trom tax – adj. steuerfrei
exemption
s. Befreiung, Freistellung, Ausnahmeregelung, Ausschluss
s. Steuerbefreiung, unechte Mehrwertsteuerbefreiung, Mehrwertsteuerbefreiung ohne Vorsteuerabzug
s. Steuerfreibetrag
exemption trom duty – s. Zollbefreiung
exercise – s. Übung, Vorgehen, Vorgangsweise, Aktion
exercise price – s. Ausübungs-, Basispreis, Strike-Preis
exhaust – v. erschöpfen, aufbrauchen, verbrauchen
exhaustible asset – s. der Substanzverringerung unterliegender / natürlicher / nicht reproduzierbarer / nicht erneuerbarer Vermögensgegenstand
exaustible resources – s. nicht erneuerbare / nicht reproduzierbare / der Substanzverringerung unterliegende Ressourcen / Energieträger
exhaustion – s. Substanzverringerung, Aufbrauchen, Ausschöpfung, Erschöpfung
exhibit – s. Ausstellungsgegenstand, Exponat
exhibit
v. aufweisen
v. ausstellen
exhibit a defect – einen Mangel aufweisen
exhibiting company – Aussteller/in, Ausstellerfirma
exhibition – s. Ausstellung
exhibition goods – s. Ausstellungsgüter, Exponate
exhibitor – s. (Messe-)Aussteller/in, Aussstellerfirma
exhortation – s. Ermahnung, Wirtschaftslenkung durch Überredung, Seelenmassage
Eximbank – Export-Import-Bank (siehe)
exit – v. aussteigen, abschichten
exit an investment – eine Beteiligung abschichten, eine Beteiligung (durch Börsengang oder Verkauf) verwerten
exit strategy – Ausstiegsstrategie
expansion – s. Expansions-, Ausweitungs-, Aufschwungsphase
expatriate manager – s. Expatriat, (aus dem Stammland seines Arbeitgebers stammender) Auslandsmanager
expenditure s. Ausgaben, Aufwendungen
expenditure method – s Verwendungsrechnung (BNP / BIP)
expenditure multiplier – s. Ausgabenmultiplikator
expense
s. Aufwand, Aufwendung(en)
s Kosten, Unkosten
s Ausgabe(n)
s. Spesen
at the expense of – auf Kosten von
incur expenses – Auspaben / Spesen haben / machen / tätigen
expense account – s. Aufwandskonto
expense budget – s. Aufwandsplan, Kostenplan
expense item – s. Aufwandsposten, Aufwendung
expiration period – s. Laufzeit / Lebensdauer einer Option
expire – v. ablaufen, erlöschen, verfallen, außer Kraft treten
period expires – Frist läuft ab
expiry – s. Ablauf, Erlöschen
exploit
v. (wirtschaftlich) verwerten / nutzen
v. abbauen
v. ausbeuten
exploitable – adj. abbaufähig, (kommerziell) verwertbar
exploitable stores of raw materials – s. Abbauvorräte

exploitation
s. (wirtschaftliche) Verwertung, Nutzung, Auswertung,
s. Abbau, Gewinnung
s. Ausbeutung, Ausnutzung, Raubbau
exploitative – adj. ausbeuterisch
export clerk – s. Exportsachbearbeiter, Exportreferent
export controls – s. Exportbeschränkungen
export credit guarantee – s. Exportkredit-, Exportrisikogarantie, (staatliche) Exporthaftung
Export Credits Guarantee Department – s. staatliche UK-Exportförderungsstelle, staatlicher UK-Exportrisikoversicherer
export credit insurance – s. Exportkreditversicherung
export controls – s. Exportbeschränkungen
export debts – s. Exportforderungen
export distributor – s. Generalexporteur
export duty – s. Export-, Ausfuhrzoll
export multiplier – s. Exportmultiplikator
exporter's retention – s. Risiko- / Verlust- / Haftungsbeteilung des Exporteurs
export factor – s. Export-Factor(-gesellschaft)
export finance – s. Exportfinanzierung, Exportfinanzierungsmittel
export guarantee – s. Exportkreditgarantie, Exportrisikogarantie
Export-Import Bank –s. staatliche US-Exportförderungsinstitution
export leasing – s. Exportleasing, grenzüberschreitendes Leasing
export licence – s. Exportlizenz, Ausfuhrgenehmigung
export marketing – s. Exportmarketing
export merchant – s. Export-, Ausfuhrhändler
export multiplier – s. Exportmultiplikator
export outlet – s. Exportmarkt, Absatzmöglichkeit im Ausland
export processing zone – s. Industrie-, Exportfreizone, freie Wirtschaftszone
export promotion
s. Exportförderung
s. Kommunikationspolitik / Werbung im Export
export quota – s. Export-, Ausfuhrkontingent
export receivable – s. Exportforderung
export subsidy – s. Exportsubvention, -stützung
export tariff – s. Export-, Ausfuhrzoll
expose
v. aussetzen
v. aufdecken, entlarven
be exposed to a risk – einem Risiko ausgesetzt sein
expose doubtful practices – zweifelhafte Praktiken aufdecken
exposure
s. Belichtung,
s. Ausgesetztsein (einer Bedrohung, einem Risiko gegenüber)
s. (das mit einem wirtschaftlichen Engagement verbundene) Risiko, Risikoausmaß
(currency) exposure – (Fremd-)Währungsposition, Währungsrisiko
exposure (to a borrower) – Kreditnehmerrisiko, Ausmaß des Kreditnehmerrisikos
exposure to market forces – freies Einwirken der Marktkräfte
exposure metre – s. Belichtungsmesser
exposure netting – s. interne Positionsaufrechnung
expropriation – s. Enteignung
ex quay (duties on buyer's account) – ab Kai (Zoll zu Lasten des Käufers)

ex quay (duty paid) – ab Kai (verzollt)
extend
v. verlängern
v. gewähren
v. sich (zusätzlich) erstrecken / (zusätzlich) erfassen
extend a credit – einen Kredit gewähren / verlängern
cover extends to physical damage – die Versicherungsdeckung erstreckt sich auch auf Sachbeschädigung(en)
extension
s. Verlängerung, Fristerstreckung
s. Gewährung
s. Nebenstelle, Klappe
s. ausgeworfener Betrag, Produkt aus Menge mal Preis
grant an extension – eine Fristverlängerung gewähren
extension of a loan – Kreditgewährung
extension of maturity – Laufzeitverlängerung, Verlängerung der Rückzahlungsfrist
extension of a forward exchange contract – Prolongation eines Devisenterminkontraktes
external accounts – s. Zahlungsbilanz
external audit – s. externe Rechnungsprüfung / Abschlussprüfung
external auditing – s. externe Rechnungsprüfung / externe Abschlussprüfung
external auditor – s. externe/r Rechnungsprüfer/in, externe/r Abschlussprüfer/in
external communication – s. externe Kommunikation
external economies of scale – s. externe Economies of Scale
external effects – s. externe Effekte, Externalitäten, Spillover-Effekte, externe Kosten und Erträge
external finance – s. Außenfinanzierung
external front – s. außenwirtschaftlicher Bereich
external hedging method – s. externe Kurssicherungsmethode / Kurssicherungstechnik
external hedging technique – s. externe Kurssicherungstechnik / Kursicherungsmethode
externalities – s. externe Effekte, Externalitäten, Spillover-Effekte, externe Kosten und Erträge
external memory – s. peripherer Speicher
external memory device – s. peripheres Speichergerät
external storage – s. peripherer Speicher, periphere Speicherung
external tariff – s. Außenzoll
external trade – s. Außenhandel
external value – s. Außenwert (einer Währung)
extractive industries – s. primärer Sektor, Urproduktion
extraordinary expenses – s. außerordentliche Aufwendungen
extraordinary general meeting – s. außerordentliche Hauptversammlung
extraordinary items – s. außerordentliche Posten / Erträge und/oder Aufwendungen
extraordinary revenues – s. außerordentliche Erträge
extrapolate – v. extrapolieren, hochrechnen, auf die Grundgesamtheit umlegen
extrusion press – s. Strangpresse
EXW – EX WORKS (siehe)
EX WORKS – AB WERK

F

face – s. Vorderseite (eines Dokumentes)
F2F – face-to-face (communication) (siehe)
face-to-face communication – s. interpersonale / nicht mediengebundene Kommunikation
face-to-face contact – s. persönlicher / direkter Kontakt
face value – s. Nennwert
facilitate – v. erleichtern
facility
s. Möglichkeit, Gelegenheit
s. Gebäude, Einrichtung, Anlage, Fazilität
s. Erleichterung
washing facility – Waschgelegenheit
production facility – Produktionseinrichtung
facility management – Immobilienverwaltung und -bewirtschaftung
payment facilitilities – bequeme Zahlungsmodalitäten, Entgegenkommen bei den Zahlungsmodalitäten
facsimile machine – s. Faxgerät, Fernkopierer, Faksimilegerät, Telekopierer
facsimile transmission – s. Faxen, Fernkopieren, Faksimileübertragung
factor
s. (Produktions-)Faktor
s. Verkaufskommissionär/in
s. Factor, Factoring-Institut, Factor-Bank
factor costs – s. Faktorkosten
factor-endowment theory – s. Theorie der Faktorausstattung, Faktorausstattungstheorie, Heckscher-Ohlin-Theorem
factor income – s. Faktor-, Leistungseinkommen
factoring – s. Factoring
factor intensity – s. Faktorintensität, Faktoreinsatzverhältnis
factor of production – s. Produktionsfaktor
factor price – s. Faktorpreis
factory – s. Fabrik, Werk
factory overhead(s) – s. Fertigungsgemeinkosten
factory supplies – s. Hilfs- und Betriebsstoffe
fail
v. nicht tun, unterlassen, versäumen
v. Bankrott machen, fallieren, Pleite gehen, Pleite machen
v. versagen, scheitern
fail to pay – nicht zahlen
failing – prep. in Ermangelung, mangels, ohne
failure
s. Unterlassung, Versämnis. Nicht-
s. Versagen, Störung, Defekt
s. Fehlschlagen, Scheitern, Mißerfolg
s. Pleite, Bankott
failure to appear at court – Nichterscheinen bei Gericht
fair – s. Messe
fair contractor – s. Messebaufirma
fair trade
s. gerechter Handel
s. gerechter Nord-Süd Handel, Fairer Handel, Fair Trade
s. fairer Wettbewerb
s. Preisbindung zweiter Hand, vertikale Preisbindung
Fair Trade Commission – s. Fair-Trade-Kommission, Wettbewerbsbehörde
fair-trade label – s. Fair-Trade-Zeichen, Fair-Trade-Siegel, Fair-Trade-Gütesiegel
fair-trade seal – s. Fair-Trade-Zeichen, Fair-Trade-Siegel, Fair-Trade-Gütesiegel
fall short – v. zurückbleiben, nicht erreichen
fall short of expectations – hinter den Erwartungen zurückbleiben
false advertising – s. irreführende Werbung
falsify – v. fälschen (abändern)
fan merchandise – s. Fan-Artikel
family brand – s. Produktgruppen-, Dach-, Familienmarke
famine – s. Hungersnot
F.A.S. – FREE ALONGSIDE SHIP (siehe)
FAS – internationaler Code für F.A.S.
farm out – v. auslagern, outsourcen, (Aufträge) an Subunternehmer/innen oder Zulieferer/innen vergeben
fashion accessories – s. Mode-Accessoires
fast buck – s. schnelles Geld, schneller Dollar
fast food industry – s. Schnellimbissbranche
fast-moving item – s. Renner, umsatzstarker Artikel, Knüller
fast seller – s. umsatzstarkes Produkt, Renner, Knüller
fatality – s. Todesfall, Todesopfer
faulty goods – s. fehlerhafte Ware
fax – s. Fax, Faxsendung
fax – v. faxen, als Fax schicken
fax machine – s. Faxgerät, Fernkopierer
fax-copier combination – Faxkopierer, Fax-Drucker-Kombination
FCA – Fellow Chartered Accountant (siehe)
FCA – FREE CARRIER (siehe)
FCIA – Foreign Credit Insurance Association (siehe)
FCL – full container load (siehe)
FCR – forwarding agent's (certificate of) receipt (siehe)
FDI – foreign direct investment (siehe)
FDI inflows – s. Zufluss ausländischer Direktinvestionen, passive Direktinvestitionen (des Auslands)
FDI outflows – s. Abfluss ausländischer Direktinvestitionen, aktive Direktinvestitionen (im Ausland)
feasibility – s. Durchführbarkeit, Möglichkeit, Wirtschaftlichkeit, wirtschaftliche Sinnhaftigkeit
feasible – adj. durchführbar, möglich, wirtschaftlich sinnvoll
feature
s. Merkmal, Charakteristikum
s. Leistungs-, Ausstattungsmerkmal, Funktion
feature – v. (als Besonderheit, als besonderes Merkmal) aufweisen, sich auszeichnen durch
Federal Funds – s. Federal Funds, Überschussliquidität der US-Banken bei der jeweiligen Zentralbank, kurzfristige Geldmarktkredite (Tagesgeld) der US-Banken
Federal Funds rate – s. Tagesgeld-Zinssatz der US-Banken; US-Leitzinssatz
federal income tax – s. Bundeseinkommensteuer
Federal Reserve Bank – s. eine der 12 Mitgliedsbanken des US Federal Reserve Systems (siehe)
Federal Reserve System – s. US-Zentralbanksystem
federal taxation – s. Bundesbesteuerung, Besteuerung durch die Bundesregierung
Federal Trade Commission – s. US-Bundeshandelskommission, US-Verbraucherschutz- und Wettbewerbsbehörde
FedWire – s. (internes und externes) Echtzeit-Zahlungsverkehrssystem der US-Federal Reservebanks
fee – s. Gebühr, Taxe, Honorar, Tantieme
fees earned – s. Honorarerträge
feed – v. zuführen, einführen, einlegen
feed paper into a typewriter – Papier in eine Schreibmaschine einlegen

feedback – s. Feedback, Rückkoppelung
feeder service – s. Zubringerdienst, -verkehr
feeding – s. (Papier-)zuführung, (Material-)Zufuhr, Beschickung
Fellow Chartered Accountant – s. Vollmitglied des UK-Institute of Chartered Accountants
felt pen – s. Filzstift
fermentation – s. Gärung, Gärprozess
ferry – s. Fähre, Fährschiff
fertiliser – (Kunst-)Dünger
fetch
v. holen
v. erzielen
fetch a price – einen Preis erzielen
fibre-optic network – s. Glasfasernetz
fictitious gain – s. Scheingewinn
fidelity insurance – s. Personen-Kautionsversicherung, Veruntreuungsversicherung, Vertrauensschaden-Versicherung
fiduciary – adj. fiduziarisch, treuhändisch
act in a fiduciary capacity – als Treuhänder tätig sein / fungieren, fiduziarisch tätig sein
field
s. Gebiet, Bereich
s. Außendienst
work in the field – im Außendienst tätig sein
field executive – s. Reisende/r, Vertreter/in, Mitarbeiter/in im Außendienst
field research – s. Feldforschung, (Durchführung von) Primärerhebungen
FIFO – first-in, first-out (method) (siehe)
file
s. (Akten-)Ordner
s. Akt
s. Datei, Datenbestand, File
file
v. ablegen, einordnen
v. einbringen, einreichen, anmelden
file a letter – einen Brief ablegen
file information by subjectmatter – Informationen nach Sachgebieten ordnen / ablegen
file a complaint – eine Beschwerde einbringen
file a petition in bankruptcy – einen Antrag auf Eröffnung eines Insolvenzverfahrens einbringen, Konkurs anmelden
filing – s. Ablage, Schriftgutablage
filing cabinet – s. Aktenschrank
filing clerk – s. Registrator/in, Ablagesachbearbeiter/in
filing code number – s. Ablagecode, -nummer
filing section – s. Ablageabteilung
filing system – s. Ablagetechnik, -form, -sytem
film unit – s. Aufnahmegerät
final accounts – s. Perioden-, Rechnungsabschluss, Finanzausweise, Abschluss der Finanzbuchhaltung
draw up final accounts – Rechnungsabschluss erstellen
final assessment – s. endgültige Steuervorschreibung
final consumer – s. End-, Letztverbraucher
final dividend – s. Schlussdividende
final user – s. End-, Letztverbraucher
Finance Act – s. UK-Budgetgesetz
finance director – s. Finanzvorstand, Vorstandsmitglied für Finanzen, Finanzabteilungsleiter/in, Finanzdirektor/in
finance lease – s Finance-Leasing(-vertrag); Finanzierungsleasing(-vertrag)
financial account – s. Kapital-, Kapitalverkehrsbilanz (neues Zahlungsbilanzsystem)
financial accounting – s. Finanzbuchhaltung
financial accounts – s. Finanzbuchhaltung (einer Firma)
financial analyst – s. Finanzanalyst, -analytiker
financial asset – s. Finanzaktivum, -vermögenswert, -anlage, Forderung(-swert)
financial budget – s. Finanzplan, -budget
financial community – s. Finanzwelt, -kreise
financial control – s. Finanzkontrolle, Finanzkontrollsystem
financial expenses – s. Finanzaufwendungen, -aufwand
financial flow account – s. volkswirtschaftl. Finanzierungsrechnung, Kreditänderungskonto
financial forwards – s. Finanztermingeschäfte, -kontrakte
financial futures – s. börsengehandelte Finanzterminkontrakte
financial institution – s. Finanzinstitution
financial instrument – s. Finanzinstrument, -titel, Wertpapier, Papier
financial intermediary – s. Finanzintermediär/in , -mittler/in, Mittler/in auf Finanzmärkten
financial leverage – s. Financial Leverage, Finanzhebel, Hebelwirkung des Fremdkapitals
financial management – s. Kapitalwirtschaft, betriebliche Finanzwirtschaft, Finanzmanagement
financial manager – s. Mitglied des Finanzteams einer Firma, Finanzmanager/in, Leiter/in der Finanzabteilung
financial market – s. Finanzmarkt
financial officer – s. Mitglied des Finanzteams einer Firma, Finanzvorstand, Finanzdirektor/in
financial option – s. Finanzoption
financial product – s. Finanzprodukt
financial ratio – s. finanzwirtschaftliche Kennzahl, Kennzahl der Finanzbuchhaltung
financial revenues – s. Finanzerträge
financial resources – s. Geld-. Finanzmittel
financial services – s. Finanzdienstleistungen
financial service provider – s. Finanzdienstleister
financial services industry – s. Finanzdienstleistungsbranche, Finanzdienstleister-Branche
financial standing – s. finanzielle Lage, Vermögensverhältnisse
financial statements – s. Perioden-, Jahresabschluss, Finanzausweise, Abschluss der Finanzbuchhaltung
financial statement analysis – s. Bilanzanalyse, Jahresabschlussanalyse
Financial Times-Stock Exchange 100 index – s. Financial-Times-100 Aktienindex
financing – s. Finanzierung, Mittelbereitstellung
financing charges – s. Finanzierungskosten
financing package – s. Finanzierungspaket
fine tuning – s. (wirtschaftspolitische) Feinsteuerung
finished goods – s. Fertigwaren, Finalgüter
finite – adj. endlich
fire brigade – s. (freiwillige) Feuerwehr
fire insurance – s. Feuer-, Brandschadenversicherung
fire risk – s. Brandrisiko
fireside shopping – s. „Einkaufen in der bequemen Atmosphäre Ihres eigenen Wohnzimmers" (Werbeslogan des Versand- und Internethandels)
firm commitment underwriting – s. feste Übernahme (einer Emission durch ein – auf eigene Rechnung handelndes – Übernahmekonsortium)
firm offer – s. festes / fixes / bindendes Angebot
first-in, first-out method – s. FIFO-Verfahren (Pauschalbewertung des Vorratsvermögens zum Einstandspreis der letzten Lagerzugänge der Rechnungsperiode)
first-stage finance – s. Erstrundenfinanzierung

first-year allowance – s. Betrag der vorzeitigen Abschreibung für das erste Jahr, vorzeitige Abschreibung für das erste Jahr
fiscal crisis (of the modern state) – s. Finanzkrise (des modernen [Versorgungs-]Staates)
fiscal drag
s. fiskalischer Bremseffekt
s. kalte Progression, progressive Abschöpfung, inflationsbedingtes Hineinwachsen in höhere Einkommenstufen
fiscal policy – s. Fiskalpolitik, Budgetpolitik
fiscal year – s. Haushaltsjahr, Rechnungsjahr, Geschäftsjahr
fishmonger – s. Fischhändler
fishyback service – s. Roll-on- / Roll-off-Verkehr
fit
s. Passform, Sitz
s. Anfall, (Wut-)Ausbruch
to be a perfect fit – wie angegossen sitzen, genau passen
by fits and starts – stoßweise, ruckweise, mit Anlaufschwierigkeiten
fixed assets – s. materielles und immaterielles Anlagevermögen
fixed-assets-to-equity ratio – s. Anlagendeckungs(-grad)
fixed cost(s) – s. Fixkosten, fixe Kosten
fixed date forward contract – s. Terminkontrakt mit fixem Fälligkeitszeitpunkt
fixed deposit – s. Festgeld
fixed exchange rate – s. fester / fixer Wechselkurs
fixed exchange rates – s. feste / fixe Wechselkurse, System fester Wechselkurse
fixed exchange rate with bands – s. festes Wechselkurssystem mit Bandbreite
fixed expense(s) – s. Fixkosten, fixe Kosten
fixed/floating (interest rate) swap – s. Zinsswapp fest/variabel
fixed-interest bearing securities – s. festverzinsliche Wertpapiere
fixed-interest securities – s. festverzinsliche Wertpapiere
fixed-line telephone – s. Festnetztelefon, Festtelefon
fixed-price offer – s. Festpreisemission, -verfahren
fixed rate (of exchange) – s. fester / fixer Wechselkurs
fixing date – s. Zinsanpassungsdatum (bei einem Rollover-Kredit)
flat
adj. flach
adj. flau, lustlos, stagnierend
adj. einheitlich, pauschal
flat-bottomed boat – s. flachbödiges Schiff, Plattbodenschiff
flat-rate tax – s. Proportionalsteuer, proportionale Steuer, Flat-Rate Tax, Einheitssteuer(satz)
flat wagon – s. Rungenwagen, -waggon
fleet of vehicles – Fuhrpark
flexiband – s. Gleitzeitbandbreite
flexible disk – s. Diskette, Floppy-Diskette, flexible Diskette, Weich-, Folienspeicherplatte
flexible exchange rate – s. flexibler / freier / floatender Wechselkurs
flexible exchange rates – s. flexible Wechselkurse, System flexibler Wechselkurse
flexible manufacturing – s. flexibles Fertigungssystem
flexible rate of exchange – s. flexibler / freier / floatender Wechselkurs
flexitime – s. Gleitzeit
flight accident policy – s. Flugunfallversicherung
float
s. Streubesitz (von Wertpapieren)
s. Postlaufkredit, Float, Summe der noch nicht endgültig verbuchten Überweisungen und Schecks
s. (zinsfreier) Wertstellungskredit
float
v. gründen
v. auflegen, begeben
v. floaten, freigeben
float a company – ein Unternehmen an der Börse platzieren, eine Firma gründen
float a currency – den Kurs einer Währung freigeben
float an issue – eine Emission begeben
flo(a)tation (of a company) – s. Börsengang, Bösenplatzierung, Gang an die Börse
floater – s. variabel verzinsliche Anleihe, Anleihe mit variabler Verzinsung, Floater
floating – s. Floaten, Floating, Freigabe (eines Wechselkurses)
floating debt – s. kurzfristige Schuld
floating exchange rate – s. flexibler/ freier / floatender Wechselkurs
floating exchange rates – s. System flexibler Wechselkurse
floating/floating (interest rate) swap – s. Zinsswap variabel/variabel
floating policy – s. Abschreibepolizze
floating rate – variabler / flexibler Zinssatz / Wechselkurs
floating rate market – s. Markt für variabel verzinsliche Finanzinstrumente
floating-rate loan – s. variable verzinslicher Kredit, Floater-Kredit
floating rate note – s. kurz- bis mittelfristige, variabel verzinsliche Schuldverschreibung
floating rate of exchange – s. flexibler Wechselkurs, freier Wechselkurs
flog off – v. verkaufen, verscherbeln, versilbern
flood – s. Überschwemmung, Überflutung
floor
s. Untergrenze, unterer Interventionspunkt
s. Zins-Floor, Floor, börsengehandelte Vereinbarung einer Zinsuntergrenze
floor buyer – s. Floor-Käufer
floor covering – s. Fußbodenbelag
floor holder – Floor-Käufer
flooring – s. Fußbodenbelag
floor seller – s. Floor-Verkäufer/in, Stillhalter/in bei einem Zinsfloor
floor writer – s. Floor-Verkäufer/in, Stillhalter/in bei einem Zinsfloor
flop – s. Flop, Versager
floppy disk – s. Diskette, Weichplatte
floppy disk device – s. Diskettenspeicher, -laufwerk
flotation (of a company) – s. Börsengang, -platzierung, Gang an die Börse
flow concept – s. Strom-, Periodengröße
flow-of-product method – s. Verwendungsrechnung (für das BNP / BIP)
flow of traffic – s. Verkehrsaufkommen
flow production – s. Fließband-, Massenfertigung
fluctuating exchange rate – s. flexibler / freier / floatender Wechselkurs
fluctuating rate of exchange – s. flexibler / freier / floatender Wechselkurs
fluidised bed combustion – s. Wirbelschichtfeuerung
FOA – F.O.B. AIRPORT (siehe)
F.O.B. AIRPORT – F.O.B. FLUGHAFEN
F.O.B. – F.O.B., FREI AN BORD
FOB – internationaler Code für F.O.B

F.O.B (named place of destination in the country of importation) - FREI . . . (benannter Bestimmungsort im Einfuhrland)
F.O.B. buyer's warehouse - frei Haus (US-Handelsklauseln 1941)
F.O.B. VESSEL - F.O.B. SCHIFF
focus - v. sich konzentrieren, ins Visier nehmen
focus on sthg. - sich auf etwas konzentrieren
focus strategy - s. Fokusstrategie
folder
s. Mappe, Schnellhefter
s. Faltprospekt, zusammengefaltete Druckschrift
follow-up letter - s. Nachfassbrief
food and drug laws - s. Lebens- und Arzneimittelgesetze
food processing - s. Lebensmittelverarbeitung
foodstuff(s) - s. Lebens-, Nahrungsmittel
food subsidy - s. Lebensmittelsubvention, -hilfe
footing - s. Stellung, Status, Grundlage
on an equal footing - gleichgestellt, gleichberechtigt
Footsie 100 index - Financial Times-Stock Exchange 100 index (siehe)
force majeure - s. höhere Gewalt
force majeure event - s. Force-Majeure-Ereignis, Höhere-Gewalt-Ereignis
forecast - s. Prognose, Vorhersage
forecast - v. vorhersagen, prognostizieren
forecasting - s. Prognoseerstellung
foreclose - v. gerichtlich für verfallen erklären
foreclose a mortgage - eine Hypothek gerichtlich für verfallen erklären, sich aus einer Hypothek befriedigen
forego - v. preisgeben, verzichten auf
benefit foregone - entgangener Nutzen
foreign banknotes and coins - s. Valuten, Sorten
foreign borrowing - s. Kreditaufnahme im Ausland
foreign control - s. Überfremdung
Foreign Credit Insurance Association - s. Verband der US-amerikanischen privaten Exportkreditversicherer
foreign currency - s. Fremdwährung, ausländische Währung, Devise(n)
foreign currency forward - s. Devisentermingeschäft
foreign currency futures - s. börsengehandelte Devisenterminkontrakte, Währungsterminkontrakte, Währungsfutures
foreign currency futures market - s. Markt für börsengehandelte Devisenterminkontrakte, Devisenterminmarkt
foreign currency gain - s. (Währungs-)Transaktionsgewinn, (Währungs-)Umwechslungsgewinn
foreign currency loan - s. Fremdwährungskredit
foreign currency loss - s. (Währungs-)Transaktionsverlust, (Währungs-)Umwechslungsverlust
foreign currency market - s. Devisen-, Währungsmarkt
foreign currency option market - s. Devisenoptionsmarkt, Markt für Devisenoptionen
foreign currency rate - s. Wechsel-, Devisen-, Fremdwährungskurs
foreign currency receivable - s. Fremdwährungsforderung, auf eine Fremdwährung lautende Forderung
foreign currency reserves - s. Devisenreserven
foreign currency risk - s. Wechselkurs-, Devisenkurs-, Kurs-, Währungsrisiko
foreign currency swap - s. (Fremd-)Währungs-, Devisenswap, Devisentausch(-geschäft)
foreign currency swap market - s. Devisenswapmarkt
foreign direct investment - s. direkte Auslandsinvestition(-en), Direktinvestition(en) im Ausland
foreign exchange - s. Fremdwährung, Devisen
foreign exchange broker - s. Devisenmakler
foreign exchange control - s. Devisenbewirtschaftung
foreign exchang covering - s. Devisenkurs-, Wechselkurssicherung, Absicherung gegen das Wechselkursrisiko
foreign exchange dealer - s. Devisenhändler/in
foreign exchange dealing - s. Devisenhandel
foreign exchange exposure - s. Währungs-, Fremdwährungs-, Devisenposition
foreign exchange futures - s. Währungsterminkontrakte, Währungsfutures
foreign exchange gain - s. (Wechsel-)Kursgewinn, Währungsgewinn
foreign exchange hedging - s. Devisenkurs-, Wechselkurssicherung, Absicherung gegen das Wechselkursrisiko
foreign exchange loss - s. (Wechsel-)Kursverlust, Währungsverlust
foreign exchange market - s. Devisenmarkt
foreign exchange option - s. Devisen-, Währungsoption
foreign exchange permit - s. Devisengenehmigung
foreign exchange rate - s. Wechsel-, Devisen-, Fremdwährungskurs
foreign exchange receipts - s. Deviseneinnahmen, -eingänge
foreign exchange reserves - s. Währungs-, Devisenreserven
foreign exchange risk - s. Wechselkurs-, Kurs-, Währungsrisiko
foreign exchange swap - s. (Fremd-)Währungsswap, Devisenswap, Devisentausch(-geschäft)
foreign fair - s. Auslandsmesse
foreign leasing - s. Auslandsleasing
foreign tax - s. Auslandssteuer, im Ausland erhobene / bezahlte Steuer
foreign tax credit - s. Anrechnung ausländischer Steuer(-n), (im Rahmen von Doppelbesteuerungsabskommen), angerechnete ausländische Steuer
foreign trade - s. Außenhandel
foreign trade zone - s. Industriefreizone, freie Wirtschaftszone
foreman - s. Vorarbeiter, Werksmeister, Bauführer
forestall - v. zuvorkommen, vorwegnehmen
forest die-back - s. Waldsterben
forex - foreign exchange (siehe)
forex dealer - s. Devisenhändler
forex option - s. Devisen-, Währungsoption
forfaiting - s. Forfaitierung
forfaiting agreement - s. Forfaitierungsvertrag
forfaitor - s. Forfaitierer, forfaitierende Bank, Forfaitierungsinstitut
forge - v. fälschen (produzieren)
forge documents - Dokumente fälschen
fork-lift truck - s. Gabelstapler
fork out - v. blechen, berappen, (Geld) herausrücken
format - s. Format, Präsentation(-sweise), Darstellung (-sweise)
formation - s. Bildung, Errichtung, Gründung
formation of a company - s. Errichtung / Gründung einer Gesellschaft
FORMULA TRANSLATION - s. FORMULA-TRANSLATION-Programmiersprache
for-profit organistion - s. gewinnorientierte Organisation, gewinnorientiertes / kommerzielles Unternehmen
FORTRAN - FORMULA TRANSLATION (siehe)
fortress - s. Festung
Fortress Europe - die Festung Europa, das abgeschottete Europa, die Abschottung Europas

fortune – s. Erfolg
forward – s. Termingeschäft, -kontrakt, Devisenterminkontrakt, -geschäft
forward – v. befördern, senden, versenden, nachsenden, weiterbefördern, weiterleiten
forward – adj. / adv. zur späteren Lieferung, auf Termin, per Termin, Termin-
sell sthg. forward – etwas auf / per Termin verkaufen
buy a commodity forward – eine Ware auf / per Termin kaufen
forward contract – Termingeschäft, -kontrakt
forward cover – s. Kurssicherung(-stransaktion) am Devisenterminmarkt
forward covering – s. Kurssicherung am Devisenterminmarkt, Terminsicherung, Terminkurssicherung
forward deal – s. Termingeschäft, -kontrakt
forward dollar – s. Termindollar
forwarder – s. Spediteur/in
forward exchange – s. Termindevisen
forward exchange contract – s. Devisenterminkontrakt, -geschäft
forward exchange rate – s. (Devisen-)Terminkurs
forward exchange market – s. Devisenterminmarkt
forward foreign exchange rate – s. (Devisen-)Terminkurs
forward-forward swap – s. Forward-Forward-Swap
forward hedging – s. Abdeckung des Währungsumwechslungsrisikos über den (Devisen-)Terminmarkt, Kurssicherung mittels (Devisen-)Termingeschäft, Terminkurssicherung
forwarding agent – s. Spediteur
forwarding agent's (certificate of) receipt – s. (Internationale) Spediteurübernahmebescheinigung
forward market – s. Termin-, Devisenterminmarkt
forward option – s. Termingeschäft mit Laufzeitoption
forward price – s. (Devisen-)Terminkurs
forward purchase – s. Termin-, Devisenterminkauf
forward quotation – s. Terminnotierung, -kurs
forward rate agreement – s. Forward Rate Agreement, außerbörslicher Zinsterminkontrakt
forward rate (of exchange) – s. (Devisen-)Terminkurs
forwards – s. Terminkontrakte, -geschäfte
forward sale – s. (Devisen-)Terminverkauf
forward trading – s. Abschluss von Termingeschäften
forward transaction – s. Termingeschäft, -kontrakt
fossile fuel – s. fossiler Brennstoff
fossile-fuel plant – s. fossiles Kraftwerk
foster – v. fördern, begünstigen
foul bill of lading – s. unreines Konnossement
found – v. gründen, errichten
founder – s. Gründer
fount – s. Schrift(-satz), Schriftart
f.p.a. – free from particular average (siehe)
f.p.a. policy – s. Versicherung(-spolizze) mit der Klausel „ohne Partikularhavarie"
fraction – s. Bruchzahl, Bruchteil
FRA – forward rate agreement (siehe)
frame
s. Bild, Bildformat, Blatt, Blattformat
s. Frame, Billard-Rahmen
framework – s. Rahmen, Rahmenbedingungen, Umfeld, Umwelt, Datenkranz
franchise
s. Integralfranchise
s. Franchise, Franchisevertrag, Franchiseverhältnis, Franchise-Rechte,
s. Träger von Franchise-Rechten
s. Kundenakzeptanz, Gefolgschaft, Kundenstock
s. (staatliche) Lizenz
franchisee – s. Franchisenehmer/in
franchising – s. Franchising
franchising fee – s. Franchisegebühr
franchisor – s. Franchisegeber/in
frank – v. freimachen, frankieren
franking machine – s. Frankiermaschine
fraud – s. Betrug, arglistige Täuschung
free – adj. / adv. frei, gratis, kostenlos
free agent – s. Freischaffende/r, Selbständige/r
FREE ALONGSIDE SHIP – FREI LÄNGSSEITE SCHIFF
free balance – s. unverzinsliche Sichteinlage, unverzinsliches Giroguthaben
free banking services – s. gebührenfreie Bankdienstleistungen
FREE CARRIER – FREI FRACHTFÜHRER
free from particular average – s. (Versicherungsdeckung) ohne Partikularhavarie / ohne Deckung der Teilschäden
free goods – s. freie Güter
freehold flat – s. Eigentumswohnung
freely flexible exchange rate – s. völlig freier Wechselkurs, System völlig freier Wechselkurse
freely floating exchange rate – s. völlig freier Wechselkurs, System völlig freier Wechselkurse
free market economy – s. freie Marktwirtschaft
free movement of capital – s. Freizügigkeit des Kapitalverkehrs
free movement of labour – s. Freizügigkeit des Arbeitsmarktes
free movement of services – s. Freizügigkeit des Dienstleistungsverkehrs
free-phone system – s. (ferngesprächs-)gebührenfreies Telefonservice, National Freeline, Anruf zum Nulltarif, 0800-Dienst
free port – s. Freihafen
frequent-flier programme – s. Vielfliegerprogramm
free sample – s. Gratisprobe, -muster
free trade area – s. Freihandelszone, -gebiet
free trade regime – s. Freihandelsordnung, -system
free trade zone – s. Industriefreizone, freie Wirtschaftszone
freight
s. Fracht, Fracht-, Transportgebühr
s. Fracht, Frachtgut
freight bookings – s. Frachtaufträge, Frachtgeschäft
FREIGHT/CARRIAGE AND INSURANCE PAID TO – FRACHTFREI VERSICHERT
FREIGHT/CARRIAGE PAID TO – FRACHTFREI
freight carrying – s. Frachtbeförderung, -verkehr
freight collect – Fracht nachnehmen, unfrei, Fracht beim Empfänger einheben
freight forwarder – s. Spediteur
freight handling – s. Fracht-, Güterumschlag
freightliner system – s. UK-Eisenbahnfrachtlinienverkehrssystem
freightliner train – s. Liniengüterzug, fahrplanmäßiger Güterzug
Freight Out – s. Ausgangsfracht(-aufwandskonto)
freight prepaid – Fracht im Voraus bezahlt, frei
freight rate – s. Frachtsatz, -rate, -tarif
freight train – s. Güterzug
frenzy – s. Wahn, Rausch,
frequency modulation – s. Frequenzmodulation
friction – s. Friktion, funktionale Störung(-en), Störungserscheinungen beim Übergang von einem Gleichgewichtszustand zu einem anderen

frictional unemployment – s. Friktions-, Fluktuations-, Bodensatzarbeitslosigkeit
friendly takeover bid – s. freundliches (mit der Geschäftsleitung der Zielgesellschaft abgestimmtes) Übernahmeangebot
fringe benefit – s. (betriebliche) Nebenleistung / Sozialleistung
frontier – s. Grenze
front-running – s. Front-Running
FT industrial ordinary index – s. Financial Times Industrieaktienindex
FT-SE 100 share index – Financial Times-Stock Exchange 100 index
FTZ – foreign trade zone (siehe)
fuel – s. Brenn-, Treibstoff
fuel supplies – s. Brennstoff-, Treibstoffvorrat
fuelwood – s. Heizholz
full absorption costing – s. Vollkostenrechnung
full container load – s. Containerladung, FCL
full count – s. Vollerhebung
full employment – s. Vollbeschäftigung
full-page ad – s. ganzseitige Anzeige
full-payout lease – s. Vollamortisationsleasing(-vertrag)
full production – s. Vollproduktion
full-scale – adj. im Großmaßstab, in natürlicher / voller Größe, vollständig entwickelt
full-service bank – s. Universalbank
full-service wholesaler – s. Vollfunktionsgroßhändler; Großhändler, der alle üblichen Großhandelsfunktionen ausübt
full-time director – s. geschäftsführendes Mitglied des Führungsgremiums einer (UK- / US-)Kapitalgesellschaft, Geschäftsführer/in, Vorstandsmitglied mit Aufsichtsratsfunktion, Aufsichtsratsmitglied mit Vorstandsagenden
full-time job – s. Vollzeitarbeitsplatz, -beschäftigung
fully-fledged – adj. vollständig, vollwertig, voll entwickelt, Voll-
fully-paid share – s. voll eingezahlte Aktie
fumes – s. Abgase
function – s. Funktion, Tätigkeitsbereich
functional distribution – s. funktionale Einkommensverteilung
functionalisation – s. Funktionalgliederung, Gliederung nach funktionellen Gesichtspunkten
functional manager – s. Funktionsmanager, für eine betriebswirtschaftliche Funktion zuständiger Manager
functional organisation – s. funktionale Organisation(-sform)
functional unit – s. funktionale Organisationseinheit
fund
s. Fonds, zweckgebundenes (Sonder-)Vermögen
s. Fonds, Kasse, Versicherungsanstalt
s. (pl.) Barmittel, finanzielle Mittel
s. (pl.) Kapital
raise funds – Mittel / Kapital aufbringen
source funds – Mittel / Kapital aufbringen
allocate funds – Mittel verwenden / einsetzen / zuteilen
no funds – ohne Deckung (Scheck)
shareholder's funds – Eigenkapital
fundamental analysis – s. fundamentale Wertpapieranalyse, Fundamentalanalyse
fundamental information – s. (wirtschaftliche) Fundamentaldaten
funding
s. Finanzierung, Mittelbereitstellung
s. Finanzmittel, Geldmittel, Kapital,
s. Fundierung, Umwandlung kurzfristiger in langfristige (fundierte) Schulden
fund-raising campaign – s. Fund-Raising-Aktion
funds-flow statement – s. Kapitalflussrechnung
funds transfer – s. Überweisung
fungible goods – s. fungible / vertretbare Ware(n)
fungicide – s. Fungizid
furniture and fixtures – s. Betriebs- und Geschäftsausstattung, Inventar
Furniture and Fixtures – s. (das Konto) Betriebs- und Geschäftsausstattung
further – v. fördern, unterstützen
fuselage – s. (Flugzeug-)Rumpf
futures – s. börsengehandelte Terminkontrakte (siehe *futures contract*)
futures contract – s. börsengehandelter Terminkontrakt (ohne effektive Lieferung), Börsen-Terminkontrakt, Futures-Kontrakt
close out a futures contract – einen Terminkontrakt glattstellen
futures contract price – Börsenterminkurs, Kurs für börsengehandelte Terminkontrakte
futures hedging – s. Kurssicherung mit börsengehandelten (Devisen-)Terminkontrakten, Hedging mit Währungs-Futures
futures option – s. Futures-Option
futures position – s. Börsen-Terminposition, Position auf dem (Devisen-)Terminmarkt
futures price – s. Börsenterminkurs, Kurs für börsengehandelte Terminkontrakte
FX – foreign exchange (siehe)
FX-dealer – s. Devisenhändler

G

gain
s. Gewinn
s. Zuwachs
gains due to currency fluctuations – s. Wechselkursgewinne, Währungsgewinne
productivity gains – Produktivitätszuwächse
gainful – adj. gewinnbringend, Erwerbs-
gainfully employed – erwerbstätig
gains from trade – s. positive Wohlfahrtseffekte des Außenhandels, Außenhandelsgewinne
gambling – s. Glücksspiel
gaming – s. Glücksspiel
gantry crane – s. Portalkran
gaseous – adj. gasförmig
gasification – s. Vergasung, Gasifizierung
coal gasification – Kohlevergasung
GATS – General Agreement on Trade in Services (siehe)
GATT– General Agreement on Tariffs and Trade (siehe)
gay market – s. Marktsegment für Homosexuelle, Schwulenmarkt
gays – s. Homosexuelle, Schwule
GDP – gross domestic product (siehe)
GDP deflator – s. BIP-Deflator, impliziter Preisindex des Bruttoinlandproduktes
GDP per head – Pro-Kopf-BIP
GE – genetically engineered (siehe)
gear – v. abstimmen, abstellen
geared to sthg. – auf etwas abgestimmt
gearing
s. Fremdkapital
s. Verschuldungskoeffizient, -grad
s. Financial Leverage, Finanzhebel, Hebelwirkung des Fremdkapitals
gearing ratio – s. Verschuldungskoeffizient, -grad
gene – s. Gen
general accounting – s. Finanzbuchhaltung
general agent – s. Generalhandlungsbevollmächtigte/r
General Agreement on Tariffs and Trade – s. Allgemeines Zoll- und Handelsabkommen, GATT
General Agreement on Trade in Services – s. Allgemeines Abkommen über den Handel mit Dienstleistungen
general average – s. Havarie-grosse, große Havarie
general average act – s. Havariehandlung, -opfer
general average contribution – s. Havarie-grosse-Beitrag / Schadensbeitrag
general average damage / loss – s. Havarie-grosse-Schaden / Verlust
general cargo – s. Stückgut (im Seeverkehr)
general cargo vessel – s. Stückgutfrachter
general costs – s. allgemeine / sonstige Kosten
general crossing – s. Blankokreuzvermerk, allgemeine Kreuzung
general inquiry – s. allgemeine Anfrage
Generalised System of Preferences – s. Allgemeines Präferenzystem / APS (des GATT)
general-line wholesaler – s. Universalgroßhändler, Sortimenter
generally accepted accounting principles – s. Grundsätze ordnungsgemäßer Buchführung und Bilanzierung
general manager – s. Generaldirektor/in, Geschäftsführer/in, Generalist/in
general meeting – s. Hauptversammlung (AG), Gesellschafterversammlung (GmbH)
General Office – s. Haupt-, Zentralbüro (eines Unternehmens)
general partner – s. Vollhafter, Komplementär
general partnership – s. offene Handelsgesellschaft, OHG
general-purpose microcomputer – s. Mehrzweck-/ Allzweckmikrocomputer
general reserve – s. freie Rücklage
general sales tax – s. umfassende / generelle Umsatzsteuer, umfassende / generelle Verbrauchsteuer
generate
v. erzeugen, hervorbringen, produzieren
v. erstellen, konzipieren
v. erwirtschaften, abwerfen
generate electricity – Elektrizität erzeugen
generate information – Informationen produzieren
information is generated – Informationen fallen an
generate documents – Dokumente erstellen
documents are generated – Dokumente / Belege fallen an
generate profits – Gewinne erwirtschaften / abwerfen
generation
s. Erzeugung, Hervorbringung, Produktion
s. Erstellung
s. Erwirtschaftung, Erwirtschaften
generic product – s. generisches / markenfreies / anonymes Produkt, Gattungsprodukt
genetically engineered – adj. genetisch verändert / modifiziert
genetically modified – adj. genetisch verändert / modifiziert
genetically modified organism – genetisch veränderter Organismus
genetic engineering – s. Gentechnik, Genmanipulation
gentlemen's agreement – s. Gentlemen's Agreement
get-together – s. Zusammenkunft, Treffen
Giffen good – s. Giffen-Gut
Giffen paradox – s. Giffen-Effekt, Giffen-Paradoxon
gift – s. Geschenk
gift tax – s. Schenkungssteuer
gigabyte – s. Gigabyte (1024 Megabyte)
gilt-edged securities – s. UK-Staatsanleihen / Staatsschuldverschreibungen
gilts – s. giltedged securities (siehe)
gilts market – s. Börsensektor für UK-Staatsanleihensektor
Gini-coefficient – s. Gini-Koeffizient (Konzentrationsmaß der Einkommensverteilung)
globalisation – s. Globalisierung
global marketing – s. globales Marketing
global quota – s. Global-, Gesamtkontingent
Global System for Mobile Communications – s. globales Mobilkommunikationssystem (GSM)
gloss over – v. bemänteln, vertuschen, beschönigen
glossy brochure – s. Hochglanzbroschüre
GM – genetically modified (siehe)
GMO – genetically modified organism (siehe)
GSM – Global System for Mobile Communications (siehe)
GNP – gross national product (siehe)
GNP deflator – s. BNP-Deflator, impliziter Preisindex des Bruttonationalproduktes
GNP per head – s. Bruttonationalprodukt pro Kopf, Pro-Kopf-Bruttonationalprodukt
goal – s. Ziel
set goals – Ziele festsetzen / festlegen
meet goals – Ziele erreichen
identify goals – Ziele ermitteln

goal-setting – s. Zielvorgabe, -findung
go bad – v. verderben, schlecht werden
going – adj. laufend, zur Zeit gültig, üblich
going wage rate – zur Zeit geltender Lohntarif
going public – s. Gang an die Börse, Erstemission
golf-ball typing element – s. Kugelschreibkopf
good faith – s. guter Glaube
in good faith – in gutem Glauben, bona fide
goods – s. Güter, Waren
goods account – s. Waren-, Warenverkehrs-, Güterbilanz
goods in process – s. Halberzeugnisse, -fabrikate, Zwischenprodukte
goods-in-transit insurance – s. Binnentransportversicherung von Gütern
Goods Inwards – s. Wareneingang(-sstelle), Warenübernahme(-stelle), Warenannahme(-stelle)
Goods Outwards – s. Versandabteilung
goods train – s. Güterzug
good will – s. Wohlwollen, Ansehen
goodwill – s. Firmenwert
go-slow – s. Bummelstreik
government agency – s. Regierungsstelle, -amt
governmental – adj. staatlich, Regierungs-
governmental bond – s. Staatsschuldverschreibung, Staats-, Bundesanleihe
government bonus – s. staatliche (Bauspar-)Prämie
government expenditure – s. Staatsausgaben
government expenditure multiplier – s. Staatsausgabenmultiplikator
government export financing – s. staatliche Exportfinanzierung
government failure – s. Staats-, Regierungsversagen
government grant – s. staatlicher Zuschuss, staatliche Zuweisung, Subvention
government insurance facilities – s. staatliche Versicherungseinrichtungen / -möglichkeiten
government-owned – adj. staatseigen, im Staatseigentum (befindlich)
government procurement – s. öffentliches Beschaffungswesen
government securities – s. Staatspapiere, -anleihen
government-sponsored – adj. staatlich gefördert, vom Staat getragen
government stock – s. Staatsschuldverschreibung, Staats-, Bundesanleihe
government transfers – s. staatliche Transferzahlungen / Einkommensübertragungen / Nicht-Leistungszahlungen
grade
s. Klasse, Sorte, Qualität, Güteklasse
s. Ausbildungsgrad, Besoldungsgruppe
grade – v. einteilen, klassieren
grade commodities – Waren nach Güteklassen einteilen, Waren klassieren
grain – s. Getreide
grant
s. Subvention, Finanzhilfe, Finanz- und Sachhilfe, Stützung(-sbetrag)
s. Schenkung,
s. Gewährung, Zuerkennung, Erteilung, Zuweisung
grant – v. gewähren, zuerkennen, bewilligen, erteilen, verleihen, übertragen
grant a credit – einen Kredit gewähren
grant an allowance – einen Preisnachlass einräumen / gewähren
grant damages – Schadenersatz zuerkennen
grant an import licence – eine Einfuhrgenehmigung erteilen
grant a right – ein Recht verleihen
grant element – s. Schenkungselement
graph – s. Graphik, graphische Darstellung, Diagramm
graph – v. graphisch darstellen
grasp – v. verstehen, erfassen
gratuitous transfer – s. unentgeltliche Vermögensübertragung
grave – adj. schwerwiegend, gewichtig, ernst
gravel – s. Kies, Sand
gravitational pull – s. (Wirken der) Schwerkraft
grazing land – s. Weideflächen, Weidland
Great Depression – s. Weltwirtschaftskrise
greenfield site – s. unverbautes Grundstück, „grüne Wiese"
greenhouse effect – s. Treibhaus-, Glashauseffekt
green label – s. Öko-, Umweltsiegel, Ökozeichen, Ökogütezeichen,
Green Revolution – s. Grüne Revolution
green tax – s. Öko-, Umweltsteuer
grievance – s. Beschwerde, Grund zur Klage, Übelstand, Missstand, Groll, Unzufriedenheit
gross – adj. / adv. brutto, Brutto-, Roh-, vor Abzug
gross of depreciation – vor Abzug der Abschreibung
gross of tax – vor Abzug der Steuer(n), unversteuert
gross cash flow – s. Brutto-Cash-Flow
gross domestic product – s. Bruttoinlandsprodukt
gross fixed assets – s. Bruttoanlagevermögen
gross income – s. Bruttoeinkommen, -gewinn, Einkommen / Gewinn vor Steuern
gross margin – s. Rohgewinn, Rohübererträg
gross national product – s. Bruttonationalprodukt, Bruttosozialprodukt, Bruttoinländerprodukt, BNP, BSP
gross private domestic investment – s. private Bruttoanlagekapitalbildung / Bruttoanlageinvestitionen
gross profit – s. Rohgewinn, Rohüberschuss
gross profit on trading – s. Rohgewinn, Rohüberschuss
gross revenue – s. Bruttosteueraufkommen
gross sales – s. unbereinigte Bruttoerlöse
gross weight – s. Bruttogewicht
gross working capital – s. Umlaufvermögen
groupage bill of lading – s. Sammelkonnossement
group company – s. Konzernunternehmen, verbundenes Unternehmen (inkludiert Mutter- und Tochtergesellschaften und assoziierte Unternehmen)
grouped consignment – s. Sammelladung
group headquarters – s. Konzernzentrale
group of companies – s. Konzern, Unternehmensgruppe
growth-gap unemployment – s. wachstumsdefizitäre Arbeitslosigkeit, auf eine langfristige systemimmanente Nachfrageinsuffizienz zurückzuführende Arbeitslosigkeit
growth rate – s. Wachstumsrate
grudging – adj. widerwillig
GSM – Global System for Mobile Communications (siehe)
GSP – Generalised System of Preferences (siehe)
guarantee
s. Garantie (im Sinne einer Gewährleistungsgarantie)
s. Garantie (im Sinne eines unabhängigen Garantievertrages)
s. (Ausfalls-)Bürgschaft
s. Nachschusspflicht
company limited by guarantee – Gesellschaft mit beschränkter Nachschusspflicht
provide a guarantee – eine Grantie stellen
post a guarantee – eine Garantie stellen
guaranteed amount – s. Garantiesumme
guarantee period – s. Garantiefrist
guarantor – s. Garantiegeber, (Ausfalls-)Bürge
guardian – s. Wächter, Schützer, Hüter
guideline – s. Richtlinie
guild – s. Gilde, Zunft, Innung

H

haemophiliac - s. Bluter/in
halfway house - Kompromiss, Übergangslösung
Hague rules - s. Haager Regeln
HagueVisby rules - s. Haager-Visby Regeln
hallmark - s. Punze, Stempel, Kennzeichen, charakteristisches Merkmal
Hamburg rules - s. Hamburger Regeln
hand - s. Hand
It is in the hands of the shareholders. - Es liegt bei den Aktionären.
hand - v. aushändigen, überreichen, übergeben
hand-held device - s. Handheld, Handheld-Gerät
hand in - v. einreichen
handle
v. durchführen, abwickeln, sich befassen mit, erledigen
v. führen
v. handhaben, anfassen, umschlagen
handle goods - Waren führen, Waren umschlagen / handhaben
handle an issue - eine Emission durchführen / abwickeln
handle a problem - mit einem Problem fertigwerden
handling
s. Umschlag (Überführung von Gütern zwischen Lager und Transportmittel und zwischen Transportmitteln)
s. innerbetrieblicher Transport, Förderwesen
s. Manipulation, Handhabung
s. Durchführung, Abwicklung, Erledigung, Bewältigung
handling charge - s. Manipulations-, Bearbeitungs-, (Seehafen-)Umschlaggebühr
handling facilities - s. (Güter-/ Fracht-) Umschlagseinrichtungen, innerbetriebliche Verkehrs-, Fördereinrichtungen, Förderanlagen
handling of an account - s. Kontoführung
hand-operated - adj. für den / mit Handbetrieb
hands-off - adj. zurückhaltend, interventionsfrei, distanziert
hands-off policy - s. nicht-interventionistische (politische) Linie
hand-picking - s. Handsammeln, händisches Einsammeln
hand-to-mouth - adj. der kurzfristigen Bedarfsdeckung dienend
handy - adj. praktisch
hard copy - s. gedruckte Maschinenausgabe, Druckausgabe, ausgedruckte Kopie, Hardcopy
hard-copy device - s. Druckgerät, Drucker, Plotter
hard currency - s. Hartwährung
hard disk
s. Hart-, Magnetplatte
s. Festplatte
hard elements - s. harte, quantifizierbare Elemente / Fakten
hard energy path - s. harte / umweltbelastende Energiepolitik
hard energy technology - s. harte / umweltbelastende Energietechnologie
hard foreign currency - s. Hartwährung, harte / starke Währung
hard loan - s. hartes Darlehen, kommerzieller Kredit, Kredit zu kommerziellen Bedingungen
hard (producer) goods - s. Investitionsgüter
hard selling - s. aggressive Verkaufsmethode(n)
hardship - s. Härte, Not, Mühsal
hardware - s. Hardware
hardware store - s. Hartwarengeschäft, Eisen- und Geschirrgeschäft
harness - v. nutzbar machen, einspannen
haul - s. Transport, Transportweg, Distanz, Entfernung
haul - v. befördern, transportieren, schleppen
haulier - s. Transportfirma, -unternehmen
hazard - s. Gefahr, Gefährdung, Risiko, Wagnis
head - s. Leiter, Vorsteher
head - v. vorstehen, leiten, führen, an der Spitze stehen
head a department - einer Abteilung vorstehen, eine Abteilung leiten
headed by a woman - unter der Leitung einer Frau
head-and-shoulder - s. Kopf-und-Schulter(-formation)
headhunter - s. Headhunter, Personalberater für Führungskräfte, „Kopfjäger"
heading - s. Überschrift, Titel, Position (Buchhaltung)
headquartered - adj. mit Sitz
headquarted in Austria - mit Sitz in Österreich
headquarters - s. Zentrale, Leitung, Hauptbüro, -geschäftsstelle, -verwaltung
head office - s. Zentrale, Leitung, Hauptbüro, -geschäftsstelle, -verwaltung
health regulations - s. Gesundheitsvorschriften
health standard - s. Gesundheitsnorm, -standard
heat insulation - s. Wärmedämmung, -isolierung
heat pollution - s. Abwärme(-last)
heavy lorry - s. Schwerlaster
heavy weather - s. schwere See, hoher Seegang
hedge
s. (Schutz-)Hecke
s. Absicherung
s. Kurssicherungsmaßnahme, -transaktion
hedge
v. (sich) absichern, sichern
v. hedgen, (Kursrisiko, Preisrisiko) abdecken
hedge against a risk - sich gegen ein Risiko absichern, ein Risiko (ab-)decken
hedge fund - s. Hedge Fund, Hedge-Fonds, Risikofonds
hedgerow - s. Hecke
hedging
s. (Inflations-)Absicherung, (Inflations-)Abdeckung
s. Hedging, (Wertpapier-)Kurssicherung, (Wechsel-/ Devisen-) Kurssicherung, Zinssicherung, (Waren-)Preissicherung, Abeckung des (Wechsel-)Kurs- / Preis- / Zinsrisikos
hedging instrument - s. Kurssicherungsinstrument, -technik, -maßnahme, Maßnahme zur Kurssicherung / Preissicherung / Zinssicherung
hedging in the money market - s. Abdeckung des Währungsumwechslungsrisikos / Kurssicherung über den Geldmarkt / durch Fremdwährungkreditaufnahme und/oder -veranlagung
hedging operation - s. Kurssicherungstechnik, -maßnahme, Maßnahme zur Kurssicherung / Preissicherung / Zinssicherung
hedging technique - s. Kurssicherungstechnik, -maßnahme, Maßnahme zur Preissicherung
hedging transaction risk in the foreign currency option market - s. Abdeckung des Währungsumwechslungsrisikos auf dem Devisenoptionsmarkt, Kurssicherung mittels Devisenoptionen
hedging transaction risk in the forward exchange market - s. Abdeckung des Währungsumwechslungsrisikos über den (Devisen-)Terminmarkt, Kurssicherung mittels (Devisen-)Termingeschäft, Terminkurssicherung

hedging transaction risk in the money market – s. Abdeckung des Währungsumwechslungsrisikos über den Geldmarkt, Kurssicherung über den Geldmarkt / durch Fremdwährungskredite und/oder Fremdwährungsveranlagungen
hedging with foreign currency futures – s. Kurssicherung mittels börsengehandelten (Devisen-)Terminkontrakten, Hedging mit Währungs-Futures
heir – s. Erbe
herbicide – s. Unkrautvertilgungsmittel, Herbizid
hereditary defect – s. Erbschaden
hidden reminder – s. verdeckte / versteckte Mahnung
hidden reserve – s. stille Rücklage
hierarchical level – s. Hierarchieebene
higher-level language – s. höhere Programmiersprache
higher-of-cost-or-market principle – s. Höchstwertprinzip
higher self – s. höheres Selbst
high-grade bond – s. erstklassige, risikoarme Anleihe / Schuldverschreibung
highlight – v. beleuchten, herausstreichen
high-resolution colour graphics – s. hochauflösende Farbgraphik
high-rise – s. Hochhaus
high street – s. Haupteinkaufsstraße
high-street – adj. Haupt-, Spitzen-
high-street location – Haupt-, Spitzenlage
high-tech – adj. hochtechnologisch, Hochtechnologie-
hike – s. Erhöhung
hike – v. erhöhen
hire
v. mieten,
v. anstellen, einstellen, in Dienst nehmen
hire purchase
s. Mietkauf (mit automatisch ausgeübter Kaufoption)
s. Ratenkauf mit Eigentumsvorbehalt
s. Ratenkauf, Ratengeschäft
historical cost – s. Anschaffungs- und / oder Herstellungskosten, Anschaffungswert
historical cost principle – s. Anschaffungswertprinzip
historical exchange rate – s. Entstehungskurs
historic(al) rate – s. historischer Kurs, Anschaffungskurs
historical rate method – s. Zeitbezugsmethode
historical rate of exchange – s. Entstehungskurs
historical standard – s. (firmeninterner) historischer Vergleichswert
HM Inland Revenue and Customs – s. UK-Steuerbehörde
hoarding – s. Anschlag-, Plakatwand, Anschlagfläche
hold one's own – v. sich behaupten
holder – s. Inhaber, Besitzer
holder of a bill of exchange – s. Wechselinhaber/in, Inhaber/in eines Wechsels
holder of a cheque – s. Scheckinhaber/in, Inhaber/in eines Schecks
holding
s. Besitz, Bestand (bes. an Wertpapieren)
s. Beteiligung, Anteil
s. Grundbesitz
holding company
s. Muttergesellschaft, Obergesellschaft, herrschendes Unternehmen
s. Holding(-gesellschaft), nicht-operative Muttergesellschaft
holiday pay – s. Urlaubsgeld
holiday with pay – s. bezahlter Urlaub
home banking – s. Abwicklung von Bankgeschäften über Heimterminals, Homebanking
home banking facilities – s. Homebanking-Service, Homebanking-Möglichkeiten
home computer – s. Heimcomputer
home consumption – s. freier (Inlands-)Verkehr (im zolltechnischen Sinn)
home currency – s. Inlandswährung, inländische Währung
home currency invoicing – s. Fakturierung in heimischer Währung
home loan – s. Baudarlehen, -kredit
home-made – adj. hausgemacht
homepage – s. Homepage, Leit-, Haupt-, Startseite
home shopping – s. Homeshopping, Heimkauf
honour – v. honorieren, einlösen, zahlen, akzeptieren
honour a bill of exchange – einen Wechsel honorieren / akzeptieren / einlösen / zahlen
honour a cheque – einen Scheck honorieren / einlösen / zahlen
hook up – v. verbinden
horizontal integration – s. horizontale Integration, horizontaler Unternehmungszusammenschluss
host
s. Gastgeber
s. große Anzahl, Menge, Unzahl
host computer – s. Host-Computer, Host-Rechner, Wirt-Rechner
host country – s. Gast-, Zielland
hostile takeover bid – s. feindliches (d. h. nicht mit der Firmenleitung der Zielfirma abgestimmtes) Übernahmeangebot
hot money – s. Fluchtgeld, heißes Geld
hourly rates – s. Stundenlöhne
house bill of lading – s. Haus-, Spediteurkonnossement
housing subsidy – s. Wohnbauförderung, Wohnungsbeihilfe
http – hypertext transfer protocol (siehe)
hull insurance – s. (See- und Luft-) Kaskoversicherung
hull policy – s. (See- und Luft-) Kaskoversicherungspolizze
human capital – s. Human-, Arbeitskapital
Human Relations movement – s. Human-Relations-Bewegung
human resources – s. Humanressourcen, Human-, Arbeitskapital
human resource(s) management – s. Humnanressourcen-Management, Personalmanagement, -wesen, -wirtschaft
hybrid computer – s. Hybridrechner
hybrid economy – s. Mischwirtschaft, hybrides Wirtschaftssystem
hybridise – v. (sich) kreuzen
hydroelectric power station – s. Wasserkraftwerk
hydroelectric scheme – s. Wasserkraftwerksprojekt, -anlage
hydropower plant – s. Wasserkraftwerk
hydrosphere – s. Hydrosphäre
hydro station – s. Wasserkraftwerk
hyperinflation – s. Hyperinflation
hypermarket – s. Hypermarkt, großer Supermarkt, Groß-, Verbrauchermarkt
hypermedia – s. Hypermedia-Technologie, Hypermedialität (Fähigkeit eines Computers, auch multimediale Dateiformate aus dem WWW herunterzuladen und darzustellen)
hypertext transfer protocol – s. Hypertext Transfer Protocol (Standard für die elektronische Interaktion bei der Übertragung von Web-Dokumenten ins Internet)

I

ICC – International Chamber of Commerce (siehe)
icon
s. Icon, Klicksymbol, Piktogramm
s. Ikone (kirchlich geweihtes Bild)
s. Ikone, Vorbild (mit Kultstatus), Kultobjekt, -person
IDA – International Development Association (siehe)
IDA Ireland – Irish Industrial Development Agency
identify – v. identifizieren, bestimmen, erfassen, ermitteln, herausfinden
identify costs – v. Kosten erfassen / ermitteln
identity – s. Identität, Nämlichkeit
proof of identity – Nämlichkeitsnachweis
idle – adj. ungenützt, brachliegend, stillliegend
idleness – s. Faulheit, Müßiggang, Trägheit
igloo-shaped container – s. Iglu-Container
illiteracy – s. Analphabetentum, Schriftlosigkeit
image
s. Bild, Mikrofilmbild
s. Image
image pricing – s. Image-Pricing, Luxuspreisstrategie, image-orientierte Preisgestaltung
image processing – s. Bilddatenverarbeitung
image transfer – s. Image-Transfer
IMF – International Monetary Fund (siehe)
immersion heater – s. Tauchsieder
impair – v. beeinträchtigen
impairment – s. Beeinträchtigung, Schädigung
imperative – adj. entscheidend, maßgeblich, unbedingt erforderlich
implement – v. durchführen, realisieren, verwirklichen, in die Tat umsetzen, vollziehen, implementieren
implement a system – ein System implementieren
implement the budget – das Budget vollziehen
implement a plan – einen Plan umsetzen / durchführen
implementation – s. Durchführung, Realisierung, Verwirklichung, Vollzug, Implementierung
implicit interest – s. kalkulatorische Zinsen
imply
v. implizieren, einschließen,
v. erschließen, unterstellen, Schluss ziehen
A is implied from B – A kann aus B erschlossen werden
imply from conduct – aus dem Verhalten schließen / konkludieren
import – s. Import, Einfuhr
import control – s. Importbeschränkung, -restriktion
import duty – s. Import-, Einfuhrzoll
import factor – Import-Factor- (Gesellschaft)
import licence – s. Importlizenz, Einfuhrgenehmigung
grant an import licence – eine Einfuhrgenehmigung erteilen
import licensing – s. Importlizenzsystem, Vergabe von Importlizenzen
import merchant – s. Einfuhrhändler/in, Importkaufmann, Importeur/in
import quota – s. Einfuhr-, Importkontingent
goods subject to an import quota – kontingentierte Einfuhren / Importe
import restriction – s. Importbeschränkung
import tariff – s. Importzoll
import tax – s. Importzoll
import VAT – s. Einfuhrumsatzsteuer
impose – v. auferlegen, belegen, einführen
impose a tax – eine Steuer auferlegen
impose a tax on sthg. – etwas besteuern / mit einer Steuer belegen
imposition – s. Auferlegung, Einführung, Verhängung
imposition of a penalty – Verhängung einer Strafe
imposition of a tax – Auferlegung einer Steuer, Besteuerung
imposition of exchange controls – Einführung von Devisenverkehrsbeschränkungen
impoverishment – s. Verarmung
imprinter – s. (Kreditkarten-) Imprinter / Schlitten
imputation system – s. Anrechnungssystem
impute – v. anrechnen, unterstellen, zuschreiben, annehmen
imputed interest – s. kalkulatorische Zinsen
imputed rent – s. (für Besteuerungszwecke) angenenommener Mietbetrag, steuerrechtliche Miete
inadequacy – s. Unzulänglichkeit, wirtschaftliche Überholung
inadmissible – adj. unzulässig
inadvertent – adj. unabsichtlich
inc. – Abkürzung für *incorporated* (siehe) in Firmennamen
incentive – s. Anreiz, Förderungsmaßnahme
incentive payments – s. Anreizzahlungen, Leistungslöhne, leistungsorientierte Entlohnung
incentive scheme – s. Anreizsytem
incidental wage costs – s. Lohn-, Personalnebenkosten
incidence – s. Inzidenz, Vorkommen, Anfall, Auftreten, Häufigkeit, Belastungswirkung
incidence of tax – s. Steuerinzidenz, steuerliche Belastungswirkung
incidental
adj. sekundär, Neben-
adj. zugehörig, verbunden
A is incidental to B – A gehört zu B, A ist mit B verbunden
incidental expenses – s. Spesen, Nebenausgaben
incision – s. Einschnitt
inclemency of the weather – s. Wetterunbill
inclement – adj. unfreundlich, rauh
income
s. Einkommen
s. Ertrag, Erträge, Erlös, Erlöse
s. Gewinn(e)
income account
s. Ertragskonto,
s. Erfolgskonto
s. (Volks-)Einkommenskonto
s. Einkommensbilanz, Bilanz der Einkommen
income approach – Verteilungsrechnung (für das BNP / BIP)
income bracket – s. Einkommensstufe
income determination – s. (Volks-)Einkommensbestimmung
income distribution – s. Einkommensverteilung
income elasticity of demand – s. Einkommenselastizität der Nachfrage
income from primary operations – s. (positives) Betriebsergebnis, Betriebsgewinn,
income gearing – s. Financial Leverage, Hebelwirkung des Fremdkapitals
income item – s. Ertragsposten
income method – s. Verteilungsrechnung (für das BNP / BIP)
incomes policy – s. (staatliche) Einkommenspolitik
income statement – s. Erfolgsrechnung, Gewinn- und Verlustrechnung, G+V-Rechnung
income statement item – s. Erfolgsposten

income statement ratio – s. Erfolgskennzahl, Kennzahl der V+G-Rechnung
income tax – s. Einkommensteuer
income tax return – s. Einkommensteuererklärung
income to net sales ratio – s. Umsatzrentabilität
incoming message – s. erhaltene Botschaft / Mitteilung
inconsistency – s. (innerer) Widerspruch, Unvereinbarkeit
incorporate
v. errichten, gründen, (amtlich ins Handelsregister / Firmenbuch als Kapitalgesellschaft) eintragen lassen, Rechtspersönlichkeit verleihen
v. einbauen, eingebaut haben, umfassen, einschließen, inkludieren
incoroporated
adj. gegründet, (als Kapitalgesellschaft im Handelsregister / Firmenbuch) eingetragen
adj. eingebaut, inkorporiert, inkludiert
incorporation
s. Gründung, Errichtung, Verleihung der Rechtspersönlichkeit, handelsrechtliche Eintragung / Registrierung
s. Einbau, Inkludierung
incorporator – s. Gründer / Gründungsmitglied einer Kapitalgesellschaft
INCOTERMS – s. INCOTERMS, Internationale Regeln für die Auslegung der handelsüblichen Vertragsformeln (International Rules for the Interpretation of Trade Terms)
increasing returns to scale – s. steigende Skalenerträge, steigendes Niveaugrenzprodukt
incur – v. auf sich nehmen, eingehen, machen
incur expenses – Aufwendungen / Ausgaben / Spesen machen
expenses are incurred – Aufwendungen entstehen / fallen an
incur an obligation – eine Verpflichtung eingehen / auf sich nehmen
incur a liability – eine Verbindlichkeit eingehen, eine Haftung übernehmen
incur debts – Schulden machen
indebtedness – s. Schuld, Schulden, Schuldenlast, Schuldverhältnis
settle an indebtedness – eine Schuld begleichen
indemnify – v. entschädigen, schadlos halten, entschädigen, freistellen
indemnify sby. against sthg. – jemanden für etwas entschädigen / schadlos halten
indemnify sby. against a liability – jemanden von der Haftung (für etwas) freistellen
independent agent abroad – s. selbständige/r Handelsvertreter/in im Ausland
independent variable – s. unabhängige / exogene / erklärende Variable
index
s. Index, Messzahl
s. Maßstab, Indikator, Anzeiger
index – v. an einen Index binden, indexieren
indexation – s. Indexbindung, Indexkopplung, automatische Valorisierung
indexation relief – s. Ausgleich der kalten Progression durch Indexbindung von Steuertarifen und/oder Freibeträgen, steuerlicher Inflationsausgleich
index currency – s. Indexwährung
index linking – s. Indexbindung, Indexkopplung, automatische Valorisierung
index strip – s. Rückenschild (eines Büroordners)
indicative bid – s. indikatives (nicht bindendes) Zeichnungsangebot im Rahmen eines Bookbuilding-Verfahrens
indirect arbitrage – s. indirekte Arbitrage, Mehrwährungsarbitrage
indirect cost(s) – s. Gemeinkosten, indirekte Kosten
indirect exporting – s. indirekter Export
indirect export promotion – s. indirekte Exportförderung
indirect guarantee – s. indirekte Garantie
indirect intervention – indirekte Intervention
indirect labour – s. Gemeinkostenlöhne, Lohngemeinkosten
indirect leasing – s. indirektes Leasing
indirect manufacturing cost – s. Fertigungsgemeinkosten
indirect material – s. Materialgemeinkosten
indirect quotation – s. Mengennotierung
indirect tax – s. indirekte Steuer
indiscriminate – adj. wahl-, unterschiedslos, unüberlegt
individual policy – s. Reise-, Einzelpolizze
indorsee – s. Indossatar/in
indorse – v. indossieren, mit einem Indossament versehen
indorse in blank – blanko indossieren, mit einem Blankoindossament versehen
indorsement – s. Indossament
indorsement in blank – s. Blankoindossament
indorser – s. Indossant/in
induce
v. motivieren, dazu bringen, veranlassen
v. induzieren, herbeiführen, hervorrufen
wage-induced – lohnkosten-induziert, durch Lohnsteigerungen hervorgerufen
industrial
adj. industriell, Industrie-, Wirtschafts-
adj. Arbeitgeber-Arbeitnehmer betreffend, Arbeits-
adj. branchenmäßig, branchenspezifisch, Branchen-
industrial average – s. (ungewichteter) Industrieaktienindex
industrial action – Arbeitskampf(-maßnahmen)
industrial conflict – s. Arbeitskonflikt, -kampf
industrial democracy – s. Wirtschaftsdemokratie
industrial design – s. Gebrauchsmuster, kleines Patent
industrial equipment – s. Maschinen, Industrieanlagen
industrial goods – s. Produktions-, Industriegüter
industrial goods marketing – s. Produktionsgüter-, Industriegütermarketing
industrialised country – s. Industrieland
industrial mix – s. Wirtschaftsstruktur, Industriestruktur
industrial park – s. Industrie-, Gewerbe-, Businesspark
industrial policy – s. Industriepolitik
industrial production – s. industrielle Produktion
industrial property
s. Immaterialgüterrechte im Sinne des gewerblichen Schutzrechtes, gewerbliche Schutzrechte
s. Betriebsobjekt(e) (Fabriken, Werkstätten usw.)
industrial rates – s. Gemeindesteuer für Industriegebäude und -grundstücke
industrial relations – s. (institutionalisierte) Arbeitgeber-Arbeitnehmer Beziehungen
industrial relations record – s. Bilanz der Arbeitgeber-Arbeitnehmer-Beziehungen
industrials – s. Industrieaktien
industrial share – s. Industrieaktie
industrial standard – s. Industrienorm
industrial structure – s. Wirtschafts-, Industriestruktur
industrial union – s. Industriegewerkschaft, IG
industrial user – s. Großabnehmer/in, gewerbliche/r Kunde/Kundin
industrial wage rate – s. Lohntarif für eine bestimmte Branche, Branchentarif
industry
s. Fertigungsindustrie

s. Wirtschaft, Wirtschaftszweig, Branche, -wirtschaft
s. Arbeitsleben
the two sides of industry - Arbeitgeber und Arbeitnehmer, die beiden Parteien im Arbeitsleben, Sozialpartner
electricity industry - Elektrizitätswirtschaft
chemical industry - Chemiebranche
industry average - s. Branchenkennzahl
industry benchmark - s. Branchenbenchmark, -richtwert
industry standard - s. Branchenschnitt, -vergleichswert, -richtwert, -referenzwert
inefficiency - s. Leerlauf, Vergeudung von Ressourcen, mangelnde Effizienz
infant industry - s. junge Industrie, junger Wirtschaftszweig
infant industry argument - s. Erziehungszollargument
infant industry tariff - s. Erziehungszoll, Schutzzoll für junge Wirtschaftszweige
infiltrate - v. infiltrieren, einsickern, einschleusen
infinitesimal - adj. infinitesimal, unendlich klein
inflation - s. Inflation, Geldentwertung, Kaufkraftverlust
inflation rate - s. Inflationsrate
inflow of capital - s. Kapitalzufluss
inflow of cash
s. Einzahlung, Einnahme
s. (pl.) Einzahlungs-, Einnahmenreihe, Einzahlungsstrom
inflow of funds - s. Zahlungsmittelzufluss, Zufluss von Zahlungsmitteln, Einzahlungen
inform
v. informieren, verständigen, benachrichtigen
v. durchdringen
information management - s. Informationswirtschaft, -management
information management unit - s. informationswirtschaftliche Organisationseinheit, Informationsmanagementabteilung
information needs - s. Informationsbedarf
information overload - s. Informationsüberangebot, -überflutung
information processing - s. Informationsverarbeitung, Datenverarbeitung im weiteren Sinn
information requirements - s. Informationsbedarf
information resources - s. Informationsquellen, -ressourcen
information retrieval - s. Retrieval, Informationsrückgewinnung, Datenabruf
information retrieval system - s. Informationsabruf-System
information system - s. Informationssystem
infrastructure - s. Infrastruktur
infringe - v. übertreten, verletzen
infringe a patent - ein Patent verletzen
infringement - s. Übertretung, Verletzung, Verstoß
inherent - adj. inhärent, innewohnend
inherent vice - s. innerer Verderb
inheritance - s. Erbschaft, Erbmasse, Nachlass
inheritance tax
s. (allgemein) Erbanfallsteuer
s. UK-kombinierte Schenkungs- und Nachlasssteuer
in-house - adj. fimenintern, hausintern, Eigen-
in-house production - s. Eigenfertigung, firmeninterne Produktion
initial cost - s. Anschaffungswert
initial order - s. Erstauftrag
initial public offering - s. Erstemission (an der Börse), öffentliche Erstemission, erstes öffentliches Zeichnungsangebot, Gang an die Börse, IPO
initiate - v. initiieren, auslösen, einleiten
injurious - adj. schädlich
injury test - s. Prüfverfahren zur Schadensfeststellung, Schadensfeststellungsverfahren
injured party - s. Geschädigte/r
ink - s. Tinte, Druckerschwärze
ink cartridge - s. (Tinten-)Druckerpatrone
ink-jet printer - s. Tintenstrahldrucker
in-kind grant - s. Sachhilfe, -subvention, Naturalsubvention
inland marine insurance - s. Binnentransportversicherung
Inland Revenue - (ehemalige) UK-Finanzverwaltung / Steuerbehörde (für direkte Steuern)
inland water transport - s. Binnenschifffahrt
inland waterway - s. Binnenwasserstraße
inland waterway bill of lading - s. Ladeschein
inland waterway carrier - s. Binnenreeder(-ei), Binnenschiffahrts-Reeder(-ei), Binnenfrachtführer
inland waterways transport - s. Binnenschiffahrt
inoperative - adj. ungültig, unwirksam
in-payment form - s. (Schalter-)Zahlschein, Erlagschein
in-process inventories - s. Lagerbestände im (Produktions-)Prozess, prozessnotwendige Lagergüter
input
s. Input, Faktoreinsatz(-menge), Produktionsfaktor(en)
s. (Daten-)Eingabe, Input
s. Lagerzugang
input - v. eingeben
input data - Daten eingeben
input device - s. Eingabegerät
input-output device - s. Ein- / Ausgabegerät, Dialoggerät
input-output ratio - s. (Faktor-)Intensität, Input-Output-Verhältnis, Mitteleinsatz-Ergebnis-Relation
input-output table - s. Input-Output-Tabelle, tabellenförmige Darstellung der interindustriellen Verflechtung
input tax - s. (Mehrwert-)Vorsteuer
inquiry s. Anfrage
make an inquiry by telephone - eine telefonische Anfrage machen, telefonisch anfragen
inquiry form - s. Anfragsformular
inquiry service - s. Auskunfts-, Informationssystern
insect pest - s. Schädlingsinsekt, schädliches Insekt
insert - v. einschieben, einführen
inside director - s. geschäftsführendes Mitglied des Führungsgremiums einer UK- / US- Kapitalgesellschaft, Geschäftsführer, Vorstandsmitglied mit Aufsichtsratsfunktion, Aufsichtsratsmitglied mit Vorstandsagenden
insolvency
s. Überschuldung, Insolvenz (auf Grund von Überschuldung), Zahlungsunfähigkeit
s. Illiquidität, Insolvenz (auf Grund von Illiquidität)
insolvent
adj. zahlungsunfähig, insolvent (auf Grund von Überschuldung)
adj. illiquid, insolvent (auf Grund kurzfristiger Illiquidität)
inspection - s. Inspektion, Überprüfung, (Waren-)Abnahme
instalment - s. Rate, Teilbetrag
pay in instalments - in Raten zahlen
buy on the instalment plan - auf Raten kaufen
instalment sale - s. Ratenkauf, -geschäft, Teilzahlungsgeschäft
instant messaging - s. Instant Messaging, Sofortbotschaftsdienste, internetbasierter Echtzeitdienst
Institute of Chartered Accountants - s. einer der UK-Berufsverbände für Wirtschaftsprüfer
institutional advertising - s. Firmenimage-, Repräsentations-, Goodwillwerbung

institutional arrangements – s. institutionelle Ordnung / Struktur
institutional investor – s. institutioneller Anleger, Kapitalsammelstelle
in-store boutique – s. In-Store-Boutique, Boutique-im-Geschäft
instruct – v. anweisen, beauftragen
instructing bank – s. Erstbank (bei einer indirekten Bankgarantie)
instruction form – s. Auftragsformular (für Dokumenteninkassi), Dokumenteninkassoauftrag
instrument – s. Urkunde, Instrument, (Wert-)Papier, Objekt (z. B. Geldmarktobjekt)
financial instrument – s. Finanzinstrument, -objekt
instrumental objective – s. Sekundärziel
instrument payable to order – s. Orderpapier
insulate – v. isolieren
insurance – s. Versicherung, Versicherungswesen
write insurance – Versicherung(en) abschließen / annehmen
effect / take out insurance for sthg. – für etwas eine Versicherung abschließen, etwas versichern
insurance agent – s. Versicherungsvertreter/in
insurance broker – s. Versicherungsmakler/in
insurance company – s. Versicherungsgesellschaft, Versicherung
insurance cover – s. Versicherungsschutz, Versicherungsdeckung, Versicherung
insurance coverage – s. Versicherungsschutz, -deckung, Versicherung
insurance coverage attaches – Versicherung(-sschutz) gilt
Insurance Expense – s. Versicherungsaufwand(-skonto), (das Konto) Versicherungsaufwand
insurance industry – s. Versicherungswirtschaft
insurance market – s. Versicherungsbörse
insurance policy – s. Versicherungspolizze, -schein
insurance premium – s. Versicherungsprämie
insured – s. Versicherte/r
insured party – s. Versicherte/r
insured percentage – s. Deckungs-, Garantiequote
insurer – s. Versicherer
insurrection – s. Aufruhr, Aufstand
intangible assets – s. immaterielles Anlagevermögen
intangible fixed assets – s. immaterielles Anlagevermögen
intangible goods – s. unkörperliche Sachen, Rechte und/oder Dienstleistungen
intangible personal property – s. unkörperliche Sachen, Forderungs- und / oder Immaterialgüterrechte
intangibles
s. immaterielles Anlagevermögen
s. unwägbare Faktoren, Imponderabilien, nicht quantifizierbare Elemente
integrated mailing machine – s. kombinierte Postbearbeitungsmaschine
integrated pest management – s. integrierte Schädlingsbekämpfung, integrierter Pflanzenschutz
Integrated Services Digital Network – s. dienst-integriertes digitales Netzwerk, ISDN
integrated transport – s. kombinierter Verkehr
integration – s. Integration, Unternehmungszusammenschluss, betriebliche Konzentrationen
intellectual property – s. Immaterialgüterrechte, geistiges Eigentum
intellectual property rights – s. Immaterialgüterrechte, geistige Eigentumsrechte
intelligent terminal – s. intelligentes Terminal / Datenendgerät
interact – v. aufeinander einwirken, miteinander umgehen
interactive – adj. interaktiv, Dialog-
interactive mode of operation – s. interaktiver Betrieb, Dialogbetrieb
interactive terminal – s. Dialoggerät
interbank lending – s. (Vergabe von) Zwischenbankkredite(n)
interbank market – s. Zwischenbankmarkt, Geldmarkt im engeren Sinn
interbank rate – s. Zwischenbankzinssatz
interbank transaction – s. Zwischenbankgeschäft, -transaktion
inter-company transaction – s. konzerninterne / firmeninterne Transaktion
interest
s. Interesse, Engagement
s. Interessenvertretung, Lobby, hinter (einer Organisation / Branche) stehende Kreise
s. Zinsen
s. Beteiligung (an einer Unternehmung), Anteil
s. Unternehmen, an dem eine Beteiligung gehalten wird, Beteiligung
s. Recht, Pfandrecht
automotive interests – Lobby der Fahrzeugindustrie, Autolobby
industrial interests – Industrielobby
bear / carry interest – Zinsen abwerfen, sich verzinsen
interest arbitrage – s. Zinsarbitrage
interest-bearing – adj. verzinslich
interest-bearing securities – s. verzinsliche Wertpapiere
interest clause – s. Zinsklausel
inter-company transaction – s. konzerninterne / zwischenbetriebliche Transaktion
interest earned – Zinserträge
interest expense – s. Zinsaufwand
Interest Expense – s. Zinsaufwand(-skonto)
interest income – s. Zinsertrag/-erträge
interest on arrears – s. Verzugszinsen
interest rate – s. Zinssatz, -fuß
interest rate collar – s. Zins-Collar, Kombination von Zinsobergrenze und Zinsuntergrenze
interest rate controls – s. Zinsregelung, Zinssteuerung, zinspolitisch Maßnahmen
interest rate differential – s. Zinsdifferenz, -gefälle
interest rate future – (börsengehandelter) Zinsterminkontrakt, Zinsfuture, Zins-Future
interest rate option – s. Zinssatzoption, Zinsoption
interest rate risk – s. Zinsrisiko, Zinssatzrisiko
interest rate swap – s. Zinsswap, Zinssatzswap
interest subsidy – s. Zinsstützung, -subvention, -förderung
interface – s. Schnittstelle
interfirm comparison – s. zwischenbetrieblicher Vergleich, Betriebsvergleich
interim dividend – s. Zwischen-, Abschlagsdividende
intermediary – s. Mittler/in, Vermittler/in, Mittelsmann, Mittelsfrau
act as intermediary – vermitteln, als Vermittler tätig sein
intermediate input – s. Vorleistung
intermodal – adj. intermodal, verschiedene Verkehrsmittel kombinierend, verkehrsträgerunabhängig
intermodal transport – s. kombinierter / intermodaler Verkehr, Kombiverkehr, intermodaler Transport
intermodal unit load – s. intermodale Ladeeinheit
internal audit – s. Innenrevision, interne Rechnungsprüfung
internal auditing – s. Innenrevision, interne Rechnungsprüfung
internal finance – s. Innenfinanzierung

internal hedging technique – s. interne Kurssicherungstechnik / Kurssicherungsmaßnahme
internalise – v. internalisieren, mit einbeziehen
internally developed goodwill – s. originärer Firmenwert
internal market – s. Binnenmarkt (EWG)
internal rate of return – s. interner Zinsfuß
internal rate of return method – s. interne-Zinsfuß-Methode, Methode des internen Zinsfußes
internal service department – s. Verwaltungs- und Finanzabteilung einer Werbeagentur
internal storage unit – s. Primär-, Haupt-, Arbeits-, Zentralspeicher
internal tariff – s. Binnenzoll
international access code – s. internationale Vorwahlnummer
International Bank for Reconstruction and Development
s. Internationale Bank für Wiederaufbau und Wirtschaftliche Entwicklung (Weltbank)
International Chamber of Commerce – s. Internationale Handelskammer
international commercial terms – s. internationale Handelsklauseln
International Development Association – s. Internationale Entwicklungsorganisation, IDA
international double taxation – s. internationale / echte Doppelbesteuerung
international funds transfer – s. internationale Banküberweisung
international leasing – s. internationales Leasing
international marketing – s. internationales Marketing
International Monetary Fund – s. Internationaler Währungsfonds, IWF
international money transfer – s. internationale Banküberweisung
International Organization for Standardization – s. Internationale Organisation für Normung, Internationale Normungsorganisation, ISO
international private law – s. interntionales Privatrecht
Internet banking – Online Banking, elektronsiches Banking, E-Banking
Internet marketing – s. Internet-Marketing, elektronisches Marketing, Online-Marketing
Internet shopping – s. E-Shopping, Internet-Shopping, Internetkauf
interpersonal skills – s. interpersonelle / zwischenmenschliche Fähigkeiten
interplay – s. Zusammenwirken, Zusammenspiel
interstatement ratios – s. kombinierte Bilanz- und Erfolgskennzahlen
intertemporal comparison – s. Zeitreihenvergleich
intervention – s. Intervention, Eingreifen, Eingriff, Lenkungsmaßnahme(n)
intervention level – s. Interventionspreis, -kurs
intervention point – s. Interventionspunkt
intimate – v. zu verstehen geben, wissen lassen
intra-group accounts payable – s. konzerninterne (Buch-)Verbindlichkeiten (aufgrund von Warenlieferungen und Leistungen)
intra-group accounts receivable – s. konzerninterne (Buch-)Forderungen (aufgrund von Warenlieferungen und Leistungen)
intra-group investment – s. konzerninterne Kapitalanlagen / Investition(en)
intra-group payables – s. konzerninterne Verbindlichkeiten (aufgrund von Warenlieferungen und Leistungen)
intra-group receivables – s. konzerninterne Forderungen (aufgrund von Warenlieferungen und Leistungen)
intra-group transaction – s. konzerninterne Transaktion, konzerninterner Geschäftsfall
intra-firm trade – s. firmeninterner / konzerninterner/ unternehmesinterner (Außen-)Handel
intra-industry trade – s. brancheninterner Handel
intranet – s. Intranet, firmeninternes / hausinternes Netz
intrapreneurial unit – s. autonome (firmeninterne) Projektgruppe
intrapreneurship – s. Unternehmertum / unternehmerisches Verhalten in (Groß-)Unternehmen
intrinsic value
s. innerer Wert, Wert an sich, Substanzwert, Materialwert
s. intrinsischer / innerer Wert einer Option
inventory – s. Lager, Lagerbestand, Lagerbestände, Vorratsvermögen, Lagergüter
inventory-carrying – s. Lagerhaltung
inventory control – s. Lagerwirtschaft, -management
inventory investment – s. Lagerinvestition
inventory loan – s. (kommerzieller) Warenlombardkredit
inventory management – s. Lagerwirtschaft, -management
inventory records – s. Lagerbuchhaltung
inventory-taking – s. Inventur, Bestandsaufnahme
inventory turnover – s. Lagerumschlag(-shäufigkeit)
invest – v. investieren, anlegen, veranlagen, hineinstecken, Kapital bilden, einsteigen
a speculator invested in a currency – ein Spekulant, der in eine Währung eingestiegen / investiert ist / hat
invest in / into a project – in ein Projekt investieren
investee – s. Target(-firma); Zielgesellschaft (einer Investition); Firma, an der eine Beteilung besteht / erworben werden soll; Investitionsempfänger; Investitionsnehmer
investing community – s. Anleger-, Investorenkreise, die Anleger / Investoren
investment
s. (Real-)Investition, Realkapitalbildung, Kapitalbindung
s. Finanzanlage, Finanzinvestition, Kapitalbindung
s. (pl.) (kurzfristige / langfristige) Finanzanlagen, Wertpapiere (des Umlauf- / Anlageververmögens)
investment appraisal – s. Investitionsrechnung
investment bank – s. Investmentbank, Effektenbank
investment certificate – s. Investmentzertifikat, Investmentanteilschein
investment company – s. Investmentgesellschaft, Investmentfonds, Kapitalanlagegesellschaft
investment expenditure – s. Investitionsaufwand, Ausgaben für Investitionen, Investition(en)
investment fund – s. Investmentfonds, Kapitalanlagegesellschaft
investment goods – s. Investitionsgüter
investment grant – s. Investitionsprämie
investment incentive – s. Investitionsanreiz, Investitionsförderung(-smaßnahme)
investment income – s. Kapitalerträge (Zinsen, Dividenden und sonstige Kapitalerträge)
investment industry – s. Investment-, Veranlagungsbranche
investment management – s. Finanzanlagenverwaltung, Verwaltung von Kapitalanlagen
investment medium – s. Anlageobjekt, Anlagemedium
investment performance – s. Investment-Performance, Investitions-, Anlageergebnis, Gesamtrentabilität einer Finanzanlage
investment ratio – s. Rentabilitätskennzahl
investments – s. Finanzanlagen
investment scheme – s. Investment-, Anlageprogramm, Anlagemodell

investment tax credit – s. Steuergutschrift / Steuerabzug / Absetzbetrag für Investitionen
investment trust – s. geschlossener Investmentfonds, Investmentfonds nach dem Gesellschaftsprinzip
investor – s. (Kapital-)Anleger/in, Investor/in, Geldgeber/in, Kapitalgeber/in
invisible account – s. Dienstleistungsbilanz
invisible earnings – s. Deviseneingänge aus dem Dienstleistungsverkehr
invisible exports – s. Dienstleistungsexporte, unsichtbare Exporte
invisible imports – s. Dienstleistungsimporte, unsichtbare Importe
invisible payments – s. Devisenausgänge aus dem Dienstleistungsverkehr
invisibles – s. Dienstleistungsverkehr
invisibles deficit – s. Dienstleistungsbilanzdefizit, -abgang, -passivum
invisibles surplus – s. Dienstleistungsbilanzüberschuss, -aktivum
invisible trade – s. Dienstleistungsverkehr
invitation for tenders – s. Ausschreibung (im engeren Sinn)
invitation to tender – s. Ausschreibung (im engeren Sinn)
invitation to treat – s. Einladung zur Stellung eines Antrages, Aufforderung zur Abgabe eines Angebotes
invoice – s. Rechnung, Faktura
prepare / make out an invoice – eine Rechnung ausstellen
settle an invoice – eine Rechnung zahlen / begleichen
invoice – v. fakturieren, in Rechnung stellen
invoice in the buyer's currency – in der Währung des Käufers fakturieren
invoice amount – s. Rechnungs-, Fakturabetrag
invoice form – s. Rechnungsformular
invoicing – s. Fakturierung
invoicing in domestic currency – s. Fakturierung in heimischer Währung
involve
v. involvieren, mit sich bringen, verbunden sein mit,
v. sich handeln um
This involves trade-offs. – Das bringt auch Nachteile mit sich.
the company involved – die Gesellschaft, um die es sich handelt; die in Frage stehende Gesellschaft
involvement – s. (emotionales) Engagement, Anteilnahme, Interesse, Verwicklung
inward directed investment – direkte Investitionen aus dem Ausland, passive Direktinvestititionen
inward investment – s. Investitions-, Kapitalzufluss, Kapitalzugang
inward processing – s. aktiver Veredelungsverkehr
IPM – integrated pest management (siehe)
IPO – initial public offering (siehe)
IPRs – s. intellectual property rights (siehe)
Irish Industrial Development Agency – s. Irische Betriebsansiedlungsgesellschaft
iron ore – s. Eisenerz
IRR method – internal rate of return method (siehe)
irredeemable bond – s. ewige Rente, Rentenanleihe
irreplaceable – adj. nicht reproduzierbar
irrevocable credit – s. unwiderrufliches Akkreditiv
ISDN – Integrated Services Digital Network (siehe)
ISO – International Organization for Standardization (siehe)
ISO mark – s. ISO-Zeichen
ISO standard – s. ISO-Norm
issue
s. Problem, Frage, Sache, Punkt, Anliegen
s. Emission / Ausgabe / Begebung (von Wertpapieren)
s. Ausstellen / Ausstellung (von Dokumenten)
s. Entnahme / Ausfolgung (von Material aus dem Lager)
issue
v. emittieren, ausgeben, begeben
v. ausstellen, eröffnen
v. entnehmen, ausfolgen
issue shares – Aktien emittieren
issue a certificate of origin – ein Ursprungszeugnis ausstellen
issue a letter of credit – ein Akkreditiv eröffnen
issued capital – s. begebenes / ausgegebenes / emittiertes Kapital
issue price – s. Emissionskurs
issuer
s. Aussteller/in
s. Emittent/in
issuer of a guarantee – s. Garantiegeber, -aussteller, Garant
issuing agency – s. ausstellende Stelle
issuing bank
s. Akkreditivbank
s. Garantiebank
issuing company – s. Emittent/in, emittierende / begebende Gesellschaft
issuing house – s. UK-Emissionsbank, Merchant Bank mit Spezialisierung auf Emissionsgeschäfte
item
s. Posten, Punkt (in einer Aufstellung)
s. Artikel, Produkt, Gut
itemise – v. Punkt für Punkt anführen, im Einzelnen angeben, detaillieren, spezifizieren, aufgliedern
itemised statement – s. detaillierte Aufstellung
item of capital equipment – s. Anlagegut
item of equipment – s. Gerät

J

JAVA – s. JAVA-Programmiersprache
jawbone – s. Wirtschaftslenkung durch Überredung, Seelenmassage
jeopardise – v. gefährden, in Gefahr bringen
jettison – v. über Bord werfen
job
s. Arbeitsplatz, Job, Beschäftigung
s. Auftrag, Aufgabe, Bearbeitung (Datenverarbeitung)
s. (Fertigungs-)Auftrag
create jobs – Arbeitsplätze schaffen
on the job – am Arbeitsplatz, während der Arbeit
perform a job – eine Aufgabe durchführen
jobber
s. (brit.)Effekteneigenhändler / Wertpapierhändler
s. (am.) Großhändler
jobber's turn – s. (Gewinn-)Spanne eines Jobbers / Effekteneigenhändlers
jobcentre – s. Arbeitsamt
job-hunting – s. Arbeitsplatz-, Stellensuche
joblessness – s. Arbeitslosigkeit
jobless rate – Arbeitslosenrate
job opportunities – s. Beschäftigungsmöglichkeiten, offene Stellen
job-order production – s. Einzel-, Kundenauftragsfertigung
job satisfaction – s. Arbeitszufriedenheit
jobseeker – s. Arbeitssuchende/r
jobseekers allowance – s. Arbeitslosenunterstützung
job-sharing – s. Jobsharing, Arbeitsplatzteilung
join – v. sich anschließen, beitreten
join forces – sich verbünden / zusammentun
joint – adj. gemeinsam, gemeinschaftlich, Gemeinschafts-, verbunden
joint and several liability – s. gesamtschuldnerische Haftung
jointly and severally liable – adj. gesamtschuldnerisch
be jointly and severally liable – gesamtschuldnerisch haften
joint venture – s. Joint Venture, Gemeinschaftsunternehmen
journal – s. Journal, Grundbuch
juggernaut – s. großer Brummer, Straßenungetüm, Großlastkraftwagen
junk bond – s. Ramsch-Anleihe, Schund-Anleihe, Risiko-Anleihe, hochverzinsliche Unternehmesanleihe mit niedriger Bonitätseinstufung
junior executive – s. Nachwuchsführungskraft
junior management – s. Nachwuchsführungskräfte
junior manager – s. Nachwuchsführungskraft
jurisdiction
s. Rechtsprechung, Gerichtsbarkeit
s. Gerichtsstand
just-in-time – adj. lagerlos, vorratsarm

K

K – s. K, Kilo ($10^3 = 1000$)
keen – adj. scharf, hart, stark, knapp
keen prices – knapp kalkulierte Preise
key – s. Taste
key account – s. Hauptkunde/-kundin, Großabnehmer/in
key account management – s. Key-Account Management, Betreuung von Schlüsselkunden
keyboard – s. Tastatur
keyboard terminal – s. Tasten-, Tastaturterminal
key in – v. eintippen
key interest rate – s. Leitzinssatz
key interest rates – s. Leitzinsen
key phone – s. Tastentelefon, Telefon mit Wahltastatur
key variable – s. Schlüssel-, Hauptvariable
killing – s. Erfolg, Reibach, Beute
make a killing – abräumen, abkassieren, das große Geld machen
kilobyte – s. Kilobyte (2^{10} – 1024 Bytes)
kind – s. Gattung, Klasse, Sorte
in kind – in natura, in Form einer Sachleistung / von Sachleistungen
investment in kind – s. Sacheinlage
in-kind allowance – s. Deputat
knock down
v. zuschlagen, den Zuschlag (bei einer Auktion) erteilen
v. zerlegen, abbauen
knock down to the highest bidder – dem Meistbietenden zuschlagen
knock-down stand – (abbaubarer) Messe-Modulstand
knocking copy – s. herabsetzende / verunglimpfende Werbung

L

label
s. Etikett, Aufschrift, Aufkleber
s. Bezeichnung, Name
s. Beschriftung, Produktkennzeichnung
s. Marke
label
v. etikettieren, beschriften, mit Etiketten versehen
v. bezeichnen, benennen
labelling – s. Etikettierung, Beschriftung, Auszeichnung, Kennzeichnung
labelling legislation – s. gesetzliche Vorschriften zur Produktkennzeichung, Produktkennzeichnungsrecht
labelling requirements – s. Produktkennzeichnungsvorschriften, -recht
labor relations – s. (am.) (institutionalisierte) Arbeitgeber-Arbeitnehmer-Beziehungen
labor union – s. (am.) Gewerkschaft
labour
s. Arbeit
s. Arbeit (als Produktionsfaktor)
s. Arbeitskräfte, Arbeitnehmer, Arbeiterschaft, Arbeiter
child labour – Kinderarbeit
labour and social standards – s. Arbeits- und Sozialstandards, Arbeits- und Sozialnormen
labour exchange – s. Arbeitsamt
labour force – s. Arbeitskräftevolumen, Arbeitskräftepotenzial, Erwerbsbevölkerung
labour-intensive – adj. arbeitsintensiv
labour productivity – s. Arbeitsproduktivität
labour relations – s. (institutionalierte) Arbeitgeber-Arbeitnehmer-Beziehungen
labour resources – s. Arbeitskraftressourcen, Arbeitskräftepotenzial
labour turnover – s. Mitarbeiterfluktuation, Fluktuationsziffer
lack – s. Mangel, Fehlen
lack of foreign exchange – Devisenmangel
lag – s. Lag, (Reaktions-)Verzögerung, Reaktionszeit, negative Phasenverschiebung
lag behind – v. nachhinken
lagging – s. Lagging, Zahlungsverzögerung
lagging indicator – s. Spätindikator, nachlaufender Konjunkturindikator
LAN – local area network (siehe)
land
s. Grundstück, Grundbesitz
s. Boden
Land – s. (das Konto) Grundstücke, Grundstückkonto
land carrier – s. Frachtführer im Landverkehr
land conveyance – s. Landfahrzeug
landing charges – s. Landungs-, Löschkosten
landlord – s. Grundbesitzer/in, Hauseigentümer/in, Vermieter/in
land-locked country – s. Binnenland
land prices – s. Grundstückpreise
lapse – v. verfallen, außer Kraft treten, hinfällig werden, Gültigkeit verlieren, ungültig werden
an offer lapses – ein Angebot verliert seine Gültigkeit
laptop – s. Laptop, Laptop-Computer, Laptop-Rechner (netzunabhängiger tragbarer PC / AT)
large caps – large cap stocks (siehe)
large cap stocks – s. Hauptwerte, Aktien von Firmen mit großer Börsenkapitalisierung
large-scale – adj. / adv. in großem Ausmaß / Stil
large-scale use – Anwendung / Einsatz in großem Stil
LASH – Lighter Aboard Ship (siehe *LASH-vessel*)
LASH-vessel – s. LASH-Schiff, Schwimmcontainerschiff
last-in-first-out method – s. LIFO-Methode (Pauschalbewertung des Vorratsvermögens zum Einstandspreis der ersten Lagerzugänge der Rechnungsperiode)
late delivery – s. verspätete Lieferung, Lieferverzug
latitude – s. Spielraum, Freiheit
launch – s. Markt-, Produkteinführung, Einführungsphase, Launch
launch – v. einführen, starten, lancieren
launch a product – ein Produkt (auf einem Markt) einführen
law
s. Gesetz
s. Recht
local laws – Gesetze / Rechtslage im Zielland
under Austrian law – nach österreichischem Recht
law of comparative advantage – s. Gesetz des komparativen (Kosten-)Vorteils
law of contract – s. Vertragsrecht
law of diminishing returns – Gesetz vom abnehmenden Ertragszuwachs
lawsuit – s. Zivilprozess, Rechtsstreit
lay down – v. festlegen, festsetzen
layoff – s. Entlassung / Abbau (von Arbeitskräften)
lay off – v. abbauen, entlassen, freisetzen
layout – s. Layout, Gestaltung, Satzspiegel
L/C – letter of credit (siehe *documentary letter of credit*)
LCD – liquid crystal display (siehe)
LCL
less-than-carload (siehe)
less-than-container load (siehe)
LDC
least developed country (siehe)
less developed country (siehe)
L/C terms – s. Akkreditivbedingungen
lead – s. Blei
lead
v. führen, leiten, lenken
v. voraneilen, vorangehen, früher kommen als
event A leads event B – Ereignis A geht dem Ereignis B voraus
lead auditor – s. Prüfungsleiter/in, Leiter/in der Abschlussprüfung
lead bank – s. Lead-Bank, federführende (Konsortial-)Bank, Konsortialführer/in
leader item – s. Lockvogelangebot
leader pricing – s. Verwendung / Einsatz von Lockvogelangeboten
leading – s. Leading, Zahlungsbeschleunigung
leading-edge – adj. innovativ, topaktuell, Spitzen-
leading-edge technology – Spitzentechnologie
leading indicator – s. Frühindikator
lead underwriter – s. Lead Underwriter, federführendes Mitglied eines Emissionskonsortiums
leaflet – s. (kleiner) Prospekt, Werbeblatt, Werbezettel
leak – v. auslaufen, austreten, entströmen, entweichen
leakproof – adj.(leck-)dicht, lecksicher, (flüssigkeits-)undurchlässig
lease – s. Leasingvertrag, Leasing

lease
v. vermieten, verpachten, leasen
v. mieten, pachten, leasen
lease contract – s. Leasingvertrag
lease of land and buildings – s. Immobilienleasing(-vertrag)
leash – s. Leine, Spielraum
keep on a long / short leash – an einer langen / kurzen Leine halten, viel / wenig Spielraum geben
leasing – s. Leasing
leasing company – s. Leasinggesellschaft
least developed country – s. armes Entwicklungsland
leave – v. verlassen, weggehen, ausscheiden
workers leaving a firm – ausscheidende Arbeitskräfte
ledger – s. Hauptbuch, Hauptbuchkontengruppe
ledger account – s. Hauptbuchkonto
legacy – s. Erbe, Vermächtnis, Altlast
legal debt – s. tatsächliche / effektive Schuld, rechtlich bestehendes Schuldverhältnis
legal entity – s. juristische Person
legalise – v. beglaubigen
legalisation
s. Beglaubigung
s. Legalisierung
legal person – s. juristische Person
legal personality – s. juristische Person, Rechtspersönlichkeit
legal reserves – s. Mindestreserven (erforderliche Mindestsichtguthaben der Kreditinstitute bei der Zentralbank)
legal tender – s. gesetzliches Zahlungsmittel
legion – s. Legion, große Zahl
Their number is legion. – Es gibt unzählige davon.
legislation – s. Legislatur, Gesetzgebung, Gesetze, gesetzliche Vorschriften, Recht
leisure – s. Freizeit
lender – s. Kreditgeber/in
lender of last resort – s. Kreditgeber / Refinanzierungsinstitut letzter Instanz (Notenbank)
lender's option – s. Zins-Put
lending – s. Kreditvergabe, Aktkivgeschäft
lending syndicate – s. Kreditkonsortium
length of notice – s. Kündigungsfrist
length of service – s. Dienstalter, Anstellungsdauer
less developed country – s. (veralteter Ausdruck für) Entwicklungsland
lessee – s. Leasingnehmer
lesser media – s. (weniger wichtige) sonstige Medien (wie Adressbücher)
lessor – s. Leasinggeber/in
less-than-carload freight – s. Stückgut
less-than-container load – s. Container-Teilladung, Container-Sammelgut LCL
less-than-wagon load – s. Stückgut
let
v. vermieten, verpachten, mieten, pachten
v. zuschlagen, Zuschlag erteilen
let a contract – den Zuschlag für einen ausgeschriebenen Auftrag erteilen
letter-box company – s. Briefkastenfirma
letterhead – s. Briefkopf, Briefkopf-, Firmenpapier
letter of advice – s. Verständigung, Aviso, Anzeige
letter of complaint – s. Beschwerde(-brief), Mängelrüge
letter of credit – s. Akkreditiv
open a letter of credit – ein Akkreditiv eröffnen
issue a letter of credit – ein Akkreditiv eröffnen
apply for a letter of credit – ein Akkreditiv beantragen
letting a contract – s. Zuschlag, Auftragserteilung
level – s. Ebene, Niveau, Höhe, Ausmaß
level – adj. eben, gleichmäßig
level playing field – gleiche Vorraussetzungen / Vorbedingungen, Waffengleichheit
level of activity – s. Ausmaß der Beschäftigung, Beschäftigungsniveau
level of aggregation – s. Aggregationsniveau
level of economic activity – s. Konjunktur(-lage), Umfang der Wirtschaftstätigkeit
level of interest rates – s. Zinsniveau
level of wages – s. Lohnniveau
lever – s. Hebel
leverage – s. Leverage, Finanzhebel, Hebelwirkung, Fremdkapitalwirkung auf die Eigenkapitalrentabilität
leverage – v. wirksam einsetzen, wirtschaftlich effizient verwerten
leveraged – adj. mit hohem Fremdkapitalanteil
leveraged buyout – s. Leveraged Buyout, (stark) fremdfinanzierte Firmenübernahme
leveraged takeover – s. Leveraged Buyout, (stark) fremdfinanzierte Firmenübernahme
levy – s. Abgabe, Steuer, Beitrag, Umlage
levy – v. einheben, erheben
levy taxes – Steuern einheben
levy import duties – Importzölle einheben
LLP – s. limited liability partnership
liabilities and capital – s. Verbindlichkeiten und Eigenkapital
liability
s. Verbindlichkeit, Schuld, Zahlungsverpflichtung, Zahllast
s. Passivposten, (pl.) Verbindlichkeiten, Passiva
s. Haftung, Haftpflicht, Pflicht, Verpflichtung
meet one's liabilities – seinen Zahlungsverpflichtungen nachkommen
meet a liability – einer Verpflichtung nachkommen
assume a liability – eine Verpflichtung übernehmen / eingehen
be under liability – haften, verpflichtet sein
liability account – s. passives Bestandskonto
liability for product guarantees – s. Produkthaftung
liability insurance – s. Haftpflichtversicherung
liability reserve – s. (etwa) Rücklage
liable
adj. haftbar, verantwortlich
adj. pflichtig, verpflichtet
adj. neigend (zu), anfällig (für)
fully liable – voll haftbar
be fully liable – voll haften
be primarily liable – als Hauptschuldner haften
be secondarily liable – subsidiär / akzessorisch haften
liable to tax – steuerpflichtig
liable to pay – verpflichtet zu zahlen
liable to problems – problemanfällig
liaison – s. Verbindung, Zusammenarbeit
maintain a liaison – eine Verbindung aufrechterhalten
LIBOR – London Interbank Offered Rate (siehe)
licence – s. Lizenz, Konzession
produce under licence – im Rahmen einer Lizenz fertigen
licence fee – s. Lizenzgebühr
license – v. Linzenz(en) vergeben, erteilen
license a patent – eine Patentlizenz erteilen / vergeben
license a process – Lizenz für ein Fertigungsverfahren erteilen / vergeben
licensee – s. Lizenznehmer/in
licensing – s. Lizenzvergabe, -gewährung, -geschäft
licensing agreement – s. Lizenzvertrag
licensor – s. Lizenzgeber/in

lien
s. Zurückbehaltungsrecht
s. Pfandrecht, Belastung eines Vermögenswertes, hypothekarische Belastung
life
s. Lebens-, Nutzungsdauer, Nutzungszeit,
s. Lagerfähigkeit, Haltbarkeit
s. Laufzeit
life assurance – s. Lebensversicherung
life cycle – s. (Produkt-)Lebenszyklus, (Produkt-)Lebenslauf
natural life cycle – natürlicher / ökologischer Lebenslauf (eines Produktes)
life expectancy – s. Lebenserwartung
life insurance – s. Lebensversicherung
life insurance policy – s. Lebensversicherungspolizze
lifestyle – s. Lebensform, -stil
life-support system – s. lebenserhaltendes System
lifetime gift – s. Schenkung unter Lebenden / inter vivos
LIFFE – London International Financial Futures Exchange (siehe)
LIFO – last-in, last-out (method) (siehe)
lift
v. anheben, heben, erhöhen
v. aufheben, abschaffen
lifting device – s. Hebevorrichtung
lighter – s. Leichter(-schiff), Lastkahn
lighterage – s. Leichtergebühr, Kosten für die Leichterung
light lorry – s. Leichtkraftwagen
lightning – s. Blitz, Blitzschlag
lime – s. Kalk
limelight – s. Rampenlicht
limitation of liability – s. Haftungsbeschränkung
limited liability partnership – s. Personengesellschaft mit beschränkter Haftung (für alle Teilhaber)
limited-line store – s. Fachgeschäft, -händler
limited partner – s. Teilhafter/in, Kommanditist/in
limited partnership – s. Kommanditgesellschaft, KG
limited-service wholesaler – s. Abholgroßmarkt, Großhändler mit beschränktem Serviceangebot
line
s. Produktlinie, Waren-, Artikelgruppe
s. Gewerbe, Sparte, Branche, Fach, Wirtschaftszweig, Tätigkeitsbereich, Beruf
s. politische Linie, Grundsatz, Richtung, Strategie
s. Übereinstimmung
s. Leitung, elektrische Leitung / Kabel, (pl.) Netz
s. Telefonanschluss
on divisional lines – nach divisionalen Grundsätzen, nach dem Geschäftsspartenprinzip
in line with – in Übereinstimmung mit
go on line – ins /ans Netz gehen
line-and-staff organisation – s. Stablinienorganisation
linear programming – s. lineares Programmieren
line authority – s. Leitungsbefugnis(se)
line management – s. Linienmanagement
line manager – s. Linieninstanzinhaber/in, Linieninstanz, Vorgesetzte/r, Boss, Chef/in
line of command – s. Befehlsweg
line of credit – s. Kreditlinie, -fazilität, -rahmen
line organisation – s. Linienorganisation
liner service – s. Liniendienst, -verkehr
line unit – s. Linieninstanz, -stelle
liquified natural gas carrier – s. Flüssiggastanker
liquid assets – s. flüssige Mittel, Liquidität
liquidated damages – s. im Vorhinein festgesetzter Schadenersatz, Vertragsstrafe / Konventionalstrafe in der Höhe des zu erwartenden Schadens
liquidating sale – s. Glattstellungsverkauf, Verkauf zur Glattstellung
liquidation – s. Abwicklung, Liquidierung, Glattstellung
liquidation dividend – Liquidationsdividende
liquidation of a futures contract – Glattstellung eines börsengehandelten Terminkontraktes
liquid crystal display – s. Flüssigkristallanzeige
liquid current assets – s. kurzfristiges Umlaufvermögen
liquidity
s. (Geld-)Liquidität, (Geld-)Flüssigkeit
s. (Markt-)Liquidität
s. flüssige Mittel
liquidity ratio – s. Liquiditätskennzahl
list price – s. Listenpreis
list
v. anführen, auflisten
v. notieren
be listed – (an der Börse) notieren
listed company – börsennotierte Gesellschaft
listed securities – börsennotierte / börsengängige Wertpapiere
listing – s. Börsennotierung, -zulassung
listing requirements – s. Voraussetzungen für die Börsennotierung / Börsenzulassung von Wertpapieren, Börsenzulassungskriterien
list price – s. Listenpreis
litigation – s. Rechtsstreit, Prozess
litosphere – s. Litosphäre
livelihood – s. Lebensunterhalt
livestock – s. (lebendes) Vieh
live up to – v. gerecht werden, entsprechen, erfüllen, halten
live up to a promise – ein Versprechen halten
LLDC – (veraltete Abkürzung für) *least developed country* (siehe)
Lloyd's – Lloyd's-Versicherungsbörse
Lloyd's broker – s. Maklermitglied bei Lloyd's
Lloyd's underwriter – s. Einzelversicherer bei Lloyd's
LLP – s. limited liability partnership (siehe)
load – v. beladen, aufladen, verladen
loading berth – s. (Schiffs-)Ladeplatz
loading broker – s. Schiffsmakler/in
loading charges – s. Ladekosten, -gebühren
loan – s. Kredit, Darlehen
raise a loan – einen Kredit aufnehmen
take out a loan – s. einen Kredit aufnehmen
grant a loan – einen Kredit gewähren
extend a loan – einen Kredit gewähren / verlängern
loan agreement – s. Kreditvertrag
loan capital – s. (mittel- bis langfristiges) Fremdkapital
loan-deposit ratio – s. Kredit-Einlagen-Relation
loan scheme – s. Kreditprogramm, -aktion
loan syndication – s. Konsortialfinanzierung
loan with strings – s. Kredit mit Verwendungsauflagen (z. B. Lieferbindung)
lobby – s. Lobby, Interessensvertretung
local
adj. lokal, örtlich, ortsansässig, nahe
adj. zum Zielland gehörend, im Zielland
local area network – s. Local Area Network, Nahverkehrsnetz, lokales Computernetz(-werk) / Rechnernetz(-werk)
local authority stock – s. Kommunalschuldverschreibung(en)
local buyer – s. ortsansässige/r Käufer/in, ortsansässige/r Einkäufer/in
local content – s. inländischer Wertschöpfungsanteil, Wertschöpfungsanteil im Ziel- /Importland

local content requirement – s. Local-Content-Verpflichtung; Local-Content-Auflage; Verpflichtung eines ausländischen Investors, einen gewissen Anteil an Vorprodukten im Zielland der Investition zu erwerben
local sales requirement – s. Local-Sales-Auflage; Verpflichtung eines ausländischen Investors, einen bestimmten Anteil der Produktion im Zielland der Investition abzusetzen
local food co-operative – s. Basiskonsumgenossenschaft
local government – s. Lokalregierung, Länder- / Gemeindeverwaltung
locate
v. (auf-)finden
v. sich niederlassen / ansiedeln, Standort wählen
located in – mit Sitz in
location – s. Standort
location pricing – s. ortsabhängige Preisgestaltung, örtliche Preisdifferenzierung
location studies – s. Standortforschung
location theory – s. Standorttheorie
lock – s. Schifffahrtsschleuse, Schleusenkammer
lock-out – s. Aussperrung (von Arbeitern)
lock out – v. aussperren
locust – s. Heuschrecke
lodge – v. einreichen, hinterlegen, deponieren, einbringen
lodge a tender – ein (Submissions-) Angebot einreichen
logging – s. Abholzen, Holzfällung, -gewinnung
logistical – adj. logistisch
logistician – s. Logistiker
logistics – s. Logistik, Marketinglogistik, physische Distribution
logo – s. Logo, Firmenzeichen, -marke
loitering – s. Trödeln, Herumlungern
London Interbank Offered Rate – s. Londoner Geldmarktzinssatz für Zwischenbankkredite, LIBOR (Richtwert für viele internationale variabel verzinsliche Kredite und Anleihen)
London International Financial Futures Exchange (LIFFE) – s. Internationale Londoner Börse für den Handel mit Finanzterminkontrakten
long
adj. lang
adj. Plus- , gedeckt
go long – eine Plusposition / eine (Währungs-)Aktivposition eingehen
long call option hedge – s. Kurssicherung durch den Kauf einer Devisenkaufoption
long-distance call – s. Ferngespräch
long end of the market – s. Marktsegment für langfristige Anleihen
long exposure – s. (Währungs-)Plusposition, (Währungs-)Aktivposition
long futures hedge – s. Kurssicherung durch den Kauf von börsengehandelten (Devisen-) Terminkontrakten
longlife milk – s. Haltbarmilch
long (option) position – s. positive Optionsposition, Plus-Optionsposition
long position – s. Hausse-, Plus-, Aktivposition
long put option hedge – s. Kurssicherung durch den Kauf einer Devisenverkaufsoption
long run – lange Sicht, Langzeit(-perspektive)
in the long run – auf lange Sicht, langfristig (gesehen)
long-run – adj. langfristig
long-term – adj. langfristig
long-term liabilities – langfristige Verbindlichkeiten
long-term creditors – s. Fremdkapitalgeber mit langfristigen Forderungen; Gläubiger, die langfristiges Fremdkapital zur Verfügung stellen
long-term currency swap – s. Währungsswap basierend auf der Kombination eines Devisen-Kassageschäfts mit einem gegenläufigen Devisen-Termingeschäft
long-term debt – s. langfristige Verbindlichkeiten, langfristiges Fremdkapital
long-term debt to total capitalisation s. (Unterform des) Verschuldungsgrad(es)
long-term investments – s. langfristige Finanzanlagen
long-term liabilities – s. langfristige Verbindlichkeiten
long-term solvency ratio – s. Kapitalstrukturkennzahl
long-transaction exposure – s. positive Netto-Währungsumwechslungsposition
look after – v. betreuen, sich kümmern um
loop – s. Schleife, Schlinge
loophole – s. Gesetzeslücke, (Steuer-)Schlupfloch
loose
adj. lose, locker
adj. unverpackt, ohne Emballage
adj. ungenau, nicht streng, weit, vage
in loose form – unverpackt
in a looser sense – in einem ungenaueren / weiteren Sinn
The term is used more loosely. – Der Ausdruck wird in einem vageren Sinn verwendet.
loose association – s. lose / nicht sehr enge Verbindung / Gruppierung / Vereinigung
loose-leaf – adj. Loseblatt-, aus losen Blättern bestehend
loose-leaf account sheet – s. lose Kontenkarte, loses Kontoblatt
loosen – v. lockern, lockerer machen, entschärfen
loosen controls – Beschränkungen lockern / entschärfen
losse substance – s. loses / unverpacktes Material
Lorenz curve – s. Lorenzkurve , graphische Darstellung eines Konzentrationsmaßes
lorry – s. Lastkraftwagen, LKW
lorry-load – s. LKW-Ladung
loss – s. Verlust, Schaden
sustain a loss – einen Verlust / Schaden erleiden
incur a loss – einen Verlust / Schaden erleiden
loss in value – s. Wertminderung
loss leader – s. Lockvogelangebot
loss-leader pricing – s. Lockvogelstrategie
loss of circulation – s. Streuverlust
loss of, or damage to, the goods – s. Verlust oder Beschädigung der Ware
lot
s. Menge, viele
s. Partie, (Waren-)Posten
to take a lot – eine Menge / eine Partie nehmen
to take the lot – alle / alles nehmen
lower-case letter – s. Kleinbuchstabe
lower intervention point – s. unterer Interventionspunkt
lower management – s. Nachwuchsführungskräfte, untere Führungsebene
lower-of-cost-or-market principle – s. Niederstwertprinzip
low-income earner – s. Kleinverdiener
loyalty – s. Treue, Loyalität
loyalty rebate – s. Treuerabatt
lubricant – s. Schmiermittel
lug – v. schleppen
luggage insurance – s. Gepäcksversicherung
lump sum – s. Pauschale, Pauschalsumme, Einmalzahlung
lump sum premium – s. Einmalprämie
lunar energy – s. Mondenergie
lure – v. anlocken

M

M1 – Geldmenge M1
M2 – Geldmenge M2
M3 – Geldmenge M3
Maastricht criteria – s. Maastricht-Kriterien
machination – s. Intrige, Machenschaft
machine code – s. Maschinensprache
machine language – s. Maschinensprache
machine operator – s. Maschinist/in, (pl.) Bedienungspersonal
Machinery – s. Maschinen(-konto)
Machinery and Equipment – s. (das Konto) Maschinen und maschinelle Anlagen
machine tool – s. Werkzeugmaschine
macroeconomic – adj. makroökonomisch
macroeconomics – s. Makroökonomie, Makroökonomik
main contractor – s. Generalunternehmer/in
magnetic core – s. Magnetkern(-speicher)
magnetic disk – s. Magnetplatte
magnetic drum – s. Magnettrommel(-speicher)
magnetic strip – s. Magnetstreifen
magnetic strip reader – s. Magnetstreifenleser
magnetic tape – s. Magnetband(-speicher)
magnetic tape block – s. Bandblock
magnetic tape reader – s. Magnetbandleser, -lesegerät
mail-handling – s. Postbearbeitung
mail order – s. Versandgeschäft, -handel
mail order firm – s. Postversandhaus, Versender, Versandhandelsgeschäft
mail order house – s. Postversandhaus, Versender, Versandhandelsgeschäft
mail-order operation – s. Versandgeschäft
mail room – s. Poststelle (einer Firma)
mailroom equipment – s. Postbearbeitungsmaschinen
mail transfer – s. briefliche Auszahlung
mainframe – s. Großrechner, Großrechenanlage
mainframe computer – s. Großrechner, Großrechenanlage
mainland Europe – s. Kontinentaleuropa
main memory – s. Zentral-, Primärspeicher
main office – s. Hauptanstalt (einer Bank), Zentrale
mainstream – adj. etabliert, normal, traditionell, konventionell, nicht alternativ, nicht ausgefallen
mainstream retailers – der traditionelle Einzelhandel
maintain
v. aufrechterhalten, beibehalten, pflegen
v. warten, instand halten, servicen
v. behaupten
maintain contacts – Kontakte pflegen
maintain a machine – v. eine Maschine instand halten / warten
maintenance – s. Erhaltung, Instandhaltung, Wartung
maintenance lease – s. Full-Service-Leasing(-vertrag)
maize – s. Mais
major – adj. größer, bedeutend, Groß-, Haupt-
major defect – s. erheblicher / nicht geringfügiger Mangel
majority – s. Mehrheit
majority interest – s. Mehrheitsbeteiligung
make-or-buy decision – s. Entscheidung über Eigenleistung oder Zukauf / firmeninterne Fertigung oder Outsourcen
maker
s. Erzeuger/in, Produzent/in
s. Aussteller/in (eines Solawechsels)
s. Optionsgeber/in
maker of an option – s. Optionsgeber/in
malnutrition – s. Unterernährung
man – v. personalmäßig ausstatten, mit Personal besetzen
managed floating – s. kontrolliertes / schmutziges / manipuliertes Floaten
management
s. Management, Geschäftsleitung, Führungskräfte
s. Unternehmensführung
s. Management, Verwaltung, Wirtschaft, Steuerung, Handhabung, Manipulation
management accounting – s. entscheidungsorientiertes Rechnungswesen, (etwa) Controlling, internes Rechnungswesen
management buyout – s. Management Buyout, Übernahme eines Unternehmens durch das eigene Management
management by exception – s. Management by Exception, Mitarbeiterführung durch Eingreifen bei größeren Ergebnisabweichungen, Unternehmensführung durch Ausnahmeeingriff, Meldung bei Abweichung
management by objectives – s. Management by Objectives, Mitarbeiterführung durch Zielvorgabe, zielgesteuerte Unternehmensführung
management by results – s. Management by Results, (Unternehmens-)Führung durch Ergebnisüberwachung
management company – s. Verwaltungsgesellschaft (eines offenen Investmentfonds)
management consultancy – s. Unternehmens-, Betriebsberatung
management consultant – s. Betriebsberater/in, Managementberater/in, Managementkonsulent/in
management consulting – s. Unternehmens-, Betriebsberatung
management fee – s. (Fonds-)Verwaltungsgebühr
management information system – s. Managementinformationssystem
management services – s. Managementberatungs- und Managementunterstützungsleistungen
management stock option scheme – s. Aktienoptionsprogramm für Manager
management style – s. Führungsstil
management technique – s. Managementtechnik
management tool – s. betriebswirtschaftliches Instrument, Instrument der Unternehmensführung
managerial personnel – s. Führungskräfte
managing director – s. Vorstandsvorsitzender mit Aufsichtsratsfunktion, Generaldirektor, Geschäftsführer (einer UK-*private limited company*)
managing partner – s. geschäftsführender Gesellschafter einer Personengesellschaft
managing underwriter – s. Lead Underwriter, federführendes Mitglied eines Emissionskonsortiums, Emissionskonsortialsführer/in
M&As – mergers & acquisitions (siehe)
mandate – s. Mandat, Auftrag, (Bank-)Vollmacht
mandate – s. (gesetzlich) vorschreiben / anordnen
mandatory – adj. obligatorisch, (gesetzlich) vorgeschrieben, zwingend
mandatory controls – s. gesetzliche Lenkungsmaßnahmen
man-hour – s. (geleistete) Arbeitsstunde
manpower – s. (verfügbare) Arbeitskräfte
manual – adj. händisch

manual operation – s. Handbetrieb, -arbeit, manuelle Tätigkeit
manual private branch exchange – s. Nebenstellenanlage für Handvermittlung
manufactured goods – s. Fertigwaren
manufactured imports – s. Fertigwarenimporte
manufacturer – s. Erzeuger, Produzent
manufacturer's agent – s. Werksvertreter/in, selbständige/r Vertreter/in einer Herstellerfirma
manufacturer's brand – s. Herstellermarke
manufacturing
s. Herstellung, Erzeugung
s. Fertigungsindustrie, sekundärer Sektor
manufacturing business – s. Industrie-, Gewerbe-, Erzeugungs-, Fertigungsbetrieb
manufacturing branch – s. Zweigwerk
manufacturing cost(s) – s. Herstellungskosten
manufacturing establishment – s. Industrie-, Gewerbe-, Erzeugungs-, Fertigungsbetrieb
manufacturing industry – s. Fertigungsindustrie, sekundärer Sektor
manufacturing management – s. Produktionswirtschaft, -management
manufacturing overhead(-s) – s. Material- & Fertigungsgemeinkosten, Fertigungsgemeinkosten
manufacturing operation – s. Fertigungsbetrieb, -unternehmen
manufacturing pattern – s. Produktionsvorlage, Werkstattzeichnung
manufacturing subsidiary – s. Fertigungs-, Produktionstochter(-gesellschaft)
manufacturing supplies – s. Hilfs- und Betriebsstoffe
manufacturing system – s. Produktions-, Fertigungssystem
margin
s. Rand, Abstand
s. Marge, Spanne, Handels-, Gewinn-, Zinsspanne, Rendite, Rentabilität
s. (Wertpapier-)Kredit, Einschuss
s. Grenze, jeweils letzte (Input- / Output-)Einheit
in the margin – am Rand (eines Papierblattes)
sales margin – Umsatzrendite, Gewinnspanne, Gewinnmarge
Value is determined at the margin. – Der Wert wird an der Grenze bestimmt.
marginal
adj. geringfügig, unbedeutend, marginal
adj. grenztheoretisch, marginal, Grenz-
marginal approach – s. grenztheoretischer Ansatz
marginal cost(s) – s. Grenzkosten
marginal costing – s. Grenzkostenrechnung, (unechtes) Direct Costing
marginal income – s. Grenzeinkommen(-steile)
marginal income tax rate – s. Grenzsteuersatz / Spitzensteuersatz auf Einkommen
marginalism – s. grenztheoretischer Ansatz, Grenztheorie
marginal product – s. Grenzprodukt
marginal productivity – s. Grenzproduktivität, -leistungsfähigkeit
marginal propensity to consume – s. marginale Konsumquote
marginal propensity to save – s. marginale Sparquote
marginal tax rate – s. Grenzsteuersatz
marginal utility – s. Grenznutzen
margin of dumping – s. Dumpingmarge, -spanne
margin of fluctuation – s. Bandbreite
marine cargo insurance – s. Seefrachtversicherung
marine hull insurance – s. Seekaskoversicherung
marine insurance – s. (brit.) Seetransportversicherung, (am.) See- und Binnentransportversicherung
take out marine insurance – eine Seetransportversicherung abschließen
marine insurance policy – s. Seetransportversicherungspolizze, See- und Binnentransportversicherungspolizze
marital status – s. Familienstand
maritime transport – s. Seetransport
mark – s. (Kenn-)Zeichen, Etikette, Kennzeichnung, Markierung, Aufschrift
mark – v. kennzeichnen, markieren, bezeichnen, beschriften
marked
adj. merklich, deutlich
adj. markiert, gekennzeichnet, mit einer Aufschrift versehen
a marked increase – eine deutliche Erhöhung
a bill marked on board – ein als Bordkonnossement gekennzeichneter Seefrachtbrief
a window marked WITHDRAWALS – ein Schalter mit der Aufschrift ABHEBUNGEN
market
s. Markt, Absatz-, Beschaffungsmarkt, Börse
s. Marktpreis, Tageswert (am Beschaffungsmarkt), Wiederbeschaffungswert
at market – zum Marktwert
at the lower of cost or market – zum Niederstwert
make a market – einen Markt machen, einen geordneten Markt (mit jederzeitiger Kauf- und Verkaufsmöglichkeit) für ein bestimmtes Wertpapier gestalten
marketability – s. Vermarktungsfähigkeit, Marktgängigkeit
marketable securities – Wertpapiere des Umlaufvermögens, börsengängige und sonst leicht verkäufliche Wertpapiere
market capitalisation – s. Markt-, Börsenkapitalisierung, Börsenwert, Gesamtkurswert (aller im Umlauf befindlichen Aktien eines Unternehmens)
market entry – s. Markteintritt, -erschließung
market failure – s. Marktversagen, Versagen des Marktes
marketing – s. Marketing, Absatzpolitik
marketing channel – s. Distributionskanal, Absatzweg
marketing department – s. Marketingabteilung, Abteilung für Marketing
marketing director – s. Marketingdirektor/in, Marketingvorstand, Vorstandsmitglied für (das Ressort) Marketing
marketing environment – s. Marketingumfeld, -klima, Rahmenbedingungen für das Marketing
marketing intelligence – s. Marktinformationen
marketing intermediary – s. Absatzmittler
marketing manager – s. Marketingmanager/in, Marketingleiter/in, Leiter/in der Marketingabteilung, für den Marketingbereich zuständige Führungskraft (die meist nicht dem Verwaltungsrat angehört)
marketing mix – s. Marketingmix
marketing research – s. Absatz-, Marketing-, Marktforschung
marketing resources – s. Marketingressourcen, die der Marketingabteilung zur Verfügung stehenden (personellen, finanziellen, materiellen) Mittel
market interest rate – s. Marktzinssatz
market maker – s. Primärhändler, Market-Maker, Marktmacher
market penetration
s. Marktpenetration, -durchdringung, -ausschöpfung, Erhaltung und Ausbau von Marktanteilen
s. Distributionsdichte
market research – s. Marktforschung
market risk – Markt-, Preisrisiko

market segmentation – s. Marktsegmentierung
market share – s. Marktanteil
market-skimming pricing – s. Abschöpfungspreisstrategie
marking – s. Beschriftung, Markierung, Kennzeichnung, Etikettierung, Auszeichnung
marking instructions – s. Markierungsanweisungen
mark-up – s. Handelsspanne, Kalkulationszuschlag
markup language – s. Markup-Sprache, Auszeichnungssprache
married couple's allowance – s. Freibetrag für Verheiratete / Ehepaare, Ehefreibetrag
marshal – s. verschieben, rangieren
marshalling yard – s. Verschiebebahnhof, (fig.) Aufmarschgebiet
mask – v. überdecken, verschleiern
Massachusetts trust – s. Massachusetts Trust, Unternehmenstreuhand, Kapitalgesellschaft in Treuhandform
mass-customisation – s. individuelle Massenproduktion, kundenspezifische Massenproduktion, (das Prinzip) „ein Maßanzug von der Stange"
mass marketing – s. Massenartikelmarketing
mass production – s. Massenproduktion, -fertigung, Serienfertigung
master – s. Kapitän (eines Handelsschiffes)
master agreement – s. Rahmenvertrag
master budget – s. Gesamtplan, -budget, Rahmenplan, Generalplan
master copy – s. Matrize, Kopier-, Druckvorlage
master franchisee – s. Master-Franchisenehmer
master of a ship – s. Kapitän eines Handelsschiffes
Master of Business Administration – s. Magister der Wirtschaftswissenschaften (mit Schwerpunkt Betriebswirtschaftslehre / Unternehmensführung)
match
v. zusammenstellen, paaren, aufeinander beziehen
v. gleichziehen, sich messen, mithalten
match the dumping prices – mit den Dumpingpreisen mithalten / gleichziehen
matching principle – s. Prinzip der periodengerechten Zurechnung von Aufwendungen und Erträgen
material
adj. erheblich, rechtserheblich, wesentlich
adj. materiell, finanziell, monetär
material injury – ernsthafter / erheblicher Schaden
material incentives – materielle / finanzielle Anreize
material requirement planning – s. Materialbedarfsplanung, MRP-Planung
materials handling – s. innerbetrieblicher Materialtransport, Förderwesen
materials management – s. Materialwirtschaft, -management
materials management department – s. Abteilung Materialwirtschaft, Materialwirtschaftsabteilung
maternity leave – s. Mutterschaftsurlaub, -karenz
mate's receipt – s. Mate's Receipt, Bordempfangsschein
matrix – s. Matrix, Matrizentabelle
matrix organisation – s. Matrixorganisation
matter under dispute – s. Streitgegenstand
mature – v. fällig werden
mature economy – s. reife / hochentwickelte Volkswirtschaft
mature market – s. gesättigter Markt
maturity
s. Fälligkeit, Fälligkeitstag, Fälligkeitstermin, Verfallstag
s. Laufzeit (eines Kredites)
s. Reifephase
maturity date – s. Fälligkeits-, Erfüllungs-, Valutatag
MBA – Master of Business Administration (siehe)
m-commerce – mobile commerce (siehe)
meaning – s. Bedeutung, Sinn
within the meaning of the law – im Sinne des Gesetzes
within the meaning of Section 3 – im Sinne von Paragraph 3
means of communication – s. Kommunikationsmittel, Methoden der Nachrichtenübermittlung
mean – v. bedeuten, beabsichtigen
means – s. Mittel
an efficient means – ein effizientes Mittel
means of conveyance – s. Transportmittel
measure
s. Maß, Maßstab, Maßeinheit
s. Maßnahme, Schritt
take measures – Maßnahmen ergreifen / setzen, Schritte tun / ergreifen
measurements – s. Abmessungen, Maße (z. B. Länge, Breite)
measure of value – s. Wertmaßstab (Funktion des Geldes)
mechanical engineering – s. Maschinenbau
mechanical occupation – s. handwerklicher Beruf
mechanisation – s. Mechanisierung
meddle – v. sich einmischen
media selection department – s. Medieneinkaufsabteilung
medical care – s. ärztliche Betreuung, medizinische Versorgung, Gesundheitswesen
medium – s. Medium, (Informations-)Träger
medium – adj. mittelgroß, durchschnittlich, Mittel-, Durchschnitts-
medium of exchange – s. Tausch-, Transaktionsmittel (Funktion des Geldes)
medium-scale establishment – s. Mittelbetrieb
medium tech – adj. mitteltechnologisch, aus dem Bereich der mittleren Technologie
medium-technology – s. mittlere Technolgie, Mitteltechnologie
medium-term – adj. mittelfristig
meeting of minds – s. Willensübereinstimmung
member
s. Mitglied
s. Gesellschafter/in (einer AG oder GmbH), Aktionär
membership fee – s. Mitgliedsgebühr
memo – s. (innerbetriebliche) Anweisung / Mitteilung
memorandum
s. Niederschrift
s. Gründungsurkunde, Gesellschaftsvertrag
memorandum of association – s. Gründungsurkunde einer UK-*registered company*, der das Außenverhältnis regelnde Teil des Gesellschaftsvertrages / der Satzung / der Statuten
memory
s. Gedächtnis, Andenken
s. Speicher(-einheit)
memory chip – s. Speicherchip
memory stick – s. Speicherstab, -stick, Mobilspeicher
Mercado Común del Sur – s. Gemeinsamer Markt des Südens, Mercosur-Zollunion
mercantile agency – s.(Handels-)Auskunftei
mercantile custom – s. Handelsbrauch
mercantile occupation – s. kaufmännischer Beruf
merchandise
s. Ware, Waren, Produkte
s. Handelsware
s. Merchandise, Merchandise-Produkt(e), Fanartikel
Some merchandise is produced ethically. – Einige Fanartikel werden nach ethischen Grundsätzen produziert.
merchandise account – s. Handelsbilanz, Bilanz des Warenverkehrs
merchandise exports – s. Waren-, Güterexporte

merchandise imports – s. Waren-, Güterimporte
merchandise inventory – s. Handelswarenbestand, -lager
merchandising – s. Warenhandel, Merchandising
Merchandise Inventory – s. Handelswarenbestand(-skonto)
merchandise management system – s. Warenwirtschaftssystem
merchandise trade account – s. Waren-, Warenverkehrs-, Handels-, Güterbilanz
merchant
s. (brit.) Großkaufmann, Großhändler, Export-Import-Kaufmann
s. (am.) Kaufmann, Händler, Ladeninhaber, Einzelhändler
s. Kreditkartenvertragspartner, Vertragshändler, Mitgliedsunternehmen einer Kreditkartenorganisation
merchant bank – s. Merchant Bank (Außenhandels- und/oder Investmentbank)
merchant middleman – s. als Eigenhändler fungierender Absatzmittler, Eigen-, Zwischenhändler
Mercosur – Mercado Común del Sur (siehe)
merger
s. (brit.) Fusion (im weitesten Sinn)
s. (am.) Fusion durch Aufnahme
mergers and acquisitions – s. Firmenübernahmen und Beteiligungen, Mergers & Acquisitions, Fusionen & Übernahmen, M&As
meritorious good – s. meritorisches /quasi-öffentliches Gut
message – s. Botschaft
meter – v. (Verbrauch) messen, (Zähler) ablesen
methane – s. Methan(-gas)
method of assessment – s. Bemessungs-, Veranlagungsmethode
method of operation – s. Betriebsart, Arbeitsweise, Art der Geschäftstätigkeit
method of payment – s. Zahlungsmethode
metomymic – adj. metonymisch
metonymic extension – Bezeichnungsübertragung auf einen naheliegenden Begriff
metric – s. Kenn-, Messzahl, Indikator
mezzanine finance – s. Mezzanin-, Zwischen-, Überbrückungsfinanzierung
MFN clause – most-favoured-nation clause (siehe)
microcomputer – s. Mikrocomputer
microdocumentation – s. Mikrodokumentation
microeconomic – adj. mikroökonomisch
microeconomics – s. Mikroökonomie, Mikroökonomik
microfiche – s. Mikrofiche, Mikrofilmblatt
microfilm – s. Mikrofilm
micro-lending – s. Mikrokreditwesen, Vergabe von Mikrokrediten
microprocessor – s. Mikroprozessor
microsegmentation – s. Mikrosegmentierung
microtargeting – s. Auswahl von Mikrozielgruppen
middleman
s. Vermittler, Mittler, Zwischenglied
s. Absatzmittler
middle management – s. mittleres Management, mittlere Führungsebene, Mitglieder der mittleren Führungsebene
middle manager – s. Mitglied der mittleren Führungsebene, mittlere Führungskraft
middle rate – s. Mittel-, Devisenmittelkurs
mid-rate – s. Mittel-, Devisenmittelkurs
migrate – v. abwandern, zuwandern
migrant – s. Migrant, (Ein-, Aus-)Wanderer
migrant worker – s. Gast-, Fremdarbeiter, ausländische Arbeiter
mill – s. Fabrik, Werk, Spinnerei
mimeograph – v. vervielfältigen
mind-boggling – adj. umwerfend, verblüffend, verwirrend
mini – minicomputer (siehe)
minicomputer – s. Minicomputer, Kleinrechner
minimum capital requirement – s. Mindestkapitalerfordernis
minimum off-take agreement – s. Mindestabnahmeverpflichtung (im Rahmen von Projektfinanzierungen)
minor – adj. geringfügig
minor defect – s. geringfügiger / nicht erheblicher Mangel
minor infringement – s. Obliegenheitsverletzung
minority interest – s. Minderheitsbeteiligung
Mint – s. Münze, Münzstätte, -amt
mint – v. prägen, münzen
minute – v. protokollieren
minute – adj. winzig, klein
minutes – s. Protokoll
keep / take minutes – das Protokoll führen
minute taker – s. Protokollführer/in
misallocation – s. Fehlleitung, Fehlinvestition, Fehlallokation
miscellaneous accounts payable – s. sonstige Verbindlichkeiten
miscellaneous accounts receivable – s. sonstige Forderungen
misconduct – s. Verfehlung
mismatch – s. Mangel an Übereinstimmung, mangelnde Übereinstimmung
misnomer – s. Fehlbezeichnung
mission statement – s. Mission Statement, (Bekanntmachung der) Firmenphilosphie
mitigate – v. mildern, dämpfen, abschwächen
mixed account – s. gemischtes Konto
mixed blessing – s. zweischneidiges Schwert
mixed container – s. Sammelcontainer
mixed economy – s. Mischwirtschaft
mixed finance – s. Mischfinanzierung, -kredite
mixed fund – s. Mischfonds
mixed merchandise account – s. ungeteiltes / gemischtes Warenkonto
mixed policy – s. kombinierte Zeit- und Reisepolizze
mnemonic notation – s. mnemonischer / mnemotechnischer Code, symbolische Befehlsbezeichnung(-sweise)
mobile – s. Mobiltelefon, Handy
mobile commerce – s. mobiler Internethandel, über mobile Internetterminals (z.B. Handys) abgewickelter elektronischer Handel, mobiler netzgestützer Handel, M-Commerce
mobile phone – s. Mobiltelefon, Handy
mobility – s. Mobilität
Model Business Corporation Act – s. US-bundesstaatliches Mustergesetz für das einzelstaatliche Recht der Kapitalgesellschaften
modem – s. Modem
mode of delivery – s. Beförderungs-, Zustellart, Liefermodus
mode of transport – s. Transport-, Beförderungsart, Transportmodus, (gewähltes) Verkehrsmittel
modify – v. modifizieren, abändern
modulation – s. Modulation
modulator – s. Modulator
module – s. Modul, Baugruppe, -teil
mom-and-pop store – s. Tante-Emma-Laden, Greißler
monetary – adj. monetär, geldmäßig, geld- und kreditpolitisch
in monetary terms – geldmäßig, in Geld ausgedrückt, pagatorisch
monetary aggregate – s. monetäres Aggregat, Geldmengendefinition, geldpolitische Variable
monetary authority – s. Währungsbehörde

monetary controls – s. geldpolitische Restriktionen / Lenkungsmaßnahmen
monetary management – s. geldpolitische Lenkung(-smaßnahmen)
monetary measures – s. geldpolitsche Maßnahmen
monetary policy – s. Geld- und Kreditpolitik, Notenbankpolitik
monetary system – s. Währungssystem
monetary union – s.Währungsunion
monetary unit – s. Währungs-, Geldeinheit
money – s. Geld
money market – s. Geldmarkt
money market deposit – s. Geldmarkteinlage
money market instrument – s. Geldmarktinstrument, -objekt, -anlage
money order – s. Geldanweisung
money supply – s. Geldmenge
monitor – s. Monitor, Bildschirm(-einheit)
monitor – v. (ständig) überwachen, verfolgen
montor orders – Aufträge / Auftragsbearbeitung überwachen / verfolgen
monopsony – s. Monoposon, Käufermonopol
moonlighter – s. Schwarzarbeiter; Arbeiter, der einer nicht gemeldeten Nebenbeschäftigung nachgeht
moot – adj. fraglich, strittig
moot point – s. Streitpunkt, umstrittene Frage
moratorium
s. (vereinbarter oder einseitig verfügter) Zahlungsaufschub, Stundung, Moratorium
s. Stopp, Stillhaltefrist
moratorium on approvals – s. Genehmigungsstopp
mortgage
s. Hypothek
s. Hypothekarkredit
mortgage banking – s. Hypothekarkreditgeschäft, Vergabe von Hypothekarkrediten
mortgage bond – s. hypothekarisch gesicherte Schuldverschreibung / Anleihe
mortgagee – s. Hypothekengläubiger/in, Pfandrechtnehmer/in
mortgage loan – s. Hypothekarkredit
mortgager – s. Hypothekenschuldner/in, Pfandrechtgeber/in
most-favoured-nation clause – s. Meistbegünstigungsklausel
most-favoured-nation principle – s. Prinzip der Meistbegünstigung
motion – s. (formeller) Antrag bei einer Sitzung
table a motion – einen Antrag (bei einer Sitzung) stellen
motion picture – s. Film
motivator – s. Motivator, Motivations- / Antriebsfaktor
motor industry – s. Autoindustrie
motor insurance – s. Kraftfahrzeugversicherung
motor trade – s. Autoindustrie
mould – s. (Guss- / Press-)Form, Gestalt
mouse-click economy – s. Internetwirtschaft, Online-Wirtschaft, Click-Wirtschaft
mouthpiece – s. Sprechmuschel
movables – s. bewegliche Sachen (und Rechte)
move – v. sich bewegen, übersiedeln, entwickeln
The price moved against him. – Der Kurs entwicklete sich zu seinen Ungunsten.
movement certificate – s. Warenverkehrsbescheinigung
moving average – s. gleitender Durchschnitt
moving bridge – s. bewegliche Brücke
MRP – material requirement planning (siehe)
MT – mail transfer (siehe)
multidomestic marketing – s. multinationales Marketing
multilateral aid – s. multilaterale (Entwicklungs-)Hilfe
multilateralism – s. Multilateralismus
multi-level trade – s. Muli-Level-Handel, mehrschichtiger Handel
multimedia – s. Multimedia, Multimedien, Medienverbund, Mixed Media
multimodal – adj. multimodal, verkehrsträgerunabhängig, verkehrsträgerneutral
multimodal transport – s. kombinierter / gebrochener Verkehr
multinational – s. Multi, multinationales Unternehmen, multinationaler Konzern
multinational company – s. multinationales Unternehmen, multinationaler Konzern, Multi
multinational corporation – s. multinationales Unternehmen, multinationaler Konzern, Multi
multinational group – s. multinationales Unternehmen, multinationaler Konzern, Multi
multinational marketing – s. multinationales Marketing
multiple
s. Vielfaches
s. Kurs-Gewinn-Verhältnis, KGV
multiple shop – s. Filialunternehmen, Filialist, Ladenkette, Filialkette
multiple-step report form – s. Staffelform
multiple store – s. Filialunternehmen, Filialist, Ladenkette, Filialkette
multiple taxation – s. Mehrfachbesteuerung
multiple voting rights – s. Mehrfachstimmrecht
multiplier – s. Multiplikator
multi-product enterprise – s. Multi-Produkt-Unternehmen
multi-stage sales tax – s. Mehrphasen-, Allphasenumsatzsteuer
municipal bond – s. Kommunalschuldverschreibung
municipality – s. Gemeinde, Stadtbehörde
mushroom – v. (kräftig) wachsen, sich wie die Schwammerln vermehren, ins Kraut schießen
mutatis mutandis – adv. sinngemäß, entsprechend, unter Berücksichtigung der geänderten Umstände / Voraussetzungen
mutual – adj. gegenseitig, wechselseitig, genossenschaftlich
mutually beneficial – von wechselseitigem / beiderseitigem Nutzen
mutual fund – s. (am.) offener Investmentfonds, Investmentfonds des Treuhandtypus, Kapitalanlagegesellschaft nach dem Fondsprinzip
mutual fund share – s. Anteil an einem offenen Investmentfonds, Investmentfondsanteil(-schein)
mutual organisation – s. genossenschaftliche Organisation
mutual savings bank – s. genossenschaftliche Sparkasse, Sparkasse auf Gegenseitigkeit
mutual understanding – s. (Willens-)Übereinkunft

N

named-perils policy – s. Einzel-Gefahren-Versicherung(-spolizze)
named port of shipment – s. benannter Verschiffungshafen
narrow-based index – s. enger / selektiver Index, Spezialindex
narrowbased sales tax – s. selektive (Einphasen-) Umsatzsteuer
national accounting – s. volkswirtschaftliche Gesamtrechnung
national account management – s. Key-Account-Management, Betreuung von Schlüsselkunden
national accounts – volkswirtschaftliche Gesamtrechnung
national debt – s. Staats-, Bundesschuld
national defence – s. Landesverteidigung
national economy – s. Volkswirtschaft
national expenditure – s. Bruttonationalprodukt nach der Verwendungsrechnung
national federation – s. Landesverband, überregionaler Verband
national giro – s. UK-Postscheck- und Postüberweisungsverkehr
National Giro Bank – s. UK-Postscheckamt / Postsparkasse
national income – s. Volkseinkornmen (im engeren und weiteren Sinn)
national income accounts – s. (System der) volkswirtschaftlichen Gesamtrechnung im engeren Sinn, Volkseinkommensrechnung (im weiteren Sinn)
national income statistics – s. Volkseinkommensstatistik
national insurance – s. UK-Sozialversicherung
national insurance contribution – s. UK-Sozialversicherungsbeitrag
nationalisation – s. Verstaatlichung
nationalised industries – s. verstaatlichte Industrie / Wirtschaftszweige / Wirtschaft
national output – s. Bruttosozialprodukt nach der Entstehungsrechnung
national product – s. National-, Sozialprodukt
National Savings Bank – s. UK-Postsparkasse
national wealth account – s. Volksvermögensrechnung
national welfare – s. nationale Wohlfahrt
natural deterioration – s. innerer / natürlicher Verderb
natural gas – s. Erdgas
natural gas well – s. Erdgassonde
natural life cycle (of a product) – natürlicher / ökologischer Lebenslauf (eines Produktes)
natural monopoly – s. natürliches Monopol
natural person – s. natürliche Person
natural pest control – s. natürliche Schädlingsbekämpfung, -regulation, -regulierung
NAV – net asset value (siehe)
need – s. (primäres) Bedürfnis, Bedarf
supply / satisfy a need – ein Bedürfnis befriedigen
negative exposure – s. (Währungs-)Minusposition, (Währungs-)Passivposition
negative externalities – s. netagive externe Effekte, soziale / volkswirtschaftliche Kosten
negative transaction exposure – s. negative Netto-Währungsumwechslungsposition
negligence – s. Fahrlässigkeit, Fehlen der verkehrsüblichen Sorgfalt, Nachlässigkeit
negligent – adj. fahrlässig, ohne die verkehrsübliche Sorgfalt
negotiability – s. Begebbarkeit, Abstraktheit (von Wertpapieren)
negotiable
adj. begebbar, abstrakt
adj. (frei) vereinbar
Terms of payment are negotiable. – Zahlungsbedingungen können frei vereinbart werden.
negotiable bill of lading – s. Order-, Namenskonnossement
negotiable instrument – s. begebbares / abstraktes Wertpapier
negotiable warehouse receipt – s. Orderlagerschein
negotiate – s. verhandeln, aushandeln, vermitteln
negotiated commission – s. frei vereinbarte Provision
negotiation
s. Negotiation, Negoziierung
s. Verhandlung
negotiation skills – s. Verhandlungsgeschick
neighbourhood association – s. (schweizerisch) Quartierverein, Nachbarschaftshilfeorganisation, Neighbourhood Association
neighbourhood store – s. Nachbarschaftsladen, Tante-Emma-Laden, Greißler
neo-protectionism – s. Neoprotektionismus, neue Form des Proktionismus
net – s. / adj. / adv. netto, Netto-, nach Abzug, ohne (weiteren) Abzug
30 days net – 30 Tage netto Kassa
2/10 net 30 – 2% bei Bezahlung innerhalb von 10 Tagen oder 30 Tage netto Kassa
net of tax – nach Abzug der Steuer(n), versteuert
net assets – s. Reinvermögen, Eigenkapital
net asset value – s. Nettoinventarwert
net cash flow
s. Netto-Cash-Flow
s. Nettozahlungsstrom, Differenz zwischen Einzahlungs- und Auszahlungsstrom
net credit sales – s. bereinigte Forderungen aus Warenlieferungen und Leistungen
net current assets – s. Nettoumlaufvermögen, Working Capital
net exports (of goods and services) – s. Außenbeitrag, Leistungsbilanzsaldo
net exposure – s. Währungsnettoposition, Netto-Währungsposition
net financial items – s. (Netto-)Finanzergebnis
net income – s. Reingewinn, Jahresüberschuss, Bilanzgewinn, Unternehmungsgewinn, positives Unternehmungsergebnis
net-income-to-net-sales ratio – s. Umsatzrentabilität bezogen auf den Jahresüberschuss
net lease – s. Leasing(-vertrag) ohne Wartungs- und Serviceleistungen des Leasinggebers
net national product at factor prices – s. Nettonationalprodukt zu Faktorpreisen, Volkseinkommen
net national welfare – s. Net National Welfare, gesamtgesellschafliche Netto-Wohlfahrt
net negative transaction exposure – s. negative Netto-Währungsumwechslungsposition
net out – v. gegenseitig aufrechnen
net position
s. Nettoposition, (Verrechnungs-)Saldo, Differenz zwischen Forderungen und Verbindlichkeiten
s. Währungsnettoposition, Netto-Währungsposition
net positive transaction exposure – s. positive Netto-Währungsumwechslungsposition
net present value method – s. Kapitalwertmethode

net profit – Reingewinn, Jahresüberschuss, Bilanzgewinn, Unternehmungsgewinn, positives Unternehmungsergebnis
net profit margin – s. Nettoumsatzrendite; Nettomarge, Nettogewinnmarge, Gewinnspanne / Umsatzrentabilität bezogen auf den Jahresüberschuss
net realisable value – s. voraussichtlich einbringbarer Forderungsbetrag
net register tonnage – s. Nettoregistertonnage
net sales – s. Umsatz-(erlöse)
netting – s. interne Positionsaufrechnung
netting of exposure – s. interne Positionsaufrechnung
net transaction risk exposure – s. Netto-Währungsumrechnungsposition
net wealth tax – s. (österr. / deutsche) Vermögensteuer
net weight – s. Nettogewicht
network
s. Netz
s. Netzplan
s. Netzwerk, Rechnernetz
network analysis – s. Netzplantechnik
net working capital – s. Nettoumlaufvermögen, Working Capital
network configuration – s. Netzwerkkonfiguration
network of branches – s. Filialnetz
network of roads – s. Straßennetz
net worth – s. Reinvermögen, Eigenkapital
net worth reserve – s. Rücklage
New Age – s. New Age, Neues Zeitalter, Wassermannzeitalter
new economy – s. neue Wirtschaft, Internet-Wirtschaft, New Economy
newly industrialising country – s. Schwellenland
new orders – s. Auftragseingang
NGO – non-governmental organisation (siehe)
nibble – s. Halbbyte
NIC – newly industrialising country (siehe)
niche strategy – s. Nischenstrategie
nitric acid – s. Salpetersäure
nitrogen dioxide – s. Stickstoffdioxid
NNW – net national welfare (siehe)
nitrous oxide – Stickstoffdioxid, Stickoxid
nitty-gritty details – s. (die schwierigen) Umsetzungsdetails
no-frills – adj. ohne Schnickschack, ohne Zusatzleistungen, Billig-
no-frills airline – Billigfluglinien
noise pollution – s. Lärmbelastung
nominal
adj. nominell, geringfügig
adj. nominal, nicht preisbereinigt, wertmäßig
adj. Erfolgs-
nominal account – s. Erfolgskonto
nominal GDP – s. nominales Bruttoinlandsprodukt / BIP
nominal GNP – s. nominales Bruttonationalprodukt / BNP
nominal share capital – s. Nominalkapital (einer AG), Stammkapital einer (GmbH)
nominal value
s. Nominalwert, Nennwert, Nominale,
s. nominaler Wert, preislich nicht bereinigte Größe
nominal wages – s. Nominallöhne
non-acceptance – s. Nichtannahme, Annahmeverweigerung
no-name product – s. generisches / markenfreies / anonymes Produkt, No-Name-Produkt
non-cancellable – s. unkündbar
non-cash expense – s. unbarer / nicht ausgabenwirksamer Aufwand
non-cash revenue – s. unbarer / nich einnahmewirksamer Ertrag
non-contributory occupational pension – s. beitragsfreie Firmen- / Betriebspension
non-convertible currency – s. nicht konvertierbare Währung
non-cumulative preference share – s. Vorzugsaktie ohne Dividendennachbezugsrecht
non-cumulative quantity discount – s. Einzelauftragsrabatt
non-cumulative tax – s. nicht-kumulative (Umsatz-)Steuer, Mehrwertsteuer
non-current investment – s. langfristige Finanzanlage
non-delivery – s. Nichtlieferung, Nichtübergabe
non-depletable resources – s. erneuerbare / unbegrenzt nutzbare Ressourcen / Energieträger
non-depreciable assets – s. nicht abnutzbare Vermögenswerte
non-discriminatory – adj. unterschiedslos, gleichförmig, gleichmäßig
non-domestic rates – s. UK-Gemeindesteuern auf Büro- und Geschäftsgebäude und Industrieobjekte
non-durable consumer goods – s. Verbrauchsgüter (im engeren Sinn)
non-durable producer goods – s. kurzlebige Produktionsgüter, Hilfs- und Betriebsstoffe
non-essentials – s. nicht lebensnotwendige Güter, Güter des gehobenen Bedarfs und Luxusgüter
non-exclusive licence – s. einfache Lizenz
non-executive director – s. nicht geschäftsführendes Mitglied des Führungsgremiums einer UK- / US-Kapitalgesellschaft, reines Aufsichtsratsmitglied
non-exhaustible resources – s. erneuerbare / unbegrenzt nutzbare Ressourcen / Energieträger
non-food items – s. Nicht-Lebensmittel- (Produkte), Non-Food-Produkte
non-governmental organisation – s. Nichtregierungsorganisation, NGO, NRO
non-interest bearing – adj. unverzinslich
non-market activities – s. nicht marktwirtschaftliche Aktivitäten / Tätigkeiten, nicht über den Markt laufende Aktivitäten / Tätigkeiten
non-negotiable cheque – s. Rektascheck
non-negotiable bill of exchange – s. Rektawechsel
non-negotiable bill of lading – s. Rektakonnossement
non-negotiable warehouse receipt – s. Lagerempfangsschein
non-notification factoring – s. stilles Factoring
non-operating expenses – s. betriebsfremde Aufwendungen
non-operating holding company – s. reine Holding, Dachgesellschaft
non-operating income – s. betriebsfremde Erträge
non-operating revenues – s. betriebsfremde Erträge
non-payout lease – s. Teilamortisationsleasing(-vertrag), Restwertleasing(-vertrag)
non-performance – s. Nichterfüllung, Nichtleistung
non-profit marketing – s. Non-Profit Marketing, Sozialmarketing
non-profit organisation – s. Non-Profit Organisation / Unternehmen
non-proprietary – adj. nicht (marken- / patentrechtlich) geschützt, nicht lizenzpflichtig, lizenzfrei, Open-Source, quelloffen
non-reciprocal – adj. einseitig, nicht reziprok, nicht gegenseitig, nicht wechselseitig
non-recourse factoring – s. echtes / regressloses Factoring
non-recurring – adj. einmalig, nicht regelmäßig erfolgend, Einzel-, außerordentlich
non-recurring transaction – s. Einzeltransaktion
non-renewable – adj. nicht erneuerbar, erschöpfbar, nicht reproduzierbar, der Substanzverringerung unterliegend
non-renewable resources – s. nicht erneuerbare / nicht

reproduzierbare / der Substanzverringerung unterliegende Ressourcen / Energieträger
non-resident – s. Gebietsfremder, Devisenausländer
non-resident benk – s. gebietsfremde Bank, Bank im Devisenausland
non-specific factor of production – s. nicht spezifischer / substitutionaler Produktionsfaktor
non-starter – s. hoffnungsloser/ aussichtsloser Fall, chancenloses Produkt
non-tariff trade barrier – s. nichttarifäres / außertarifäres Handelshemmnis
non-traded goods and services – s. nicht (international) gehandelte Waren und Dienstleistungen
non-traded option – s. Freiverkehrsoption, nicht-börsengehandelte Option, bankmäßige (Devisen-)Option
non-voting share – s. stimmrechtslose Aktie
non-wage labour costs – s. Lohn-, Personalnebenkosten
non-wasting asset – s. nicht der Substanzverringerung unterliegender / reproduzierbarer / Vermögensgegenstand
no-par-value share – s. Quoten-, Anteilsaktie, nennwertlose Aktie
normal value – s. Normalwert
notary public – s. Notar
notation
s. Vermerk, Anmerkung
s. Schreibweise
note
s. Banknote
s. Wechsel, Solawechsel, Schuldschein
s. kurz- bis mittelfristige Schuldverschreibung
notebook – s. Notebook
notebook-size computer – s. Computer im Taschenformat, Notebook
note dispenser – s. Geldausgabevorrichtung
note-issuing bank – s. Notenbank
notes payable – s. Schuldwechsel, Wechselverbindlichkeiten (aufgrund von Warenlieferungen und Leistungen)
Notes Payable – s. (das Konto) Schuldwechsel / Wechselverbindlichkeiten (aufgrund von Warenlieferungen und Leistungen)
Notes Payable – Miscellaneous – s. (das Konto) sonstige Wechselverbindlichkeiten
notes receivable – s. Besitzwechsel, Wechsel, Wechselforderungen, Rimessen
Notes Receivable – s. Rimessen(-konto), Besitzwechsel(-konto)
notice – s. Kündigung, Kündigungsfrist
without notice – fristlos
until further notice – bis auf weiteres, bis auf Widerruf
notice deposit – s. Kündigungsgeld
notice of assessment – s. Steuerbescheid
issue a notice of assessment – einen Steuerbescheid erlassen
notice of dishonour – s. Notanzeige, Benachrichtigung über die Nichtzahlung bzw. Annahmeverweigerung eines Wechsels / Schecks
notice of withdrawal – s. Kündigungsfrist (bei Termin- und Spareinlagen)
notice period – s. Kündigungsfrist
notification – s. Verständigung
notification factoring – s. offenes Factoring
notify – v. verständigen, in Kenntnis setzen, unterrichten
notion – s. Begriff, Idee, Vorstellung
notional amount – s. nomineller / fiktiver / virtueller Kapitalbetrag
not negotiable
adj. (beim Scheck) mit Ausschluss des Gutglaubensschutzes
adj. (beim Wechsel) Rekta-, nicht durch Indossament und/oder Übergabe übertragbar
bill marked not negotiable – Rektawechsel
not-negotiable bill of lading – s. (nicht begebbare) Konnossementskopie
NOW account – s. kombiniertes Spar- und Scheckkonto
NPV method – net present value method (siehe)
nuclear fission – s. Kernspaltung
nuclear fusion – s. Kernfusion
nuclear power – s. Atom-, Kernkraft
nuke – s. Atomkraftwerk
numerator – s. Zähler (einer Bruchzahl)
numerical control – s. NC-Steuerung, numerische Steuerung, Computersteuerung
numerical data – s. numerische Daten
NYSE – New York Stock Exchange

O

oats – s. Hafer
obviate – v. unötig / überflüssig machen
object – s. Gegenstand, Objekt
objective – s. Ziel
set objectives – Ziele setzen / festsetzen / festlegen
identify objectives – Ziele ermitteln
Objective One area – s. Ziel-eins-Gebiet
object leased – s. Vermietungsobjekt, Gegenstand des Leasingvertrags
object program – s. Maschinensprachenprogramm, Zielsprachenprogramm
obligation – s. Verpflichtung
meet obligations – Verpflichtungen nachkommen
obligatory period – s. Grundmietzeit
observational method – s. Beobachtung(-smethode)
obsolescence – s. Überholung, Veralten, Überalterung
obstacle – s. Hindernis
obtain – v. erhalten, bekommen, beschaffen, erzielen
obtain better prices – bessere Preise erzielen
obtainable – adj. erhältlich, erzielbar
prices obtainable abroad – im Ausland erzielbare Preise
occupant – s. Inhaber, Benutzer
occupation – s. Beschäftigung, Beruf
occupational disease – s. Berufskrankheit, berufsbedingte Krankheit
occupational distribution of income – s. berufsspezifische Einkommensverteilung
occupational licensing – s. gewerberechtliche(s) Genehmigung(-sverfahren)
occupational pension – s. Firmen-, Betriebspension
occupier (of a property) – s. Besitzer / Nutzer eines Immobilienobjektes
occur – v. geschehen, eintreten, erfolgen, durchgeführt werden
occurrence – s. Eintritt (eines Ereignisses), Ereignis
ocean bill of lading – s. Konnossement, (begebbarer) Seefrachtbrief
ocean cargo policy – s. Seefrachtversicherung(-spolizze)
ocean marine cargo insurance – s. Seefrachtversicherung
ocean marine hull insurance – s. Seekaskoversicherung
ocean marine insurance – s. Seeversicherung
(ocean) marine insurance policy – s. Seetransportversicherungspolizze
O-chart – organisation chart (siehe)
OCR optical character recognition (siehe)
odd – adj. seltsam, ungerade, unrund
odd number – s. unrunde Zahl
OECD – Organization for Economic Cooperation and Development (siehe)
OEM – original equipment manufacturer (siehe)
OFGAS – Office of Gas Supply (ehemalige Aufsichtsbehörde der britischen Gaswirtschaft)
off – adj. aus(-geschaltet), „nein"
OFGEM – Office of Gas and Electricity Markets (Aufsichtsbehörde der britischen Gas- und Elektrizitätswirtschaft)
off-balance sheet – adj. außerbilanziell, nicht in der Bilanz ausgewiesen
off-balance sheet item – s. außerbilanzieller Posten
off-balance sheet liabilities – außerbilanzielle Verbindlichkeiten
offer
s. Antrag
s. Anbot, Angebot, Offerte
s. Brief-, Verkaufs-, Devisenbrief-, Devisenverkaufskurs
make an offer – einen Antrag / ein Angebot machen
submit an offer – ein Angebot unterbreiten
refuse an offer – ein Angebot ablehnen
turn down an offer – ein Angebot ablehnen
offer
v. anbieten, offerieren
v. (sich) bieten, leisten
we offer you firm – wir bieten Ihnen fest an
offer resistance – Widerstand leisten
offer an opportunity – eine / die Gelegenheit bieten
offer price – s. Brief-, Verkaufs-, Devisenbrief-, Devisenverkaufskurs
offer rate – s. Brief-, Verkaufs-, Devisenbrief-, Devisenverkaufskurs
offer without obligation – s. freibleibendes / unverbindliches Angebot
offered price – s. Brief-, Verkaufs-, Devisenbrief-, Devisenverkaufskurs
offered rate – s. Brief-, Verkaufs-, Devisenbrief-, Devisenverkaufskurs
offeree – s. Antragnehmer, Oblat, Adressat eines Antrages
offer for sale
s. Fremdemission auf eigene Rechnung, Emissionsvermittlung auf eigene Rechnung, feste Übernahme einer Emission durch ein Emissionskonsortium
s. öffentliche Zeichnungsangebot
offeror – s. Antragsteller, Anbieter
offer subject to confirmation – s. freibleibendes / unverbindliches Angebot
offer with a (fixed) time limit for acceptance – s. befristetes Angebot
offer without engagement – s. freibleibendes / unverbindliches Angebot
off-high-street location – s. Billiglage, Nebenlage
office
s. Büro
s. Amt
office of president – das Amt des Vorstandsvorsitzenden
office block – s. Bürogebäude
office equipment – s. Büroausstattung (Büromaschinen & Bürogeräte & Büromöbel)
Office Equipment – s. (das Konto) Büroausstattung
Office Expense – s. (das Konto) Büroaufwand
office manager – s. Büroleiter/in, Bürovorsteher/in
office personnel – s. Büropersonal
office supplies – s. Bürobedarf, -material, -artikel
officer
s. Organ / Mitglied der Geschäftsleitung einer Kapitalgesellschaft
s. Referent/in, Bevollmächtigte/r, Beauftragte/r
environmental officer – Umweltbeauftragter
office worker – s. Büroarbeiter/in, Büroangestellte/r
official exchange rate – s. amtlicher / offizieller Wechselkurs
official gold and foreign currency reserves – s. offizielle (Gold- und) Währungsreserven
official interest rate – s. Leitzinsatz
offline – adj. / adv. off-line, offline, rechner-, server-netzunabhängig
offline storage – rechnerunabhängiger Datenspeicher

work off-line - offline arbeiten
offload - v. abladen
off-premises - adj. / adv. außerhalb der Geschäftsräumlichkeiten / des Betriebsgeländes
off-season - s. tote Saison, Vor- und Nachsaison
offset - s. Parallel-, Kopplungsgeschäft
offset - v. ausgleichen, kompensieren, aufwiegen, aufrechnen, in Gegenrechnung bringen, verrechnen
offset claims - Forderungen gegenseitig aufrechnen
offsetting sale - s. Glattstellungsverkauf, Verkauf zur Glattstellung
offsetting transaction - s. Gegengeschäft, börsenmäßiges Deckungsgeschäft, Glattstellungstransaktion, -geschäft
OFWAT - Office of Water Services (UK-Wasserwirtschaftsaufsichtsbehörde)
oil rig - s. Ölbohrturm
oil spill - s. Ölkatastrophe, -havarie, -austritt, -verschmutzung, Tankerunfall
oil well - s. Öl-, Erdölsonde
old age allowance - s. Altersfreibetrag
oligopoly - s. Oligopol
oligopolistic market - s. oligopolistischer Markt, Oligopol
omission - s. Auslassung, Unterlassung
on - adj. aktiv, ein(-geschaltet), „ja"
on-board bill of lading - s. Bordkonnossement
oncarriage / on-carriage - s. Weiterbeförderung, Weitertransport, anschließende Beförderung
oncarrier - s. Nachbeförderer, Anschlussfrachtführer, -spediteur, Weiterbeförderer
on-demand bond - s. Bankgarantie auf erstes Anfordern
one-off - adj. einmalig, nicht wiederholbar, Einzel-, Einmal-
one-off exercise - s. Einzelaktion, Einzelvorgang, Einmalaktion
one-off operation - s. Einzelaktion, Einmalprozess, singuläre Aktivität
one-stage channel - s. einstufiger Vertrieb(-skanal)
one-stop shopping - s. One-Stop-Shopping, Komplettangebot, „Alles unter einem Dach"
one-to-one marketing - s. Eins-zu-eins-Marketing, Individual-, Einzelkundenmarketing, One-to-One-Marketing
one-year forward rate - s. ein-Jahres-Terminkurs, Terminkurs per ein Jahr
on-lend - v. weiterverleihen
online / one-line - adj./ adv. on-line, online, rechnerabhängig, internetgestützt
online marketing - Online Marketing
work on-line - online arbeiten
go on-line - ins / ans Netz gehen
online broking - s. Online-Maklergeschäft, Online-Brokergeschäft
online commerce - s. Online-Handel, E-Commerce, elektronischer Handel, Internethandel
online consulting - s. Online-Unternehmensberatung
online file - s. rechnerabhängige Datei, Oneline-Datei
online insurance - s. Online-Versicherung(-swesen), E-Versicherung, Internet-Versicherungsgeschäft
online marketing - s. Online Marketing, elektronisches Marketing, Internet-Marketing
online recruiting - s. Online-Personalbeschaffung
online shopping - E-Shopping, Internet-Shopping, Internetkauf, Online-Kauf
oneline stock trading - s. Online-Aktienhandel / Börsenhandel
online storage device - s. Online-/ rechnerabhängige Speichereinhiet
on site - adv. vor Ort, an Ort und Stelle, auf dem Betriebsgelände, in den Geschäftsräumlichkeiten

OPEC - Organisation of Petroleum Exporting Countries
open account - s. offene Rechnung
on open account - gegen offene Rechnung
amount owing on open account - offene (ungesicherte) Buchforderung(en)
on / under open account terms - gegen offene Rechnung
open cheque - s. Barscheck
open container - s. offener Container
open corporation - s. (etwa) Aktiengesellschaft
open cover - s. Pauschaldeckung
open-end fund - s. (am.) offener Investmentfonds, Investmentfonds des Treuhandtypus, Kapitalanlagegesellschaft nach dem Fondsprinzip
opening bank - s. Akkreditivbank
opening stock - s. Anfangsbestand
open-market operation - s. Offen-Markt-Operation
open outcry - s. offener (Preis-)Zuruf, offener (Preis-)Ausruf
open reserve - s. offene Rücklage
open tendering - s. öffentliche Ausschreibung
operate - v. arbeiten, tätig sein, laufen, Leistungen erstellen, betreiben, führen, verwalten
operate at full capacity - voll ausgelastet arbeiten
operate a business ein Geschäft betreiben
operate on sthg. - etwas bearbeiten
operate an information system - ein Informationssystem verwalten / betreiben
operating cash flow - s. operativer Cash Flow
operating cost(s)
s. Betriebskosten, betriebliche Aufwendungen
operating department - s. Betriebs- / Leistungsabteilung
operating expense(s)
s. Betriebsaufwand, betriebliche Aufwendungen
operating income
s. (positives) Betriebsergebnis, Betriebsgewinn,
s. betriebsbedingte Erträge
operating lease - s. Operatingleasing(-vertrag)
operating loss - s. negatives Betriebsergebnis, Betriebsverlust
operating parent - s. operative / in der betrieblichen Leistungserstellung tätige Mutter(-gesellschaft)
operating profit - s. (positives) Betriebsergebnis, Betriebsgewinn, (etwa) EBIT-Gewinn
operating profit ratio - s. Umsatzrentabilität / Umsatzmarge bezogen auf das Betriebsergebnis, (etwa) EBIT-Marge
operating rate - s. Kapazitätsauslastung, -nutzungsgrad, Beschäftigungsgrad
operating ratio - s. Betriebsaufwand als Prozentsatz des Umsatzes, (etwa) Betriebskostendeckung
operating revenues - s. betriebsbedingte Erträge
operating software - s. Systemsoftware, Betriebssystem
operation - s. Betrieb, Geschäftstätigkeit, Arbeitsvorgang, Tätigkeitsbereich, (finanzielle) Transaktion, Führung, Leitung, (pl.) betriebliche Leistungserstellung
operational
adj. leistungswirtschaftlich, zum Leistungserstellungsbereich gehörend, operativ
adj. operational, quantifizierbar, rechnerisch nachvollziehbar
operational assets - s. betrieblich genutztes / produktives Anlagevermögen
operational auditing - s. Operational Auditing, (etwa) Wirtschaftlichkeits- und Rentabilitätsprüfung
operational budget - s. leistungswirtschaftliches Budget, leistungswirtschaftlicher Plan
operational definition - s. operationale Definition
operational department - s. Betriebs- / Leistungsabteilung
operational planning - s. operative Planung

operational task(s) – s. Leistungserstellung, Linienfunktion
operations – s. Geschäftstätigkeit, betriebliche Leistungserstellung
operations control – s. Betriebskontrolle, -kontrollsystem, operative Kontrolle, operatives Kontrollsystem
operations research – s. Operations Research, (quantitative Methoden der) Unternehmensforschung
operator
s. Bedienungsperson, Maschinist/in
s. Unternehmer/in
s. Marktteilnehmer/in, Händler/in, (Börsen-)Spekulant/in
opinion
s. Meinung, Ansicht, Anschauung
s. Gutachten, Stellungnahme, (Bestätigungs-)Vermerk, Befund
opinion poll – s. Meinungsumfrage
opportunity cost – s. Opportunitäts-, Alternativkosten, alternative Kosten
opt – v. optieren, wählen, sich entscheiden
opt for sthg. – sich für etwas entscheiden
opt out – aussteigen, draußen bleiben
optical character recognition – s. optische Zeichenerkennung
optical disk – s. optische Speicherplatte
optical fibre – s. Glasfaser, optische Faser
optical scanner – s. optischer Scanner, optisches Lesegerät
optimum coverage – s. optimale Reichweite
option
s. Option, (Wahl-)Möglichkeit
s. Option, Wertpapier-, Devisenoption
We have no option. – Wir haben keine Wahl.
exercise an option – eine Option ausüben
option buyer – s. Optionskäufer/in, -inhaber/in, -nehmer/in
options exchange – s. Optionsbörse
option fee – s. (Options-)Prämie
option forward – s. Termingeschäft mit Laufzeitoption
option hedging – s. Kurssicherung mittels Devisenoptionen
option holder – s. Optionskäufer/in, -inhaber/in, -nehmer/in
option on a swap – s. Option auf einen (Zins-)Swap, Swaption
option period – s. Optionszeitraum, -frist, -laufzeit
option premium – s. Optionsprämie, -preis
option price – s. Optionspreis, -prämie
option seller – s. Optionsverkäufer/in, -schreiber/in, -geber/in, -stillhalter/in
option taker – s. Optionskäufer/in, -inhaber/in, -nehmer/in
option writer – s. Optionsverkäufer/in, -schreiber/in, -geber/in, -stillhalter/in
OR – operations research (siehe)
order
s. Befehl, Anweisung
s. Auftrag, Bestellung
s. Order
s. Ordnung, Reihenfolge
unconditional order – unbedingte Anweisung
place an order – einen Auftrag erteilen
meet / execute / fill / carry out an order – einen Auftrag ausführen
cancel an order – einen Auftrag stornieren
confirm an order – einen Auftrag bestätigen
supply goods against an order – Waren aufgrund eines Auftrages liefern
order placed against an offer – aufgrund eines Angebotes erteilter Auftrag
made out to shipper's order – an Order des Befrachters ausgestellt
call a meeting to order – den Ordnungsruf erteilen, eine Sitzung formell eröffnen
in this order – in dieser Reihenfolge
order assembly – s. Auftragszusammenstellung
order bill
s. Orderwechsel
s. Order-, Namenskonnossement
order bill (of exchange) – s. Orderwechsel
order book
s. Auftragsbuch, -ordner
s. Auftragsbestand, Bestand an unerledigten Aufträgen
order cheque – s. Namens-, Orderscheck
order instrument – s. Orderpapier
order intake – s. Auftragseingang, Zugang an Aufträgen
order of a court – s. Gerichtsbeschluss
order processing – s. Auftragsbearbeitung, -abwicklung
order processing clerk – s. Auftragsbearbeiter/in
ordinary dividend – s. Stammdividende
ordinary resolution – s. Beschluss mit einfacher Mehrheit
ordinary share – s. Stammaktie
ordinary share capital – s. Stammaktienkapital
ordinary shareholder – s. Stammaktieninhaber/in
ore – s. Erz
ore-deposit – s. Erzlagerstätte, Erzvorkommen
ore carrier – s. Erzfrachter
organic
adj. organisch
adj. biologisch, Bio-, Natur-
organic cultivation – s. biologischer Landbau, biologische Landwirtschaft, Biolandbau, -landwirtschaft
organic farming – s. biologischer Landbau, biologische Landwirtschaft, Biolandbau, -landwirtschaft
organic farmer – s. Biobauer, Biobäuerin, Bio-Landwirt/in, biologischer Landwirtschaftsbetrieb
organic fertiliser – s. Natur-, Biodünger
organic food – s. biologische Nahrungsmittel / Lebensmittel, Bio-Lebensmittel
organic produce – s. biologische Nahrungsmittel / Lebensmittel / Produkte, Bioprodukte
organisation
s. Organisation
s. Unternehmen, Firma
organisational development – s. Organisationsentwicklung
organisational goals – s. Organisations-, Unternehmensziele
organisational level – s. Organisations- / Hierarchieebene
organisational procedures – s. organisatorische Abläufe, Organisationsregeln, Ablauforganisation
organisational structure – s. Aufbauorganisation, Organisationsstruktur
organisational unit – s. Organisationseinheit
organisation chart – s. Organigramm, Organisationsschaubild
Organization for Economic Cooperation and Development – s. Organisation für wirtschaftliche Zusammenarbeit und Entwicklung, OECD
original cost – s. Anschaffungskosten und / oder Herstellungskosten
original equipment manufacturer – s. Original Equipment Manufacturer, (in gewissen Branchen) Zulieferer, Originalteilhersteller
originate
v. stammen, entspringen, Usprung haben
v. erstellen, produziere
goods originating in the USA – aus den USA stammende Waren; Waren, die ihren Ursprung in den USA haben
originate texts – Texte erstellen / produzieren
origin method – s. Entstehungsrechnung (für das BNP / BIP)

origin of goods – s. Ursprung von Waren
origin principle – s. Ursprungslandprinzip
OTC – over-the-counter (siehe)
OTC option – over-the-counter option (siehe)
other business – s. Allfälliges (bei Sitzungen)
other expenses –s. betriebsfremde Aufwendungen
other income
s. betriebsfremde Erträge
s. sonstige Einkommen
other revenues – s. betriebsfremde Erträge
outdoor media – s. Medien der Außenwerbung
outflow of capital – s. Kapitalabfluss
outflow of cash
s. Auszahlung, Ausgabe
s. (pl.) Auszahlungs-, Ausgabenreihe, Auszahlungs-, Ausgabenstrom
outflow of funds – s. Abfluss von Zahlungsmitteln, Auszahlungen, Ausgaben,
outgoing message – s. ausgesandte Botschaft / Mitteilung
outlet
s. Laden, Geschäft, Verkaufsstelle
s. Markt, Absatzmöglichkeit, Investitionsmöglichkeit
output
s. Output, Produktion(-smenge), Leistung
s. (Daten-)Ausgabe, (Daten-)Output
s. Lagerabgang
output – v. ausgeben
output data from a system – Daten aus einem System ausgeben
output approach – s. Entstehungsrechnung (für das BNP / BIP)
output device – s. Ausgabegerät
output measure – s. Entstehungsrechnung (für das BNP / BIP)
output method – s. Entstehungsrechnung (für das BNP / BIP)
output tax – s. Bruttoumsatzsteuer, Umsatzsteuer vor Vorsteuerabzug
outright
adj. direkt, glatt, völlig, total, bedingungslos
adj. / adv. ohne Rückgriff
adj. Solo-
outright forward rate – s. Solo-Terminkurs, Outright-Terminkurs
outside director – s. nicht geschäftsführendes Mitglied des Führungsgremiums einer UK- / US-Kapitalgesellschaft, reines Aufsichtsratsmitglied
outside services – s. zugekaufte Dienstleistungen
outsource – v. auslagern, outsourcen, (Aufträge) an Subunternehmer / Zulieferer vergeben
outsource production – Produktion auslagern
outsourcing – s. Outsourcing; Einsatz von Subunternehmern / Zulieferern; Auslagern von Aufträgen / Leistungen / Geschäftsbereichen
outstanding
adj. offen, nicht bezahlt, aushaftend
adj. außerordentlich, bedeutend
balance outstanding from time to time – jeweils offener / aushaftender Saldo / Betrag
outstanding account – s. offene / unbezahlte Rechnung, offene Forderung
outstanding receivable – s. offene Forderung / Rechnung
outward direct investment – s. direkte Investitionen im Ausland, aktive Direktinvestitionen (im Ausland)
outward investment – s. Investitions-, Kapitalabfluss, Kapitalabgang
outward processing – s. passiver Veredelungsverkehr
overall – adj. gesamt, Gesamt-, Total-,
overall quota – Gesamt-, Globalkontingent
overall deficit – Gesamtdefizit
overall return – Gesamtrendite
overbanking – s. Oberbanking, zu hohe (Bank-)Filialdichte
overcharge – s. Überfakturierung, überhöhter Rechnungsbetrag
overdraft
s. Kontokorrentkredit
s. Kontoüberziehung, Überziehungskredit
overdraw – v. überziehen
overdraw an account – ein Konto überziehen
overdue – adj. überfällig
overhead(s) – s. Gemeinkosten, indirekte Kosten
overhead cost(s) – s. Gemeinkosten, indirekte Kosten
overhead rate – s. Gemeinkostenzuschlag
overheated – adj. überhitzt
over-invoice – v. überfakturieren
overlap – v. (sich) überlappen / überschneiden
overnight money – s. Tagesgeld
override – v. außer Kraft setzen, (rechtlichen) Vorrang haben vor, größere Rechtskraft haben als
A overrides B – A hat rechtlichen Vorrang vor / größere Rechtskraft als B
overseas – adj. / adv. Auslands-, im Ausland, ausländisch
overseas agent – s. selbständiger Handelsvertreter/in im Ausland / Auslandsvertreter/in
overseas trade – s. Außenhandel
over-the-counter – adj. / adv. (wörtlich) über den Ladentisch, nicht börsengehandelt, außerbörslich, bankgehandelt, bankmäßig
over-the-counter market – s. Freiverkehr(-sbörse), außerbörslicher Handel,
over-the-counter option – s. Freiverkehrsoption, nicht börsengehandelte Option, bankmäßige Devisenoption
overtaxation – s. Überbesteuerung, überhöhte Besteuerung
overtime – s. Überstunden
overtime pay – s. Überstundenlohn(-satz), -zuschlag, -entgelt, -entlohnung
overvalued – adj. überbewertet
owe – v. schulden
a debt is owing – ein Betrag wird geschuldet
owner-occupied dwelling – s. Eigenheim, Eigentumswohnung
owner-occupier – s. Eigenbesitzer
owners' equity – s. Eigenkapital
owners'-equity-to-total-assets ratio – s. Eigenkapitalanteil, -quote
owners' funds – s. Eigenkapital, -mittel
ownership – s. Eigentum, Eigentumsrecht, -verhältnisse
ownership rights – s. Eigentumsrechte
own label – s. Eigen-, Haus-, Händler-, Handelsmarke
oxygen – s. Sauerstoff
ozone – s. Ozon
ozone-depleting – adj. ozonschichtschädigend, ozonzerstörend

P

pack – s. Packung, Schachtel, Packerl
package – s. Packung, Paket, Packstück, Frachtstück, Kollo, Verpackung
packaging – s. Aufmachung, Packungsgestaltung
packet – s. (Daten-)Paket
packet switching – s. Paketvermittlungstechnik
packing – s. Verpackung, Verpacken
packing container – s. Verpackung(-sbehälter)
packing list – s. Packliste
paid-up capital – s. eingezahltes Grund- / Stammkapital
pallet – s. (Lade-)Palette
palletisation – s. Palettisierung, Umstellung auf / Verwendung von Paletten
palmtop – s. (älterer Ausdruck für) *personal digital assistant* (siehe)
paper-based – adj. auf Formularbasis
paper bid – s. Umtausch-Übernahmeangebot, (öffentliches) Übernahmeangebot mit Bezahlung des Übernahmepreises in Form von Wertpapieren (Aktien) der bietenden Firma
paper clip – s. Büroklammer
paper-folding machine – s. Papierfalt-, Brieffaltmaschine
paper gain – s. Buchgewinn, nicht realisierter Gewinn
paper jam – s. Papierstau
paperless – adj. papierlos, elektronisch, online
paperless office – papierloses Büro
paperless job-hunting – Online-Stellensuche
paper loss – s. Buchverlust, nicht realisierter Verlust
paper punch – s. Locher
paper tape – s. Lochstreifen
par – s. Nennwert, Pariwert, pari
issue shares at par – Aktien al pari emittieren
issue shares below par – Aktien unter pari / mit einem Disagio emittieren
issue shares above par – Aktien über pari / mit einem Agio emittieren
paradox of value – s. Wertparadoxon
paragon – s. Vorbild, Ausbund
parallel market – s. Parallelmarkt
parcel
s. Paket, Postpaket
s. Grundstück, Parzelle
s. (Waren-)Posten
parcel service – s. Paketdienst
parent – s. Mutter(-gesellschaft), Konzernmutter
parent company – s. Mutter(-gesellschaft), Konzernmutter
parent currency – s. Konsolidierungs-, Mutterwährung, Währung der Konzernmutter
parity – s. fester Wechselkurs, (Währungs-)Parität
part – s. Bestandteil, Komponente
part delivery – s. Teillieferung
partial – adj. partiell, teilweise, Teil-
partial loss or damage – s. Teilverlust, -schaden
participating preference share – s. Vorzugsaktie mit zusätzlicher Gewinnbeteiligung
particular average – s. Partikularhavarie, Teilschaden
particular average loss – s. Partikularhavarie, Teilverlust, Teilschaden
part-load goods – s. (Eisenbahn-)Stückgut
partly-owned subsidiary – s. Beteiligungstochter, Teiltochter
partly-paid share – s. nicht voll / teilweise eingezahlte Aktie
partner
s. Partner/in, Geschäftspartner/in
s. Teilhaber/in / Gesellschafter/in einer Personengesellschaft
partners' equity – s. Anteil an einer Personengesellschaft
partnership – s. Personengesellschaft
partnership agreement – s. Gesellschaftsvertrag (einer Personengesellschaft)
part payment – s. Teilzahlung
parts per million – s. Teile pro Million
part-time agent – s. nebenberuflicher Sammelbesteller/in
part-time director – nicht geschäftsführendes Mitglied des Führungsgremiums einer UK- /US-Kapitalgesellschaft, reines Aufsichtsratsmitglied
part-time job – s. Teilzeitarbeitsplatz, -beschäftigung
part with – v. sich trennen von, herausgeben
part with goods – sich von der Ware trennen, die Ware herausgeben
party – s. (Vertrags-)Partei
party to the contract – s. Vertragspartei
par value – s. Nennwert
PASCAL – s. PASCAL-Programmiersprache
pass – v. übergehen, ausfallen lassen
pass the dividend – die Dividende ausfallen lassen
passage of time – s. Zeitablauf
passbook – s. Sparbuch
passbook savings account – s. Sparkonto
passenger liner – s. Passagierlinienschiff
passenger train – s. Personenzug
passing of property – s. Eigentumsübergang
passing of the title to the goods – s. Eigentumsübergang
pass on – v. weitergeben, abwälzen
pass on a cost increase – eine Kostenerhöhung (auf die Kunden) abwälzen
password – s. Losungswort
past-due – adj. überfällig
paste – v. kleben, einkleben, einfügen
patent – s. Patent
grant a patent – ein Patent erteilen
take out a patent – ein Patent nehmen
patentee – s. Patentinhaber/in
patent holder – s. Patentinhaber/in
patron – s. (Stamm-)Kunde/Kundin
patronage – s. (Bestehen einer längerfristigen) Kundenbeziehung, Kundschaft
pattern
s. (Stoff-)Muster
s. Struktur, Verlaufsstruktur, -muster
pattern of industry – s. Industrie-, Branchenstruktur
pay – s. Bezahlung, Entlohnung
pay – v. zahlen, bezahlen
pay a sum into an account – eine Summe auf ein Konto einzahlen
pay for goods – Ware bezahlen
payable – adj. zahlbar, zu zahlen
payable at sight – adj. zahlbar bei Sicht
payables – s. (Buch- und Wechsel-)Verbindlichkeiten (aufgrund von Warenlieferungen oder Leistungen)
Pay-As-You-Earn system – s. Lohnsteuerabzugssystem, -verfahren
payback method – s. Amortisationsvergleichsrechnung, Pay-Off-Rechnung, Payback-Rechnung
payback period – s. Amortisationszeit, -dauer, Kapitalrückflussdauer, Payback-Periode

P.A.Y.E. system – Pay-As-You-Earn system (siehe)
P.A.Y.E. tax – s. Lohnsteuer
payee – s. (Zahlungs-)Empfänger/in, Begünstigte/r, Remittent/in, Nehmer/in
paying agency – s. auszahlende Stelle, Zahlstelle
paying bank – s. Zahlstelle
payment – s. Zahlung, Begleichung, Zahlungsausgleich, -leistung
effect / make payment – Zahlung leisten / durchführen
payment is effected / made – Zahlung erfolgt
in payment of an invoice – zur Begleichung einer Rechnung
payment by results – s. Leistungslohn, leistungsorientierte Entlohnung
payment in advance – s. Vorauszahlung, Zahlung im Voraus
payment in cash
s. Barzahlung
s. Barleistung, Barbezug, monetäres Entgelt
payment in kind – s. Sachleistung, -entgelt, -bezug, Naturalleistung
payment (of a bill of exchange) – s. Zahlung (eines Wechsels)
payment on invoice – s. Zahlung bei Rechnungserhalt
payment on receipt of goods – s. Zahlung bei Erhalt der Ware
payment on receipt of invoice – s. Zahlung bei Rechungserhalt
payment record – s. (etwa) Zahlungsmoral
payment term – s. Zahlungsziel
pay packet – s. Lohntüte, -sackerl
payout – s. Ausschüttung, Dividendenzahlung
payout ratio – s. Ausschüttungsquote
payroll
s. Lohn-, Gehaltsliste
s. Lohnsumme
s. Beschäftigte
pay-roll accounting – s. Lohnverrechnung, Lohnbuchhaltung(sabteilung)
payroll section – s. Lohnbuchhaltung(-sabteilung)
payroll tax
s. (einbehaltene) Lohnsteuer
s. Sozialversicherungsabgabe
s. Lohnsummensteuer
PAYTERMS – s. PAYTERMS, standardisierte internationale Zahlungsbedingungen
pay up v. (endlich) zahlen, einzahlen
PBX – private branch exchange (siehe)
PC – personal computer (siehe)
PCSs – personal communication services (siehe)
PDA – s. personal digital assistant (siehe)
PE – private equity (siehe)
peak out – v. den Höhepunkt erreichen (und überschreiten)
pecuniary resources – s. Geldmittel
peer – s. Gleichgestellte/r
peer pressure – s. Gruppendruck
peg – s. fester / fixer Wechselkurs
peg – v. fixieren, festlegen
pegged exchange rate – fester / fixer Wechselkurs
pegged rate – s. fester / fixer Wechselkurs
penalise – v. bestrafen
penalty – s. Strafe, Vertrags-, Konventionalstrafe
penalty clause – s. Vertragsstrafenklausel
penalty for late payment – s. Verzugs-, Strafzinsen
penalty interest (for late payment) – s. Verzugs-, Strafzinsen
penalty tariff – s. Strafzoll
pence rate – s. Preisnotierung
pending – adj. anhängig, schwebend
pending lawsuit – schwebendes / anhängiges Verfahren
penetration pricing – s. Penetrationspreisstrategie
penetration rate – s. Penetrationsrate, Nutzeranteil, Distributionsdichte
pension fund – s. Pensionskasse, Pensionsversicherungsanstalt
pension scheme – s. Pensionsplan, -programm
per capita – adj. Pro-Kopf , pro Kopf
per capita GDP – s. Pro-Kopf Bruttoinlandsprodukt, Pro-Kopf-BIP
per capita GNP – s. Bruttonationalprodukt pro Kopf, Pro-Kopf-Nationalprodukt
per capita income – s. Pro-Kopf-Einkommen
per capita wealth – s. Pro-Kopf-Vermögen
percentage – s. Prozentsatz, -wert, -zahl
percentage of cover – s. Deckungs-, Garantiequote
percentage of loss insured – s. Deckungs-, Garantiequote
percentage rule – s. Prozentregel, -kriterium
percentage share – s. Prozentanteil
perception – s. Perzeption, Sichtweise, Wahrnehmung
customer perception – Kundenwahrnehmung
perfect competition – s. vollständiger / vollkommener Wettbewerb
perfect hedge – Perfect Hedge, perfekte Immunisierung gegen mögliche (Wechsel-)Kursschwankungen
perfect knowledge of the market – s. genaue Kenntnisse des Marktes, (absolute) Markttransparenz
perfect market – s. vollkommener Markt
perfect substitute – s. (völlig) gleichwertiges Ersatzgut / Substitut
perform – v. erfüllen, durchführen, erbringen
perform auditing – (Abschluss-)Prüfungen durchführen, Prüfungstätigkeit ausüben
perform a contract – einen Vertrag erfüllen
perform a service – eine Dienstleistung erbringen
performance
s. Erfüllung
s. Leistung, Abschneiden, Resultat, Ergebnis
performance bond – s. Liefer-, Leistungs-, Erfüllungsgarantie
post a performance bond – eine Liefergarantie stellen
call a performance bond – eine Liefergarantie in Anspruch nehmen
performance of a contract – s. Vertragserfüllung
peril – s. Gefahr, Risiko
perils of the sea – s. Seerisken, Gefahren der See
period
s. Periode, Zeitraum, Zeitdauer
s. Fälligkeit, Fälligkeitstermin
period cost(s) – s. Periodenkosten
periodic expense – s. Periodenkosten, -aufwand
periodic income – s. Periodenertrag, -erträge
period of assessment – s. Veranlagungszeitraum
period of grace – s. rückzahlungsfreie Periode, rückzahlungsfreier Teil der Kreditlaufzeit
period of notice – s. Kündigungsfrist
peripheral – adj. peripher, weniger wichtig, dezentral, nicht zentral, Neben-
peripheral device – s. periphere Einheit, Peripheriegerät
peripheral equipment – s. periphere Einheiten, Peripherie
peripheral field – s. Nebengeschäftsfeld, kein Kerngeschäftsfeld
peripherals – s. periphere Einheiten, Peripherie
peripheral unit – s. periphere Einheit, Peripheriegerät
perishable – adj. leicht verderblich
perishable product – s. leicht verderbliches Produkt

perishables – s. leicht verderbliche Produkte
permanent investments – s. Finanzanlagevermögen, langfristige Finanzanlagen, Wertpapiere des Anlagevermögens
permissible – adj. zulässig, erlaubt
persistent – adj. anhaltend, hartnäckig, gewohnheitsmäßig
persistent dumping – s. Dauerdumping, langfristiges Dumping
personal accident insurance – s. Unfall-, Personenschadenversicherung
personal allowance – s. (persönlicher / auf den persönlichen Umständen eines Steuerpflichtigen beruhender) Freibetrag
personal code – s. persönlicher (Identifikations-)Code
personal computer – s. Personalcomputer, PC
personal communication services – s. persönliche Kommunikationsdienste, Personal Communication Services, Mobilfunkdienste der digitalen Mobilfunknetze
personnel consulting – s. Personalberatung
personnel consulting agency – s. Personalberatungsagentur, Personalberater
personal consumption – s. privater Konsum
personal digial assistant – s. Handcomputer, Handheld, Handheld-Gerät, Handheld-Computer, PDA
Personal Identification Number – s. persönlicher Identifikationscode, PIN-Code
personal distribution of income – s. personelle Einkommensverteilung
personal income – s. persönliches Einkommen (aus selbständiger und unselbständiger Erwerbstätigkeit)
personal income tax – s. Einkommensteuer
personal injury – s. Körperverletzung, Personenschaden
personal lending – s. Vergabe von Privatkrediten, Privatkreditgeschäft
personal loan – s. Privatkredit
personal property – s. bewegliche Sachen und Rechte
personal savings rate – s. persönliche Sparquote, Sparquote der privaten Haushalte
personal selling – s. persönlicher Verkauf
personal touch – s. persönliche Note
personnel – s. Personal, Mitarbeiter
Personnel – s. Personalabteilung, Personalwirtschaft
personnel administration – s. Personalwirtschaft, -management
personnel budget – s. Personalbudget
personnel consulting – s. Personalberatung
personnel consulting agency – s. Personalberatungsfirma, -gesellschaft, -agentur
personnel costs – s. Personalkosten, -aufwand
personnel development – s. Personalentwicklung
personnel – s. Personalwirtschaft, -management, -wesen
personnel manager – s. Leiter/in der Personalabteilung, Personalchef/in
persuade – v. überreden, überzeugen
persuasion – s. Wirtschaftslenkung durch Überredung, Seelenmassage, Persuasion
pertain – v. verbunden sein (mit), gehören (zu)
pervade – v. durchdringen
pervasive – adj. allgegenwärtig, überall vorhanden, durchdringend
pest – s. Ungeziefer, Planzenschädling, Schädling
pest control – s. Schädlingsregulation, -bekämpfung
pesticide – s. Pflanzenschutz-, Schädlingsbekämpfungsmittel, Pestizid
pesticide-resistent – adj. pestizid-resistent
pest-resistent – adj. schädlingsresistent
petition in bankruptcy – s. Antrag auf Eröffnung eines Insolvenz- / Konkursverfahrens
petrification – s. Versteinerungsphase , Phase der Bodensatznachfrage / Restnachfrage
PFI – Private Finance Initiative (siehe)
pharmaceutical division – s. Pharma-Abteilung, Pharma-Divison, Geschäftsfeld Pharma
phase in – v. langsam / schrittweise einführen
phase out – v. auslaufen lassen, langsam / schrittweise abbauen
phone banking – s. Phone-Banking, Telefon-Banking
phosphorus – s. Phosphor
photographic supplies – s. Photobedarf
photovoltaic cell – s. photovoltaische Zelle, Solarzelle
photovoltaic conversion – s. photovoltaische (Energie-)Umwandlung
photovoltaic conversion meter – s. Messgerät für photovoltaische Energieumwandlung
photovoltaics – s. Photovoltaik, photovoltaische Technologie / Geräte
photovoltaic tiles – s. photovoltaische Dachziegel, Sonnenziegel
physical – adj. physisch, körperlich, materiell, echt, tatsächlich, real
physical asset – s. Gegenstand des materiellen Vermögens / Sachanlagevermögens, materieller Vermögensgegenstand
physical delivery – s. körperliche Übergabe, effektive Lieferung
physical damage – s. Sachschaden, -schäden
physical distribution – s. physische Distribution, (Marketing-)Logistik
physical entity – s. physikalische Einheit
physical life – s. technische Nutzungsdauer
physicals – s. Warentermingeschäfte mit effektiver Lieferung
physical shrinkage – s. Substanzverringerung
physical transfer – s. Ortsveränderung, Transport
picketing – s. Aufstellung / Einsatz von Streikposten
picking – s. Selektion, Warenentnahme (aus einem Lager)
pickup truck – s. Pickup, Pritschenwagen, Pritsche
piece rate – s. Akkord-, Stücklohn
piece rate system – s. Akkordlohn-, Stücklohnsystem, Akkordentlohnung,
pie chart – s. Torten-, Kreis-, Kuchendiagramm
pier – s. Pier, Landungbrücke
piggyback service – s. Huckepack-Verkehr
pile up – v. anhäufen, ansammeln
pilferage – s. Beraubung, vollständige oder teilweise Entwendung des Inhaltes eines Packstückes
pillar – s. Säule, Stütze, Standbein
pilot version – s. Versuchs-, Test-, Pilotversion
PIN – Personal Identification Number (siehe)
pipeline –
s. Pipeline, Rohrleitung
s. Vorlauf(-phase), Nachschub, (Überweisungs-)Weg
in the pipeline – in Vorbereitung, im Kommen / Anrollen
research and development pipeline – Nachschub an neuen Produkten (im Forschungs- und Entwicklungsstadium)
piping hot – adj. brennheiß
piracy – s. Piraterie; unerlaubte Vervielfältigung von Werken und Leistungen, die durch ein Urheberrecht oder ein verwandtes Schutzrecht geschützt sind; Raub geistigen Eigentums; Immaterialrechtsgüterverletzung
pitch – v. festsetzen
The issue price was pitched too low. – Der Emissionskurs wurde zu niedrig festgesetzt.
place – v. platzieren, unterbringen

place an advertisement - eine Annonce platzieren / unterbringen / schalten
placement – s. Platzierung, Unterbringung, Vermittlung
placement agency – s. Stellenvermittlungsbüro, -agentur
place of abode – s. Aufenthalt(-sort)
place of delivery – s. Lieferort
place of destination – s. Bestimmungsort
place of issue – s. Ausstellungsort
plain envelope – s. neutrales Kuvert
plain vanilla instrument – s. einfaches Finanzinstrument ohne besondere Merkmale, Grundform eines Finanzinstruments
planned obsolescence – s. geplante Produktveralterung
planning permit – s. Baugenehmigung
plant – s. Werk, Fabrik, Betrieb, Anlage, Betriebsgebäude, Betriebsgebäude und Betriebsgrundstücke
plant and equipment – s. Betriebsgebäude, Maschinen und maschinelle Anlagen
plant assets – s. materielles Anlagevermögen, Sachanlagen
plantation – s. Plantage
plant closure – s. Betriebsstilllegung, -schließung, Werks-, Fabriksschließung
plant exports – s. Anlagenexporte
plant layout – s. Werksplan, -grundriss
plant site – s. Werks-, Betriebsgelände
plasma screen – s. Plasmabildschirm
plastics division – s. Plastik-Abteilung
platen – s. (Schreibmaschinen-)Walze
player – s. Mitspieler/in, Akteur/in
civil-society player – zivilgesellschaftlicher Akteur
plc – public limited company (siehe)
pledge – s. Pfandvertrag, (Faust-)Pfand
pledge
v. bindendes Versprechen abgeben, feierlich und förmlich versprechen, bindend zusagen
v. verpfänden
pledge as security – v. als Sicherheit / Besicherung verpfänden, in Pfand geben
PL1 – s. Programming Language ONE (Programmiersprache)
plotter – s. Plotter, Kurvendrucker, -schreiber
ploughback – s. Selbstfinanzierung, Gewinnthesaurierung
plough back – v. reinvestieren, thesaurieren
plowback – s. Selbstfinanzierung, Gewinnthesaurierung
plume – s. Rauchfahne
point of collection – s. (Müll-)Sammelstelle
point of sale – s. Point of Sale, Verkaufsort, Ort des Verkaufs
point of sale system – s. POS-System, Datenerfassungskassa, Warenwirtschaftssystem
point of shipment – s. Versandort, -stelle
poison – s. Gift
poisonous – adj. giftig, toxisch
poison pill – s. Poison Pill, Giftpille, Übernahmeabwehr(-maßnahme)
police – v. überwachen
policing problem – Überwachungsproblem
policy
s. Politik, politischer Kurs, politische Richtung, (Richt-)Linie, Grundsatz, Programm, Strategie
s. (Versicherungs-)Polizze, Versicherungsschein
adopt a policy – eine Politik / eine politische Linie einschlagen
pursue a policy – eine Politik / Linie verfolgen
draw up a policy – eine Polizze ausfertigen
issue a policy – eine Polizze ausstellen
policyholder – s. Versicherungsnehmer/in, Polizzeninhaber/in
policy maker – s. politische/r Entscheidungsträger/in, politische Entscheidungsinstanz, verantwortliche/r Politiker/in
policy of easy money – s. expansive Geldpolitik
policy of tight money – s. restriktive Geldpolitik
policy period – s. Laufzeit einer (Versicherungs-)Polizze
political economist – s. Vertreter der politischen Ökonomie
political economy – s. politische Ökonomie
political risk – s. politisches Risiko
politics – s. Politik, Staatskunst, politische Grundsätze/ Ansichten
poll
s. (schriftliche) Abstimmung, Wahl
s. Umfrage, Befragung
opinion poll – s. Meinungsumfrage
poll tax – s. Kopfsteuer, Lokalsteuer, Gemeindeabgabe
pollutant – s. Schadstoff, Kontaminant
pollute – v. (die Umwelt) verschmutzen
pollution – s. Umweltverschmutzung
pollution-restistant – adj. schadstoff-, verschmutzungsresistent
polycentric marketing – s. polyzentrisches Marketing
polyculture – s. Mehrfruchtwirtschaft, Polykultur (Gegensatz: Monokultur)
pool
s. Pool, Ansammlung, Bestand, Fundus, (gemeinsame) Kasse, Topf, Reservoir
s. Gemeinschaft, Zusammenschluss
s. Kartell höherer Ordnung (z. B. Gewinnverteilungs-Kartell)
pool of cash – Barbestand, Mittelfundus, (gemeinsamer) Geldtopf
pool of labour – Arbeitskräftereservoir
car pool – Fahrgemeinschaft
pool – v. zusammenlegen, bündeln, vereinigen
pooling of risks – s. (Bildung einer) Risikogemeinschaft, Risikobündelung
pool of cash – s. Barmittel-, Liquiditätsvorrat, Mittelpool, (gemeinsamer) Geldtopf
pool of tax revenues – s. Steuertopf
pool table – s. Billardtisch
poor
adj. arm, mittellos
adj. schwach, dürftig
a poor record / performance – eine schwache Leistung
population
s. Bevölkerung, Einwohner
s. Grundgesamtheit
pop-up – s. Popup, sich automatisch öffnendes Internet-/ Werbefenster
pop up – v. plötzlich auftauchen
port – s. Hafen
portable – s. Portable (im weiteren Sinn), tragbarer Computer
portable telephone – s. tragbares Telefon, Mobiltelefon
portal – s. Webportal, Startseite, Portalseite, Link-Seite
port basin – s. Hafenbecken
port clerks – s. Hafenverwaltungspersonal
porterage – s. Rollgeld, Rollfuhrgebühr
portfolio
s. Portefeuille, Bestand an Wertpapieren und / oder sonstigen Finanzanlagen
s. (Produkt-)Portfolio, Produktpalette eines Unternehmens
s. Geschäftsportfolio, Gesamtheit der Geschäftsbereiche eines Unternehmens
portfolio investments – s. indirekte Investitionen, Finanzinvestitionen
portfolio value – s. Substanz-, Depotwert
port of destination – s. Bestimmungshafen
port of discharge – s. Lösch-, Entladehafen
port of loading – s. Lade-, Versandhafen

port of shipment – s. Versand-, Verschiffungshafen
port rates – s. Hafengebühren
POS – point of sale (siehe)
position – s. (Wertpapier-, Devisen-)Position
take a position – eine Position eingehen
positive exposure – s. (Währungs-)Plusposition, (Währungs-) Aktivposition
positive externality – s. positiver externer Effekt, positive Externalität, externer Nutzen
positive transaction exposure – s. positive Netto-Währungsumwechslungsposition
possession – s. Besitz
take possession of goods – Waren / Ware übernehmen / abnehmen
possessor – s. Besitzer
post
v. aufgeben, zur Post bringen, per Post schicken
v. anschlagen, aufkleben
v. buchen
v. stellen
post a list – eine Liste anschlagen
post the ledger – im Hauptbuch buchen
post a bond – eine (Bank-)Garantie stellen
post a guarantee – eine Garantie stellen
postal order – s. Postbon, Postanweisung (für kleine Beträge)
posted price – s. Listenpreis
poster – s. Plakat
poster advertising – s. Plakatwerbung
POS terminal – s. POS-Terminal, Datenerfassungskassa
post-mortem
s. Leichenbeschau
s. Nachbesprechung, Manöverkritik, Nachanalyse, Post-Mortem-Analyse
Post Office – s. Post
Post Office Savings Bank – s. (ehemalige Bezeichnung der UK-) Postsparkasse
post room – s. Poststelle, -abteilung
post-room staff – s. Poststellenmitarbeiter/in
post-shipment finance – s. Ausfuhrfinanzierung (im engeren Sinn), Fakturen-, Refinanzierungskredite
poundage – s. Steuersatz in Pence pro Pfund
power
s. Befugnis, Amtsgewalt
s. (politische, physische) Gewalt
s. Energie
s. (math.) Potenz
three to the power of zero – drei hoch null
power station – s. Kraftwerk
ppm – parts per million (siehe)
PPP
Public Private Partnership (siehe)
purchasing power parity (siehe)
precipitation – s. Niederschlag
precision – s. Präzision, Genauigkeit
with any degree of precision – auch nur einigermaßen genau
precision marketing – s. Präzisionsmarketing
precursor – s. Vorläufer
predatory – adj. räuberisch, Raub-
predatory animal – s. Raubtier
predatory competition – s. Verdrängungswettbewerb
predatory dumping – s. räuberisches Dumping, Raubdumping
predatory pricing – s. Verdrängungswettbewerb
predecessor – s. Vorgänger/in, Vorläufer/in
predetermine – v. im Vorhinein festlegen
pre-empt – v. (im Voraus) in Beschlag nehmen / für sich in Anspruch nehmen
preference dividend – s. Vorzugsdividende
preference share – s. Vorzugsaktie
preference shareholder – s. Vorzugsaktieninhaber/in
preference share capital – s. Vorzugsaktienkapital, Vorzugskapital
preferential – adj. Vorzugs-, bevorzugend
preferential duty – s. Vorzugs-, Präferenzzoll
preferential tariff – s. Vorzugs-, Präferenzzoll
preferential tariff agreement – s. Vorzugs-, Präferenzzollabkommen
preferential treatment – s. Vorzugsbehandlung, Bevorzugung, Einräumen von Vergünstigungen / (Zoll-)Präferenzen
preferred stock – s. Vorzugsaktien, Vorzugskapital
premature – adj. vorzeitig
premises – s. Geschäftsräumlichkeiten, Betriebsgebäude und -grundstück(-e)
premium
s. Versicherungsprämie
s. Report, (Termin-)Aufschlag
s. Agio
s. Aufpreis, (Preis-)Zuschlag
s. Werbegeschenk, kleine Zugabe
s. Spitzen-, Qualitäts-, Prestige-
The dollar is at a premium against the euro. – Der Dollar weist einen Report gegenüber dem Euro auf
The three-month dollar is quoted at a premium. – Der Dreimonatsdollar notiert mit einem Report / wird mit einem Report gehandelt
sell at a premium – über pari stehen
stand at a premium to asset value – höher notieren als der Substanzwert
be at a premium – geschätzt / gefragt sein, hoch im Kurs stehen
to put a premium on sthg. – auf etwas besonderen Wert legen
premium brand – s. Spitzen-, Prestigemarke
premium price – s. Hoch-, Spitzen-, Prestigepreis
premium quality – s. Spitzenqualität
premium rate – s. Prämiensatz, Versicherungstarif
prepaid expense – s. eigene Vorauszahlung(en), transitorische(s) Aktivum/ Aktiva, aktive/r Rechnungsabgrenzungsposten
prepaid income – s. erhaltene Vorauszahlungen, transitorische Passiva, passive Rechnungsabgrenzungsposten
prepaid rent
s. im Voraus (von der Berichtsfirma) bezahlte Miete, geleistete Mietvorauszahlung (transitorisches Aktivum, aktiver Rechnungsabgrenzungsposten)
s. im Voraus (bei der Berichtsfirma) eingegangene Miete, erhaltene Mietsvorauszahlung (transitorisches Passivum, passiver Rechnungsabgrenzungsposten)
prepaid revenues – s. erhaltene Vorauszahlungen, transitorische Passiva, passive Rechnungsabgrenzungsposten
prepayment – s. Vorauszahlung
preparation
s. Vorbereitung
s. Erstellung, Ausarbeitung, Ausfertigung
preparation of financial statements – Erstellung von Rechnungsabschlüssen
prepare
v. vorbereiten, fertigmachen
v. erstellen, ausfertigen, ausarbeiten
prepare financial statements – Rechnungsabschluss / Rechnungsabschlüsse erstellen
prepare documents – Dokumente ausfertigen
prepayment – s. Vorauszahlung

pre-qualification exercise – s. Vorqualifikation (bei einer beschränkten Ausschreibung)
prerequisite – s. Voraussetzung, Vorbedingung
prerogative – s. Vorrecht
present
v. präsentieren, darbieten
v. vorlegen
present a cheque – einen Scheck vorlegen
presentation – s. Vorlage, Vorlegung, Präsentation
on presentation – bei Vorlage
present value – s. Bar-, Gegenwarts-, Kapitalwert
preside – v. Vorsitz führen
pre-tax profit – s. vorsteuerlicher Gewinn, Gewinn vor Steuern
pre-shipment finance – s. Produktionsfinanzierung, Finanzierung der Produktionsphase, Produktionskredite
president – s. Vorstandsvorsitzende/r mit Aufsichtsratsfunktion, Generaldirektor/in, wichtigster *executive director* einer US-Aktiengesellschaft, Geschäftsführer/in einer US-GmbH
press-button selection – s. (Einzelbild-)Wahl per Knopfdruck
presumption – s. Vermutung, Annahme
prevail – v. herrschen, vorherrschen, gelten
prevailing prices – die zur Zeit herschenden / geltenden Preise
previous holder – s. Vormann, früherer Inhaber
price – s. Preis, Kurs
charge a price – einen Preis verlangen
a price is quoted – ein Preis wird angegeben, ein Kurs notiert
sthg. commands a price – für etwas wird ein Preis verlangt, etwas wird (nur) entgeltlich abgegeben
compete on price – über den Preis konkurrieren
price control – s. Preisregelung, -lenkung
price differential – s. Preisdifferenzial, -differenz, -gefälle
price-earnings multiple – s. Kurs-Gewinn-Verhältnis, KGV
price-earnings ratio – s. Kurs-Gewinn-Verhältnis, KGV
price elasticity of demand – s. Preiselastizität der Nachfrage
price elasticity of supply – s. Preiselastizität des Angebots
price fixing
s. Festsetzung von Preisen, Preisfestsetzung
s. Preisabsprache, -kartell
s. (vertikale) Preisbindung
price freeze – s. Preisstopp
price guideline – s. Preisleitlinie, (pl.) indikative Preisplanung
price hike – Preiserhöhung
price index – s. Preisindex
price list – s. Preisliste
price pattern – s. Kursverlauf(-smuster)
price policy – s. Preis- und Konditionenpolitik
price restraint – s. zurückhaltende Preispolitik, Zurückhaltung bei den Preisen
price ring – s. Preiskartell
price-taker – s. Preisnehmer, Mengenanpasser
price ticket – s. Preiszettel, -etikett
pricing – s. Preis- und Konditionenpolitik, Preisgestaltung, -festlegung
pricing model – s. Preismodell
pricing policy – s. Preispolitik, -gestaltung(-spolitik)
pricing studies – s. preispolitische Analysen
prima facie evidence – s. Anscheinsbeweis, Prima-facie-Beweis
primary – adj. primär, hauptsächlich, Haupt-, Primär-
be primarily liable – als Hauptschuldner haften
primary agricultural products – unverarbeitete / halbverarbeitete Agrarprodukte
primary commodity – s. (international gehandelter) Rohstoff
primary contract – s. Hauptvertrag
primary data – s. Primärdaten
primary dealer – s. Primärhändler/in
primary duties – s. Hauptpflichten
primary energy – s. Primärenergie
primary industry – s. primärer Sektor / Wirtschaftszweig
primary liability – s. Haftung als Hauptschuldner/in, Primärhaftung, Haupthaftung
primary market – s. Primär-, Emissionsmarkt
primary sector – s. primärer Sektor, Urproduktion
primary storage unit – s. Primär-, Haupt-, Arbeitsspeicher
prime borrower – s. Kreditnehmer mit erstklassiger Bonität, erste Adresse
prime rate – s. Zinssatz für erste Adressen, Primarate
principal
s. Kreditsumme, Darlehenssumme, Kapital
s. Geschäftsherr, vertretene Firma, vertretene Person, Auftraggeber/in
s. Outsourcing-Auftraggeber, auslagernde Firma, Auslagerer
s. Akkreditivsteller/in
s. Hauptschuldner/in
s. Garantiesteller/in
principal amount – s. Kreditsumme, Darlehenssumme, Kapital
principal debtor – s. Hauptschuldner/in, Garantiesteller/in
principle of fair presentation – s. Grundsatz der Bilanzwahrheit
principle of non-discrimination – s. Nichtdiskriminierungsprinzip
printer – s. Drucker
printer-copier combination – s. Druck/Kopierer-Kombination, Kopierdrucker, Druckkopierer
printing device
s. Druckgerät, -vorrichtung, -teil
s. Sende-, Eingabeteil
printing element – s. Typenträger, Schreibelement
printout – s. Ausdruck, Druckausgabe
prior – adj. /adv. vorher, voherig, früher, vorrangig
prior consent – vorherige Zustimmung
prior party – s. Vormann (im Wechselregress)
private
adj. privat, nicht staatlich
adj. nicht börsennotiert, nich an der Börse notiert
take a company / corporation private – eine Gesellschaft von der Börse abziehen,
go private – von der Börse abgehen
private branch exchange – s. Nebenstellenanlage, (firmeneigene) Telefonzentrale
private brand – s. Eigen-, Haus-, Händler-, Handelsmarke
private circuit – s. private / firmeneigene Verbindungsleitung
private company
s. private Firma, Firma in Privatbesitz
s. nicht börsennotierte Gesellschaft
private corporation
s. private Firma, Firma in Privatbesitz
s. nicht börsennotierte Gesellschaft
private consumption – s. Privatkonsum, Konsum der privaten Haushalte
private costs – s. private / interne Kosten, Privatkosten
private equity – s. Private Equity, Beteiligung an nicht börsennotierten Unternehmen, Beteiligungsfinanzierung für nicht börsennotierte Unternehmen
private equity firm – s. Private-Equity-Firma
private equity fund – s. Private-Equity-Fonds, Private-Equity-Beteiligungsfonds

Private Finance Initiative – s. Private Finance Initiative, private Finanzinitiative
private industry – s. Privatwirtschaft
private insurer – s. privater Versicherer, private Versicherungsgesellschaft
private investor – s. Privatanleger
private label – s. Eigen-, Haus-, Händler-, Handelsmarke
private limited company – s. (etwa) Gesellschaft mit beschränkter Haftung
privately held company – s. nicht börsennotierte Gesellschaft
privately held corporation – s. nicht börsennotierte Gesellschaft
private placement – s. Privatplatzierung (von Wertpapieren)
private placing – s. Privatplatzierung (von Wertpapieren)
private sector – s. Privatwirtschaft, privater Unternehmenssektor
PE firm – private equity firm (siehe)
private property – s. Privateigentum
private sector – s. Privatwirtschaft, privater Unternehmenssektor
privatisation – s. Privatisierung, Entstaatlichung
privatise – v. privatisieren, entstaatlichen
problem-oriented language – s. problemorientierte Programmiersprache, Quellensprache
procedure – s. Vorgangsweise, Verfahren
proceedings – s. Geschehen, Verfahren
formal proceedings – formelles Verfahren
institute legal proceedings – (Gerichts-)Verfahren einleiten
proceeds – s. Erlös (besonders aus Einzeltransaktionen wie Kreditaufnahmen / Einlösung von Schecks u. ä.)
process control – s. Prozesssteuerung, Steuerung von technischen Prozessen
processing – s. (Weiter-)Verarbeitung, Bearbeitung, Veredelung
procure – v. beschaffen, akquirieren, vermitteln
procure documents – Dokumente beschaffen
procure orders – Aufträge vermitteln / akquirieren
procurement – s. Beschaffung(-swesen / -swirtschaft)
procurement agency – s. Vermittlungsagentur
procurement budget – s. Beschaffungsbudget, -plan
procurement management – s. Beschaffungswirtschaft, -management
procurement policy – s. Beschaffungspolitik
procurement tying – s. Lieferbindung (bei der Bereitstellung von Entwicklungshilfemitteln)
produce – s. landwirtschaftliche Erzeugnisse, Frischware(n)
produce
v. produzieren, herstellen
v. vorweisen, herzeigen
produce documents – Dokumente vorweisen
producer – s. Erzeuger/in, Hersteller/in, Produzent/in
producer brand – s. Herstellermarke
producer goods – s. Produktionsgüter
product – s. Produkt, Leistung
product advertising – s. Produktwerbung
product-based – adj. produktorientiert
product buy-back – s. Produktabnahmegeschäft, Produktrückkauf, Buy-Back-Geschäft
product development – s. Produktentwicklung
product differentiation
s. Produktdifferenzierung (gegenüber Angeboten der Konkurrenz)
s. Produkt-, Sortimentsdifferenzierung, Produktmodifikation
product feature – s. Produktmerkmal, (Leistungs-)Merkmal eines Produktes
product guarantee – s. Produktgarantie
product innovation – s. Produktinnovation
product liability insurance – s. Produkthaftungsversicherung
production
s. Erzeugung, Fertigung, Herstellung, Produktion (im engeren Sinn)
s. Förderung, Abbau (von Bodenschätzen)
s. Produktion (im weiteren Sinn), Wertschöpfung, Nutzenstiftung
s. Vorweisen, Herzeigen (von Dokumenten)
production account – s. Produktionskonto
production budget – s. Produktionsbudget
production control – s. Produktions-, Fertigungssteuerung
production cost(s) – s. Herstellungs-, Produktionskosten
production department – s. Produktions-, Fertigungsabteilung, Fertigung
production effect – s. Produktions-, Schutzeffekt
production facilities – s. Produktionseinrichtungen, -anlagen
production – s. Produktionswirtschaft, -management
production of documents – s. Vorweisen von Dokumenten
production quota – s. Produktionsquote, -kontingent
production run – s. (Produktions-)Serie
productive output method – s. Leistungsabschreibung (auf der Basis von Leistungseinheiten)
productivity – s. Produktivität, Ergiebigkeit, Ertragskraft, Rentabilität
productivity gain – s. Produktivitätszuwachs
product liability – s. Produkthaftung
product life cycle
s. (Marketing-) Produktlebenszyklus / Produktlebenslauf
s. (ökologischer) Produktlebenszyklus / Produktlebenslauf
product line – s. Produktlinie, Warengruppe
product manager – s. Produkt-, Markenmanager, Brand-Manager
product mix – s. Produktions-, Leistungs-, Verkaufsprogramm, Sortiment
product mix simplification – s. Sortimentsbereinigung
product modification – s. Produktmodifikation
product-mix pricing – s. sortimentbezogene Preisgestaltung, Preisbestimmung im Produktmix, Verbundkalkulation, kalkulatorischer Ausgleich (im Sortiment)
product policy – s. Produktpolitik
product positioning – s. Produktpositionierung
product range – s. Produktions-, Leistungs-, Verkaufsprogramm, Sortiment
product research – s. Produktforschung
professional partnership – s. Erwerbsgesellschaft
profit – s. Gewinn, (Netto-)Ertrag, Profit
profitability – s. Rentabilität, Wirtschaftlichkeit, Ertragskraft, Gewinnträchtigkeit
profitability ratio – s. Rentabilitätskennzahl
profit and loss account – s. Erfolgsrechnung, Gewinn- und Verlustrechnung, G+V-Rechnung
profit budget – s. Gewinnplan
profit contribution – s. Gewinnbeitrag
profit for tax purposes – s. handelsrechtlicher / steuerlicher Gewinn
profit-making concern – s. gewinnorientiertes Unternehmen
profit margin – s. Gewinnspanne, -marge, Umsatzrentabilität, -rendite, -marge
profit margin ratio – s. Gewinnspanne, -marge, Umsatzrentabilität, -rendite, -marge
profit on ordinary activities – s. Gewinn / Ergebnis der gewöhnlichen Geschäftstätigkeit
profit-sharing – s. Gewinnbeteiligung (der Arbeitnehmer/innen)
pro forma invoice – s. Proformarechnung

programme aid – s. Programmhilfe
programming language – s. Programmiersprache
progress – v. Terminüberwachung durchführen, verfolgen
progress orders – bei Aufträgen die Terminüberwachung durchführen, Auftragstermine / Lieferantentermine überwachen / verfolgen
progressive tax – s. progressive Steuer
progress payments – s. Fortschrittszahlungen, Zahlungen nach Baufortschritt / Leistungsfortschritt
prohibitive duty – s. Prohibitivzoll
prohibitive tariff – s. Prohibitivzoll
project – v. prognostizieren, vorhersagen
projected sales – prognostizierter Umsatz
project aid – s. Projekthilfe
project finance – s. Proiektfinanzierung, Cash-Flow-basierte Finanzierung
projection – s. Extrapolation, Vorhersage, Prognose
project team – s. Projektgruppe
proliferation – s. Verbreitung
promissory note – s. eigener Wechsel, Solawechsel
promote
v. fördern, unterstützen, forcieren
v. Reklame machen, Verkauf / Absatz forcieren
v. kommunikationspolitische Aktivitäten durchführen
v. gründen
v. befördern
promote an employee – einen Arbeitnehmer befördern
promoter – s. Firmengründer
promotion
s. Förderung, Unterstützung
s. Vorrückung, Beförderung
s. Kommunikationspolitik
s. Verkaufsförderung
s. Aktion, Promotion, Verkaufsförderungsaktion
promotional – adj. Kommunikations-, kommunikationspolitisch, Werbe-
promotional activity – s. kommunikationspolitische Aktivität(en) / Maßnahmen, Werbeaktivität(en)
promotional budget – s. Kommunikationsbudget
promotional device – s. Instrument der Kommunikationspolitik, kommunikationpolitisches Instrument, Werbemethode
promotional mix – s. Kommunikations-Mix
promotional pricing – s. Promotionspreisstrategie, Niedrigpreisstrategie
promotional tool – s. Instrument der Kommunikationspoltik, kommunikationpolitisches Instrument, Werbemethode
promotion run – s. Verkaufsförderungs-Aktion, Promotion-Aktion
proneness to crises – s. Krisenanfälligkeit
proof of identity – s. Identitätsnachweis
propensity to consume – s. Konsumquote, Konsumneigung
propensity to import – s. Importquote, Importneigung
propensity to save – s. Sparquote, Sparneigung
propensity to tax – s. (marginale) Steuerquote
property
s. Eigentum, Eigentumsrecht
s. Immobilien, Realitäten
s. Vermögensgegenstand, (Immobilien-/ Bau-)Objekt:
s. (pl.) Immobilienaktien
property in the goods – Eigentum an der Ware
property company – s. Immobiliengesellschaft
property developer – s. Immobilienverwerter, Immobilienverwertungsgesellschaft, Property Developer
property development – s. Immobilienverwertung, Property Development
property fund – s. Immobilienfonds
property income – s. Besitzeinkommen, arbeitsloses Einkommen
property market – s. Immobilien-, Realitätenmarkt
property, plant and equipment – s. materielles Anlagevermögen; Grundstücke, Gebäude, Maschinen und maschinelle Anlagen
property sector – s. Immobiliensektor, -branche
property share – s. Immobilienaktie
property tax
s. Vermögensteuer
s. Grundsteuer
proportional tax – s. proportionale Steuer, Flat-Rate Tax, Einheitssteuer
proportionate – adj. proportional
proposal form – s. Antragsformular, Versicherungsantrag(-sformular)
proposer – s. (Versicherungs-)Antragsteller/in
proprietary
adj. Eigentums-, eigen
adj. (marken- / patentrechtlich) geschützt, lizenzpflichtig
proprietary interest – s. Anteil, Beteiligung, Eigenkapital
proprietor – s. Eigentümer/in
proprietor's equity – s. Eigenkapital
pro rata – adj. / adv. anteilsmäßig
prospect
s. potenzielle/r Kunde/Kundin, (Kauf-)Interessent/in
s. (meist im Plural) Aussicht(en), Zukunftsperspektiven
prospective customer – s. potenzielle/r Kunde/Kundin, (Kauf-)Interessent/in
prospectus – s. Aktien- / Emissionsprospekt
protection – s. Schutz, (Ab-)Sicherung, Abdeckung
protection from transaction risk – s. Abdeckung des Währungsumwechslungsrisikos
protectionism – s. Protektionismus
protektionist – adj. protektionistisch
protectionist reciprocity – s. wechselseitiger Protektionismus
protectionist device – s. protektionistisches / handelspolitisches Schutzinstrument
protection of the environment – s. Umweltschutz
protection to the bona fide holder – s. Gutglaubensschutz
protective duty – s. Schutzzoll
protective effect – s. Schutz-, Produktionseffekt
protective tariff – s. Schutzzoll
protest – s. (Wechsel-)Protest
protest – v. protestieren, protestieren lassen
protest a bill of exchange – einen Wechsel protestieren / protestieren lassen
protest for non-acceptance – s. Protest mangels Annahme
protest for non-payment – s. Protest mangels Zahlung
protracted – adj. anhaltend, langwierig, sich hinziehend
protracted default – s. anhaltender Zahlungsverzug
provide
v. bestimmen, festsetzen, vereinbaren, ansetzen, regeln
v. vorsorgen, vorsehen, ansetzen
v. beschaffen, beliefern
the amounts provided for depreciation – die für Wertminderung angesetzten Beträge
as provided in the contract – wie im Vertrag vorgesehen / vereinbart / geregelt
provider of capital – s. Geldgeber/in, Kapitalgeber/in
provision
s. Bestimmung, Klausel, Vorschrift
s. Bereitstellung, Versorgung
s. Wertberichtigung

s. (Abschreibungs-)Aufwand
s. Rückstellung
provision for bad debts – s. Wertberichtigung für uneinbringliche und dubiose Forderungen / Forderungsausfälle
Provision for Bad Debts – s. (das Konto) Wertberichtigung zu Forderungen, Delkredererückstellung(-skonto)
provision for depreciation – s. Abschreibung, Abschreibungsaufwand
Provision for Depreciation – s. (das Konto) Wertberichtigung zum Anlagevermögen
proxy
s. (vom Aktieninhaber erteilte) Stimmrechtsvollmacht
s. (zur Stimmabgabe) Bevollmächtigte/r
PSBR – Public Sector Borrowing Requirement (siehe)
PSDR – Public Sector Debt Repayment (siehe)
psychographic variable – s. psychographische Variable
psychological pricing – s. psychologische Preisgestaltung / Preispolitik
public
adj. öffentlich, staatlich
adj. Publikums-
adj. börsennotiert, an der Börse notiert
take a company public – eine Gesellschaft an die Börse bringen
go public – an die Börse gehen
going public – s. Gang an die Börse, Börseneinführung
public company – s. börsennotierte Gesellschaft, Publikumsgesellschaft
public corporation
s. (brit.) wirtschaftliche Unternehmung der öffentlichen Hand, verstaatlichte Gesellschaft
s. öffentlich-rechtliche Körperschaft
s. (am.) börsennotierte Gesellschaft, Publikumsgesellschaft
public finance – s. öffentliche Finanzwirtschaft, Staatsfinanzen, Finanzwissenschaft
public good – s. öffentliches Gut, öffentliche Leistung
public investment corporation – s. staatliche Holding- und Beteiligungsgesellschaft
publicity
s. Publicity, öffentliche Aufmerksamkeit
s. Publizität-, Offenlegung(spflicht)
publicity requirements – s. Publizitätspflicht, -vorschriften
public limited company – s. (etwa) Aktiengesellschaft
publicly held corporation – s. (am.) börsennotierte Gesellschaft, Publikumsgesellschaft
public offering – s. öffentliches Zeichungsangebot (für Wertpapiere)
Public Private Partnership – s. Public Private Partnership, Öffentlich Private Partnerschaft, ÖPP
public procurement – s. öffentliches / staatliches Beschaffungswesen
public relations – s. Public Relations, PR, Öffentlichkeitsarbeit
public relations consultant – s. PR-Konsulent/in, PR-Berater/in
public sector – s. öffentlicher Sektor, Staat
Public Sector Borrowing Requirement – s. Finanzierungsbedarf / Kreditbedarf der öffentlichen Hand
Public Sector Debt Repayment – s. Schuldentilgung / Finanzierungsüberschuss der öffentlichen Hand
public sector deposits – s. Einlagen der öffentlichen Hand
public service – s. öffentliche Versorgungsleistung (-einrichtung)
public utility – s. öffentlicher Versorgungsbetrieb, öffentliches Versorgungsunternehmen
public utility company – s. öffentlicher Versorgungsbetrieb, öffentliches Versorgungsunternehmen
public warehouse – s. Lagerhaus, gewerblicher Lagerhalter
publishing house – s. Verlag, Verlagsgesellschaft, Verleger
punch – s. Locher
punch – v. lochen
punched card – s. Lochkarte
punched tape – s. Lochstreifen
punitive damages – s. (zusätzlicher) Schadenersatz mit Strafcharakter, Strafaufschlag (zur normalen Konventionalstrafe)
punitive tariff – s. Strafzoll
purchase book – s. Wareneingangsbuch
purchased goodwill – s. derivativer Firmenwert
purchase price – s. Kaufpreis
purchasing – s. Einkauf, Beschaffung
purchasing department – s. Einkaufs-, Beschaffungsabteilung
purchasing director – s. Leiter/in der Einkaufsabteilung, Einkaufsleiter/in, für den Einkauf zuständiges Vorstandsmitglied / Verwaltungsratsmitglied, Einkaufsdirektor/in
purchasing manager – s. Leiter/in der Einkaufsabteilung, Einkaufsleiter/in, Einkaufsmanager/in, (nicht dem Verwaltungsrat angehörende) für den Einkauf zuständige Führungskraft
purchasing power – s. Kaufkraft
purchasing power parity – s. Kaufkraftparität
pure competition – s. vollständiger Wettbewerb
pure holding company – s. reine Holdinggesellschaft, Dachgesellschaft
pure competition – s. vollständiger / vollkommener Wettbewerb
pure underwriting – s. Emissionsgarantie, Emission durch ein Verkaufskonsortium mit Haftung für den Emissionserfolg
push-button selection – s. Wahl auf Knopfdruck
push-tug assembly – s. Schubverband (von Lastkähnen)
put – s. Verkaufsoption
put across – v. darstellen, präsentieren, „verkaufen"
put aside – v. zur Seite legen, separieren
put aside money for a rainy day – Geld für schlechte Zeiten auf die hohe Kante legen
put option – s. Verkaufsoption, Put-Option, Put
put premium – s. Verkaufsoptionsprämie, Put-Preis
put seller – s. Verkäufer/in einer Verkaufsoption, Stillhalter/in (in Geld), Put-Verkäufer/in
put writer – s. Verkäufer/in einer Verkaufsoption, Stillhalter/in (in Geld), Put-Verkäufer/in

Q

quadruplicate – s. vierfache Ausfertigung
qualification
s. Qualifikation, Eignung, Kompetenz, Befähigung
s. Einschränkung, Vorbehalt, einschränkende Klausel
qualified
adj. qualifiziert, kompetent, geeignet, befähigt
adj. eingeschränkt, bedingt
unqualified success – uneingeschränkter Erfolg
qualified acceptance – s. „modifizierte" Annahme, Annahme unter einschränkenden oder ergänzenden Bedingungen
qualified auditor's report – s. eingeschränkter Bestätigungsvermerk des Abschlussprüfers / der Abschlussprüferin
qualified majority – s. qualifizierte Mehrheit
qualified minority – s. qualifizierte Minderheit
qualify –
v. (sich) qualifizieren, Anspruch haben / erwerben
v. einschränken, näher bestimmen
qualify for incentives – einen Anspruch auf Förderungsmaßnahmen haben / erwerben
quality circle – s. Qualitätszirkel
quality control – s. Qualitätskontrolle
quality management – s. Qualitätswesen, -management, -wirtschaft
quantity demanded – nachgefragte Menge
quantity discount – s. Mengenrabatt
quantity discount schedule – s. Mengenrabattstaffel
quanitity supplied – s. angebotene Menge
quarry – s. Steinbruch
quarrying – s. Abbau von Steinen, Industrie der Steine und Erden
quarterly – adj. vierteljährlich, Vierteljahres-
quarterly account – s. Vierteljahres-, Quartalsabschluss, vierteljährlicher Abschluss
quaternary sector – s. Quartärsektor, vierter Sektor, gehobener Dienstleistungssektor
quasi-public good – s. quasi-öffentliches / meritorisches Gut
quay – s. Kai, Schiffslandeplatz
query – v. in Frage stellen, hinterfragen
question mark – s. Fragezeichen, Nachwuchsprodukt
questionnaire – s. Fragebogen
quick assets – s. kurzfristiges Umlaufvermögen, Umlaufvermögen ohne Lagervermögen
quick current assets – s. kurzfristiges Umlaufvermögen
quick ratio – s. Liquidität 2. Grades
quorum – s. Quorum, beschlussfähige Anzahl von Anwesenden
quota
s. Quote, Anteil
s. Kontingent, mengenmäßige Beschränkung
s. Soll, Vorgabe, Liefer-, Verkaufssoll
goods subject to a quota – kontingentierte Ware
The quota is exhausted. – Das Kontingent ist ausgeschöpft.
fixing sales quotas – Festlegung von Verkaufszielen
quotation
s. Preisangabe, Preis
s. Angebot
s. Notierung
quotation and trading system – s. Börsennotierungs- und -handelssystem
quotation form – s. Angebotsformular
quote – v. zitieren, (Preise) angeben, Angebot machen
be quoted – an der Börse notieren
quoted company – börsennotierte Gesellschaft
Three-month dollars are quoted at a premium. – Dreimonats-Dollar werden mit einem Report gehandelt / weisen einen Report auf.
rate of exchange quoted on a direct / indirect basis – Preisnotierung / Mengennotierung
quoted company – s. börsennotierte Gesellschaft
quoted securities – s. börsennotierte / börsengängige Wertpapiere
quoted share – s. börsennotierte Aktie

R

racial distribution of income – s. rassenspezifische Einkommensverteilung
rack jobber – s. Regalgroßhändler/in
rack-jobbing – s. Regalgroßhandel, -handel
radio link – s. Richtfunk(-verbindung), drahtlose Verbindung / Übertragung
radiate – v. strahlen, abstrahlen
radiation – s. Strahlung
radio pager – s. Radio Pager, Piepserl
rail
s. Schiene, Bahn
s. Reling (eines Schiffes)
by rail – mit der Bahn
pass the ship's rail – die Reling des Schiffes überschreiten
rail carrier – s. Frachtführer im Eisenbahnverkehr, Eisenbahnunternehmen, Eisenbahn
rail consignment note – s. Eisenbahnfrachtbrief
rail freight
s. Eisenbahnfracht(-gut)
s. Eisenbahnfracht(-gebühr)
rail terminal – s. (Fracht-)Bahnhof
railway company – s. Eisenbahngesellschaft
raise
v. erhöhen, hinaufsetzen
v. aufbringen, auftreiben
raise funds – Geldmittel / Kapital aufbringen
RAM – random access memory (siehe)
R&D – research and development (siehe)
random – adj. zufällig, zufallsgesteuert, Zufalls-
at random – nach dem Zufallsprinzip, zufallsgesteuert
random access storage (device) – s. Randomspeicher, RAM, Direktzugriffsspeicher, direkt adressierbarer Speicher
random sample – s. zufallsgesteuerte Stichprobe, Zufallsstichprobe
range
s. Auswahl, Sortiment, (Leistungs-)Angebot, (Leistungs-)Programm, Vielfalt
s. Bereich, Umfang, Reichweite, Spielraum, Bandbreite
range of goods – s. Produktions-, Verkaufsprogramm, Sortiment, Produktpalette, Angebot
range of prices – s. Preisbereich, -klasse
rank – s. Rang, Klasse, Reihe, Gruppe
join the ranks of industrialised countries – sich in die Gruppe der Industrieländer einreihen
rank
v. rangieren, (an einer Stelle) liegen, (einen Rang) einnehmen
v. einordnen, reihen, einreihen
rank first – an erster Stelle liegen
rank for dividend – dividendenberechtigt sein
rank companies according to total assets – Unternehmen nach der Bilanzsumme reihen
ranking – s. Rangordnung, Ranking
rape – s. Raps
rate
s. Prozentsatz
s. Kurs, Preis, Tarif
s. (pl.) Zinssätze
s. Quote
s. Geschwindigkeit, Tempo
s. Ausmaß, Umfang
rateable – adj. anteilig, anteilsmäßig
rateable value – s. Steuer-/ Einheitswert / Bemessungsgrundlage für die ehemalige UK-Gemeindesteuer
rate capping – s. Begrenzung der UK-Lokalsteuersätze nach oben hin
rate of deliveries – s. Ausmaß der Auslieferungen / der versandten Aufträge
rate of exchange – s. Wechsel-, Devisen-, Fremdwährungskurs
rate of inflation – s. Inflationsrate
rate of interest – s. Zinssatz, -fuß
rate of labour turnover – s. Fluktuationsziffer, Mitarbeiterfluktuation
rate of remuneration – s. Lohn-/ Gehaltstarif
rate of turnover – s. Umschlagshäufigkeit
rate poundage – s. (ehemaliger) UK-Gemeindesteuersatz, Grundsteuerhebesatz
rates
s. (pl.) ehemalige UK-Lokal- / Gemeinde- / Grundsteuern
s. Zinsen, Zinssätze
rate for banknotes and coins – s. Valutenkurs
ratify – s. ratifizieren, bestätigen, zustimmen
rating
s. Bewertung,
s. Bonitätseinstufung, -bewertung, Rating, Kreditwürdigkeit,
s. Börsenbewertung, Einstufung durch die Börse, Börsenkurs
s. Rating, Analystenempfehlung
rating agency – s. Rating-Agentur, Bonitätsagentur
rating authority – s. UK-Gemeindesteuerbehörde
rating book – s. Rating Book, Ratingbuch, (Kredit-)Bewertungsbuch
ratio – s. Kenn-, Verhältniszahl
ratio analysis – s. Kennzahlenanalyse
ration – v. rationieren, mengenmäßig beschränken, bewirtschaften
rationale – s. (Grund-)Prinzip, Begründung
rationalisation – s. Rationalisierung, Effizienzverbesserung
rationalise – v. rationalisieren, effizienter machen
rationing – s. Rationierung, Bewirtschaftung
ratio of current liabilities to capital – s. Anteil des kurzfristigen Fremdkapitals am Eigenkapital
ratio of current liabilities to owners' equity– s. Anteil des kurzfristigen Fremdkapitals am Eigenkapital
ratio of fixed assets to net worth – s. Anlagendeckung (-sgrad)
ratio of loans to deposits – s. Kredit-Einlagen-Relation
ratio of operating income to net sales – s. Umsatzrentabilität / Umsatzmarge bezogen auf das Betriebsergebnis
ratio of total liabilities to total assets – s. Fremdkapitalanteil, -quote, Anspannungskoeffizient Kapitalanspannung
raw material – s. Rohstoff, -material
raw wool – s. Rohwolle
razor blade – s. Rasierklinge
reader – s. Lesegerät
read-only memory – s. ROM-Speicher, Festspeicher(-einheit)
ready-to-occupy factory – s. bezugsfertige Fabrik
read-write head – s. Lese/Schreib-Kopf
reafforestation – s. Wiederaufforstung
real
adj. real, Real-, preislich bereinigt, mengenmäßig
increase in real terms – realer Anstieg, Realerhöhung, inflationsbereinigte Erhöhung

real account – s. Bestandskonto
real estate – s. Grundeigentum, -besitz, Immobilien, Liegenschaften, unbewegliche Sachen
real estate agent – s. Immobilienmakler
real estate investment trust – s. (geschlossener) Immobilienfonds
real estate mortgage – s. Immobilienhypothek, Hypothek auf Immobilien
real estate tax – s. Grundsteuer
realign – v. adjustieren, neu festsetzen
real investment – s. Realinvestition(en), Sachkapitalbildung
realisable value – s. Veräußerungswert, erzielbarer Marktwert
real property – s. Grundeigentum, -besitz, Immobilien, Liegenschaften, unbewegliche Sachen
real-time application – s. Echtzeitanwendung, -verarbeitung
real-time processing – s. Echtzeitverarbeitung
real value – s. Realwert, preisbereinigter / inflationsbereinigter Wert
real wages – s. Reallöhne
rear – v. aufziehen, züchten
reasonable – adi. vernünftig, angemessen
reassure – v. beruhigen, beschwichtigen
rebate
s. Nachlass, Ermäßigung
s. (im Nachhinein gewährter) Preisnachlass
receipt
s. Erhalt, Abnahme, Entgegennahme, Übernahme (von Waren)
s. Eingang (von Geldern)
s. (pl.) Einnahmen, Eingänge, (Export-)Erlöse
s. Empfangsbestätigung, Quittung
receivables – s. (Buch- und Wechsel-)Forderungen (aufgrund von Warenlieferungen und Leistungen)
receivables loan – s. Zessions-, Debitorenkredit, durch Forderungszession besicherter Kredit,
receivables outstanding – s. offene Forderungen
receivables-to-sales ratio – s. Außenstandsdauer der Forderungen, Forderungsdauer, Zahlungsdauer
receivables turnover – s. Debitorenumschlag(-shäufigkeit), Forderungsumschlag(-häufigkeit)
receive – v. erhalten, einnehmen
receive money – Geld einnehmen
money is received – Geld geht ein
received bill of lading – s. Übernahme-, Empfangskonnossement
received for shipment bill of lading – s. Übernahme-, Empfangskonnossement
receiver
s. Empfänger/in
s. Telefonhörer
s. Konkursmasseverwalter/in, Vermögensverwalter/in
receiving device – s. Empfangsgerät, Empfangsteil (eines Gerätes)
receiving terminal – s. Empfangsgerät
recession – s. Rezession
recipient – s. Empfänger/in
reciprocal – adj. reziprok, gegenseitg, wechselseitig
reciprocity – s. Reziprozität, Gegenseitigkeit, Wechselseitigkeit
recital – s. Lieder- , Klavierabend
recognise – v. ausweisen, verbuchen, buchhalterisch erfassen
recognise bad debts – uneinbringliche / dubiose Forderungen gesondert ausweisen
recommended retail price – s. empfohlener Endverbraucherpreis, unverbindlicher/ nicht kartellisierter Richtpreis
record
s. Rekord, Spitzenleistung, Höchstwert
s. Aufzeichnung, Niederschrift, schriftlicher Bericht, Beleg, Protokoll, Verzeichnis, Liste
s. Ergebnis(se), (bisherige) Leistung(en), „Bilanz"
the environmental record of a firm – die Umweltbilanz / die Umweltleistungen einer Firma
record – v. aufzeichnen, (schriftlich) niederlegen, aufnehmen, erfassen, speichern, verbuchen
recorded in the balance of payments – in der Zahlungsbilanz erfasst
record-keeping – s. Führen von Aufzeichnungen, Informationsspeicherung
recourse – s. Rückgriff, Regress
take recourse – Rückgriff nehmen
have recourse to a prior party – gegen einen Vormann Regress nehmen
without recourse – ohne Rückgriff, rückgriff-, regresslos
recover
v. sich erholen
v. wiedererlangen, zurückerhalten, hereinbringen, ersetzt bekommen, (zurück-)verdienen
recover costs – Kosten wieder hereinbringen, Abschreibung verdienen
recoverable – adj. einbringbar, ersetzbar, zu ersetzen
The loss is recoverable. – Der Verlust kann ersetzt werden / wird ersetzt.
The amount is recoverable under the policy. – Der Betrag kann auf Grund der Polizze ersetzt werden / wird auf Grund der Polizze ersetzt.
Costs are recoverable. – Kosten können eingebracht / verdient werden.
recovery
s. Wiedererlangung, Wiederbeschaffung, Einbringung, Rückgewinnung,
s. Ersatzleistung, Entschädigung, Rückvergütung, Bergung
s. Gesundung, Erholung
s. Rückfluss, Rückgewinnung (von Kapital), Verdienen (der Abschreibung)
s. Konjunkturaufschwung, Erholungsphase
recovery of fixed costs – Verdienen / Rückgewinnung der Fixkosten
recovery of bad debts – Einbringung von zweifelhaften Forderungen
recreational facilities – s. Freizeiteinrichtungen
recruit – v. anwerben, beschaffen, rekrutieren
recruit employees – Personal beschaffen / anwerben
recruitment – s. Personalbeschaffung, -anwerbung
rectitude – s. Rechtschaffenheit, Verantwortungsbewusstsein
recur – v. sich wiederholen, wiederkehren, immer wieder stattfinden / auftreten
recycle – v. rezyklieren, recyceln, wiederverwerten
recycling – s. Recycling, Rezyklierung, Wiederverwertung
recycling society – s. Wiederverwertungs-, Recyclinggesellschaft
red – s. rote Zahlen, Verlustzone
in the red – in den roten Zahlen, in der Verlustzone
redeem – v. zurückzahlen, tilgen, einlösen, auslösen
redeem a bond – eine Anleihe tilgen / zurückzahlen
redeemable – adj. tilgbar, rückzahlbar
redeemable preference share – s. tilgbare Vorzugsaktie, Vorzugsaktie mit Tilgungsoption
redemption – s. Tilgung, Zurückzahlung, Rückkauf, Einlösung, Auslösung
redemption price – s. Rückzahlungsbetrag, Rücknahme- / Tilgungskurs (einer Anleihe)

redevelopment – s. bauliche Neugestaltung, Neubebauung, bauliche Sanierung, (Immobilien-)Sanierung, (Immobilien-)Revitalisierung, Redevelopment
rediscount – v. rediskontieren
redistribution – s. Umverteilung
redistribution of income – s. Einkommensumverteilung
redistributive – adj. redistributiv, umverteilend, Umverteilungs-
red tape – s. Amtsschimmel, bürokratische Ineffizienz, Bürokratie
reducing-charge method – s. degressive Abschreibung
reduction
s. Reduktion, Verringerung, Senkung
s. Verkleinern, Verkleinerung
reduction in wages – Lohnsenkung
redundancy
s. Redundanz, Überflüssigkeit
s. Abbau von Arbeitskräften, Freisetzung, Entlassung (auf Grund von objektiven wirtschaftlichen Tatbeständen)
redundancy payment – s. Abfertigung (bei Entlassung aus objektiven wirtschaftlichen Gründen)
redundant – adj. redundant, überflüssig, überschüssig, abgebaut
redundant elements – redundante Elemente
redundant workers – abgebaute / abzubauende Arbeiter
make workers redundant – Arbeitskräfe abbauen
refer
v. sich beziehen
v. bezeichnen
v. weiterleiten
refer to a letter – sich auf einen Brief beziehen
referring to your letter – unter Bezugnahme auf Ihren Brief
refer to sthg. as X – etwas als X bezeichnen
sthg. is referred to as X – etwas wird als X bezeichnet
Your inquiry was referred to me. – Ihre Anfrage wurde an mich weiter geleitet.
reference
s. Bezugnahme
s. Weiterleitung, Zuweisung
s. Nachschlagen, Konsultieren, Benutzung von Informationssystemen, Informationssuche, Retrieval
refinance
v. (sich) refinanzieren
v. umschulden, umfinanzieren
refinance a loan – einen Kredit umschulden / durch einen günstigeren Kredit ablösen
refinancing
s. Refinanzierung
s. Umschuldung, Kreditablösung
refinancing loan – s. Refinanzierungskredit
reflation
s. Reflation, Aufschwungphase,
s. expansive Konjunkturpolitik, Konjunkturbelebungsmaßnahmen
reflationery – adj. reflationär, stimulierend, konjunkturbelebend, expansiv
reformat – v. umformatieren
reforest – v. (wieder) aufforsten
refrain – v. unterlassen, bleiben lassen, nicht tun
refrain from taxable actions – steuerbare Handlungen unterlassen
refrigerated container – s. Kühlcontainer
refrigerated facilities – s. Kühleinrichtungen, -häuser, -räume
refrigerated unit – s. gekühlter (Verkaufs-)Automat
refrigerated vessel – s. Kühlschiff
regardless of – prep. ungeachtet, ohne Rücksicht auf
regime – s. Ordnung, Regelung, System
region
s. (Klein-)Region, Teilregion eines Landes
s. (mehrere Länder umfassende) Großregion
regional economic integration – s. regionale Wirtschaftsintegration
regionalism – s. Regionalismus, regionale (wirtschaftliche) Integration / Integrationsbestrebungen / Integrationspolitik
regional pattern – s. Regionalstruktur, regionale Verteilung
regional policy – s. Regionalpolitik
registered company – s. durch Eintragung ins Handelsregister / Firmenbuch auf der Rechtsgrundlage des Gesellschaftsrechtes errichtete Gesellschaft
registered office – s. (im Handelsregister / Firmenbuch) eingetragene offizielle Zustelladresse einer UK-Kapitalgesellschaft, (etwa) Firmensitz
registered share – s. Namensaktie
registered unemployed – s. registrierte Arbeitslose, beim Arbeitsamt als arbeitsuchend gemeldete Erwerbspersonen
register of members – s. Aktienbuch, Verzeichnis der Aktionäre / Gesellschafter
Register of Companies – s. UK-Handelsregister / Firmenbuch
registration – s. Eintragung (z. B. ins Handelsregister / Firmenbuch)
regressive – adj. regressiv
regressive tax – s. regressive Steuer
regrettables – s. Schadenskosten, instrumentelle Ausgaben, Ausgaben zur Kompensation von negativen Wohlfahrtseffekten
regulation – s. Verordnung, Durchführungsverordnung, Verwaltungsvorschrift, Vorschrift
regulation of promotional activities – s. Reglementierung kommunikationspolitischer Aktivitäten
regular course of business – s. gewöhnliche Geschäftstätigkeit
regulatory agency – s. Aufsichtsbehörde
regulatory audit – s. durch eine Aufsichtsbehörde (z. B. durch die Securities and Exchange Commission) vorgeschriebene (Abschluss-)Prüfung
regulatory body – s. Aufsichtsbehörde
regulatory environment – s. gesetzliche / ordnungspolitische Rahmenbedingen
reimburse – v. zurückzahlen, rückerstatten, erstatten
reimburse sby. for sthg. – jemandem etwas erstatten
reimbursement – s. (Rück-)Erstattung, Vergütung, Rückzahlung
reinstate – v. wieder einsetzen, wieder aufnehmen, reaktivieren, wieder einbuchen
reinstate a risk – ein Risiko wieder in eine Polizze aufnehmen
reinstate an account – eine Forderung wieder einbuchen / reaktivieren
REIT – real estate investment trust (siehe)
reject – v. ablehnen, zurückweisen, nicht annehmen, Annahme verweigern
reject goods – die Annahme von Waren verweigern
rejection – s. Ablehnung, Zurückweisung, Annahmeverweigerung, Nichtannahme,
wrongful rejection – ungerechtfertigte Annahmeverweigerung
rejection of an offer – s. Ablehnung eines Antrages / Angebotes
rejection of goods – s. Annahmeverweigerung / Nichtannahme von Waren

rejection rate – s. Ausschussrate
relationship marketing – s. Kundenbeziehungsmarketing, Customer Relationship Marketing, Management von Kundenbeziehungen, Kundenbeziehungsmanagement
relative market share – s. relativer Marktanteil
relaunch – s. Relaunch, Neustart, (Einführung einer) Produktvariation
relax – v. lockern
relax controls – Restriktionen lockern
relax a condition – eine Bestimmung / Beschränkung lockern
release – v. freigeben, freisetzen, auflösen, abgeben, herausgeben, übergeben, aushändigen, ausfolgen
release capital – Kapital freisetzen
release reserves – Rücklagen auflösen
release documents to sby. – Dokumente an jemanden freigeben, jemandem Dokumente aushändigen
release gases – Gase freisetzen / emittieren
release warehoused items – eingelagerte Waren ausfolgen / herausgeben
relevant – adj. einschlägig
relief – s. Erleichterung, Befreiung, Vergünstigung, Begünstigung
relieve – v. befreien, entbinden
relieved from V.A.T. – mehrwertsteuerbefreit
relinquish – s. aufgeben, preisgeben, verzichten auf
relocate – v. übersiedeln, umziehen, verlegen, verlagern
relocation grant – s. Übersiedlungsbeihilfe
remainder – s. Rest(-bestand, -betrag)
remaining life
s. Restlaufzeit (Wechsel)
s. restliche Nutzungsdauer, Restnutzungsdauer
remedial – adj. Abhilfe-, Korrektur-
remedial action – s. Abhilfemaßnahme(n), Mängelbeseitigung, Sanierung
remedy
s. Abhilfe, Gegenmaßnahme, Mittel, Heilmittel, Gegenmittel,
s. Rechtsbehelf, Rechtsmittel
remedy – v. abhelfen, beheben, in Ordnung bringen, heilen
reminder – s. Zahlungserinnerung, Mahnung
remit – v. (Geld) übermitteln / übersenden / überweisen
remit proceeds by cheque – Erlös per Scheck übermittlen
remittance
s. übermittelter Betrag
s. Zahlungsübermittlung, Überweisung, Übersendung von Zahlungsmitteln
remittances by migrant workers – s. Gastarbeiterüberweisungen, -transfers
remitting bank
s. überweisende Bank
s. Einreicherbank
remitting person – s. Zahler/in, Überweiser/in
remote copier – s. Fernkopierer, Faxgerät, Telekopierer
remote copying – s. Faxen, Fernkopieren, Faksimileübertragung
remote peripheral device – s. Gerät der Fernperipherie, (pl.) Fernperipherie
removable disk – s. Wechselplatte
removal
s. Entlassung, Absetzung, Abberufung, Eliminierung
s. Fortschaffen, Wegschaffen, Abtransport
s. Übersiedlung, Standortverlegung
removal grant – s. Übersiedlungsbeihilfe
remove – v. entfernen, eliminieren
remunerate – v. entlohnen
remuneration – s. Entgelt, Vergütung, Entlohnung

render
v. machen
v. erbringen
v. legen, vorlegen
v. fällen, treffen
v. wiedergeben, übersetzen
render impossible – unmöglich machen
render a service – eine Dienstleistung erbringen
render an account –eine Rechnung (vor)legen, abrechnen
render a decision – ein Urteil fällen, eine Entscheidung treffen
renewable – adj. erneuerbar, unerschöpflich
renewable resource – s. erneuerbare Ressource
renewable soft energy – s. erneuerbare / sanfte Energie
rent
s. Miete, Pacht
s. (volkswirtschaftliche) Rente
rent earned – s. (verdiente) Mieterträge / Pachterträge
rental – s. Leasingrate
rental payment – s. Leasingrate
rent control – s. Mietenregelung, Mieterschutz
Rent Expense – s. Mietaufwand(-skonto)
rentier – s. Rentier; jemand, der von seinem Besitzeinkommen lebt; „Kuponschneider", Bezieher eines arbeitslosen Einkommens
re-ordering point – s. Melde-, Bestellbestand, kritischer Lagerbestand
reorder level – s. Melde-, Bestellbestand, kritischer Lagerbestand
repair facilities – s. Reparatureinrichtungen, -anlagen
repair work – s. Reparaturarbeiten
repatriated profits – s. repatriierte Gewinne, ins Land der Muttergesellschaft rückgeführte Gewinne
repatriation of profits – s. Gewinnrepatriierung, -rückführung
repayment – s. Rückzahlung, Tilgung
repayment term – s. Laufzeit (eines Kredites)
repayment schedule – s. Tilgungs-, Rückzahlungsplan
repeal – v. aufheben, außer Kraft setzen
repeal an act – ein Gesetz aufheben / außer Kraft setzen
repeat order – s. Nachbestellung
replacement
s. Ersatz, Ersatzlieferung, -leistung
s. Ersatz-, Wiederbeschaffung
replacement demand – s. Ersatznachfrage
replant – v. neu bepflanzen, neu anpflanzen
replenish – v. auffüllen, ergänzen, wieder aufstocken
replenish supplies – Vorräte ergänzen
report – s. Bericht
render a report – einen Bericht legen
report
v. berichten, melden, angeben
v. ausweisen, bilanzieren, Rechnung legen
v. unterstehen
report costs – Kosten ausweisen
report sthg. as a liability – etwas als Verbindlichkeit/ Passivposten ausweisen / bilanzieren
report to the president – dem Generaldirektor unterstehen
report income – Einkünfte (in einer Steuererklärung) angeben
report form – s. Staffelform
reporting – s. Berichtslegung, Berichtswesen
reporting basis – s. Meldepflicht, Meldung
on a monthly reporting basis – mit monatlicher Meldung
reporting business unit – s. Berichtsfirma, -unternehmen, rechnungslegendes Unternehmen
reporting country – s. Berichtsland

reporting function – s. Berichtswesen
repository – s. Aufbewahrungsort, Hort, Lager
representative – s. (Handels-)Vertreter/in
reprocessing – s. Wiederaufbereitung, neuerliche Verarbeitung
repudiate – v. zurückweisen, ablehnen
repudiate a contract – die Vertragserfüllung ablehnen, vom Vertrag zurücktreten
re-radiate – v. zurückstrahlen
resettlement of birds – s. Wiederansiedlung von Vögeln
revenue budget – s. Ertragsplan, -budget
revival – s. Aufschwung, Erholungsphase
request – s. Bitte, Ersuchen, Gesuch, Verlangen, Antrag
on request – auf Verlangen
at his request – auf sein Verlangen
comply with a request – einer Bitte nachkommen / entsprechen
requirement
s. Voraussetzung, Bedingung, erforderliche Eigenschaft, Erfordernis, Anforderung
s. (pl.) Bedarf
meet requirements – Erfordernissen / Anforderungen entsprechen, Bedingungen erfüllen,
annual requirements – Jahresbedarf
requisition
s. Mittel-, Materialanforderung
s. Materialanforderungsschein
resale price maintenance – s. Preisbindung zweiter Hand / der zweiten Hand / für Wiederverkäufer, vertikale Preisbindung
reschedule – v. umschulden
rescheduling (of debts) – s. Umschuldung
rescind – v. aufheben, rückgängig machen, für ungültig erklären, wandeln
rescind a contract – einen Vertrag rückgängig machen / aufheben / wandeln
rescission of a contract – s. Vertragsauflösung, -wandlung
research and development – s. Forschung und Entwicklung, F&E
research department – s. Forschungsabteilung
research and development pipeline – s. Nachschub an neuen Produkten (im Forschungs- und Entwicklungsstadium), Innovationsnachschub
reserve
s. Reserve, Vorrat
s. Rücklage
reserve account – s. Rücklagenkonto
reserve asset – s. Reserveaktivum, -medium
reserve currency – s. Reserve-, Leitwährung
reserve requirements – s. Mindestreserven (Mindestguthaben der Kreditinstitute bei ihrer Zentralbank)
reserves of gold and foreign currencies – s. Gold- und Devisenreserven
reset date – s. Zinsanpassungsdatum (bei einem Rollover-Kredit)
residence
s. (tatsächlicher) Wohnsitz
s. Wohnstätte, Wohnung
resident – s. Gebietsansässiger, Deviseninländer
residential development – s. Wohnhausanlage
residential property – s. Wohngebäude, -objekt
residual – adj. restlich, Rest-
residual risk – Restrisiko
residual value – Restwert
resignation – s. Rücktritt, (freiwilliges) Ausscheiden
resolution – s. Beschluss, Entschließung
take a resolution – einen Beschluss fassen
resort – s. Zuflucht, Ausweg, Möglichkeit
the last resort – die letzte Möglichkeit
lender of last resort – Kreditgeber letzter Instanz
resort – v. Zuflucht nehmen, zurückgreifen, (als letzten Ausweg / letzte Alternative) wählen
resort to litigation – den Gang zum Gericht als letzten Ausweg wählen, gerichtliche Schritte ergreifen
resource efficiency – s. Ressourceneffizienz
resources – s. Mittel, Ressourcen, Produktionsfaktoren, Einsatzgüter, Inputs
respond – v. antworten, reagieren
respondent – s. Befragte/r, Proband/in, Untersuchungsperson
response – s. Antwort, Reaktion
in response to sthg. – als Reaktion auf etwas
in response to your letter – in Beantwortung Ihres Schreibens
response rate – s. Rücklaufquote
responsiveness – s. Reaktionsbereitschaft, Reagibilität, Ansprechbarkeit
rest
s. Rest, Saldo
s. Telefongabel
rest of the world – s. Ausland
restrain – v. in Schranken halten, zügeln, bändigen, zurückhalten, bremsen
restraint of trade – s. Wettbewerbsbeschränkung
restrictive indorsement – s. Rektaindossament, -klausel, negative Orderklausel
restrictive practices – s. Wettbewerbsbeschränkung, wettbewerbshemmende Vorgangsweisen / Praktiken
retail banking – s. Mengengeschäft / Kleinkundengeschäft der Banken, Bankleistungen für Lohn- und Gehaltsempfänger und gewerbliche Kleinkunden
retail branch office network – s. (Bank-)Filialnetz
retail concern – s. Einzelhandelsunternehmen
retail customer
s. Letztverbraucher/in, Endverbraucher/in, Kunde/Kundin eines Einzelhandelsgeschäftes
s. Kleinkunde (einer Bank)
retailer
s. Einzelhändler/in
s. Kreditkartenvertragspartner/in, Vertragshändler/in, Mitgliedsunternehmen einer Kreditkartenorganisation
retailer('s) brand – s. Eigen-, Haus-, Händler-, Handelsmarke
retail establishment – s. Einzelhandelsgeschäft
retail format – s. Einzelhandelsformat, -form, -konzept
retailing – s. Einzelhandel, Detailverkauf
retail needs – s. Einkaufswünsche (eines Normalverbrauchers)
retail organisation – s. Einzehandelsunternehmen, -firma, -gesellschaft
retail outlet – s. Einzelhandelsgeschäft, Verkaufsladen
retail price – s. Einzelhandelspreis
retail price index – s. Verbraucherpreisindex, Index der Verbraucherpreise, Lebenshaltungskosten-Preisindex
Retail Price Index – s. UK-Verbraucherpreisindex
retail sales – s. Einzelhandelsumsätze
retail shop – s. Einzelhandels-, Detailgeschäft
retain – v. ein-, vor-, bei-, zurückbehalten
retain title – Eigentum(-srecht) vorbehalten
retain a format – ein Format beibehalten
retain profits – Gewinne nicht auschütten / thesaurieren
retained earnings – s. thesaurierte / nicht ausgeschüttete Gewinne, Rücklagen
Retained Earnings – s. Rücklagen(-konto)
retained percentage of loss – s. Risiko- / Verlust- / Haftungsbeteilung (des Exporteurs)

retained profit – s. thesaurierter / nicht ausgeschütteter Gewinn
retaliate – v. zurückschlagen, Vergeltung üben, sich rächen
retaliation – s. Vergeltung, Rache
retaliatory – adj. vergeltend, Vergeltungs-, Rache-
retaliatory duty – Vergeltungs-, Retorsionszoll
retaliatory measure – s. Vergeltungsmaßnahme
retaliatory protectionism – s. (System) protektionistische Vergeltungsmaßnahmen
retaliatory tariff – s. Vergeltungs-, Retorsionszoll
retention – s. Beibehaltung, Behalten, Zurückhalten, Vorbehalt
retention of title – s. Eigentumsvorbehalt
retire
v. (aus Altersgründen) ausscheiden, in Pension gehen
v. ausscheiden, aus dem Verkehr ziehen, einziehen, ausbuchen
retire an asset – einen Vermögensgegenstand ausscheiden / ausbuchen
retire shares – Aktien einziehen
retirement – s. Ausscheiden (aus Altersgründen), Pensionierung, Versetzung in den Ruhestand
retirement age – s. Pensionsalter
retraining – s. Umschulung
retraining grant – s. Umschulungsbeihilfe
retrieval – s. Retrieval, Informationsrückgewinnung, Datenabruf
retrieve – v. auffinden, wiederfinden, abrufen
retrieve information – Informationen auffinden / abrufen
retrofitting – s. Ausstattung im Nachhinein, nachträgliche Ausstattung
return
s. Rücksendung, Retournierung, Rückgabe
s. (pl.) Retourware
s. (amtlicher) Bericht, Erklärung, Aufstellung, Meldung, Ausweis
s. (finanzieller) Ertrag, Rendite, Verzinsung
s. (produktionswirtschaftlicher / landwirtschaftlicher) Ertrag
in return for sthg. – als Gegenleistung für etwas
by return of post – postwendend
tax return – Steuererklärung
return on sales – Umsatzrentabilität, Umsatzrendite, Umsatzmarge
returnable glass bottle – s. Mehrwegflasche
return load – s. Rückfracht
return of capital – s. Rückgabe des Gesellschaftsvermögens
return on capital invested – s. Gesamtkapitalrentabilität, ROI
return on equity – s. Eigenkapitalrentabilität
return on investment – s. Return on Investment, ROI, (Gesamt-)Kapitalrentabilität
return on investment ratio – s. Kapitalrendite, Kapitalverzinsung (meist Gesamtkapitalrendite, aber auch als Überbegriff für die verschiedenen Arten der Kapitalrendite)
return on sales – s. Umsatzrentabilität, -rendite, Gewinnmarge, -spanne, Umsatzmarge
return on total assets – s. Gesamtkapitalrentabilität, ROI
return on total capital employed – s. Gesamtkapitalrentabilität, ROI
return ratio – s. Rentabilitätskennzahl
returns to scale – s. Skalenerträge, Niveaugrenzprodukt
reuse – s. Wiederverwendung
reuse – v. wieder verwenden
reusing – s. Wiederverwendung
revaluation (of a currency) – s. Aufwertung einer Währung (bes. einer Währung mit festem Wechselkurs)
revaluation-prone – adj. aufwertungsanfällig, -verdächtig
revalue
v. neu bewerten
v. aufwerten (bes. eine Währung mit festem Wechselkurs)
revenue
s. Ertrag, (Umsatz-)Erlös(e)
s. (pl.) (Staats-)Einnahmen, Steueraufkommen
revenue account
s. Erfolgskonto
s. Ertragskonto
revenue authorities – s. Steuerbehörden, Fiskus
revenue budget – s. Ertragsplan, -budget
revenue duty – s. Finanzzoll
revenue effect – s. fiskalischer Effekt
revenue item – s. Ertragsposten
revenue-neutral – adj. aufkommensneutral
revenue raiser – s. Steuerquelle, Quelle für Staatseinnahmen
revenue reserve – s. freie Rücklage
revenue tariff – s. Finanzzoll
reverse – v. umkehren, wenden, ins Gegenteil verkehren
reverse the charges – die Gesprächsgebühr dem angerufenen Teilnehmer verrechnen
reverse charge call – s. R-Gespräch, Rückgespräch
reverse side – s. Rückseite
review – v. überprüfen, rezensieren, neu festsetzen
revise – v. revidieren, korrigieren, novellieren
REVISED AMERICAN FOREIGN TRADE DEFINITIONS – US-Handelsklauseln
revival – s. Aufschwung, Erholungsphase
revocable credit – s. widerrufliches Akkreditiv
revocable (documentary) letter of credit – s. widerrufliches Dokumentenakkreditiv
revocation – s. Widerruf, Zurücknahme, Aufhebung
revocation of an offer – s. Widerruf eines Antrages / Angebotes
revoke – v. widerrufen, zurückziehen, aufheben, zurücknehmen
revoke an offer – einen Antrag zurückziehen / widerrufen
revolving credit – s. Revolving-Kredit, revolvierender Kredit
reward – v. belohnen, entlohnen
ribbon – s. (Farb-)Band
rider – s. (Kartei-)Reiter
rife – adj. weit verbreitet
be rife – weit verbreitet sein, grassieren, überhand nehmen
right
s. (subjektives) Recht, Anspruch
s. Bezugsrecht
grant a right – ein Recht verleihen
have a legal right to sthg. – einen gesetzlichen Anspruch auf etwas haben
right of combination – s. Koalitionsfreiheit, Versammlungsrecht
right of control – s. Verfügungsrecht, -gewalt
right of disposal – s. Verfügung(-sgewalt), Disposition
right of disposal in transit – s. nachträgliche Verfügung, Absenderanweisung
right of recourse – s. Rückgriffs-, Regressrecht
rights issue – s. Bezugsrechtsemission, -ausgabe
right to control the goods – s. Verfügungsgewalt über die Ware
rigid – adj. starr, rigid, inflexibel, unelastisch
rigid disk – s. Festplatte
rigidly fixed exchange rate – s. völlig fester Wechselkurs, System völlig fester Wechselkurse
rigour – s. Schärfe
ring binder – s. Ringordner

riot
s. Zusammenrottung, Aufruhr, Tumult
s. (pl.) innere Unruhen, Ausschreitungen
risk – s. Risiko, Gefahr
run a risk – ein Risiko eingehen
at his risk and expense – auf seine Kosten und Gefahr
at seller's risk – auf Gefahr des Verkäufers
passing of risks – Risiko-/Gefahrenübergang
risk-averse – adj. risikoscheu
risk management – s. Risikomangement
risk management instrument – s. Riskomanagementinstrument
risk of burglary – s. Einbruchsrisiko
risk of carriage – s. Transportrisiko
risk of expropriation or confiscation – s. Enteignungs- oder Konfiskationsrisiko
risk of fraud – s. Betrugsrisiko
risk of insolvency (of the buyer) – s. Insolvenzrisiko
risk of non-acceptance – s. Annahmerisiko
risk of non-payment – s. Zahlungs-, Kreditrisiko
risk of obsolescence – s. Überalterungs-, Obsoleszenzrisiko
risk of protracted default – s. Risiko des anhaltenden Zahlungsverzugs
risk-taker – s. Risikonehmer/in, -träger/in
rite – s. Ritus, Zeremonie
riverine wetland forest – s. Auwald an einem Fluss
river tug – s. Flussschlepper
road carrier – s. Frachtführer im Straßengüterverkehr, Lkw-Frächter
road consignment note – s. Frachtbrief im Straßengüterverkehr, Straßenfrachtbrief
road feeder service – s. Zubringerdienste auf der Straße
road haulage company – s. Straßengüterverkehrsunternehmen, LKW-Frächter
road haulier – s. Straßengüterverkehrsunternehmen, LKW-Frächter
road pricing – s. Road Pricing, Einhebung von (kilometerabhängigen) Straßenbenützungsabgaben
road vehicle – s. Straßenfahrzeug
robot – s. Roboter
robotics – s. Robotik, Robotertechnik, Robotertechnologie
rocker blotter – s. Löschwiege
ROE – return on equity (siehe)
ROI – return on investment (siehe)
roller rail – s. Gleitschiene
rolling back – s. Zurückdrängen
roll-on / roll-off – s. Roll-on/Roll-off-Verkehr, Ro/Ro-Verkehr
roll over – v. verlängern, prolongieren
rollover credit – s. Rollover-Kredit
rollover date – s. Zinsanpassungsdatum (bei einem Rollover-Kredit)
ROM – read-only memory (siehe)
Ro-Ro – roll-on / roll-off (siehe)
ROS – return on sales (siehe)
route – s. Route, Transport-, Seeweg
routine inquiry – s. allgemeine Anfrage
royal charter – s. Freibrief der Krone, Genehmigung durch die Krone
Royal Mint – s. Königliche Münze (UK-Münzamt)
royalties earned – s. Erträge aus Lizenzgebühren / Autorenhonoraren
royalty – s. Lizenzgebühr, Autorenhonorar, Pacht-, Förderzins
RPI – Retail Price Index (siehe)
rubber – s. Gummi
rubber-stamped – adj. (mit einem Gummistempel) abgestempelt
rule
s. Regel, Richtschnur, Grundsatz, Vorschrift, Bestimmung
s. (pl.) Geschäftsordnung,Verfahrensordnung, Satzung, Usancen, Handelsbrauch
rule – v. vorherrschen, herrschen, gelten
rate ruling on the balance sheet date – der am Bilanzstichtag geltende Kurs
rule of thumb – s. Faustregel
rules of origin – s. Ursprungsregeln
rules of procedure – s. Geschäftsordnung
ruling language – s. (offizielle) Vertragssprache
run
s. Dauer, Laufzeit, Sicht
s. Run, Ansturm
in the long run – auf lange Sicht, langfristig (gesehen)
in the short run – auf kurze Sicht, kurzfristig (gesehen)
run on a bank – Run / Ansturm auf eine Bank
run on a currency – s. Run auf eine Währung, massive Baissespekulation gegen eine Währung
runaway inflation – s. galoppierende Inflation
run down – v. abbauen, reduzieren
rural commune – s. landwirtschaftliche Kommune
ruthless – adj. rücksichtslos, unerbitterlich

S

Safe deposit – s. Depotverwahrung, Verwahrung (von Wertgegenständen durch eine Bank)
safe-deposit vault facilities – s. Tresor- und Schließfach-Service, Tresor- und Schließfach-Verwahrungsmöglichkeiten
safeguard – s. Schutz, Absicherung, Schutzmaßnahme
safeguard – v. schützen, absichern
safeguard measure
s. Schutzmaßnahme
s. (GATT-konforme) Schutzmaßnahme gegen Importe
safety regulations – s. Sicherheitsvorschriften
stafety standard – s. Sicherheitsnorm
safety stocks – s. Sicherheits-, Mindestbestand, eiserner Bestand
sailing – s. (Linienfrachter-) Abfahrtstermin
salaried employee – s. (Privat-)Angestellte/r
Salaries Expense – s. Gehaltsaufwand(-skonto), Gehälter
salary – s. Gehalt
sale
s. Verkauf, Kaufvertrag
s. Schlussverkauf, Räumungsverkauf
complete a sale – einen Verkauf tätigen
sale according to sample – s. Kauf nach Probe
sale-and-leaseback – s. Sale-and-Leaseback (-Vertrag)
sale by sample – s. Kauf nach Probe
sale on approval – s. Kauf auf Probe
sale on commission – s. Kommissionsverkauf, Kommissionsgeschäft
sale on deferred terms – s. Zielverkauf
sales
s. Umsatz, Umsatzerlöse, Handelswarenerlöse
s. Absatz
Sales – s. (das Konto) Umsatzerlöse, Umsatzerlöskonto, (das Konto) Handelswarenerlöse
sales analysis – s. Umsatzanalyse
sales budget – s. Absatz-, Umsatzplan
sales day book – s. Warenausgangsbuch
sales engineer – s. Verkaufsingenieur/in, technische/r Verkäufer/in
sales force – s. Vertreterorganisation, Mitarbeiter im Außendienst
sales-force promotion – s. Verkaufsförderung für Mitarbeiter / eigene Handelsvertreter, vertreterorientierte Verkaufsförderung, Vertreter-Promotion
sales ledger – s. Debitorenbuch, Debitorenbuchhaltung
sales ledger application – s. Debitorenbuchhaltungs-Programm(-paket)
sales letter – s. Werbebrief
sales literature – s. Verkaufsliteratur, Werbeliteratur, Prospektmaterial
salesman – s. Handlungsreisende/r, Reisende/r
sales manager – s. Verkaufsleiter/in, Leiter/in der Verkaufsabteilung
sales manual – s. Verkaufsleitfaden, Leitfaden für Verkäufer/innen und Vertreter/innen
sales office – s. Verkaufsbüro
sales organisation – s. Absatz-, Vertriebsorganisation
sales person – s. Verkäufer/in, Handlungsreisende/r, Vertreter/in
sales personnel – s. Verkaufspersonal
sales promotion – s. Verkaufsförderung, Sales Promotion
sales quota – s. Verkaufsquote, -vorgabe, -ziel
sales rep – sales representative (siehe)
sales representative – s. (unselbständiger) Handelsvertreter/in, Handlungsreisende/r, Reisende/r
sales revenue – s. Verkaufserlös(e)
sales series – s. Werbebriefserie, Folge von Werbebriefen
sales slip – s. Verkaufsbeleg, Kassazettel, Paragon
sales talk – s. Verkaufsgespräch
sales tax – s. Umsatzsteuer; (US-) Einphasenumsatzsteuer / Verkaufssteuer
sales transaction – s. Verkauf(-stransaktion)
sales volume
s. mengenmäßiger (Gesamt-) Absatz, Absatzmenge,
s. Umsatzwert, (Gesamt-)Umsatz
sales voucher – s. Verkaufsbeleg, Kassazettel, Paragon
salvage value – s. Rest-, Schrottwert
sample
s. Muster, Probe
s. Stichprobe, statistische Teilmenge
up to sample – dem Muster entsprechend
sale by sample – Kauf nach Probe
select a sample – eine Stichprobe ziehen / auswählen
sanitary regulations – s. Gesundheitsvorschriften, Gesundheitsschutzvorschriften
saturated – adj. gesättigt
saturation – s. Sättigung, Sättigungsphase
saving
s. Sparen, Spartätigkeit
s. Einsparung
s. (pl.) Ersparnisse
savings account – s. Sparkonto
savings and loan association – s. US-Bausparkasse
savings bank – s. Sparkasse
savings deposit – s. Spareinlage
savings rate – s. Sparquote
savings scheme – s. Sparprogramm
scale
s. Skala, Maßstab
s. Tabelle, Tarif(-tabelle)
s. Umfang, Ausmaß, Maßstab
on a large scale – in großem Maßstab / Umfang / Stil
medium-scale establishment – Mittelbetrieb
full-scale – im Großmaßstab, in natürlicher / voller Größe
scale of rates – s. (Steuer-)Tarif
scanner – s. Scanner, Abtastvorrichtung, Lesegeräte, -stift; Leser
scanning device – s. Scanner, Abtastvorrichtung, Lesegeräte, -stift; Leser
scarce – adj. knapp
schedule
s. (Zeit-)Plan
s. Liste, Tabelle, Verzeichnis
s. Einkunftsart, Einkommensklasse
scheduled flight – s. Linienflug
scheduled services – s. Linienverkehr, fahrplanmäßiger Verkehr
schedule of payments – s. Zahlungsplan, Tilgungsplan
scheme – s. Plan, Projekt, Entwurf, Programm, System
bonus saving scheme – s. Prämiensparprogramm
scheme of arrangement – s. Ausgleich / Vergleich(-svorschlag)
scheme of composition – s. Ausgleich / Vergleich(-svorschlag)
school district – s. Schulbezirk

school leaver – s. Schulabgänger/in
scope – s. Umfang, Geltungsbereich, Anwendungsbereich, Spielraum
scope of an agreement – s. Vertragsumfang
scope of authority – s. Umfang der (Vertretungs-)Vollmacht
scope of licence – s. Lizenzumfang
Scottish Enterprise – schottische Betriebsansiedlungsagentur (SE)
scrap – s. Schrott
scrap
v. verschrotten, ausrangieren
v. aufheben, abschaffen
scrap value – s. Schrott-, Restwert
screen – v. auswählen, aussortieren, selektieren, (heraus-)filtern
ethically screened – nach ethischen Gesichtspunkten ausgewählt / verwaltet
unsreened investment – nicht nach ethischen Gesichten ausgewählte / verwaltete Veranlagungen
screening – s. Vorauswahl, Grobauswahl, Produktideenfilterung
script – s. Schrift(-system)
scrubber – s. (Gas-)Wäscher, (Gas-)Waschanlage
scrutinise – v. genau überprüfen
scrutiny – s. genaue Überprüfung
SE – Scottish Enterprise (siehe)
sea cargo – s. Seefracht(-gut)
sea carriage – s. Seefrachtverkehr
sea carrier – s. Verfrachter, Seefrachtführer, Reeder, Reederei
sea change – s. grundlegende Veränderung, grundlegender Wandel
sea freight
s. Seefracht(-gut)
s. Seefracht(-gebühr)
seal – v. verschließen, versiegeln
sealed enveloped – verschlossener / versiegelter Umschlag
search machine – s. (Internet-)Suchmaschine
search process – s. Suchvorgang
seasonal adjustment – s. saisonale Bereinigung
seasonal discount – s. Saisonrabatt, Frühbezugsrabatt
seasonal goods – s. Saisonartikel
seasonally adjusted – s. saisonal bereinigt
seasonal pattern of employment – s. saisonaler Beschäftigungsverlauf
seasonal unemployment – s. saisonale Arbeitslosigkeit
sea voyage – s. Seereise
sea water – s. Meerwasser
sea waybill – s. (nicht begebbarer) Seefrachtbrief
seaworthy – adj. seetüchtig
SEC – Securities and Exchange Commission (siehe)
seclusion – s. Abschirmung, Abgeschiedenheit
secondary – adj. sekundär, zweitrangig, subsidiär
secondarily liable – adj. subsidiär haftbar
secondary liability – s. subsidiäre Haftung, Subsidiärhaftung (eines Ausfallsbürgen)
secondary data – s. Sekundärdaten
secondary industry – s. sekundärer Sektor, Fertigungsindustrie
secondary market – s. Sekundär-, Zirkulationsmarkt
secondary picketing – s. Einsatz von betriebsfremden Streikposten
secondary sector – s. sekundärer Sektor, Fertigungsindustrie
secondary storage – s. peripherer Speicher, Sekundär-, Hintergrundspeicher
second-stage finance – s. Zweitrundenfinanzierung
secrecy clause – s. Geheimhaltungsklausel
secretary
s. Sekretär/in
s. „Gesellschaftssekretär" (Position, die Wesenszüge eines Prokuristen, Syndikus und eines geschäftsführenden Aufsichtsratsmitgliedes vereint)
Secretary of State – s. Mitglied der Regierung eines US-Bundesstaates, das unter anderem mit der Leitung des Handelsregisters betraut ist
Secretary of the Treasury – s. US-Finanzminister
secret reserve – s. stille Rücklage
section
s. Referat, (Unter-)Abteilung, Gruppe
s. Paragraph
under Section 5 – aufgrund / gemäß Paragraph 5
section supervisor – s. Unterabteilungsleiter/in
sectoral index – s. Branchen-, Sektorindex
sectors of the economy – s. Wirtschaftssektoren, Sektoren der Volkswirtschaft
secure – v. sichern, absichern, besichern
v. befestigen, niederhalten
v. beschaffen, gewinnen, sicherstellen
secured by a mortgage – durch eine Hypothek besichert
secured by a platen – durch eine Schreibwalze niedergehalten
secure supplies – (sich) Vorräte beschaffen
secured loan – s. besicherter / gedeckter Kredit
Secure Electronic Transaction – s. Secure Electronic Transaction, Protokoll für die sichere Übertragung von Zahlungsinformationen über das Internet
securities analysis – s. Wertpapieranalyse
Securities and Exchange Commission – s. US-Wertpapier- und Börsenaufsichtsbehörde
securities-based – adj. auf Wertpapierbasis, wertpapiergestützt
securities dealer – s. Wertpapierhändler/in, Wertpapierhandelshaus
securities firm – s. Wertpapier-, Effektenfirma (z.B. Investmentbank, Maklerfirma)
securities market – s. Wertpapiermarkt, -börse, Effektenbörse
securities outstanding – s. im Umlauf befindliche Wertpapiere (Anzahl der emittierten und noch nicht zurückgekauften Wertpapiere eines Unternehmens)
securities underwriting – s. Emissionsgarantie(-geschäft), Underwriting, Fremdemission (-sgeschäft)
securitisation – s. (verstärkter Trend zur) Verbriefung / Titrierung / Umwandlung in Asset-Backed Securities
securitised – adj. verbrieft, titriert, in Wertpapierform
securitised receivables – verbriefte Forderungen
security
s. (Kredit-)Sicherung, Sicherheit, Sicherheitsleistung
s. Wertpapier
security of supplies – s. Versorgungssicherheit
security price – s. Wertpapierkurs
seed – s. (Planzen-)Samen
seed money – s. Seed-(Venture-) Kapital
seeds – s. Samen, Saatgut
seize – v. ergreifen, packen, beschlagnahmen
seize an opportunity – die Gelegenheit beim Schopfe packen
selective tendering – s. beschränkte Ausschreibung
selenium cell – s. Selenzelle
self-actualisation – s. Selbstverwirklichung
self-actualisation needs – s. Selbstverwirklichungsbedürfnisse
self-diagnosis capability – s. Selbstdiagnosefunktion, automatische Fehleranzeige
self-esteem – s. Selbstachtung, Selbstwert(-gefühl)

self-employment – s. selbständige Erwerbstätigkeit, berufliche Selbständigkeit
self-financing – s. Selbstfinanzierung, Gewinnthesaurierung
self-help group – s. Selbsthilfegruppe
self-regulation – s. freiwillige Selbstbeschränkung
self-service banking – s. Selbstbedienungs-Banking, Selbstbedienung im Bankwesen (elektronische Zahlungsverkehrs- und Informationsleistungen)
self-service store – s. Selbstbedienungsgeschäft, -laden
self-service outlet – s. Selbstbedienungsgeschäft, -laden
self-sufficiency – s. Selbstgenügsamkeit, Autarkie, wirtschaftliche Unabhängigkeit, Selbstversorgung
self-sufficient – adj. autark, selbstgenügsam, wirtschaftlich unabhängig
seller – s. Verkäufer
sellers' market – s. Verkäufermarkt
selling cost(s) – s. Vertriebsaufwand, -kosten
selling expense(s) – s. Vertriebsaufwand-, -kosten
selling point – s. Verkaufsargument, (kommunizierter) Verbrauchernutzen
selling rate – s. Brief-, Verkaufs-, Devisenbrief-, Devisenverkaufskurs
sell on credit – v. auf Ziel verkaufen
sell short – v. leer verkaufen, einen Leerverkauf / Leerverkäufe tätigen
sell-side – adj. anbieterseitig
B2B sell-side storefront – anbieterseitiges, internetbasiertes Geschäftsportal für Business-to-Business-Transaktionen
SEM – Single European Market (siehe)
semantics – s. Semantik, Bedeutungslehre, Bedeutungsstruktur
semiconductor – s. Halbleiter
semiconductor storage device – s. Halbleiterspeicher
semi-convertible currency – s. beschränkt konvertible Währung
semi-finished goods
s. Halberzeugnisse, Halbfabrikate, Zwischenprodukte
s. Halbzeug
semi-manufactured goods
s. Halberzeugnisse, Halbfabrikate, Zwischenprodukte
s. Halbzeug
semis – s. Halbzeug
semi-trailer – s. Sattelanhänger, Sattelauflieger
semi-variable costs – s. semivariable Kosten
senior clerk – s. Sachbearbeiter/in, Referatsleiter/in
senior executive – s. leitende/r Angestellte/r, Mitglied der oberen Führungsebene
senior management – s. obere Führungsebenen, Senior Management, Mitglieder der oberen Führungsebene
sensible – adj. vernünftig, rational
sensitive – adj. sensibel, empfindlich, heikel
light-sensitive – lichtempfindlich
sensitive goods – s. sensible / als schutzwürdig eingestufte Waren
sensitivity – s. Sensibilität, Grad der Schutzwürdigkeit
sequential access – s. sequentieller Zugriff
sequential access storage device – s. sequenzielles Speichergerät, Speichergerät mit sequenziellem Zugriff
serious injury – s. ernsthafter Schaden
servant – s. Arbeitnehmer, Dienstnehmer, Bediensteter
service
s. Dienstleistung, Dienst, Kundendienst
s. Wartung
s. Versorgungsleistung, Versorgungseinrichtung
s. (Verkehrs-)Verbindung, (Verkehrs-)Einrichtung
perform / render a service – eine Dienstleistung erbringen, einen Dienst erweisen

service
v. pflegen, warten, abschmieren
v. betreuen
service a machine – eine Maschine warten / abschmieren
service an account – einen Kunden / einen Werbeetat betreuen
service-based – adj. dienstleistungsorientiert, Dienstleistungs-
service charge – s. Bankgebühr (für Zusatzleistungen)
service contract – s. Wartungsvertrag
service engineer – s. Kundendienstleistungsingenieur/in, - mechaniker/in
service fee – s. Bankgebühr (für Zusatzleistungen)
service-hour method – s. Leistungsabschreibung (auf der Basis von Maschinenstunden / Laufstunden)
service industry – s. Dienstleistungsbranche, -gewerbe, (pl.) Dienstleistungssektor
service life – s. Nutzungsdauer, Nutzungszeit
service marketing – s. Dienstleistungsmarketing
service organisation – s. Dienstleistungsunternehmen, Dienstleister
service provider – s. Dienstleister/in
financial service provider – Finanzdienstleister/in
services account – s. Dienstleistungsbilanz
sevices deficit – s. Dienstleistungsdefizit, Defizit in der Dienstleistungsbilanz
services surplus – s. Dienstleistungsüberschuss, Überschuss in der Dienstleistungsbilanz
set
s. (Dokumenten-)Satz
s. (mathematische) Menge,
s. Sammlung, Gruppe, (zusammengehörige) Reihe
set of accounts – Kontengruppe
set of budgets – Budgetreihe
set of acts – Gesetzesreihe
set of rules – Regelwerk
SET – Secure Electronic Transaction (siehe)
set aside – v. zur Seite legen, aussondern, reservieren, (den Rücklagen / Rückstellungen) zuführen
set against – v. aufrechnen, gegenüberstellen
A must be set against B. – A muss gegen B aufgerechnet warden.
set of bill of lading – s. Satz Konnossemente, Konnossementensatz
set off – v. aufrechnen, skontrieren, anrechnen
set off advance payments against final assessment – Vorauszahlungen gegen die endgültige Steuervorschreibung aufrechnen
settle
v. bezahlen, begleichen, regulieren, glattstellen, abwickeln
v. regeln, ordnen, in Ordnung bringen, beilegen, schlichten
settle an account – eine Rechnung begleichen
settle a claim – einen Schaden regulieren
settle a deficit – ein Defizit ausgleichen
settle a dispute – einen Streitfall regeln / beilegen
settle a complaint – eine Beschwerde regeln
settle a futures contract – einen börsenmäßigen Terminkontrakt glattstellen
settlement
s. Begleichung, Bezahlung (des Kaufpreises), Zahlungsausgleich, Erbringung der Zahlungsleistung,
s. Erfüllung, Glattstellung
s. Regelung, Schlichtung, Vergleich, Regulierung
effect settlement – Zahlung leisten, die Zahlungsleistung erbringen

settlement date
s. Zahlungstermin, -datum, Datum der Zahlungsleistung / des Zahlungseinganges
s. Fälligkeits-, Erfüllungs-, Valutatag (eines Devisengeschäftes)
s. Liefer-, Erfüllungstags, Liefertermin (eines börsengehandelten Devisenterminkontraktes)
settlement of a claim – s. Schadensregulierung
settlement of a debt – s. Begleichung einer Schuld
settlement of a financial obligation – s. Erfüllung einer Zahlungsverpflichtung
settlement transaction – s. Anschaffung / Lieferung (des notwendigen Devisenbetrags)
set up – v. errichten, gründen
severable – adj. teilbar, trennbar
severance of employment – s. Beendigung eines Arbeits- / Dienstverhältnisses
sexual distribution (of income) – s. geschlechtsspezifische Einkommensverteilung
shadow economy – s. Schatten-, Schwarz-, Untergrundwirtschaft
share
s. Anteil
s. Aktie
s. Beteiligung
share buy-back – s. Aktienrückkauf (durch den Emittenten)
share capital – s. Aktienkapital, Grundkapital (AG), Stammkapital (GmbH)
shareholder – s. Aktionär/in, Gesellschafter/in einer GmbH / einer Kapitalgesellschaft
shareholders' equity – s. Eigenkapital (einer Kapitalgesellschaft)
shareholders' funds – s. Eigenkapital (einer Kapitalgesellschaft)
shareholder value
s. Shareholder Value, Aktionärswert, -nutzen, -rendite, Eigentümerwert, Gesamtrendite für Aktionäre
s. Shareholder-Value-Philosophie
share option
s. Aktienoption (als derivatives Finanzinstrument)
s. Mitarbeitaktienoption, Aktienoption (als Vergütungselement)
share price – s. Aktienkurs
share qualification – s. Aktienqualifikation, Pflichtaktien, satzungsgemäß vorgeschriebene Beteiligung der Verwaltungsrats- / Vorstandsmitglieder an ihrer Gesellschaft
shares in circulation – s. im Umlauf befindliche Aktien
shed – v. abwerfen, loswerden, verlieren
sheet of film – s. (Mikro-)Filmblatt
shelf – s. Regal, Regalbrett, Fachbrett
shelf-life – s. Lagerfähigkeit, Lebensdauer
shell-stand – s. Einheitsstand, Normstand, Einheitsmessestand
shell-stand scheme – s. Einheitsstand-, Normstandprogramm
shelter – s. Obdach, Unterkunft, Wohnung
shift – s. Verschiebung, Umstellung, Verlagerung
shift
v. (sich) verschieben, (sich) verlagern
v. verschieben, verlagern, abwälzen, überwälzen
shift a tax – eine Steuer überwälzen
shift production abroad – Produktion ins Ausland verlagern
shift rates – s. Schichtlohn(-tarif)
shipment – s. Sendung, Lieferung, Versand
shipowner – s. Reeder, Reederei
shipped bill of lading – s. Bordkonnossement
shipper
s. Versender, Absender
s. Befrachter, Verschiffer, Ablader
shipping
s. Schifffahrt
s. Verschiffung, Verladung
s. Versand, Versendung
s. Beförderung
shipping advice – s. Versandanzeige
shipping certificate – s. Haus-, Spediteurkonnossement
shipping charges – s. Versandkosten, -spesen
shipping clerk – s. Expedient
shipping company – s. Reederei, Schifffahrtsgesellschaft
shipping conference – s. Schifffahrtskonferenz, Frachtratenkartell
shipping department – s. Versandabteilung
shipping documents – s. Versanddokumente
prepare shipping documents – Versanddokumente ausfertigen
shipping manager – s. Leiter/in der Versandabteilung
shipping mark – s. Versandmarkierung, Signierung
ship's sweat – s. Schiffsschweiß, Kondenswasser
shop around – v. (sorgfältige) Preis- und Qualitätsvergleiche durchführen, sich (bei verschiedenen Lieferanten/ Geschäften) umsehen, Preise und Qualität sondieren
shop-floor participation – s. Mitbestimmung am Arbeitsplatz, basisorientierte Mitbestimmung
shop-floor worker – s. Arbeiter an der Werkbank, Produktionsarbeiter
shopfront – s. Geschäftsfassade
shopping basket – s. Warenkorb
shopping cart – s. Einkaufswagen
shopping centre – s. Einkaufszentrum
shopping goods – s. Gebrauchsgüter, langlebige Konsumgüter, langlebige Haushaltsbedarfsgüter
shopping item – s. Gebrauchsgut, Gebrauchsartikel, langlebiges Konsumgut / Haushaltsgut
short
adj. kurz, kurzfristig
adj. knapp, unzureichend
adj. leer, Leer-, Baisse-, Minus-
sthg. is in short supply – etwas ist knapp / unzureichend vorhanden
sell stocks / currencies short – Aktien / Devisen leer verkaufen
short call position – s. Minus- / negative Kaufoptionsposition
shortcoming – s. Mangel, Fehler, Unzulänglichkeit, Pflichtversäumnis
short end of the market – s. Marktsegment der kurzfristigen Anleihen
shorter working week – s. kürzere Wochenarbeitszeit, Arbeitszeitverkürzung
short exposure – s. Passivposition, Minusposition, passive / negative Position
short-form report – s. Bestätigungsvermerk des Abschlussprüfers / der Abschlussprüferin
shorthand notes – s. stenographische Aufzeichnungen
shorthand typist – s. Stenotypist/in
shortlist – s. engere Auswahl
shortlist – v. in die engere Wahl ziehen
short option position – s. negative Optionsposition, Minus-Optionsposition
short position – s. Baisse-Position, Baisse-Engagement, Minusposition, Passivposition, Umfang der noch nicht abgedeckten Leerverkäufe

short put postion – s. Minus-Verkaufsposition, negative Verkaufsoptionsposition
short sale – s. Leerverkauf
short-sea trade – s. große Küstenfahrt
short seller – s. Leerverkäufer/in
short selling – s. Leerverkauf
short-term investments – s. kurzfristige Finanzanlagen, Wertpapiere des Umlaufvermögens
short-term liabilities – s. kurzfristige Verbindlichkeiten
short-term notes receivable – s. kurzfristige Wechselforderungen
short-term securities – s. kurzfristige Wertpapiere, Kurzläufer
short-transaction exposure – s. negative Netto-Währungsumwechslungsposition
show of hands – s. (Wahl / Abstimmung durch) Handheben
shrink – v. schrumpfen, schrumpfen lassen
shrink back to a healthy size – gesundschrumpfen (lassen)
shunt – v. rangieren, verschieben
shut out – v. ausschließen
shuttle service – s. Pendelverkehr
sickness benefit – s. Krankengeld
sick pay – s. Krankengeld
side effect – s. Nebenwirkung
sidetrack – s. Gleisanschluss, Industriegleis
siding – s. Gleisanschluss, Industriegleis
sight – s. Sicht
after sight – nach Sicht
not in sight – s. nicht in Sicht
sight bill – s. Sichtwechsel
sight deposit – s. Sicht-, Kontokorrenteinlage
sight draft – s. Sichtwechsel, -tratte
Single (European) Market – s. (europäischer) Binnenmarkt
sign.
s. (mathematisches) Vorzeichen
s. Zeichen, Siegel
signatory – s. Unterzeichner/in, Signatarstaat
silent partner – s. von der Geschäftsführung und Vertretung ausgeschlossener, voll haftender Gesellschafter einer UK-Personengesellschaft
simple arbitrage – s. direkte Arbitrage, Zweiwährungsarbitrage
simple majority – s. einfache Mehrheit
simplification of the product mix – s. Sortimentsbereinigung
single capacity – s. (saubere) Funktionstrennung (zwischen Börsenmakler und -händler)
single European currency – s. europäische Einheitswährung, Euro
single-factor productivity – s. Teilproduktivität, partielle Produktivität
single market – s. (europäischer) Binnenmarkt
single-pane window – s. einfach verglastes Fenster, Einfachglasfenster
single person allowance – s. Freibetrag für alleinstehende Personen
single sale guarantee – s. Einzelgarantie
single-stage sales tax – s. Einphasenumsatzsteuer
single-unit firm – s. Einbetriebsunternehmen
single-user machine – s. Einplatzgerät, -anlage
sinking fund – s. Tilgungsfonds, -rücklage
size distribution of income – s. personelle Einkommensverteilung
skim off – v. abschöpfen
skim-the-cream pricing – s. Abschöpfungspreisstrategie
sky-writing – s. Himmelsschrift
slack – s. ungenütztes volkswirtschaftliches Potenzial, (Ausmaß der) Unterbeschäftigung, freie Kapazitäten und/oder Arbeitslosigkeit
take up the slack – brachliegendes Potenzial einsetzen / nützen
slack – adj. flau, lustlos
slack season – s. tote Saison, Sauregurkenzeit
slapstick – s. Klamauk
slapstick – adj. lustig, klamaukhaft, saftig, drastisch
sleeping partner – s. von der Geschäftsführung und Vertretung ausgeschlossener, voll haftender Gesellschafter einer UK-Personengesellschaft
slice of income – s. Einkommensstufe
slip
s. (Papier-)Zettel
s. Versicherungsantrag bei Lloyd's
slope – s. Neigung, Kurvenneigung
slope – v. sich neigen
slope upwards – sich nach oben neigen, ansteigen
slope downwards – sich unten neigen, abfallen
downward-sloping demand curve – abfallende Nachfragekurve
slot – s. Schlitz
slot machine – s. (Waren-, Spiel-)Automat
slowdown – s. konjunkturelle Abschwächung, Konjunkturverlangsamung, Nachlassen der Konjunktur
slow-moving item – s. umsatzschwacher Artikel, Ladenhüter
slump – s. drastischer Rückgang, Konjunktureinbruch, starke Rezession, Wirtschaftskrise
small and medium-sized enterprises – s. Klein- und Mittelbetriebe, Klein- und Mittelunternehmen, KMUs
small change – s. Kleingeld, Wechselgeld
small-scale establishment – s. Kleinbetrieb
SMEs – small and medium-sized enterprises (siehe)
smooth – adj. glatt, ohne Hindernisse
smudge – v. sich verwischen
sneakers – s. Tennis-, Turnschuhe
snoop – v. ausspionieren, herumschnüffeln
snoop on competitors – Konkurrenten ausspionieren
soar – v. in die Höhe schießen, explodieren
social accounting – s. volkswirtschaftliche Gesamtrechnung
social accounts
s. Sozialbilanz(en), gesellschaftsbezogene Rechnungslegung
s. volkswirtschaftliche Gesamtrechnung
social benefits – s. soziale / volkswirtschaftliche Erträge, volkswirtschaftlicher Nutzen
social costs
s. soziale / volkswirtschaftliche Kosten, Sozialkosten
s. negative Externalitäten, externe Kosten
social dumping – s. Sozialdumping
social indicator – s. Sozialindikator
socially responsible investment – s. ethisch-ökologisches / nachhaltiges / sozial verantwortliches / sozial verträgliches Investment, SRI, ethische Geldveranlagung
socially responsible investment fund – s. ethisch-ökologischer Fonds, Nachhaltigkeitsfonds, sozial verantwortlicher Fonds, SRI-Fonds
socially responsible marketing – s. soziales / sozial verantwortliches Marketing
social responsibility – s. soziale Verantwortung
social marketing – s. Sozialmarketing, Non-Profit Marketing
social outlays – s. soziale / volkswirtschaftliche Kosten
social science – s. Sozial-, Gesellschaftswissenschaft
social security benefit – s. Sozialversicherungsleistung
social security contribution – s. Sozialversicherungsbeitrag
social security fund – s. Sozialversicherung(-sfonds / -kasse)
social security tax – s. Sozialversicherungsbeitrag
social unrest – s. soziale Unruhen
societal marketing – s. soziales / sozial verantwortliches Marketing,

society
s. Gesellschaft (im Sinne der Soziologie)
s. Genossenschaft
s. Verein, Gesellschaft (im Sinne eines Vereins)
Society for Worldwide Interbank Financial Telecommunications (SWIFT) – s. Gesellschaft für Interntionale Banküberweisungen, SWIFT
social-technical system – s. sozialtechnisches System
sod – s. Rasen, Rasenstück
break the sod – Spatenstich durchführen
SOE – state-owned enterprise (siehe)
soft approach – s. sanfte Methode / Strategie
soft copy – s. Softcopy, weiche / elektronische Kopie, Bildschirmausgabe
soft-copy device – s. Ausgabegerät für weiche Kopien
soft currency – s. weiche Währung, Weichwährung
soft currency receivable – s. Weichwährungsforderung, Forderung in einer Weichwährung,
soft elements – s. weiche / nicht quantifizierbare Elemente / Faktoren
soft energy – s. sanfte Energie(-politik)
soft energy path – s. sanfte Energiepolitik / Energieoption / Energiestrategie
soft energy technology – s. sanfte Energietechnologie
soft loan – s. weiches Darlehen
soft path – s. sanfter Weg, sanfte Methode / Strategie / Politik
soft (producer) goods – s. kurzlebige Produktionsgüter, Hilfs- und Betriebsstoffe
software – s. Software, Programme
software house – s. Softwarehaus, Softwarehersteller
softwood lumber – s. Weichholz
soil – s. Boden, Erdreich, Erde
soil erosion – s. Bodenerosion
soil nutrients – s. Bodennährstoffe
soil pollution – s. Bodenverschmutzung
solar cell – s. Solar-, Sonnen-, Photovoltaikzelle, photovoltaische Zelle
solar collector – s. (thermischer) Solarkollektor / Sonnenkollektor
solar electricity – s. Solarstrom
solar energy – s. Sonnen-, Solarenergie
solar panel – s. Solarmodul, -panel
solar power – s. Sonnenenergie
solar satellite – s. (Sonnen-)Energiesatellit
sole agency – s. Alleinvertretung, Generalvertretung
sole agent – s. Alleinvertreter/in, Gebiets- oder Bezirksvertreter/in, Generalvertreter/in
sole director – s. alleiniges Mitglied des Verwaltungsrates einer UK-/US-Kapitalgesellschaft
sole distributor – s. Alleinvertriebsberechtigte/r, Vertragshändler/in, Generalvertreter/in
sole distributorship – s. Alleinvertrieb(-srecht), Generalvertretung
sole earner's (tax) credit – s. Alleinverdienerabsetzbetrag
sole importer – s. Alleinimporteur
sole proprietorship – s. Einzelunternehmung
sole trader – s. Einzelkaufmann, Einzelunternehmung
solicit – v. verlangen, erbitten, sich bemühen um, akquirieren
solicited offer – s. verlangtes Angebot
solicitor – s. Rechtsanwalt, Rechsanwältin
solid-state sensor – s. Halbleitersensor
solid waste – s. Festmüll, fester Abfall
solution – s. Lösung, Verdünnung
weak solution of sulphuric acid – schwache Schwefelsäurelösung
sophisticated – adj. (geistig) anspruchsvoll, hochentwickelt, raffiniert, kompliziert
source document – s. (Buchhaltungs-)Beleg
source of cash – s. Geld-, Finanzierungsquelle
source of funds – s. Mittelherkunft, Finanzierungsquelle
source program – s. Quellensprachenprogramm, in einer höheren Programmiersprache formuliertes Programm
sourcing
s. Beschaffung, Aufbringung
s. Wahl der Bezugsquelle, Lieferantenwahl
sourcing of funds – s. Mittel-, Kapitalaufbringung
sovereignty – s. Souveränität, Hoheitsgewalt, Herrschaft
soy – s. Soya
soy as cattle feed – Soya als Viehfutter
soybeans – s. Soyabohnen
space productivity – s. Flächenproduktivität
spam message – s. Spam, Spam-Botschaft, unerwünschte elektronische Nachricht
spark off – v. auslösen
spatial distribution – s. räumliche Verteilung / Anordnung, Standortwahl, Verteilung der Standorte
spawn – v. (in reichlichem Maße) hervorbringen
speaker recognition system – s. Stimmerkennungssystem
special accounts receivable – s. sonstige Forderungen
special agent – s. Sonderbevollmächtigte/r
special crossing – s. Vollkreuzung, besondere Kreuzung
special deposits – s. Mindestreserven (Mindestguthaben der Kreditinstitute bei der Zentralbank)
Special Drawing Right – s. Sonderziehungsrecht
special economic zone – s. Sonderwirtschaftszone
special indorsement – s. Vollindossament
special inquiry – s. bestimmte / spezifische / gezielte Anfrage
specialist
s. Spezialist/in, Fachmann, Fachfrau, Experte, Expertin
s. Börsenmakler/in mit Selbsteintrittsrecht (d. h. mit Berechtigung zu Geschäften auf eigene Rechnung) an der New York Stock Exchange
speciality wholesaler – s. Spezialgroßhändler
special policy – s. Reisepolizze, Einzelpolizze
special resolution – s. Beschluss mit qualifizierter Mehrheit
special shareholder meeting – s. außerordentliche Hauptversammlung
special stockholder meeting – s. außerordentliche Hauptversammlung
specific – adj. spezifisch, auf Mengenbasis berechnet
specification – s. genaue technische Beschreibung / Angabe, nähere Darlegung, Einzelaufstellung, Patentbeschreibung
specification documents – s. Ausschreibungsunterlagen
specific cost identification – s. Identitätspreisverfahren, Einzelbewertung von Vorratsvermögen
specific duty – s. spezifischer Zoll, Mengenzoll
specific factor of production – s. spezifischer (und daher eher limitationaler) Produktionsfaktor
specific guarantee – s. Einzelgarantie
specific inquiry – s. bestimmte Anfrage
specific performance – s. (Vertrags-)Erfüllung in natura, Naturalerfüllung, spezifische / effektive Vertragserfüllung, Specific Performance
specific policy – s. Reise-, Einzelpolizze
specified-perils policy – s. Einzel-Gefahren-Versicherung
specify – v. spezifizieren, im Detail angeben, näher bezeichnen
specimen signature – s. Unterschriftsprobe
speculation – s. Spekulation
speculative frenzy – s. Spekulationswahn, -rausch

speculator – s. Spekulant
spending pattern – s. Ausgabenstruktur, Verteilung der Ausgaben
spill – v. ausschütten, verschütten
spine (of a file) – s. Rücken / Rückenteil (eines Büroordners)
spirit duplicating – s. Hektographie, Umdruckvervielfältigung
splitting uranium – s. Uranspaltung
split-rate system – s. System des gespaltenen Körperschaftsteuersatzes
spoil – v. verderben, schlecht werden
goods that spoil quickly – Waren, die rasch verderben
spoil the market – den Markt verderben
sponsor
s. Sponsor/in, Förderer, Förderin, Gönner/in
s. Auftraggeber/in, Geldgeber/in, Kostenträger/in, Projektträger/in, Bauträger/in
s. Firmenpate, Firmenpatin, Firmengründer/in
s. Emissionsträger/in, Konsortialführer/in
sponsor – v. sponsern, protegieren, fördern, unterstützen, finanzieren
sponsorship – s. Sponsoring
sporadic dumping – s. sporadisches Dumping
spot – adj. / adv. sofort lieferbar und zahlbar, Kassa-, Loko-
buy a foreign currency amount spot – einen Fremdwährungsbetrag in der Kassa / per Kassa kaufen
spot delivery – s. Kassalieferung, sofortige (Aus-)lieferung
spot dollar – s. Kassadollar
spot exchange – s. Kassadevisen
spot exchange rate – (Devisen-)Kassakurs
spot-forward swap – s. Spot-Forward-Swap
spot market – s. Kassamarkt, Devisenkassamarkt
spot market hedging – s. Abdeckung des Währungsumwechslungsrisikos über den Geldmarkt, Kurssicherung über den Geldmarkt / durch Fremdwährungkreditaufnahme und/oder Fremdwährungsveranlagung
spot price – s. Kassapreis, -kurs, -notierung
spot rate (of exchange) – s. (Devisen-)Kassakurs
spot transaction – s. Kassageschäft, Devisenkassageschäft
spot value – s. Kassakurs, Devisenkassakurs
spouse – s. Gattin, Gatte
spread – s. (Zins-)Spanne, (Kurs-)Marge
spread – v. streuen, verteilen
spread risk – Risiko streuen
spread costs over the service life – Kosten über die Nutzungsdauer verteilen
spread sheet – s. Spreadsheet, Tabelle(-nsoftware), Matrix, Tabellenrechnung
square – s. Quadrat, Viereck
square – v. in Einklang / unter einen Hut bringen
square – adj. viereckig, quadratisch
square foot – s. Quadratfuß
SRI fund – socially responsible investment fund (siehe)
stack – v. (auf-)stapeln, sammeln
staff
s. Belegschaft, Belegschaftsmitglieder, Personal
s. Stab, Stabstelle
staff – v. mit Personal ausstatten / besetzen, personell ausstatten / besetzen
staff benefits – s. (freiwillige) betriebliche Sozialleistungen / Nebenleistungen, betriebliches Sozialleistungsprogramm, betriebliche Wohlfahrtseinrichtungen und -aktivitäten
staff department – s. Stabsstelle
staff manager – s. Stabstellenleiter/in, Leiter/in einer Stabsstelle
staff relationship – s. Stabsbeziehung, Beziehung zwischen Stabsstellen und Linieninstanzen
staff unit – s. Stabsstelle
staff welfare programme – s. betriebliches Sozialleistungsprogramm
stag – s. Konzertzeichner/in
stage – s. Phase, Entwicklungsstufe, Abschnitt
stage of decline – s. Niedergangsphase
stage of transit – s. Transportabschnitt, Teilstrecke
stage payments – s. Fortschrittszahlungen, Zahlungen nach Baufortschritt, Zahlung nach Leistungsfortschritt
stagflation – s. Stagflation, Zusammentreffen von (hoher) Arbeitslosigkeit und Inflation
staggering – adj. schwindelerregend, enorm
stain – v. beschmutzen, beflecken
stake
s. Wetteinsatz
s. (finanzielle / emotionale) Beteiligung,
to have a stake in sthg. – an etwas beteiligt sein
stakeholder – s. Stakeholder, Anspruchsberechtiger, (Mitglied einer) Interessensgruppe, Koalitionär
stamp book – s. Rabattbuch
stamp duty – s. Stempelgebühr
stance – s. Haltung, Einstellung
stand – s. Stand, Messe-, Ausstellungsstand
stand designer – s. (Messe-)Stand-Designer/in, Messestand-Architekt/in
stand-alone – adj. großrechnerunabhängig, nicht vernetzt, eigenständig, unabhängig, Einzel
stand-alone piece of equipment – (nicht vernetztes) Einzelgerät
standard
s. Zielvorgabe, Plansoll, Mindestanforderung
s. Norm, Richtzahl, Richtwert, Vergleichswert
standard cost(s) – s. Standardkosten, Plankosten
standard costing – s. Standardkostenrechnung, Plankostenrechnung
standard of living – s. Lebensstandard
standardisation – s. Normung, Standardisierung
standardised option – s. börsengehandelte / standardisierte Option, Börsenoption
standard phrase – s. Textbaustein
standard ratio – s. Richtzahl, -wert, Vergleichswert
standard time allowance – s. Zeitvorgabe
stand-by arrangement – s. Kreditzusage, Ziehungsrecht
stand-by letter of credit – s. Stand-by Letter of Credit (ein der Garantie ähnliches US-Sicherungsinstrument)
standing – s. Status, Stellung, Ansehen, Bonität, Ruf, Wert
have equal standing – gleichwertig / gleichberechtigt sein
standing charges – s. feststehende Aufwendungen, Fixkosten
standing committee – s. ständiger Ausschuss
standing order (mandate) – s. Dauerauftrag
create a standing order mandate – einen Dauerauftrag erteilen
cancel a standing order mandate – einen Dauerauftrag widerrufen
standing order form – s. Dauerauftragsformular
staple
s. Heftklammer
s. Hauptartikel
staple exports – Hauptausfuhrartikel
consumer staples – Standardkonsumartikel
stapler – s. Heftmaschine
stapling – s. Heften
stapling machine – s. Heftmaschine
star – s. Stern, Star, Spitzenprodukt

start-up
s. Firmengründung, Neugründung,
s. Start-Up, Unternehmen in der Gründungsphase, neu gegründete Firma, Jungfirma
start-up finance – s. Start-up-Kapital, Startkapital, Gründungsfinanzierung
stash away – v. verstecken, horten
state – s. (Betriebs-)Zustand
statement
s. Angabe, Erklärung, Darlegung, Feststellung, Behauptung, Aussage
s. Bericht, Aufstellung, Liste, Ausweis, Übersicht, (Konto-)Auszug
statement of account
s. Aufstellung der offenen Posten
s. Kontoauszug
statement of changes in financial position – s. Bewegungsbilanz, Kapitalflussrechnung
statement of changes in financial position on a cash basis
s. Bewegungsbilanz
statement of changes in financial position on a working capital basis – s. Kapitalflussrechnung
statement of financial position – s. (Unternehmens-)Bilanz
statement request – s. Kontoauszugsanforderung
state of the art – s. Stand der Technik
state-of-the-art – adj. dem neuesten Stand der Technik entsprechend, auf der Höhe der Zeit
state-owned enterprise – s. staatliches Unternehmen, Staatsunternehmen
state sales tax – s. US-einzelstaatliche Einphasenumsatzsteuer / Verkaufssteuer
state taxation – s. einzelstaatliche Besteuerung, Besteuerung durch die US-Einzelstaaten
stationery
s. Bürobedarf, Büromaterial, Büroartikel
s. Schreibwaren, Papierwaren
statistical device – s. statistische Methode / Vorgangsweise
statistical estimation – s. statistische Schätzung
status information – s. Bonitätsauskunft / -auskünfte
status inquiry – s. Erkundigungsschreiben, Auskunftsgesuch, Anfrage um Bonitätsauskunft
statute – s. (vom Parlament geschaffenes) Gesetz
statutory – adj. gesetzlich, gesetzlich vorgeschrieben
statutory audit – s. gesetzliche / aktienrechtliche / gesetzlich vorgeschriebene Abschlussprüfung
statutory company – s. „Gesellschaft öffentlichen Rechtes" (Rechtsform für in Privatbesitz befindliche Versorgungsunternehmen mit Monopolcharakter)
statutory meeting – s. gesetzlich vorgeschriebene Gründungsversammlung einer AG oder GmbH
statutory powers – s. Gesetzesvollmacht
statutory regulations – s. gesetzliche Vorschriften
statutory report – s. gesetzlich vorgeschriebener Gründungsbericht einer UK-*registered company*
S.T.D. – subscriber trunk dialling (siehe)
stencil – s. (Wachs-)Matrize
cut a stencil – eine Wachsmatrize beschriften
stencil duplicating – s. Wachsmatrizen-, Schablonenverfahren
stifle – v. ersticken, dämpfen, abwürgen
still picture – s. Standbild
stimulatory – adj. stimulierend, expansiv, (konjunktur-)belebend
stimulus – s. Anregung, Anreiz, Ansporn, (Auslöse-)Impuls, Antrieb
stipulate – v. ausbedingen, vertraglich festsetzen, vereinbaren, abmachen
stipulation – s. Vereinbarung, Abmachung, Bedingung, Klausel
stock
s. Lager, Lagerbestand, Vorratsvermögen
s. Aktienkapital, Grundkapital, Stammkapital
s. Aktien, Stammaktien
s. Wertpapier(e)
buy sthg. for stock – etwas auf Lager legen
carry stocks – Lager führen / halten
goods in stock / on stock – vorrätige Waren
stock – v. auf Lager halten, führen, vorrätig haben, (für Verkaufszwecke) lagern
stock consumer products – Konsumartikel führen
stock appreciation – s. Aufwertung / Werterhöhung des Lagervermögens
stockbroker – s. Börsen-, Kurs-, Effektenmakler/in
stock buy-back – s. Aktienrückkauf (durch den Emittenten)
stock certificate – s. Aktienzertifikat, Bescheinigung über den Besitz einer bestimmten Anzahl von Aktien
stock concept – s. Bestandsgröße, Zeitpunktgröße
stock control – s. Lagerplanung, -wirtschaft, Steuerung der Lagermenge
stock dividend – s. Stockdividende, Dividende in Form von Gratisaktien
stock exchange – s. Effektenbörse
stock exchange index – s. Börsenindex
stock exchange member – s. Börsenmitglied
stock exchange quotation – s. Börsen-, Börsenzulassung eines Wertpapieres
stock forwards – s. Aktientermingeschäfte, -kontrakte
stockholder – s. Aktionär/in, Gesellschafter/in einer GmbH, Gesellschafter einer Kapitalgesellschaft
stockholders' equity – s. Eigenkapital(-Bilanzposition)
stockholders' funds – s. Eigenkapital(-Bilanzposition)
stockholding – s. Lagerhaltung
stock index – s. Aktienindex
stock index futures – s. Terminkontrakt auf einen Aktienindex, Aktienindex-Terminkontrakt
stockist – s. Fachhändler, Fachgeschäft
stockjobber – s. Effekteneigenhändler/in, Börsenmakler/in auf eigene Rechnung
stockless production – s. lagerlose Fertigung
stock level – s. Lagerbestand, Höhe des Lagerbestandes
stock movement – s. Lagerbewegung, Veränderung des Lagerbestandes
stock on hand – s. (vorhandener / verfügbarer) Lagerbestand
stock option
s. Aktienoption (als derivatives Finanzinstrument)
s. Mitarbeitaktienoption, Aktienoption als Vergütungselement
stockout – s. Fehlmenge
stock price – s. Aktien-, Wertpapierkurs
stock records – s. Aufstellung der Lagerbestände, Lagerbuchhaltung
stock savings bank – s. private, als Aktiengesellschaft organisierte Sparkasse
stock-taking – s. Inventur
stockturn – s. Lagerumschlag(-shäufigkeit)
stock turnover – s. Lagerumschlag(-shäufigkeit)
stop – v. aufhalten, stoppen, sperren
stop a cheque – einen Scheck sperren
storage
s. Lager, Lagerhaltung
s. Speicher, Speicherung
s. Aufbewahren, Aufbewahrung
storage area – s. Lagerplatz, -fläche

storage charge – s. Lagergebühr
storage device – s. Speichergerät, -einheit
storage facilities – s. Lagerfazilitäten, -einrichtungen, Lagerservice
storage medium – s. Speichermedium, Informationsträger
storage unit – s. Speichergerät
store
s. Geschäft, Laden
s. Vorrat, Bestand, Fundus
s. Lagerhaus, Speicher
store – v. lagern, aufbewahren, speichern
store in a dry place – trocken lagern
store brand – s. Eigen-, Haus-, Händler-, Handelsmarke
store of information – s. (Bestand / Fundus an) Informationsmaterial
store of value – s. Thesaurierungs-, Wertaufbewahrungsmittel (Funktion des Geldes)
stow – v. beladen, verstauen,
stowage
s. Stauung, Verstauen, Ladung
s. Laderaum
s. Staugeld, Stauerlohn
straight – adj. direkt, gerade
straight bill of lading – s. Rektakonnossement
straight-line method – s. lineare Abschreibung(-smethode)
strand – v. stranden
stranded investment – s. Stranded Investment(s), nicht amortisierbare Investition(en), in den Sand gesetzte Investition(en)
stranding – s. Strandung
stranglehold – s. Würgegriff
strategic – adj. strategisch, langfristig
strategic business unit – s. strategischer Geschäftsbereich, SGB
strategic trade – s. strategischer Handel, strategische Außenhandelspolitik
strata – s. Schichten, Lagen, Formationen
strategic alliance – s. strategische Allianz
stratum – s. Schicht, Lage, Formation
streamline – v. rationalieren, effizienter machen
strict liability – s. strikte (Delikts-)Haftung
strike – s. Streik
strike
v. schlagen, treffen
v. streiken
v. saldieren, ermitteln
strike the return on capital – die Kapitalrentabilität ermitteln
strike pay – s. Streikgeld
strike price – s. Ausübungspreis / Basispreis / Strike-Preis (einer Option)
strike rate of interest – s. Ausübungszinssatz (einer Zinsoption)
strike record – s. Streikbilanz
string – s. Auflage, Bedingung
loan with strings – mit Auflagen verbundener Kredit
stringent – adj. streng, hart
strong currency – s. harte / starke Währung, Hartwährung
strong foreign currency – s. harte / starke Währung, Hartwährung
structural change – s. Strukturwandel
structural unemployment – s. strukturelle Arbeitslosigkeit
stumbling block – s. Stolperstein
subagent – s. Untervertreter/in
subassembly – s. Baugruppe
subassign – v. (Forderungen an einen zweiten oder dritten Factor) weiterzedieren
subaward – v. ([Teile eines] Auftrag[s]) an Subunternehmer weitervergeben
subcaption – s. (Bilanz.-) Unterposition / Untergruppe
subcontract – v. auslagern, outsourcen, (Aufträge) an Subunternehmer oder Zulieferer vergeben
subcontracting – s. Einsatz von Subunternehmern oder Zulieferern, Auslagern von Aufträgen / Leistungen / Geschäftsbereichen, Outsourcing
subcontractor – s. Subunternehmer/in, Zulieferer/in
subject matter insured – s. Versicherungsgegenstand, versicherter Gegenstand
subject of a contract – s. Gegenstand eines Vertrages, Vertragsgegenstand
subject to – prep. vorbehaltlich
subject to – adj. unterworfen, unterliegend, abhängig, -pflichtig, geltend, vorbehalten, geregelt
subject to risks – Risken unterliegend / ausgesetzt
subject to fluctuations – Schwankungen unterliegend
subject to tax – steuerpflichtig
subject to change without notice – Änderungen vorbehalten
subject to being unsold – Zwischenverkauf vorbehalten
subject to prior sale – Zwischenverkauf vorbehalten
The order is subject to a discount. – Für den Auftrag gilt ein Preisnachlass.
The offer is subject to price ruling on date of dispatch. – Für das Angebot gilt der am Versandtag geltende Preis.
subject to his approval – vorbehaltlich seiner Zustimmung
sub-market – s. Teilmarkt, Marktsegment
submersion – s. Überflutung
submission – s. Einreichung, Unterbreitung, Vorlage
submission of tenders – s. Angebotseinreichung, Einreichung von Submissionsangeboten
submit – v. unterbreiten, vorlegen, einreichen
subordinate – adj. untergeordnet
subordinate unit – s. untergeordnete Organisationseinheit
subrogate – v. einsetzen, (an die Stelle) setzen, eintreten, übergehen
The insurer is subrogated to the rights of the insured. – Der Versicherer tritt in die Rechte des Versicherten ein. / Die Rechte des Versicherten gehen auf den Versicherer über.
subrogation – s. Subrogation, Eintritt des Versicherers in die Rechte des Versicherten
subscribe
v. zeichnen
v. abonnieren
v. (symbolsich) unterschreiben, beipflichten
subscribe to a view – einer Ansicht / Meinung beipflichten
subscribe (for) shares – Aktien zeichnen
subscriber
s. Abonnent/in
s. Fernsprechteilnehmer/in, (System-)Teilnehmer/in
s. (zahlendes) Mitglied, Klient/in, Kunde/Kundin
s. Zeichner (Wertpapiere)
subscriber trunk dialling – s. Selbstwählfernverkehr
subscription
s. Abonnement, Mitgliedschaft
s. Mitgliedsbeitrag
s. Beitrag, Spende
s. Zeichnung (von Wertpapieren)
operate on a subscription basis – nach dem Abonnementsystem arbeiten
subsequently – adv. im Folgenden, daraufhin
subsidiary – s. Tochtergesellschaft, Tochter

subsidiary budget – s. Teilplan, -budget
subsidiary company – s. Tochtergesellschaft, Tochter
subsidiary objective – s. Sekundärziel
subsidise – v. subventionieren, stützen
subsidised exports – s. subventionierte / geförderte Exporte
subsidised loan – s. zinsgestützter / geförderter / subventionierter Kredit
subsidy – s. Subvention, Finanzhilfe, Finanz- und Sachhilfe, Stützung(-sbetrag), Zuschuss
substantial transformation – s. (zollrechtlich relevante) wesentliche Veränderung in der Beschaffenheit (einer Ware)
substantiate – v. beweisen, nachweisen, belegen, bekräftigen, begründen, untermauern
substitute – s. Ersatz(-artikel), Ersatzgut, substitutives Gut, Substitut
sub-subsidiary – s. Enkelgesellschaft
subsystem – s. Subsystem, Untersystem
succinct – adj. knapp, bündig
sue – v. klagen, Klage einreichen
sue for damages – auf Schadenersatz klagen
suggest
v. vorschlagen, anraten
v. andeuten, unterstellen
v. behaupten
suggested retail price – s. empfohlener Endverbraucherpreis, unverbindlicher / nicht kartellisierter Richtpreis
suggestion
s. Vorschlag, Empfehlung, Anregung
s. Andeutung, Unterstellung
suit
s. Klage, Klagesache, Rechtsstreit
s. Farbe (beim Kartenspiel)
file a suit – eine Klage einbringen / erheben
follow suit – Farbe nachspielen, nachziehen, nacheifern, einem Beispiel folgen
suitor – s. Bewerber/in, Bieter/in bei einem Firmenübernahmeangebot
sulphuric acid – s. Schwefelsäure
sum insured – s. Versicherungssumme
summarise – v. zusammenfassen
summary – s. Zusammenfassung
summary law suit – s. Schnellverfahren
summer sale – s. Sommerschlussverkauf
summit
s. Gipfel, Höhepunkt, Kuppe
s. Gipfeltreffen, Gipfelkonferenz
summit meeting – s. Gipfeltreffen
sum-of-the-years'-digits method – s. digitale Abschreibung, arithmetisch degressive Abschreibung
sunrise industry – s. Hoffnungssparte, -branche, aufsteigender / zukunftsträchtiger Wirtschaftszweig
sunset industry – s. absterbender Wirtschaftszweig
sunspot theory – s. Sonnenfleckentheorie (des Konjunkturzyklus)
superfiche – s. Superfiche
superimpose – v. hinzufügen
superimposed clause – (wörtlich) nachträglich hinzugefügte Klausel, einschränkende Vorbehaltsklausel auf einem unreinen Konnossement
superior – s. Vorgesetzte/r
superior – adj. überlegen, höher gestellt, übergeordnet
superior unit – s. übergeordnete Organisationseinheit
supermarket – s. Supermarkt
supersede – v. ersetzen, verdrängen, ablösen
supervise – v. beaufsichtigen, überwachen
supervisor – s. (unmittelbarer) Vorgesetzter, Aufseher
supervisory board – s. Aufsichtsrat (einer deutschen / österreichischen Aktiengesellschaft / großen GmbH)
supplement – s. Zusatz, Anhang, Nachtrag, (Zeitungs-)Beilage
supplement – v. ergänzen
supplementary benefit – s. Ausgleichszulage
supplementary budget – s. Teilplan, -budget, Unterplan, -budget
supplementary material – s. Gemeinkostenmaterial, zusätzlich (zu den Rohstoffen bei der Produktion) benötigtes Material
supplementary wage costs – s. Lohn-, Personalnebenkosten
supplier – s. Lieferant/in, Lieferer, Verkäufer/in, Anbieter/in
supplier credit – s. Lieferkredit, Lieferantenkredit, Liefervertragskredit
supply
s. Angebot
s. Vorrat
s. Lieferung, Anlieferung, Versorgung
s. (pl.) Hilfs- und Betriebstoffe, Zulieferungen, Nachschub
s. (pl.) Lieferungen und Leistungen (im Sinne der Mehrwertsteuer)
in short supply – knapp, beschränkt verfügbar
in abundant supply – reichlich / im Überfluss vorhanden
in fixed supply – nur in bestimmter Menge vorhanden
supply – v. liefern, versorgen, bereitstellen
supply chain – s. Beschaffungs-, Wertschöpfungskette
supply chain management – s. Supply Chain Management, Beschaffungskettenmanagement
supply curve – s. Angebotskurve
supply elasticity of price – s. Angebotselastizität des Preises
supply function – s. Angebotsfunktion
supply market – s. Beschaffungsmarkt
supply-sider – s. Vertreter/in der angebotsorientierten Volkswirtschaftslehre
supporting staternent – s. Ergänzungsrechnung (zum Periodenabschluss)
surgical supplies – s. Operationsbedarf
surface area – s. Oberfläche
surface transport – s. Oberflächentransport, Land- und Seetransport
surplus – s. Überschuss, Aktivum
show a surplus – einen Überschuss aufweisen, aktiv sein
be in surplus – einen Überschuss aufweisen, aktiv sein
surplus on invisibles – s. Dienstleistungsüberschuss
surplus stock – s. überschüssige (Lager-)Bestände
surrrender – s. Ablieferung, Abtretung
surrender – v. abliefern, übergeben
survey
s. Überblick, Übersicht
s. Erhebung, Studie, Untersuchung
s. Tatbestands- und Schadensaufnahme
conduct a survey – eine Erhebung durchführen
survey report – s. Schadensattest, Tatbestandsaufnahme
surveyor – s. Havariekommissar, Schadenssachverständiger
survival – s. Weiterbestand, Überleben
survive – v. überleben
sustain – v. ertragen, ausstehen, erleiden
sustain a loss – einen Schaden erleiden
sustainable – adj. aufrechterhaltbar, dauerhaft, nachhaltig, zukunftsbezogen, zukunftsverträglich, zukunftsfähig, systembewahrend
sustainable development – s. nachhaltige / zukunftsfähige Entwicklung
sustainability – s. Nachhaltigkeit, Zukunftsfähigkeit, -verträglichkeit, Tragfähigkeit, Belastbarkeit
swap
s. Tausch(-geschäft)

s. Swap (Zinsswap, Währungsswap), Swapgeschäft, gegenseitige Übernahme von Rechten und Pflichten, Forderungstausch
swap market - s. Swapmarkt, Swap-Markt
swap-option - s. Swaption, Option auf einen (Zins-)Swap
swap participant - s. Swap-Teilnehmer/in, Swap-Partei
swap rate - s. Swapsatz, Devisentauschsatz
swaption - s. Swaption, Option auf einen (Zins-)Swap
SWIFT
s. Society for Worldwide Interbank Financial Telecommunications (siehe)
s. SWIFT-(Überweisungs-)System
swift - adj. rasch, schnell
SWIFT transfer - s. SWIFT-Auszahlung, SWIFT-Überweisung
swing - s. Fluktuation, Schwankung
symbol
s. Symbol
s. (pl.) Bilddaten
symbolic delivery - s. symbolische Übergabe
syndicate - s. Konsortium, Syndikat
syndicate - v. ein Konsortium bilden, syndizieren
syndicate a loan - ein Bankenkonsortium für die Vergabe eines Kredites bilden, einen Kredit (unter den Mitgliedern eines Bankenkonsortiums) aufteilen / syndizieren
syndicated loan - s. Konsortialkredit, syndizierter Kredit
syndicate member
s. Konsortialmitglied, Konsorte
s. Einzelversicherer bei Lloyd's
syndicate of underwriters - s. Konsortium von Einzelversicherern bei Lloyd's
syndication - s. Syndizierung, Konsortialbildung, Co-Finanzierung
synergy - s. Synergie, Verbundvorteil(e)
synthetic fertiliser - s. Kunstdünger
systems approach - s. Systemansatz
system software - s. Systemsoftware, Betriebssystem
system thinking - s. Systemansatz

T

tab – s. Indexzunge, Tab, (Kartei-)Reiter
table – s. Tabelle, Aufstellung
table – v. auf den Tisch legen, vorbringen, einbringen, stellen
table a motion – einen Antrag (bei einer Sitzung) stellen
T-account – s. T-Konto
tacit agreement – s. stillschweigende Übereinkunft
tactical – adj. taktisch, kurzfristig
tailor – v. zuschneiden, abstimmen
tailor products to a sub-market – Produkte auf einen Teilmarkt abstimmen
tailored option – s. Freiverkehrsoption, nicht-börsennotierte Option, bankmäßige (Devisen-)Option
tailor-made – adj. maßgeschneidert, auf den Kunden zugeschnitten, außerbörslich
tailor-made option – s. Freiverkehrsoption, nicht börsennotierte Option, bankmäßige (Devisen-)Option
take-home pay – s. effektiv ausbezahlter Lohn
takeover bid – s. (öffentliches) Übernahmeangebot, Übernahmeangebot für eine Firma, Firmenübernahmeangebot
tangible – adj. greifbar, körperlich, materiell, konkret
tangible capital assets – s. materielles Anlagevermögen
tangible fixed assets – s. materielles Anlagevermögen, Sachanlagen
tangible personal property – s. bewegliche Sachen
tap
v. (ein-)tippen
v. anzapfen, erschließen, in Anspruch nehmen
tap new markets – neue Märkte erschließen
tape – s. (Magnet- / Klebe-)Band
target – s. (quantitatives) Ziel, Vorgabe, Sollwert
target audience – s. Zielpublikum, -gruppe
target company – s. Zielgesellschaft (einer Investition oder Übernahme), Übernahmeziel,
target group – s. Zielgruppe
targeting – s. Zielgruppenauswahl
target pest – s. Zielschädling
tariff – s. Zoll, Zollgebühr, -abgabe
tariff barrier – s. Zollschranke
tariff concession – s. Zollvergünstigung, -vorteil, -präferenz
tariff discrimination – s. unterschiedliche Zollbehandlung, Zolldifferenzierung
tariff escalation – s. Zolleskalation, Tarifeskalation
tariff heading – s. Zolltarifnummer
tariff legislation – s. Zollgesetze
tariff rate – s. Zollsatz
tarnish – v. beflecken
task system of pay – s. Zeitakkord
tax – s. Steuer, Abgabe, Gebühr, Beitrag
for tax purposes – im steuerlichen Sinn
impose a tax – eine Steuer auferlegen / erheben
levy a tax – eine Steuer erheben
tax
v. besteuern
v. in Anspruch nehmen, strapazieren
taxable – adj. steuerbar, steuerpflichtig
taxable action – s. steuerbare Handlung
taxable income – s. steuerpflichtiges Einkommen
taxable person – s. steuerpflichtige Person, Steuerpflichtige/r
tax advisor – s. Steuerberater/in
tax allowance – s. Steuerfreibetrag, Sonderausgabe
taxation – s. Besteuerung
tax avoidance – s. Steuervermeidung, -umgehung
tax band – s. Steuer-, Progressionsstufe
tax base – s. Steuerobjekt, -bemessungsgrundlage
tax bracket – s. Steuer-, Progressions-, Einkommensstufe
tax break – Steuersubvention, -begünstigung, -vergünstigung, -befreiung, -erleichterung
tax burden – s. Steuerlast, -belastung, -schuld
tax credit – s. Absetzbetrag, Steuergutschrift, (steuerlicher) Anrechnungsbetrag
tax deduction – s. Steuerfreibetrag, Sonderausgabe, abzugsfähiger (Betriebs-)Aufwand
tax evasion – s. Steuerhinterziehung. -betrug
tax exemption – s. Steuerbefreiung
tax haven – s. Steuerparadies, -oase
tax holiday – s. zeitlich begrenzte Steuerbefreiung
tax incidence – s. Steuerinzidenz, steuerliche Belastungswirkung
tax jurisdiction
s. Steuerhoheit
s. Steuerhoheitsträger
tax law – s. Steuergesetz, -recht
tax legislation – s. Steuergesetzgebung, -gesetze, -recht
tax liability
s. Steuerpflicht
s. Steuerschuld, Zahllast
taxman – s. Steuerbeamter, (fig.) Fiskus, Finanzamt
tax management – s. betriebswirtschaftliche Steuerlehre und -praxis, Steuerwirtschaft
tax object – s. Steuerobjekt
tax rate – s. Steuersatz
tax regime – s. Steuersystem, steuerliche Regelungen
tax relief – s. Steuersubvention, -begünstigung, -vergünstigung, -befreiung, -freibetrag
tax resistance – s. Steuerwiderstand
tax return – s. Steuererklärung
file a tax return – eine Steuererklärung einreichen
tax revenue – s. Steueraufkommen
tax stamp – s. Stempelmarke
tax treatment – s. steuerliche Behandlung
T/C – traveller's cheque (siehe)
technical aid – s. technische (Entwicklungs-)Hilfe
technical analysis – s. technische (Wertpapier-)Analyse
technical analyst – s. Chartist, technischer Analyst, technisch orientierter Analyst
technical insolvency – s. Illiquidität, Insolvenz (auf Grund von Illiquidität)
technical standard – s. technische Norm
technological unemployment – s. technologische Arbeitslosigkeit
technology transfer – s. Technologietransfer
telecommunication device – s. Nachrichtenübermittlungs-, Telekommunikationsgerät
telecommunications – s. Nachrichtenwesen, Nachrichtenverbindung, Telekommunikation
telecommuting – s. Telependeln, Teleworking, computergestützte Heimarbeit
telecommuter – s. Telependler/in, -arbeiter/in
teleconferencing – s. Teleconferencing, (Abhaltung von) Telefon- und Bildschirmkonferenzen, Telekonferenzdienste
telecopying – s. Fernkopieren, Faksimileübertragung, Faxübermittlung
telefax transceiver – s. Fernkopierer, Telekopierer, Faxgerät

telegraphic money order – s. telegraphische Geldanweisung
telegraphic transfer – s. telegraphische Auszahlung / Anweisung, Telex-Auszahlung
telephone answering machine – s. Telefonbeantworter, Anrufbeantworter
telephone banking – s. Phone-Banking, Telefon-Banking
telephone call – s. Telefonanruf, -gespräch
telephone directory – s. Telefonbuch
telephone shopping – s. Telefonshopping, Telefonkauf
teleprinter – s. Fernschreiber, Fernschreibmaschine
teleshopping – s. Teleshopping, Fernseh-, Telekauf
Teletex – s. Teletex, öffentlicher Bürofernschreibdienst
Teletext – s. Teletext
teletypewriter – s. Fernschreiber, Fernschreibmaschine
teleworking – s. Teleworking, Telependeln, computergestützte Heimarbeit
telex
s. Fernschreibdienst, Telex
s. Telex, Telexschreiben
telex equipment – s. Telexgeräte, Fernschreiber
telex machine – s. Fernschreiber
telex operator – s. Teletypist/in
telex transfer – s. Telexauszahlung, telegraphische Ausszahlung
telex transfer rate – s. Wechselkurs für telegraphische / Telex-Auszahlungen
teller – s. Schalterbeamter /-beamtin (in einer Bank), Kundenbetreuer/in am Bankschalter
teller functions – s. Aufgabenbereich eines / einer Schalterbeamten / Schalterbeamtin
temperate zone – s. gemäßigte Klimazone
temporary admission – s. Temporary Admission, vorübergehende (abgabenfreie) Einfuhr
temporary exportation of goods – s. Ausgangsvormerkverkehr
temporary importation of goods – s. Eingangsvormerkverkehr
temporary investments – s. Wertpapiere des Umlaufvermögens, kurzfristige Finanzanlagen
temporary investments of cash – s. kurzfristige Finanzanlagen, Wertpapiere des Umlaufvermögens
tenant – s. Mieter
tend – s. tendieren, (zu etwas) neigen
tender
s. Submissionsangebot
s. Ausschreibung(-sverfahren)
put a contract out to tender – einen Auftrag ausschreiben, eine Ausschreibung machen
file a tender – ein Submissionsangebot einreichen
tender – v. anbieten, Angebot machen, zur Verfügung stellen, andienen
tender bond – s. Bietungsgarantie, Ausschreibungsgarantie
post a tender bond – eine Bietungsgarantie stellen
tender documents – s. Ausschreibungsunterlagen
tenderer – s. Submittent, Anbieter/in
tender guarantee – s. Bietungs-, Ausschreibungsgarantie
tendering
s. Ausschreibung (im weiteren Sinn)
s. Angebotsabgabe, Unterbreitung von Submissionsangeboten, Teilnahme an einer Ausschreibung
s. Andienung
tender-inviting party – s. ausschreibende Stelle / Firma
tender issue – s. (Wertpapier-)Emission im Submissionsweg / im Tenderverfahren
tender notice – s. Ausschreibungsanzeige, Ausschreibungsankündigung
tender offer – s. (öffentliches) Übernahmeangebot für eine Firma, Firmenübernahmeangebot
tender procedure – s. Auschreibungsverfahren
tenor
s. Inhalt (eines Dokumentes), Wortlaut
s. Laufzeit (eines Wechsels / einer Anleihe)
term
s. Fachausdruck, -terminus, Bezeichnung, Wort
s. (pl.) Ausdrucksweise, Form, Hinsicht
s. Zeit, Periode, Klausel, Preis
s. Bedingung, Periode, Frist, Laufzeit
in nominal terms – nominal, preislich nicht bereinigt
in terms of money – in Geld ausgedrückt, geld-, wertmäßig
short-term – kurzfristig
long-term – langfristig
on these terms – zu diesen Bedingungen
come to terms – sich einigen
term – v. bezeichnen, benennen
terminal
s. Datenendgerät, Terminal
s. Endpunkt, Terminal, Endbahnhof, Endstation
s. (Container-)Terminal, (Fracht-)Abfertigungsanlage, -gebäude, Tankerbelade-, Tankerentladeanlage
terminate – v. beenden, ablaufen, enden
an offer is terminated – ein Antrag / Angebot erlischt
termination – s. Bendigung
termination of a contract – s. Beendigung eines Vertragsverhältnisses
termination of a contract of employment – s. Beendigung eines Arbeitsverhältnisses
term loan – s. mittel- bis langfristiger Kommerzkredit
term of credit
s. Kreditlaufzeit
s. Zahlungsziel
term of office – s. Amtszeit
term of patent – s. Patentlaufzeit
term of payment
s. Zahlungsziel
s. (pl.) Zahlungsbedingungen
terms of delivery – s. Lieferbedingungen
terms of trade – s. (reales) außenwirtschaftliches Austauschverhältnis, Terms of Trade, ToT
terms to the trade – s. (Zahlungs-)Bedingungen für den Handel / Wiederverkäufer
territory – s. (Vertrags-)Gebiet, Territorium
tertiary sector – s. tertiärer Sektor, Dienstleistungssektor
test
s. Test
s. Kriterium
test campaign – s. Test-, Probekampagne
testify – v. bezeugen
test marketing – s. Durchführung von lokalen Markttests, Testmarketing
textbook – s. Lehr-, Schulbuch
theft – s. Diebstahl
theft insurance – s. Diebstahlsversicherung
thermal pollution – s. Abwärmelast, Abwärmebelastung, thermische Umweltbelastung
thermal power station – s. Wärmekraftwerk, thermisches Kraftwerk
threat – s. Drohung, Bedrohung
threaten – v. drohen, bedrohen
three-month forward dollar – s. Dreimonats-Dollar, Termindollar mit Dreimonatsfälligkeit
third currency – s. Drittwährung, Drittlandswährung
third country currency – s. Drittlandswährung
third party – s. Dritte/r, dritte Person, Drittinstitution

third-party insurance – s. Haftpflichtversicherung
third-stage finance – s. Drittrundenfinanzierung
thrift – s. Sparinstitut, Sparkasse, Bausparkasse
through bill of lading – s. Durchkonnossement
through traffic – s. Direktverkehr (ohne Wechsel des Transportmittels)
through transport – s. Direkttransport (ohne Wechsel des Transportmittels)
throwaway society – s. Wegwerfgesellschaft
thyroid cancer – s. Schilddrüsenkrebs
tick – v. ticken, funktionieren, laufen
This makes him tick. – Das motiviert ihn. / So tickt er.
tidal power plant – s. Gezeitenkraftwerk
tie up – v. binden, fest anlegen
tie up capital – Kapital binden
capital tied up in stocks – im Lagervermögen gebundenes Kapital
tied aid – s. liefergebundene (Entwicklungs-)Hilfe
tight – adj. eng, streng, knapp, straff
tightly organised – straff organisiert, durchorganisiert
tighten – v. verschärfen, restringieren, kontrahieren
tighten controls – Restriktionen verschärfen
tight money – s. Politik des knappen Geldes, restriktive / kontraktive Geldpolitik
timber carrier – s. Holzfrachter, Holzfahrer
timber tract – s. Waldgebiet
time and motion study – s. Zeit- und Bewegungsstudie
time bill – s. „Zielwechsel", (umfasst Tag-, Nachsicht- und Datowechsel)
time bill payable a specified period of time after date – s. Datowechsel
time bill payable at a specified period of time after date – s. Nachsichtwechsel
time bill payable at a fixed date – s. Tagwechsel
time CD – time certificate of deposit (siehe)
time certificate of deposit – s. Terminkassenobligation
time charter – s. Zeitcharter
time-consuming – adj. zeitraubend
time deposit – s. Termineinlage
time draft – s. „Zielwechsel"
timekeeping
s. Arbeitszeitdiziplin, Einhaltung von Arbeitszeitvorgaben
s. Arbeitszeiterfassung, Überwachung der Einhaltung von Arbeitszeitvorgaben,
bad timekeeping – Unpünktlichkeit, Zuspätkommnen
time limit – s. Frist
time limit for acceptance of an offer – s. Anbotsfrist
time of delivery – s. Lieferzeit, Lieferfrist
time of payment – s. Zahlungszeitpunkt
time policy – s. Zeitpolizze, Zeitversicherung
time pricing – s. zeitabhängige Preisgestaltung, zeitliche Preisdifferenzierung
time rates – s. Zeitlohn
time series – s. (statistische) Zeitreihe
time value – s. Zeitwert
time value of an option – Zeitwert einer Option
time value of money – Zeitwert des Geldes
timing – s. Timing, Wahl des (richtigen) Zeitpunktes
tinker – v. herumbasteln, kleine Änderungen vornehmen
tinker with the economic system – am Wirtschaftssystem herumbasteln
tin-lined – s. mit Zinnblech ausgelegt
TIR – Transport International Routier
TIR carnet – s. Carnet TIR, Zollbegleitschein(-heft) für den internationalen Straßengüterverkehr
tissue – s. (organisches) Gewebe
title
s. Titel, Bezeichnung
s. (Eigentums-)Recht
title to goods – Eigentum(-srecht) an der Ware
take title to goods – Eigentum an der Ware erwerben
toiletries market – s. Toilettenartikelmarkt
toll-free number – s. gebührenfreie Telefonnummer, 0800-Nummer
toll-free system – s. (ferngesprächs-)gebührenfreies Telefonservice, National Freeline, Anruf zum Nulltarif, 0800-Dienst
toner – s. Toner, Kopierpulver
top – s. Kammzug
top loader container – s. Open-Top Container
top-notch – adj. erstklassig, Spitzen-
top management
s. Top-Management, Führungsspitze, oberste Führungsebene
s. obere Führungsebene, Mitglieder der oberen Führungsebene
top manager
s. Spitzenmanger, Mitglied der obersten Führungsebene
s. leitender Angestellter, Mitglied der oberen Führungsebene
tops of wool – s. Kammzüge
top tax bracket – s. Progressionsspitze, Einkommensstufe mit dem Spitzensteuersatz
top up – v. auffüllen, nachfüllen
ToT – Terms of Trade (siehe)
total assets – s. Gesamtvermögen, Bilanzsumme
total debt to shareholders' funds – s. Verschuldungsgrad, -koeffizient
total-factor productivity – s. Gesamtproduktivität
total-liabilities-to-owners'-equity ratio – s. Verschuldungsgrad, -koeffizient
total loss – s. Totalverlust, Gesamtverlust
total loss of, or damage to, the goods – s. Totalverlust oder -beschädigung der Ware
total price – s. Gesamtpreis, Kaufpreis, -summe
total quality management – s. Total Quality Management, umfassendes Qualitätsmanagement
total return to shareholders – s. Aktionärsrendite, Gesamtrendite für Aktionäre
tourism – s. Tourismus, Fremdenverkehr(-swesen)
tourist industry – s. Fremdenverkehr(-swirtschaft)
tow – v. schleppen
township – s. Gemeinde, Orts-, Stadtgemeinde
tow rope – s. Schleppseil
toxic – adj. giftig, toxisch
TQM – total quality management (siehe)
trace – s. Spur
trace – v. (Spur) verfolgen, (einer Spur) nachgehen, nachforschen
traceable – adj. (zurück-)verfolgbar
track – s. Gleis, Geleise
track – v. verfolgen, überwachen
order tracking – Auftragsverfolgung, -überwachung
track record – s. Ergebnis, bisherige Leistung, „Bilanz"
tract – s. Gebiet, Landstrich, Fläche
tract of rainforest – Regenwaldgebiet, -fläche
tractive unit – s. Zugmaschine, Sattelschlepper
tractor – s. Traktor, Zugmaschine, Sattelschlepper
trade
s. Handel (im engeren Sinn)
s. Gewerbe, Sparte, Beruf, Branche
s. Geschäft(-e), Geschäftstätigkeit, wirtschaftliche Tätigkeit, betriebliche Leistungserstellung
s. Börsentransaktion
s. Frachtschiffverkehr(-sroute)

trade
v. handeln
v. notieren, gehandelt werden
trade in goods – mit Waren handeln
The pound is trading for $1.82. – Das Pfund notiert mit / bei 1,82 Dollar.
trade – adj. Geschäfts-, Firmen-
trade visitor – Firmenbesucher/in (einer Messe)
trade acceptance – s. (akzeptierter) Warenwechsel / Kundenwechsel
trade accord – s. Handelsabkommen
trade account – s. Handelsbilanz, Bilanz des Warenverkehrs, Warenverkehrsbilanz
trade accounts payable – s. (Buch-)Verbindlichkeiten auf Grund von Warenlieferungen und Leistungen)
trade accounts receivable – s. (Buch-) Forderungen auf Grund von Warenlieferungen und Leistungen
trade association – s. Fachverband, Unternehmerverband, Interessenvertretung (der Unternehmer einer Branche)
trade balance – s. (Saldo der) Handelsbilanz, Warenverkehr(-ssaldo)
trade balancing requirement – Trade-Balancing-Requirement, Verknüpfung von Export- und Importvolumina (Verpflichtung eines Auslandsinvestors, Exporte aus dem Zielland in einem Mindest-Verhältnis zu den zugelassenen Importen von Vormaterialen zu halten).
trade barrier – s. Handelshemmnis, -schranke, Hindernis für den Außenhandel
trade creation – s. Trade Creation, Handelsschaffung
trade credit – s. Lieferantenkredit, Lieferkredit, Liefervertragskredit
trade creditor
s. Lieferant/in, Gläubiger/in auf Grund von Warenlieferungen und Leistungen, Lieferantenkreditgeber
s. (pl.) Verbindlichkeiten auf Grund von Warenlieferungen und Leistungen
trade cycle – s. Konjunkturzyklus, Wirtschaftszyklus
trade debt – s. Verbindlichkeiten auf Grund von Warenlieferungen und Leistungen
trade debtor
s. Warenschuldner, Kunde (der Waren oder Dienstleistungen auf Kredit bezogen hat)
s. (pl.) Forderungen auf Grund von Warenlieferungen und Leistungen
trade deficit
s. Außenhandels-, Handelsbilanzdefizit, Handelsbilanzpassivurn
s. Leistungsbilanzdefizit-, -passivum
trade deflection – s. Trade Deflection, Handelsablenkung
trade discount – s. Händler-, Wiederverkäufer-, Stufenrabatt
trade diversion – s. Trade Diversion, Handelsumlenkung
trade effect – s. Handelseffekt
trade fair – s. Messe, Fachmesse
trade flow – s. Handelsstrom
trade gap – s. (strukturelles) Defizit / Abgang in der Güterbilanz / Leistungsbilanz
trade hurdle – s. Handelshemmnis
trade in – v. in Zahlung geben
trade investor – s. strategische/r Investor/in (aus derselben Branche wie die Target-Firma)
trademark – s. eingetragenes Waren- / Dienstleistungszeichen, eingetragene Marke, Registrier-, Benutzungsmarke
trademark law – s. Markenrecht
trademark licensing – s. Markenlizensierung
trade not aid – Handel statt (Entwicklungs-)Hilfe
trade notes payable – s. Wechselverbindlichkeiten auf Grund von Warenlieferungen und Leistungen
trade notes receivable – s. Wechselforderungen auf Grund von Warenlieferungen und Leistungen
trade-off
s. Abtausch
s. Substitution; Substitutionsmöglichkeiten bei den Zielerreichungsgraden von Konfliktzielen; Zielkonflikt, negative Korrelation; Kompromiss (bei der Lösung von Zielkonflikten); Notwendigkeit, ein Ziel (teilweise) auf Kosten eines anderen zu erreichen
s. Nachteil, negative Nebenwirkung, Schattenseite, Kehrseite der Medaille
trade-off between butter and guns – s. substititutive Beziehung zwischen Butter (zivilen Gütern) und Kanonen (militärischen Gütern), „je mehr Kanonen, desto weniger Butter – und umgekehrt"
trade off – v. abtauschen, substitutieren
commodity A is traded off against commodity B – Gut A wird durch Gut B (graduell) subsititutiert
trade pact – s. Handelsabkommen
trade payables – s. Verbindlichkeiten auf Grund von Warenlieferungen und Leistungen
trade policy – s. (Außen-)Handelspolitik
trade press – s. Branchen-, Fachpresse
trade promotion – s. händlerorientierte / handelsorientierte Verkaufsförderung, Händler-Promotion
trader
s. Unternehmer/in, Geschäftsmann, Geschäftsfrau, Gewerbetreibende/r, Kaufmann
s. Händler/in, Wertpapierhändler/in, Devisenhändler/in
trade receivables – s. Forderungen aus Warenlieferungen und Leistungen
trade reference – s. Firmenreferenz
trade-related intellectual property rights – s. handelsbezogene intellektuelle Eigentumsrechte
trade-related investment measures – s. handelsbezogene Investitionsmaßnahmen / Investitionshemnisse
Trades Union Congress – s. UK-Gewerkschaftsbund
trade surplus
s. Außenhandels-, Handelsbilanzüberschuss, Handelsbilanzaktivum
s. Leistungsbilanzüberschuss, -aktivum
trade terms – s. Handelsklauseln
trade union – s. Gewerkschaft
trade unionism – s. Gewerkschaftsbewegung
trade visitor – s. Firmenbesucher/in (einer Messe)
trade-weighted value (of a currency) – s. außenhandelsgewichteter Außenwert (einer Währung)
trading account – s. Rohüberschussrechnung
trading bloc – s. Handelsblock, regionales Handelsabkommen, regionale Gruppierung (WTO-Terminologie)
trading certificate – s. Genehmigungsbescheid für eine UK-Kapitalgesellschaft
trading channel – s. Vertriebs-, Absatzweg, Distributionskanal
trading community – s. Händlerschaft, Händlerkreise
trading day – s. (Börsen-)Handelstag
trading down – s. Umstellung auf ein weniger hochwertiges Sortiment, Trading-Down
trading floor – s. Börsensaal, -parkett
trading hours – s. Handels-, Börsenstunden
trading loss
s. negatives Betriebsergebnis, Betriebsverlust,
s. (Wertpapier-) Handelsverlust
trading pattern – s. Umsatzverlauf(-muster), Verlauf der Handelstätigkeit (an der Börse)

trading profit
s. (brit.) (positives) Betriebsergebnis, Betriebsgewinn
s. (Wertpapier-) Handelsgewinn
trading session – s. Börsensitzung, Handelstag
trading stamp – s. Rabattmarke
trading stamp centre – s. Rabattmarkenzentrum
trading up – s. Sortimentsaufwertung, Trading-Up
traffic control – s. Verkehrsleitsystem(e), Verkehrslenkung, -steuerung
trailer – s. (Lkw-) Anhänger
trailer unit – s. Lastwagenzug
train – v. ausbilden
train-ferry – s. Eisenbahnfähre. Eisenbahnfährschiff, Trajekfähre
train-ferry service – s. Eisenbahnfährverkehr
train of barges – s. Schleppzug
trait – s. (Charakter-)Zug, Merkmal, Kennzeichen
tramp rates – s. Trampfrachtraten
tramp ship – s. Tramp, Trampschiff (Frachtschiff ohne feste Route)
transact – v. tätigen, durchführen, abwickeln, abschließen
transact business – Geschäfte tätigen / abschließen / abwickeln
insurance business transacted – abgeschlossene Versicherungen
transaction – s. Transaktion, Geschäft(-sfall), Abschluss
carry out a transaction – ein Geschäft durchführen / ausführen
transaction costs – s. Transaktionskosten
transaction currency risk – s. Währungsumwechslungs-, Transaktions-, Konvertierungsrisiko
transaction (exchange) gain – s. (Währungs-)Transaktions-, (Währungs-)Umwechslungsgewinn
transaction (exchange) loss – s. (Währungs-)Transaktions-, (Währungs-)Umwechslungsverlust
transaction exchange risk – s. Währungsumwechslungs-, Transaktions-, Konvertierungsrisiko
transaction exposure – s. Währungsumwechslungsposition
transaction on concurrent terms – s. Zug-um-Zug-Geschäft
transaction risk – s. Währungsumwechslungs-, Transaktions-, Konvertierungsrisiko
trans-border transaction – s. grenzüberschreitende Transaktion
transcend – v. übersteigen, überschreiten, darüber hinausgehen
transcript – s. Abschrift, Kopie
transfer
s. (rechtsgeschäftliche) Übertragung von Rechten und Vermögensgegenständen, Wertübertragung, Leistung
s. Transfer, Nichtleistungszahlung, unentgeltliche Leistung
s. Überweisung
s. Umbuchung, Dotation, Dotierung
s. Umladung, Umschlag, Transfer
s. Übergabe
transfer to reserves – Dotierung der Rücklagen
transfer
v. transferieren, übertragen, verlagern
v. überweisen
v. dotieren
v. abtreten, zedieren
transferable – adj. übertragbar, transferierbar, abtretbar
transferee – s. Übertragungsempfänger/in, Übernehmer/in, Zessionar/in
transfer of documents – s. Übergabe von Dokumenten
transfer of property – s. Eigentumsübertragung
transfer of technology – s. Technologietransfer
transferor – s. übertragende Partei, Zedent/in
transfer payments – s. Transferzahlungen
transfer price – s. (konzerninterner) Verrechnungspreis
transfer pricing – s. Verwendung / Einsatz konzerninterner Verrechnungspreise
transfer risk – s. Konvertierungs- und Transferrisiko
transfer to reserves – s. Dotierung der Rücklagen
transfer trail – s. Überweisungsweg, Dokumentenpfad einer Überweisung
transit – s. Transport
in transit – während des Transportes, beim Transport
transit costs – s. Transportkosten
transit insurance – s. Binnentransportversicherung von Gütern
transition – s. Übergang, Wandel, Überleitung
transition period – s. Übergangsphase, Umsetzungsfrist
transit time – s. Transportdauer
translation
s. Übersetzung, Umsetzung
s. Umrechnung, Währungs-, Fremdwährungsumrechnung
translation exposure – s. Währungsumrechnungsposition
translation gain – s. (Währungs-)Umrechnungsgewinn
translation loss – s. (Währungs-)Umrechnungsverlust
translation risk – s. (Währungs-)Umrechnungsrisiko
transmission capacity – s. Übertragungskapazität
transmission of funds – s. Zahlungs- und Überweisungsverkehr
transmission terminal – s. Übertragungsendgerät
transmit – v. übertragen, übermitteln, überweisen
transnational corporation – s. multinationaler / transnationaler Konzern
transpersonal – adj. transpersonal, das Alltags-Ich überschreitend, zum höheren Selbst gehörend
transplant – s. verpflanzen, transplantieren
transport – s. Transport, Beförderung
transportable – adj. transportierbarer / transportabler Personalcomputer
transportation insurance – s. Transportversicherung
transport documents – s. Transportdokumente, Versanddokumente im engeren Sinn (insb. alle Frachtbriefe, Konnossemente)
transport facilities – s. Transporteinrichtungen, -dienste
transship – v. umladen
transshipment – s. Umladung, Umladen
trap – s. Falle
globalisation trap – Globalisierungfalle
travel agency – s. Reisebüro
travel agent – s. Reisebürounternehmen
Travel Expense – s. Reise- und Fahrtaufwand(-skonto), (das Konto) Reise- und Fahrtaufwand
traveller's cheque – s. Reisescheck
tray
s. Tablett, Träge, Karton
s. (Kartei-)Kästchen, Karteibehälter
egg tray – Eierkarton
treasurer – s. Finanzdirektor/in, für den Finanzbereich zuständiges Vorstandsmitglied
Treasury – s. US-Finanzministerium / Schatzamt
treasury bill – s. Schatzwechsel
Treasury bond – s. US-Bundesschuldverschreibung, Staatsanleihe
Treasury note – s. US-Schatzschein
treasury stock – s. eigene Aktien / Anteile
Treaties of Rome – s. Römerverträge (Verträge zur Gründung der Europäischen Wirtschaftsgemeinschaft und der Europäischen Atomgemeinschaft)

treaty – s. (völkerrechtlicher) Vertrag
Treaty of Rome – s. Römervertrag (Vertrag zur Gründung der Europäischen Wirtschaftsgemeinschaft)
trend line – s. Trendlinie
trial balance – s. Rohbilanz, Summen- und/oder Saldenbilanz
trial order – s. Probeauftrag, Kauf zur Probe
trillion – s. Billion, 10^{12}
triangular compensation – s. Fremdkompensation
TRIMs – Trade-related Investment Measures (siehe)
triple A rating – s. Triple-A Rating, höchste Bonitätsstufe
triplicate – s. dreifache Ausfertigung
trip policy – s. Flugunfalleinzelpolizze, Flugunfallversicherung pro Flug
TRIPs – (Agreement on) Trade-Related Aspects of Intellectual Property Rights (siehe)
trip transit policy – s. (Binnentransport-)Einzelpolizze
trolley – s. Einkaufswagen
trouper – s. lang gedienter Mitspieler, lang gedientes Produkt
truck
s. Lastkraftwagen, Lkw
s. Eisenbahnwaggon
trucking-firm – s. Lkw-Transport-Unternehmen, Frächter, Lkw-Frächter, Straßentransportunternehmen
truckload – s. Lkw-Ladung
true and fair view – s. ein den tatsächlichen Verhältnissen entsprechendes Bild (einer Gesellschaft), Bilanzwahrheit
trunk call – s. Ferngespräch
trunk route – s. Hauptstrecke
trust
s. Vertrauen
s. Treuhand(-verhältnis)
s. Vermögensverwaltungs-Trust (eine der Stiftung ähnliche der Verwaltung von Sondervermögen dienende Organisationsform)
s. wettbewerbshemmender Unternehmenszusammenschluss, Kartell, Monopol
trust company – s. Treuhandgesellschaft, -bank, Vermögensverwaltungsgesellschaft
trust deed – s. Treuhandvertrag, Urkunde über die Errichtung einer Treuhand / eines Treuhandverhältnisses
trustee – s. Treuhänder/in
trustee bank – s. Depotbank (eines offenen Investmentfonds)
trustee company – s. Depotgesellschaft, -bank
trustee savings bank – s. UK-(gemeinnützige) Sparkasse
trustee securities – s. mündelsichere Wertpapiere
trust fund – s. Treuhandfonds, treuhändisch verwaltete Vermögensmasse
trust services – s. Treuhandgeschäfte, Vermögensverwaltung (für Kunden)
truth in advertising – s. „Wahrheit in der Werbung"; Verpflichtung, unrichtige Werbeaussagen zu vermeiden
truth in costing – s. Kostenwahrheit
truth in lending – s. „Wahrheit bei der Kreditgewährung", Verpflichtung zur wahrheitsgemäßen Angabe der tatsächlichen Kreditkosten (bes. bei Ratengeschäften)
truth in packaging – s. „Wahrheit bei der Verpackung und Aufmachung", Verbot von Mogelpackungen und falscher oder irreführender Produktkennzeichnung
TT – telegraphic transfer (siehe)
TT – telex transfer (siehe)
TT rate – s. Wechselkurs für telegraphische / Telex-Anweisungen, Devisenkurs
TUC – Trades Union Congress (siehe)
tug – s. Schlepper, Schleppschiff
tug-of-war – s. Tauziehen
tunnel – Tunnel(-formation), Zone horizontaler Konsolidierung
turn
s. Wendung, Wendepunkt, Umkehr
s. Spanne, Marge (eines Werpapierhändlers)
in turn – wiederum
turnkey contract – s. Vertrag für eine schlüsselfertige Anlage, Turnkey-Vertrag
turnkey project – s. schlüsselfertige Anlage, schlüsselfertiges Projekt, Turnkey-Projekt
turnover
s. Umschlagshäufigkeit
s. Umsatz
s. (Mitarbeiter-)Fluktuation
turn over – v. umschlagen
Inventory is turned over six times a year. – Der Lagerstand wird sechsmal pro Jahr umgeschlagen.
turnover ratio – s. Umschlagskennzahl
turnover tax – s. (Bruttoallphasen-)Umsatzsteuer
turnound – s. Schiffsumlauf, Hafenabfertigungszeit
TV spot – s. TV-Spot, (kurze) Werbeeinblendung im Fernsehen
two-bin method – s. Zwei-Behälter-Methode
two-stage channel – s. zweistufiger Vertrieb(-skanal)
two-tier – adj. gespalten, zweischichtig, zweistufig, zweiteilig
two-tier board system – s. Zweiteilung des Führungsgremiums der österr. u. deutschen Aktiengesellschaft, Trennung zwischen Aufsichtsrat und Vorstand
two-tier network – s. zweistufiges Rechnernetz
type – v. tippen, mit der Maschine schreiben
type bar – s. Typenhebel
typewriter – s. Schreibmaschine
typewriter ribbon – s. Farbband
typing pool – s. zentrales Schreibbüro, zentrale Schreibstelle
typing service – s. Schreibdienst

U

ULCC – s. ultra large crude carrier (siehe)
ultimate borrower – s. Letztkreditnehmer/in, Endkreditnehmer/in
ultimate consumer – s. Letztverbraucher/in, Endverbraucher/in
ultimate lender – s. Letztkreditgeber/in, Endkreditgeber/in
ultrafiche – s. Ultrafiche
ultra large crude carrier – s. ULCC-Tanker
umbrella brand – s. Produktgruppen-, Dach-, Familienmarke
umbrella organisation – s. Dachverband
unadjusted trial balance – s. Rohbilanz / Summen- und/oder Saldenbilanz vor Um- und Nachbuchungen
UNCITRAL – United Nations Commission on International Trade Law (siehe)
unclaimed dividend – s. nicht behobene Dividenden
uncollectibility – s. Uneinbringlichkeit
uncollectible accounts – s. uneinbringliche Forderungen (auf Grund von Warenlieferungen und Leistungen)
uncollectibles – s. uneinbringliche Forderungen (auf Grund von Warenlieferungen und Leistungen)
unconditional order – s. unbedingte Anweisung
unconfirmed irrevocable letter of credit – s. unbestätigtes unwiderrufliches (Dokumenten-)Akkreditiv
unconfirmed revocable letter of credit – s. unbestätigtes widerrufliches Akkreditiv
unconscious – s. das Unbewusste / Unterbewusste
the collective unconscious – das kollektive Unbewusste
uncrossed cheque – s. Barscheck
UN Conference on Environment and Development – s. UN-Konferenz für Umwelt & Entwicklung
UN Conference on Human Settlements – s. UN-Konferenz für menschliche Ansiedlungen
UNCTAD – United Nations Conference on Trade and Development (siehe)
under – prep. auf Grund, gemäß, nach, im Rahmen von, bei
under this method – bei dieser Methode / Vorgangsweise
under Austrian law – nach österreichischem Recht
a claim made under such bond – ein im Rahmen einer solchen Bankgarantie erhobener Anspruch
undercharge – s. Unterfakturierung, zu niedriger Rechnungsbetrag
underground economy – s. Schatten-, Schwarz-, Untergrundwirtschaft
under-invoice – v. unterfakturieren
underlying – adj. zugrundeliegend
underlying – s. Basis-, Referenzwert, Underlying
underlying asset – s. Basis-, Referenzwert, Underlying
underlying contract (of sale) – s. Grundgeschäft
underlying loan – s. Underlying Kredit
underlying transaction – s. Grundgeschäft
underpin – v. stützen, untermauern
under-report – s. zu wenig (Einkommen etc) angeben / melden / erklären
under-reporting income – Minderangabe / Mindermeldung von (steuerpflichtigem) Einkommen
undertake
v. unternehmen, durchführen
v. sich verpflichten
undertake investments – Investitionen durchführen
undertake to pay – sich verpflichten, zu zahlen; sich zur Zahlung verpflichten
undertaking
s. Versprechen, Zusage, (eingegangene) Verpflichtung, Zusicherung
s. Unternehmen, Firma
s. Vorhaben, Projekt
underutilisation – s. Unterauslastung, schlechte Auslastung
undervalued – adj. unterbewerwert
underwrite
v. garantieren
v. versichern
underwriter
s. Versicherer, bes. Einzelversicherer bei Lloyd's
s. Versicherungsspezialist im Rahmen eines Konsortiums bei Lloyd's
s. Underwriter, Emissionsgarant/in, Emissionsmittler/in, Übernehmer/in einer Wertpapieremission
underwriting
s. Underwriting, Emissionsgarantie, Fremdemission, Übernahme von Emissionsgarantieen, Fremdemissions(-geschäft)
s. Versicherung, Versichern, Versicherungsgeschäft, versicherungstechnisches Geschäft
underwriting commission – Emissionsprovision
conduct underwriting – Versicherungsgeschäfte tätigen
underwriting profit – versicherungstechnischer Gewinn
underwriting agent – s. geschäftsführendes Mitglied eines Konsortiums von Einzelversicherern bei Lloyd's
underwriting commission – s. Emissionsprovision
underwriting group – s. Emissionskonsortium
underwriting member – s. Einzelversicherer bei Lloyd's, Mitglied eines Emissionskonsortiums
underwriting membership – s. Mitgliedschaft als Versicherer bei Lloyd's
underwriting syndicate
s. Konsortium von Einzelversicherern bei Lloyd's
s. Emissions-, Übernahmekonsortium
undisclosed partner with limited liability – s. stiller Gesellschafter
unearned income – s. Besitzeinkommen
unemployment – s. Arbeitslosigkeit
unemployment benefit – s. Arbeitslosenunterstützung
unemployment rate – s. Arbeitslosenrate
unfettered – adj. unbehindert
unfriendly takeover bid – s. feindliches (d. h. nicht mit der Leitung der Zielfirma abgestimmtes) Übernahmeangebot
unhedged – adj. ungesichert, nicht abgesichert, ungedeckt
Uniform Customs and Practices for Documentary Credits – s. Einheitliche Richtlinien und Gebräuche für Dokumentenakkreditive, ERA
Uniform Resource Locator – s. Uniform Resource Locator, Webseitenadresse
Uniform Rules for a Combined Transport Document – s. Einheitliche Richtlinien für ein kombiniertes Transportdokument
unilateral aid – s. unilaterale (Entwicklungs-)Hilfe
unilateral transfers
s. Übertragungsbilanz, Bilanz der Transferleistungen, Bilanz der unentgeltlichen Leistungen
s. Übertragungen, Transferleistungen, unentgeltliche Leistungen
unincorporated business – s. Unternehmen ohne eigene Rechtspersönlichkeit (z. B. Einzelunternehmung)

unique selling proposition – s. Alleinstellungsmerkmal; spezifischer, unverwechselbarer Produktnutzen; Unique Selling Proposition: USP
union – s. Gewerkschaft
union dues – s. Gewerkschaftsbeiträge
unit
s. Maschine, Gerät, (technische) Einheit
s. (Mengen-)Einheit, Stück, Kostenträger
s. (betriebswirtschaftliche / Unternehmens-)Einheit, Betrieb(-swirtschaft), Unternehmen, Wirtschaftssubjekt
s. Investmentfondsanteil, Investmentzertifikat
unitary elasticity – s. Elastizitätsgrad „eins", Elastizität = 1
unit contribution margin – s. Deckungsbeitrag pro Einheit / pro Stück, Stück-Deckungsbeitrag
unit cost(s) – s. Stückkosten
unit depletion rate – s. Betrag der Substanzwertabschreibung pro Mengeneinheit (z.B. abgebaute Tonne, abgebauten Kubikmeter)
United Nations Commission on International Trade Law – s. Kommission für Internationales Handelsrecht der Vereinten Nationen. UNCITRAL
United Nations Conference on Trade and Development – s. Handels- und Entwicklungskonferenz der Vereinten Nationen, UNCTAD
unitholder – s. Fondsanteilinhaber/in, Inhaber/in eines Fondsanteils / von Fondsanteilen
unitisation – s. Bildung von Einheitsladungen / Ladeeinheiten
unitised freight – s. (Frachtgut in Form von) Ladeeinheiten
unitised load – s. Einheitsladung, Ladeeinheit
unit labour costs – s. Lohnstückkosten, Stücklohnkosten
unit load – s. Einheitsladung, Ladeeinheit, (logistische) Transporteinheit
unit of currency – s. Währungseinheit
unit of data – s. Informations-, Dateneinheit
unit of time – s. Zeiteinheit
unit price
s. Preis pro Mengeneinheit, Stückpreis
s. Grundpreis (im Einzelhandel)
unit pricing – s. Grundpreisauszeichnung
unit sales – s. mengenmäßiger Umsatz, Absatz, verkaufte Stückzahlen
unit shop – s. Einzelgeschäft
unit train – s. Einheitsgüterzug
unit variable cost – s. variable Stückkosten
units-of-output method – s. Leistungsabschreibung
unit trust – s. geschlossener Investmentfonds / Investmentfonds nach dem Gesellschaftsprinzip
universal bank – s. Universalbank
Universal Serial Bus – s. universelles Bussystem, Schnittstellen-Standard zum Anschluss von Erweiterungen an PCs
universe – s. (statistische) Grundgesamtheit
unlevel – adj. uneben, ungleich
unlevel playing field – ungleiche Voraussetzungen / Vorbedingungen, fehlende Waffengleichheit
unlicensed worker – s. Pfuscher
unlimited company – s. Gesellschaft mit unbeschränkter Haftung
unlisted company – s. nicht börsennotierte Gesellschaft
unlisted number – s. Geheimnummer
unlisted option – s. Freiverkehrsoption, nicht börsennotierte Option, bankmäßige (Devisen-)Option
Unlisted Securities Market – s. Londoner Freiverkehrsbörse
unload – v. ausladen, entladen, löschen
unloading charges – s. Löschgebühren, Löschkosten
unloading point – s. Auslade-, Löschplatz
unmanned – adj. ohne (firmenseitiges) Bedienungspersonal
unofficial strike – s. inoffizieller Streik, wilder Streik
unprocessed goods – s. unverarbeitete Produkte
unqualified acceptance – s. „nicht modifizierte" Annahme, Annahme ohne einschränkende oder ergänzende Bedingungen
unqualified auditor's report – s. uneingeschränkter Bestätigungsvermerk des Abschlussprüfers / der Abschlussprüferin
unrealised gain – s. nicht realisierter Gewinn
unrealised loss – s. nicht realisierter Verlust
unreflected – adj. unüberlegt, unbedacht
unrequited – adj. ohne Gegenleistung, unentgeltlich
unsecured corporate bond – s. unbesicherte Unternehmensanleihe
unsecured loan – s. Blankokredit, unbesicherter Kredit
unskilled labour – s. Hilfsarbeiter, ungelernte Hilfskräfte
unsolicited offer – s. unverlangtes Angebot
unsustainable – adj. nicht nachhaltig, nicht zukunftsfähig
unweighted average – s. ungewichteter / nicht gewichteter Durchschnitt
unweighted index – s. ungewichteter Index
update – v. auf den neuesten Stand bringen, updaten
upmarket – adj. / adv. gehoben, höherwertig, für kaufkräftige Kunden
move upmarket – Sortiment aufwerten / auf kaufkräftige Kunden umstellen
upper intervention point – s. oberer Interventionspunkt
upscale – adj. gehoben, exklusiv, in der gehobenen Preisklasse
upscale retailer – s. Einzelhänder / Einzelhandelsfirma in der gehobenen Preisklasse
upstream – adj. vorgelagert
upstream from the point of production – der Produktion (in der Wertschöpfungskette) vorgelagert
upvaluation – s. Aufwertung (einer Währung)
upvalue – v. aufwerten
urban decay – s. Verfall der Städte
URL – Uniform Resource Locator (siehe)
USB – Universal Serial Bus (siehe)
USB memory stick – s. USB-Speicherstick, USB-Mobilspeicher
useful life – s. betriebswirtschaftliche Nutzungsdauer/ Nutzungszeit
USM – Unlisted Securities Market (siehe)
USP – unique selling proposition (siehe)
utilisation – s. Auslastung, (Aus-)Nutzung, Verwendung, Einsatz
utilities
s. Versorgungsanschlüsse (z. B. Strom, Gas, Wasser)
s. Versorgungsbetriebe, -unternehmen
utility
s. Nutzen, Nützlichkeit
s. Versorgungsbetrieb, -unternehmen
utility power lines – s. öffentliches Elektrizitätsversorgungsnetz

V

vacancy
s. freie / offene Stelle
s. unvermietetes / leerstehendes Zimmer / Gebäude / Haus / Objekt
vacate – v. räumen, frei machen,
vaccine – s. Impfstoff
valid – adj. gültig, noch nicht abgelaufen
validate
v. rechtskräftig machen
v. bestätigen
validity – s. Gültigkeit
validity period – s. Gültigkeitsdauer
valuables – s. Wertgegenstände
valuation – s. Bewertung
valuation account – s. Wertberichtigungskonto
valuation allowance – s. Wertberichtigung
valuation officer – s. Veranlagungsreferent
valuation practices – s. Bewertungspraktiken, -methoden
valuation reserve – s. Wertberichtigung(-skonto)
value – s. Wert, Preis
good value (for money) – preiswert
value – v. bewerten, wertschätzen
value added – s. Wertschöpfung, Veredelung(-squote)
value added tax – s. Mehrwertsteuer
value creation – s. Wertschöpfung
value date – s. Fälligkeits-, Erfüllungstag, Valuta, Valutadatum,Werstellung(-sdatum)
value dating – s. Wertstellung, Valutierung
value for customs purposes – s. Zollwert
value-for-money – adj. preiswert, preisgünstig, preisleistungs-orientiert
value insured – s. Versicherungswert
value sales – s. (wertmäßiger) Umsatz
van – s. Lieferwagen
vanguard – s. Vorhut, Vorreiter/innen
variable cost(s) – s. variable Kosten, proportionale Kosten
variable interest note – s. variabel verzinsliche (kurzfristige) Anleihe
variable-interest securities – s. variabel verzinsliche Wertpapiere, Wertpapiere mit variabler Verzinsung
variable-rate loan – s. variabel verzinslicher Kredit
variance – s. Abweichung
variance analysis – s. Abweichungsanalyse, Soll-Ist-Vergleich
variety – s. Vielfalt
vat – s. großes Fass, Bottich
VAT – value added tax (siehe)
VAT regime – s. Mehrwertsteuersystem
VAT return – s. Umsatzsteuererklärung, -voranmeldung
VC – venture capital (siehe)
VDU – visual display unit (siehe)
vehicle
s. Fahrzeug
s. spezieller Werbeträger, spezielles Medium
s. Investitions-, Investmentmedium, Anlageform
vegetable oil – s. Pflanzenöl
vending machine – s. Verkaufs-, Warenautomat
vendee – s. Käufer/in
vendor – s. Verkäufer/in, Lieferant/in
vendor rating – s. Lieferantenbewertung
vendor selection – s. Lieferantenauswahl
venture – s. Unternehmen, Vorhaben, Wagnis
venture capital – s. Venture-Kapital, Wagniskapital, Beteiligungsfinanzierung für junge innovative Unternehmen
venture capital fund – s. Venture-Kapital-Fonds, Wagniskapitalfonds
venture funding – s. Wagnisfinanzierung, Venture-Kapital-Finanzierung, Venture-Kapital
venture group – s. autonome Projektgruppe (vor allem innerhalb eines bürokratischen Großunternehmens)
VER – voluntary export restraint (siehe)
vertical integration – s. vertikale Integration, vertikaler Unternehmungszusammenschluss
very large crude carriers – s. VLCC-Tanker
vessel – s. Schiff, Seefahrzeug
vest – v. verleihen, übertragen
vest title in sby. – Eigentum(-srechte) auf jemanden übertragen
vest powers in sby. – jemanden mit Befugnissen ausstatten
powers are vested in the board – Befugnisse liegen beim Verwaltungsrat
veterinary regulations – s. veterinärmedizinische Vorschriften
viability – s. Lebensfähigkeit, Bestand, Sinnhaftigkeit, (wirtschaftliche) Durchführbarkeit, Rentabilität
vice-president – s. Manager/in, Bereichsleiter/in, (für einen bestimmten Bereich verwantwortliches) Vorstandsmitglied, -direktor/in, -chef/in
vice-president for information systems & chief information officer – s. Informationsvorstand
vice president human resources – s. Personalleiter/in, Personalvorstand
vice-president in charge of marketing – s. Marketingmanager/in, Leiter/in der Marketingabteilung, Marketingvorstand
vice-president in charge of procurement – s. Leiter/in des Beschaffungswesens / Einkaufs-, Beschaffungsvorstand
vice-president in charge of production – s. Produktionsleiter/in, Leiter/in der Produktions- / Fertigungsabteilung, Produktionsvorstand
vice-president in charge of purchasing – s. Leiter/in der Einkaufsabteilung, Einkaufsleiter/in, Einkaufsvorstand
vice-president marketing – s. Marketingmanager/in, Leiter/in der Marketingabteilung, Marketingvorstand
vicissitudes of life – s. Wechselfälle des Lebens
victim – s. Opfer, Gegenstand eines Übernahmeangebotes
victualling – s. Verproviantierung (von Seeschiffen)
video-conferencing – s. Videokonferencing (Einsatz von) Videokonferenzen
videophone – s. Videotelefon
video screen – s. Bildschirm
videotex – s. Videotex
view – s. Aussicht, Ansicht, Meinung
in view of – angesichts
in my view – meiner Meinung nach
with a view to – mit der Absicht
with a view to developing new products – mit der Absicht, neue Produkte zu entwickeln
viewphone – s. Videotelefon, Fernsehtelefon
vinegar – s. Essig
violate – v. missachten, verletzen, übertreten, verstoßen gegen
violate the most-favoured-nation principle – gegen das Prinzip der Meistbegünstigung verstoßen

violation – s. (Gesetzes-)Übertretung, Verstoß, Verletzung, Missachtung
violation of intellectual property rights – Verletzung von Immaterialgüterrechten
virtual
adj. praktisch, faktisch, quasi
adj. virtuell
virtually impossible – praktisch unmöglich
virtual shop – s. virtuelles Geschäft(-slokal)
visible account – s. Handels-, Warenverkehrsbilanz, Bilanz des Warenverkehrs
visible exports – s. Warenexporte, sichtbare Exporte
visible imports – s. Warenimporte, sichtbare Importe
visible trade surplus – s. Handelsbilanz-, Außenhandelsüberschuss
visual display unit – s. optische Datenanzeige, Datensichtgerät, Bild-Terminal, Bildschirm
visual image – s. Bild, bildliche Darstellung
vital – adj. (lebens-)wichtig, entscheidend
VLCC – s. Very Large Crude Carrier (siehe)
vocational training – s. Berufsausbildung, berufliche Ausbildung
voice – s. (gesprochene) Sprache
voice data – s. Tondaten, Sprachdaten, Sprache
voice-grade telephone line – s. für Tondatenübertragung geeignete Telefonleitung
Voice over Internet – s. Internettelefonie
Voice over Internet Protocol – s.Voice-over-Internet-Protocol, Internettelefonie-Protokoll
voice processing – s. Tondaten-, Sprachdatenverarbeitung
void – adj. nichtig
render null and void – null und nichtig machen
VoIP – Voice over Internet Protocol (siehe)
volatile – adj. schwankend, fluktuierend, unstet
volcanic eruption – s. Vulkanausbruch
volume
s. Volumen, Umfang, Ausmaß, Menge
s. Beschäftigung(-sgrad)
volume index – s. Mengenindex
volume sales – s. mengenmäßiger Umsatz, Absatz
voluntary export quota – s. freiwilliges Exportkontingent
voluntary export restraint – s. freiwillige Exportbeschränkung
voluntary labour – s. freiwillige / ehrenamtliche Mitarbeiter
voluntary liquidation – s. freiwillige Abwicklung / Liquidation
voluntary offer – s. unverlangtes Angebot
voluntary sector – s. Dritter / autonomer / freiwilliger Sektor
voluntary winding up – s. freiwillige (Firmen-)Liquidation
vote
s. Stimme
s. Abstimmung
s. Stimmrecht
put sthg. to the vote – über etwas abstimmen (lassen)
voting power – s. Stimme, Stimmrecht
voting share – s. Aktie mit Stimmrecht
voting stock – s. Aktien(-kapital) mit Stimmrecht
voucher
s. Beleg
s. Bon, Gutschein
voyage – s. (See-)Reise
voyage charter – s. Reisecharter
voyage policy – s. Reisepolizze, Einzelpolizze, Reiseversicherung
vulnerable to crises – adj. krisenanfällig

W

w.a. – w.a., with average (siehe)
w.a. policy – Versicherung(-spolizze) mit der Klausel „einschließlich Partikularhavarie"
wad – s. Bündel
wage – s. Lohn
wage claim – s. Lohnforderung
wage control – s. Lohnregelung, staatliche Lohnbeschränkung
Wage Expense – s. Lohnaufwand(-skonto), Löhne
wage freeze – s. Lohnstopp
wage guideline – s. Lohnleitlinie
wage-price spiral – s. Lohn-Preis-Spirale
wage rate – s. Lohnsatz, -tarif
wage restraint
s. Lohnregelung
s. Mäßigung / Zurückhaltung bei Lohnforderungen
wage systems – s. Lohnformen, -systeme
wagon-load – s. Wagenladung
waive – v. verzichten / nicht bestehen auf
waive the period of notice – nicht auf der Einhaltung der Kündigungsfrist bestehen
waiver – s. Verzicht, Erlass, Befreiung
waiver to a rule – Befreiung von einer Vorschrift / Regelung, Verzicht auf die Einhaltung einer Vorschrift / Regelung
wake – s. Kielwasser
in the wake of – im Gefolge von
walkout – s. Streik, Ausstand
Wall Street – s. Wall Street (Zentrum des New-Yorker Finanzbezirks, US-Finanzzentrum)
WAN – wide area network (siehe)
want – s. (sekundäres) Bedürfnis
satisfy wants – Bedürfnisse befriedigen
satisfaction of human wants – Befriedigung menschlicher Bedürfnisse
WAP – Wireless Application Protocol (siehe)
ward – s. Mündel
warehouse,
s. Lagergebäude, Lager, Speicher
s. Lagerhaus(-firma), gewerblicher Lagerhalter
warehouse – v. einlagern, lagern, auf Lager geben / nehmen, speichern
warehouse club – s. Warehouse Club, Abholmarkt für private und gewerbliche Mitglieder
warehouse keeper – s. Lagerhalter
warehouse receipt – s. Lagerempfangsschein
warehouse-to-warehouse clause – s. Haus-zu-Haus-Klausel
warehouse-to-warehouse insurance – s. Haus-zu-Haus-Versicherung
warehouse warrant – s. Orderlagerschein
warehousing – s. Lagerhaltung
warrant
v. rechtfertigen
v. garantieren, gewährleisten
warranty
s. Gewährleistung
s. Garantie (im Sinne einer Gewährleistungsgarantie)
war risk – s. Kriegsrisiko
war risk insurance – s. Kriegsrisikoversicherung
waste
s. Vergeudung, Verschwendung, mangelnde Sparsamkeit, Ineffizienz
s. Abfall, Abfälle, Müll
waste disposal – s. Abfallbeseitigung, -entsorgung
waste heat – s. Abwärme, Wärmeverlust
waste material – s. Abfall(-stoff)
wasting asset – s. der Substanzverringerung unterliegender / natürlicher / nicht reproduzierbarer / nicht erneuerbarer Vermögensgegenstand
watermill – s. Wassermühle
water pollution – s. Wasserverschmutzung
water supply – s. Wasserversorgung(-ssystem)
water vapour – s. Wasserdunst
wave power – s. Wellenkraft, -energie
wave power station – s. Wellenkraftwerk
waybill – s. Frachtbrief
weak currency receivable – s. Weichwährungsforderung, Forderung in einer Weichwährung
wealth – s. Vermögen, Reichtum, Wohlstand
wealth-creating effect – s. (positive) Vermögenswirkung
wear and tear – s. Verschleiß, Abnutzung
wear out – v. sich abnutzen / vernutzen, der Abnutzung / dem Verschleiß unterliegen
website – s. Webseite
weed – s. Unkraut
weeding – s. (Unkraut-)Jäten
weed out – v. eliminieren
weedy relatives – verwandte Pflanzensorten im Unkrautbereich
weekly rates – s. Wochenlohn(-tarif)
weight
s. Gewicht, Last
s. Gewicht, Bedeutung, Relevanz
s. Gewicht, Gewichtungsfaktor (bei einem Index)
weight – v. gewichten
weighted – adj. gewichtet, gewogen
weighted average – gewichter / gewogener Durchschnitt
weighted index – gewichteter / gewogener Index
weighting – s. Gewichtung, Anwendung von Gewichtungsfaktoren (bei einem Index)
weighty – adj. gewichtig, wichtig
welfare – s. Wohlfahrt
welfare effects – s. Wohlfahrtseffekte
welfare services – s. Wohlfahrtseinrichtungen und -aktivitäten, Sozialleistungen
well-being – s. Wohlergehen, Wohlfahrt
welfare state – s. Wohlfahrtsstaat
well-heeled – adj. betucht, reich
wetland forest – s. Auwald
wharf – s. Kai, Lade-, Löschplatz
wharfage – s. Kaigebühren, -lagergeld
white-collar employee – s. (Privat-)Angestellte/r
white-collar union – s. Gewerkschaft der Privatangestellten
white knight – s. (wörtlich) weißer Ritter, Retter in letzter Not, alternativer Firmenübernehmer, alternatives Übernahmeangebot
whole food – s. Vollwertkost
wholesale
adj. Großhandels-, zum Großhandel gehörend
adj. / adv. im Großen, in großem Stil, umfassend, in Bausch und Bogen
wholesale bank – s. Großkunden-, Geldmarktbank
wholesale banking – s. (kommerzielles) Großgeschäft der Banken), Geldmarktgeschäft
wholesale market (for money) – s. Geldmarkt

wholesale price – s. Großhandelspreis
Wholesale Price Index – s. Großhandels-Preisindex
wholesaler – s. Großhändler/in, Großhandelsfirma, Grossist/in
wholesaling middleman – s. Absatzmittler/in mit Großhandelsfunktion, Großhändler/in als Absatzmittler/in
wholesome – adj. gesund(-heitsfördernd)
whole turnover guarantee – s. Pauschalgarantie
wholly-owned subsidiary – s. hundertprozentige / 100%ige Tochter(-gesellschaft), Volltochter(-gesellschaft)
wide area network – s. Wide Area Network, Wan-Netz, nicht lokales Rechnernetz, Fernetz, Weitverkehrsnetz
wideband cable – s. Breitbandleitung
wideband coaxial cable – s. Breitbandkoaxialleitung
width of range – s. Breite des Produktionsprogrammes / Sortiments, Sortimentsbreite
wildcat strike – s. inoffizieller / wilder Streik
wind converter – s. Windkraftanlage
wind up – v. auflösen, liquidieren
wind up a company – eine Gesellschaft auflösen / liquidieren
wind up compulsorily – per Gerichtsbeschluss / zwangsweise liquidieren
compulsory winding up – Zwangsliquidation, -auflösung
wind power – s. Windenergie
wind turbine – s. Windturbine
winter sale – s. Winterschlussverkauf
Wireless Application Protocol – s. Wireless Application Protocol (Standard für die Bereitstellung von internetbasierten Informationen und Diensten für Mobilfunkendgeräte)
wireless shopping – s. Mobil-Shopping, M-Shopping, mobiler Einkauf, Handy-Einkauf
with average – (Versicherungsdeckung) einschließlich Partikularhavarie / einschließlich Deckung der Teilschäden
withdraw
v. zurückziehen, widerrufen
v. abheben, entnehmen
withdraw an offer – ein Angebot widerrufen
withdraw profits – Gewinne entnehmen
withdraw money – Geld (von einem Konto) abheben
withdraw goods from a warehouse – Waren aus einem Lagerhaus entnehmen
withdrawal
s. Abhebung (vom Bankkonto), Abhebungsmöglichkeit
s. Gewinnentnahme (bei Einzelunternehmen & Personengesellschaften)
s. (Waren-)Entnahme
s. Entzug, Kontraktionsgröße, Sickergröße
s. Bindungsfrist
withhold – v. einbehalten, zurückbehalten, (an der Quelle) abziehen / besteuern, nicht auszahlen
withholding tax – s. Quellensteuer, (vom Arbeitgeber einbehaltene) Lohnsteuer, (von der ausschüttenden / zinsenzahlenden Gesellschaft einbehaltene) Kapitalertragsteuer
withholding tax on dividends – s. Kapitalertragsteuer (auf Dividenden)
wood-carving – s. Holzschnitzerei
woodland – s. Waldland, Waldung, Wald
word – v. formulieren, ausdrücken, in Worte fassen
a severely worded collection letter – ein scharf formuliertes Mahnschreiben
World Shop – s. Weltladen
World Trade Organization – s. Welthandelsorganisation, WTO
wording – s. Formulierung, Wortlaut
word processing – s. Textverarbeitung
word processing system – s. Textverarbeitungsanlage
word processor – s. Textverarbeitungsanlage
worker co-operative – s. selbstverwaltetes Unternehmen, Unternehmen in Arbeitselbstverwaltung, Produktiv-, Arbeitergenossenschaft
worker director – s. Arbeitnehmervertreter im Verwaltungsrat / Aufsichtsrat
worker participation – s. Arbeitnehmermitbestimmung
workers' productive society – s. Produktiv-, Arbeitergenossenschaft
work-force – s. Belegschaft, Personal (einer Produktionsfirma)
working capital
s. Umlaufvermögen
s. Nettoumlaufvermögen, Working Capital
working capital management – s. Working Capital Management, Management des Umlaufvermögens
working capital ratio – s. Liquidität 3. Grades
working hours – s. Arbeitszeit
work in process – s. im Bau befindliche Anlagen, Halberzeugnisse, Halbfabrikate, Zwischenprodukte
work in progress – s. im Bau befindliche Anlagen, Halberzeugnisse, Halbfabrikate, Zwischenprodukte
workmanship – s. Verarbeitung, Ausführung
work measurement – s. Arbeitsstudien, Leistungsmessung
works
s. Werk, Anlage, Fabrik
s. (öffentliche) Arbeiten
work schedule
s. Arbeitszeit(-einteilung)
s. Arbeitsfolgeplan / -ablaufplan
work scheduling – s. Ablaufplanung (im Fertigungsbereich), Arbeitsvorbereitung
worksheet – s. Abschlussbogen
workshop – s. Werkstatt
works manager – s. Betriebsleiter/in Werksleiter/in, Fabriksleiter/in
workstation – s. Bildschirmarbeitsplatz
work-to-rule – s. Dienst nach Vorschrift, Aktion „Vorschrift"
World Bank – s. Weltbank
World Trade Organization – s. Welthandelsorganisation, WTO
World Wide Web – s. World Wide Web (graphische Oberfläche des Internet)
worth – s. Wert
two billion dollars worth of goods – Waren im Werte von zwei Milliarden Dollar
worth – adj. wert
goods worth two billion dollars – Waren im Wert von zwei Milliarden Dollar
wrapping – s. Hülle, Umhüllung, Verpackung
wrinkle – s. Kniff, Variation, Detail
write down – s. (direkt) abschreiben, Buchwert herabsetzen
write-off
s. Abschreibung
s. Abschreibungsquote, Abschreibungsbetrag, Abschreibungsaufwand
annual write-off – jährlicher Abschreibungbetrag
write off – v. (vollständig) abschreiben
write off the costs of an asset – (Anschaffungs-)Kosten eines Anlagegutes abschreiben
write off assets –Anlagegüter abschreiben
write-off method – s. Abschreibungsmethode
writer of an option – s. Optionsgeber/in, Optionsverkäufer/in
writing down – s. direkte Abschreibung
writing-down allowance – s. Absetzung für Abnutzung, AfA
wrong goods – s. falsche Ware, Aliudlieferung, Anderslieferung
WTO – World Trade Organization (siehe)
www – World Wide Web (siehe)

XY

xeno-market – s. Xeno-Markt (Markt für Währungspositionen in einem Fremdland)
yardstick – s. Maß(-stab)
yield
s. Rendite, Effektivverzinsung
s. (produktionswirtschaftlicher / landwirtschaftlicher) Ertrag
yield
v. abwerfen, bringen, erbringen, ergeben
v. nachgeben, zurückweichen
yield per hectare – s. Hektarertrag
yield to redemption – s. Effektivverzinsung (unter Berücksichtigung aller Ausstattungsmerkmale eines Wertpapieres)
young urban professionals – s. Yuppies (junge, berufstätige (meist kinderlose) Städter mit relativ hohem Einkommen)
youth appeal – s. Anziehungskraft für die Jugend
youth market – s. Jugendmarkt
yuppies – young urban professionals (siehe)

Z

zero-coupon bond – s. Null-Koupon-Anleihe, Zero-Bond
zero rate – s. Nullsatz, (Steuer- / Zoll-)Befreiung
zero-rated – adj. echt mehrwertsteuerbefreit, mehrwertsteuerbefreit mit Vorsteuerabzug
zero-rating – s. echte Mehrwertsteuerbefreiung, Mehrwertsteuerbefreiung mit Vorsteuerabzug
zero-stage channel – s. direkter / nullstufiger Vertrieb(-skanal), Direktvertrieb(-skanal)
zoning regulation – Flächenwidmung(-splan)

KEYWORDS BY SUBJECT MATTER

ACCOUNTING

account[1], account[2] (pl.), account[3] (pl.), accounting, accounting cycle, accounting principles, accounts payable, accounts receivable[1] – general, accounts receivable[2] – valuation, accruals and deferrals, assets, auditing, balance sheet, balance sheet ratios, cash[1], contingent liability, cost accounting, cost of goods sold, credit[4], credit note, current assets, current liabilities, current ratio, debit note, debt[2], depletion, depreciation[1], depreciation[2], depreciation[3] (for tax purposes), depreciation methods, equity capital, expense, financial ratios[1] – general, financial ratios[2] – types, financial statements, fixed assets, funds[2], income statement, income statement ratios, intangible fixed assets, investment, liabilities, long-term liabilities, notes payable, notes receivable, opportunity cost, payables, provision, receivables, reserve, revenue, sales[1], valuation account, working capital.

BANKING AND MONEY

automated teller machine, bank charges, bank deposits, bank draft, banking services, bank lending, bank statement, building society, buyer credit, cash dispenser, central bank, certificate of deposit, cheque card, clearing bank, commercial bank, confirmed irrevocable (documentary) letter of credit, correspondent bank, credit[1], credit[2], credit agreement, credit card, creditor, credit transfer, currency[2], current account[2], debit card, debtor, direct debiting, discount[4], discount house, discount loan, discounting (of a bill of exchange), documentary collection, documentary draft, documentary letter of credit, electronic banking, electronic funds transfer, eurocheque, Euro-markets, export credit guarantee, factoring, financial services, forfaiting, Girobank, guarantee[2], guarantee[3], home banking, interest[1], international funds transfer, merchant bank, money, money market, money supply, NOW account, open-market operation, principal[1], principal[4], project finance, refinancing[1], refinancing[2], remittance, retail banking, revocable (documentary) letter of credit, savings account, securitisation, security (for a loan), standing order, telephone banking, traveller's cheque, unconfirmed irrevocable (documentary) letter of credit, value dating.

BUSINESS ADMINISTRATION / MANAGEMENT

bankruptcy, board of directors, break-even analysis, budgeting, business administration, business organisation[1] – general, business organisation[2] – objectives, capacity, capacity utilisation, capital investment analysis, capital structure, cash flow, company[1] – general aspects, company[2] – types of company, company[3] – legal aspects, management and control, company[4] – advantages and disadvantages, company[5]– legislation, control, controller, corporate culture, corporate governance, corporate strategy, credit inquiry, credit inquiry agency, executive, information management, intrapreneurship, inventory, inventory management, investment[1], key account management, labour turnover, line management, location, management[1], management[2], management consultancy, manufacturing management, materials management, meetings, officer, order book, order intake, organisation, overdraft, personnel management, portfolio[2], productivity, product manager, profit-sharing, promotion[2], public relations, quality management, ratio, rationalisation, record, robotics, staff[2], stakeholder, stock[1], storage, strategic alliance, subcontracting, supply[2], turnover[1], turnover[2], turnover[3], wholesale banking.

BUSINESS COMMUNICATION

advice of dispatch, bank reference, business communication, catalogue, circular letter, complaint, confirmation, credit inquiry, e-mail, firm offer, follow-up letter, inquiry, invoice, meetings, multimedia, offer[2] (of goods), offer without engagement, order (for goods), pro forma invoice, radio pager, reminder (concerning payment), sales letter, telephone, telephone answering machine, telephone call, telex, unsolicited offer, word processing.

BUSINESS ORGANISATION

agenda, annual general meeting, antitrust law, board of directors, business organisation[1] – general, business organisation[2] – objectives, cartel, commune, company[1] – general aspects, company[2] – types of company, company[3] – legal aspects, management and control[1], company[4] – advantages and disadvantages, company[5] – legislation, controllership, co-operative society, corporate governance, corporation[1], corporation[2], corporation[3], equity capital[1], franchise[1], group of companies, holding company, incorporation (of a company), interest[2], line management, management[1], management[2], merger, mergers and acquisitions, minutes, multinational company, non-governmental organisation, officer, organisation, partnership, public corporation, purchasing (management), share, shareholder, sole trader, staff[2], stock[2], takeover bid, transfer price, trust[1], trust[2], worker co-operative, worker participation.

COMPUTER / ELECTRONIC DATA PROCESSING TELECOMMUNICATIONS

analogue, batch processing, binary system, bit, byte, central processing unit, computer, computer-aided design & computer-aided manufacturing / CAD & CAM, chip card, computer applications in business, computer graphics, computer program, data processing, data transmission, desktop computer, digital, distributed data processing, e-commerce, e-mail, fax, file[3], format, hard copy, hardware, information management, interface, Internet, magnetic disk, mainframe, modem, multimedia, network, new economy, off-line, on-line, optical character recognition, packet switching, peripherals, personal computer, plotter, printer, programming language, random access memory, real-time processing, robotics, soft copy, software, storage device, telephone banking, teleshopping, terminal, visual display unit.

CONTRACT (GENERAL)

breach of contract (of sale), contract, contract of agency, contract of carriage, contract of employment, contract of insurance, contract of sale, damages, default, delay in payment, discrepancies between legal systems, index linking, performance of the contract (of sale), pricelist, term[1], term[2].

CONTRACT OF SALE

acceptance (of an offer), acceptance (of goods), account[5], account[8], advice of dispatch, bank reference, bond[2], breach of contract (of sale), cash discount, cash with order, catalogue, C.O.D., complaint, confirmation, consignment[1], contract currency, contract of sale, contract penalty, counter-offer, countertrade, credit[1], credit[3], credit information, credit inquiry, debit note, debtor, default, defective goods, delay in delivery, delivery (of goods), delivery period, discount[1], down payment, estimate, firm offer, guarantee[1], house bill of lading, INCOTERMS, inquiry, instalment, instalment sale, invitation to treat, invoice, list price, marking, method of payment, offer[1], offer[2] (of goods), offer without engagement, open account, order (for goods), performance bond, performance of the contract (of sale), price, principal[4], principal[5], pro forma invoice, progress payments, prospect[1], prospective customer, quantity discount, rebate, rejection (of goods), reminder (concerning payment), replacement, return[3] (pl.), sale by sample, sale on approval, sale on deferred terms, sales letter, sample[1], seasonal discount, standing order, statement of account, supplier, supplier credit, tender, tender bond, terms of delivery, terms of payment, through bill of lading, time of payment, trade reference, trade terms, trial order, unsolicited offer, wrong goods.

DEVELOPING COUNTRIES / DEVELOPMENT ECONOMICS / DEVELOPMENT AID

alternative trading organisation, buffer stock, development aid, developing country, development agency, fair trade[1], fair trade[2], fair-trade label, non-governmental organisation, preferential tariff, soft loan, transfer of technology, unilateral transfers.

ECONOMICS (GENERAL AND MICRO-ECONOMICS)

appreciation, barter, commodity, consumer goods, demand, demand curve, economics[1], economics[2], economic systems, economies of scale, economies of scope, economy[1], economy[2], elasticity, externalities, factors of production, flow concept, forecasting, goods, franchise[3], industry[1], industry[2], infrastructure, line[2], marginalism, micro-economics, monopoly, nominal, opportunity cost, price, producer goods, production, productivity, property[1], property[2], purchasing power, rationing, real, reflation, Retail Price Index, saving, sectors of the economy, service industries, slump, stock concept, supply[1], supply curve, trade[2], trade[3], trade-off, underground economy, voluntary sector.

ECONOMICS (MACRO-ECONOMICS)

accelerator principle, account[4], aggregate, autarky, disposable (personal) income, distribution of income, economic indicator, globalisation, gross domestic product, gross national product, inflation, labour force, micro-economics, money supply, multiplier, national accounting, national income, property sector, purchasing power parity, savings rate, slump, social costs, trade cycle, unemployment, unemployment rate.

ECONOMICS (ECONOMIC POLICY)

anti-dumping tariff, austerity, budget, controls, counter-cyclical policy, deflation[1], deregulation, development agency, discrepancies between legal systems, economic indicator, economic integration, economic policy, fiscal policy, incomes policy, index linking, industrial policy, investment incentive, monetary policy, privatisation, rationing, regional policy, regulation of promotional activities, state-owned enterprises, subsidy, unit pricing.

ENVIRONMENT/ ENERGY

acid precipitation, agribusiness, biodegradable substance, biotechnology, eco-label, ecology, ecosphere, energy conservation, energy crisis, environment, environmental auditing, externalities, genetic engineering, greenhouse effect, green taxes, hard energy path, hard energy technology, nuclear power[1] – economic aspects, nuclear power[2] – present situation, nuclear power[3] – pros and cons, organic farming, photovoltaic conversion, planned obsolescence, pollution, recycling, renewable resources, social costs, soft energy path, soft energy technology, sustainable development.

FINANCIAL MANAGEMENT/ BUSINESS FINANCE

accounts payable, accounts receivable[1] – general, accounts receivable[2] – valuation, balance sheet ratios, break-even analysis, budgeting, buyer credit, buyout, capital investment analysis, capital structure, cash[1], cash flow, cash management, commercial paper, controller, credit[2], creditor, creditors' funds, creditworthiness, current ratio, debt[1], debt[2], discount[4], discounting (of a bill of exchange), discount loan, dividend, equity capital, equity securities, export finance, factoring, financial management, financial ratios[1] – general, financial ratios[2] – types, forfaiting, fund[1], fund[2], funding[1], funding[2], funds[1], funds[2], gearing, going public, guarantee[3], income statement ratios, insolvency, interstatement ratios, issuing shares, leasing, liabilities, liquidity, long-term liabilities, market capitalisation, mergers and acquisitions, mortgage, notes payable, notes receivable, overdraft, payables, ploughback, preference share, private equity, project finance, receivables, refinancing[1], refinancing[2], rescheduling (of debts), return[2], rights issue, risk, securities, securitisation, security (for a loan), share, share buy-back, shareholder value, stock[2], swap[1], swap[2], working capital.

FINANCIAL AND SIMILAR INSTRUMENTS

acceptance (of a bill of exchange), bank guarantee, bearer cheque, bill of exchange, certificate of deposit, cheque, commercial paper, crossed cheque, discount[4], dishonoured bill, document of title, drawer (of a bill of exchange), drawer (of a cheque), forwards, futures, indorsement, negotiable instruments, order bill, order cheque, payee (of a bill of exchange), payee (of a cheque), payment (of a bill of exchange), portfolio[1], promissory note, securitisation, share, sight bill, time bill, warehouse warrant.

INSURANCE

act of God, all-risks cover, average[3], aviation insurance, cargo insurance, claim, consequential loss insurance, contract of insurance, deductible, floating policy, force majeure, f.p.a., franchise[4], general average, goods-in-transit insurance, hull insurance, insurance, insurance agent, insurance broker, insurance policy, insurance premium, liability insurance, Lloyd's, marine insurance, motor insurance, (ocean) marine insurance policy, open cover, particular average, premium subrogation, risk, surveyor, transportation insurance, underwriter[1], voyage policy, w.a., war risks insurance.

INTERNATIONAL ECONOMY (FOREIGN EXCHANGE)

arbitrage, buying rate, conversion, currency[1], devaluation (of a currency), direct quotation, discount, exchange control, exchange rate, exchange rate systems, exchange risk[1] – general, exchange risk[2] – hedging transaction risk: hedging decision, exchange risk[3] – hedging transaction risk: hedging techniques, exchange risk[4] – protection from transaction risk (covering), fixed exchange rate, floating rate of exchange, foreign exchange, foreign exchange market, forward rate (of exchange), hedging[2], hedging transaction risk in the foreign currency futures market, hedging transaction risk in the foreign currency option market, hedging transaction risk in the forward exchange market, hedging transaction risk in the money market, hot money, indirect quotation, offer[3], premium[2], purchasing power parity, revaluation (of a currency), selling rate, spot rate (of exchange), trade-weighted value (of a currency), transfer risk.

INTERNATIONAL ECONOMY (MACRO-ECONOMIC ASPECTS)

balance of payments, account[4], balance of trade, capital account, current account[1], financial account, foreign direct investment, gains and losses from trade, globalisation, income account, invisible account, terms of trade, unilateral transfers.

INTERNATIONAL TRADE (EXPORTING AND IMPORTING)

bill of lading, bond[2], buffer stock, buyer credit, certificate of origin, C.&F.-COST AND FREIGHT ... (named port of destination), C.I.F.-COST, INSURANCE, AND FREIGHT ... (named port of destination), clean collection, commercial invoice, confirmed irrevocable (documentary) letter of credit, consignee[2], consignment, consignment stock, consignor[2], consular invoice, correspondent bank, countertrade, customs invoice, customs procedure, DELIVERED AT FRONTIER ... (named place of delivery at frontier), DELIVERED DUTY PAID ... (named place of destination in the country of importation), DELIVERED EX QUAY, DELIVERED EX SHIP, direct exporting, distributing agent, documentary collection, documentary draft, documentary letter of credit, documents against acceptance, documents against payment, dumping, export credit guarantee, export credit insurance, export distributor, exporting, export finance, export marketing, export merchant, EX WORKS ... (ex factory, ex mill, ex plantation, ex warehouse, etc.), F.A.S.-FREE ALONGSIDE SHIP (named port of shipment), F.O.B.[1]-FREE ON BOARD ... (named port of shipment), F.O.B.[2], forfaiting, forward rate (of exchange), FREE CARRIER ... (named point), FREIGHT/CARRIAGE AND INSURANCE PAID TO ... (named point of destination), FREIGHT/CARRIAGE PAID TO ... (named point of destination), guarantee[2], import licence, import merchant, import quota, INCOTERMS, international marketing, joint venture, licensing, lighter, market entry, marking, origin of goods, performance bond, principal[3], principal[5], pro forma invoice, promissory note, representative, revocable (documentary) letter of credit, risk, shipped bill of lading, shipping documents, strategic alliance, subcontracting, temporary exportation of goods, temporary importation of goods, tender, tender bond, through bill of lading, trade terms, transfer risk, unconfirmed irrevocable (documentary) letter of credit, value dating.

INTERNATIONAL TRADE (DOCUMENTS)

account[5], bill of lading, certificate of origin, claused bill of lading, clean bill of lading, commercial invoice, consignment note, consular invoice, copy[2], customs invoice, document of title, export finance, export marketing, house bill of lading, import license, received bill of lading, origin of goods, sea waybill, shipped bill of lading, shipping documents.

INTERNATIONAL TRADE POLICY

ad valorem duty, arbitration, bonded warehouse, countervailing tariff, customs duty, customs procedure, customs union, devaluation (of a currency), dumping, exchange control, exchange rate, export credit guarantee, export credit insurance, export licence, fixed exchange rate, floating rate of exchange, free trade, globalisation, import duty, import licence, import quota, most-favoured-nation clause, non-tariff trade barrier, preferential tariff, protective tariff, protectionism, retaliatory tariff, revaluation (of a currency), revenue tariff, specific duty, temporary importation of goods, trade policy, trading bloc.

INVESTMENT AND SECURITIES MARKETS

average[2], bear, Big Bang, blue chips, bond[1], buyout, cash[4], certificate of deposit, commercial paper, commodity exchange, derivatives, discount[3], dividend, equity securities, financial market, forwards, fund[2], futures, gilt-edged securities, hedging[1], going public, investment[2], investment[3], investment bank, investment funds, investor, issuing shares, market capitalisation, market maker, option, portfolio[1], preference share, premium[3], primary market, rating[1], rating[2], return[2], rights issue, securities, securities analysis, securities markets, securitisation, share, share buy-back, shareholder value, short sale, socially responsible investment, speculation, stag stock[3], stockbroker, stock exchange, stock exchange indices, stock exchange members, stock exchange quotation, stockjobber, swap[2], underwriter[2], underwriting, value dating, yield.

LABOUR

contract of employment, employee benefits, employment services, flexitime, industrial relations, labour force, labour turnover, lock-out, motivation, non-wage labour costs, personnel consulting, personnel management, profit-sharing, promotion[2], recruiting, redundancy, social security tax, staff[1], strike, take-home pay, trade union, unemployment, unemployment rate, wage, wage systems, worker co-operative, worker participation, work-to-rule.

MARKETING (GENERAL)

account[6], account[8], barter, bulk goods, buyers' market, consignee[1], consignor[1], consumerism, e-commerce, export marketing, franchise[2], franchising, international marketing, joint venture, key account management, licensing, market, market entry, marketing, marketing research, market segmentation, market share, merchandise, prospect[1], prospective customer, sales force, sellers' market, survey, target group, trade[1].

MARKETING (PRODUCT)

brand, branding, commodity, consumer goods, diversification, line[1], intellectual property, planned obsolescence, portfolio[2], producer goods, product, product differentiation, product innovation, product liability, product life cycle[1], product life cycle[2], product line, product manager, product mix, product policy, product positioning, property[2], simplification of the product mix, trading down, trading up, unique selling proposition.

MARKETING (PRICE)

instalment, instalment sale, loss leader, markup, monopoly, price-list, price policy, quantity discount, rebate, resale price maintenance, retail price, seasonal discount, trade discount, trading stamp, transfer price, unit pricing.

MARKETING (DISTRIBUTION)

alternative trading organisation, auction, automatic selling, cash-and-carry wholesaler, channel of distribution, department store, discount store, distribution, franchise[1], franchising, home shopping, logistics, mail order, market entry, multiple store, order processing, point of sale system, rack jobber, retailer, sales representative, sole distributorship, stockist, supermarket, teleshopping, unit shop, warehouse club, wholesaler.

MARKETING (INTERMEDIARIES)

agent, broker, commercial agent, consignee[2], consignment[2], consignor[2], contract of agency, dealer, delcredere agent, distributing agent, exclusive dealer, export distributor, import merchant, marketing intermediary, merchandising[1], merchandising[2], merchandising[3], principal[2], representative, sales force, sole agent.

MARKETING (PROMOTION)

account[7], account executive, advertising, advertising agency, advertising copy, advertising medium, brand, branding, circular letter, copy[3], direct marketing, eco-label, fair-trade label, follow-up letter, packaging, personal selling, premium[4], premium[5], product positioning, promotion[3], promotion[4], promotional mix, public relations, regulation of promotional activities, sale, sales letter, sales literature, sales promotion, sponsorship, trade fair, trading stamp.

OFFICE

audio typist, bar chart, copier, copy[1], copy[2], fax, file[1], file[2], filing, mail room equipment, office, office equipment, office supplies, office personnel, pie chart, radio pager, telephone, telephone answering machine, telephone call, telex, typewriter, typing pool, word processing.

PAYMENT

acceptance (of a bill of exchange), bearer cheque, bill of exchange, cash[2], cash[3], cash discount, cash with order, certified check, cheque, cheque card, chip card, clean collection, clean payment, C.O.D., collection, collection agency, commercial invoice, confirmed irrevocable (documentary) letter of credit, credit[3], credit card, credit transfer, crossed cheque, debit card, delay in payment, direct debiting, documentary collection, documentary draft, documentary letter of credit, documents against acceptance, documents against payment, down payment, drawee (of a bill of exchange), drawee (of a cheque), drawer (of a bill of exchange), drawer (of a cheque), electronic banking, electronic funds transfer, eurocheque, export finance, instalment, instalment sale, method of payment, money, open account, order bill, order cheque, payee (of a bill of exchange), payee (of a cheque), payment in advance, payment (of a bill of exchange), payment on receipt of goods, payment on receipt of invoice, principal[3], pro forma invoice, promissory note, remittance, revocable (documentary) letter of credit, sale, sight bill, standing order, statement of account, terms of payment, time bill, time of payment, transfer risk, traveller's cheque, unconfirmed irrevocable (documentary) letter of credit.

STATISTICS

average[1], deflation[2], index, index linking, sample[2], seasonal adjustment, survey.

TAXATION

capital gain, capital gains tax, corporation tax, death tax, depreciation[3] (for tax purposes), direct tax, double taxation, excise tax, green taxes, income tax – personal, indirect tax, progressive taxation, property tax, rates, sales tax, social security tax, tax allowance, taxation, tax avoidance, tax credit, tax evasion, tax haven, tax liability[1], tax liability[2], turnover tax, value added tax.

TRANSPORT / PACKING / MARKING

bill of lading, carriage[1], carriage[2], carriage of goods by air[1] – economic aspects, carriage of goods by air[2] – advantages and drawbacks, carriage of goods by air[3] – legal aspects, carriage of goods by rail[1] – economic aspects, carriage of goods by rail[2] – legal aspects, carriage of goods by road, carriage of goods by sea[1] – general course of business, carriage of goods by sea[2] – economic aspects, carriage of goods by sea[3] – legal aspects, carriage of goods on inland waterways, carrier, claused bill of lading, clean bill of lading, combined transport, consignee[1], consignment[1], consignment note, consignor[1], container[1], container[2], courier and parcel services, docks, forwarding agent, freight[1], freight[2], general cargo, house bill of lading, lighter, package, packing, pallet, piggyback service, received bill of lading, roll-on / roll-off, shipped bill of lading, shipper, through bill of lading, transport, unitisation.